WINDOWS™
PROGRAMMING SECRETS

WINDOWS™
PROGRAMMING SECRETS

Kris Jamsa

Osborne **McGraw-Hill**
Berkeley, California

Osborne **McGraw-Hill**
2600 Tenth Street
Berkeley, California 94710
U.S.A.

For information on translations and book distributors outside of the U.S.A., write to Osborne **McGraw-Hill** at the above address.

A complete list of trademarks appears on page 683.

Windows™ Programming Secrets

 234567890 DODO 8987

ISBN 0-07-881262-3

CONTENTS

INTRODUCTION

If DOS is the most significant software development in recent years, then Microsoft Windows is quite possibly the second. Microsoft Windows provides the user with a user-friendly working environment that has a consistent interface and allows applications to run concurrently. With Windows, users are no longer required to memorize nebulous DOS commands and syntax; because it is menu driven, Windows greatly increases the user's ability to learn the program while decreasing his or her fear of computers. At the same time, Windows maximizes the computer's processing capabilities since it allows the user to execute several programs simultaneously.

Numerous companies have recognized the importance of the user interface provided by Microsoft Windows, and its popularity suggests that it will have a significant role in the future of microcomputer operating systems, user environments, and application programs. If Windows does become the standard for PC work environments, as many think it will, the need for applications that run under Windows will be tremendous. The programmer who has a solid understanding of the Windows program-development process will find it an important asset.

This book examines the development of Windows applications programs and each of the tools provided in the Microsoft Windows Software Development Kit. The text also presents applications that utilize each of the major functional aspects of Windows: menus, keyboard input, dialog boxes, the Clipboard interface, fonts, and GDI (graphics device interface) functions.

Each program presented in this text provides a template for your applications. Several programming examples are provided in Pascal as well as C. Don't hesitate to modify the routines to increase your understanding of Windows.

Diskette Package

All of the routines provided in this text are available on diskette. Included with the diskette is a diskette folder that is ideal for carrying your floppy diskettes when you travel or go to work or school. The complete cost of the diskette package is $12.45 plus $2.50 for shipping and handling ($5.00 for foreign orders).

Please send me the diskette package that accompanies *Windows Programming Secrets*. My payment of $14.95 ($12.45 plus $2.50 for shipping and handling or $5.00 for foreign orders) is enclosed.

Name _____

Address _____

City _____ State _____ ZIP _____

Kris Jamsa Software, Inc.   Box 26031   Las Vegas, Nevada 89126

PART

I

PROGRAMMING
TECHNIQUES

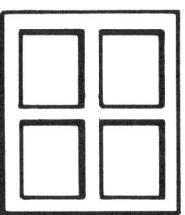

1

GETTING STARTED WITH WINDOWS

Before you examine the Windows program development capabilities, it is important first to review the process of moving through the screens and menus of Windows, by using either a mouse or the keyboard. Later chapters will examine how to develop programs that support this capability. For now, simply refresh your memory with the user's perspective of Windows.

What Is Windows?

"What is Windows?" Let's examine that question from three points of view: a general overview, the user's perspective, and through the eyes of the software developer.

In general, Windows is an operating environment that layers itself upon DOS to provide the user with a friendly, menu-driven interface. With Windows the user is able to execute multiple programs simultaneously in an integrated environment, which results in a consistent user view of computer applications. The integration provided by Windows also provides the ability to share information between unrelated programs (via the Clipboard). See Figure 1-1 for a graphic depiction of these concepts.

In addition to providing this integrated, menu-driven environment, Windows includes the following desktop applications:

☐ Calculator provides a simple calculator.

☐ Cardfile allows you to organize facts on index cards.

☐ Clock displays an analog clock with the current system time.

☐ Notepad allows you to create a "to do" list.

☐ Reversi is a challenging board game.

☐ Terminal provides terminal emulation for bulletin-board access.

Windows, however, is primarily a user's interface to the computer. No longer are users required to memorize nebulous DOS commands and syntax. As a result, their learning curve is much shorter and their fear of computers is reduced dramatically.

For a program to be successful, the user must feel comfortable with it. You must always keep foremost in your mind the audience for whom the program is being developed and then develop it with that perspective in mind. If you consider the more successful software packages in recent years (for example, Windows, SideKick, and Turbo Pascal), each provides the target user with a nonthreatening environment.

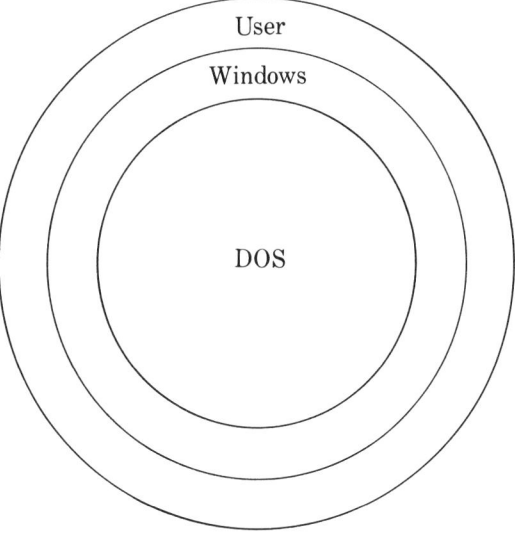

Figure 1-1. Windows layered over DOS

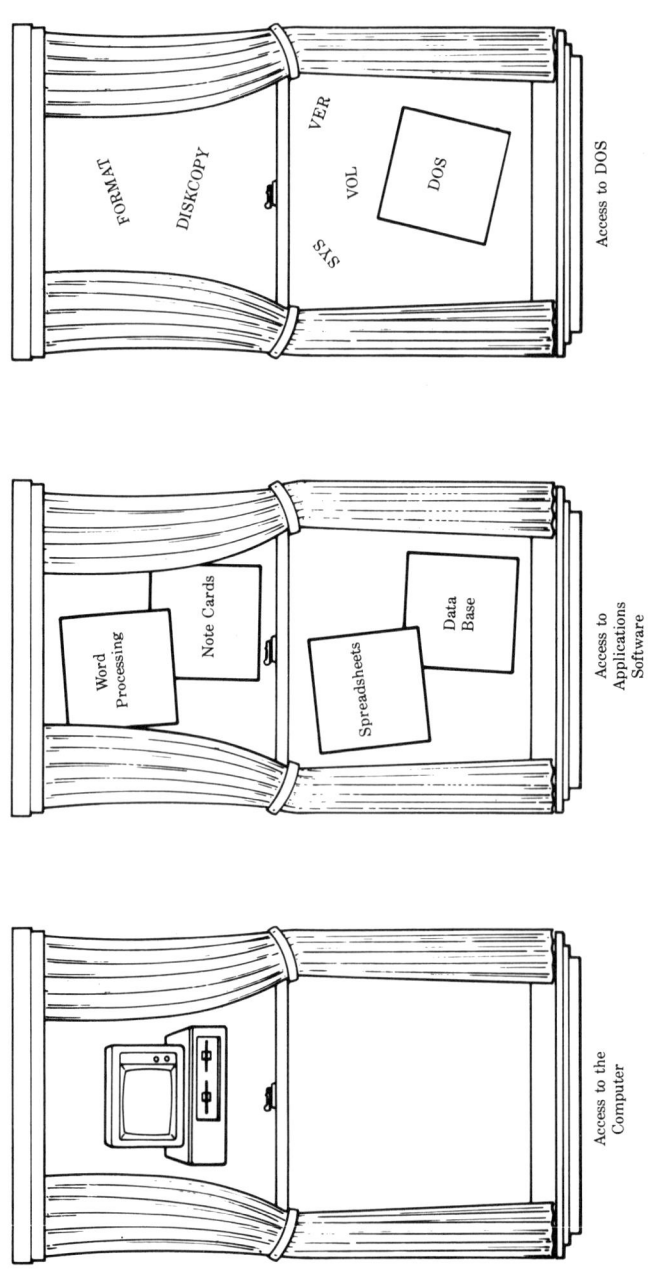

Figure 1-2. User's view of Windows

Windows achieves this because all programs that run under Windows present themselves in the same fashion. As you will see, the consistent user interface of Windows allows you to install new packages in the Windows environment that execute in a manner that is not threatening to the user. Figure 1-2 shows the user's perspective of Windows.

To the programmer, Windows provides a tremendous opportunity to learn the internal workings of one of the most successful programs ever developed. Windows is laying the foundation for future releases of DOS. The features that Windows incorporates (such as concurrency, message passing, and a consistent, user-friendly interface) will

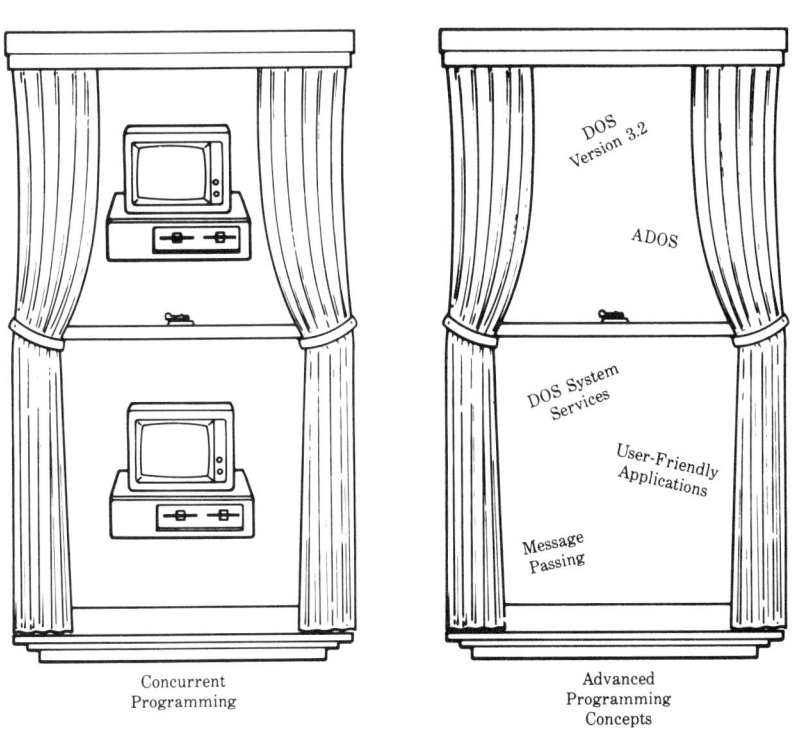

Concurrent
Programming

Advanced
Programming
Concepts

Figure 1-3. Programmer's view of Windows

have a significant impact on the development of DOS. Those programmers who are conversant with the programming of Windows applications will have a significant head start on the remainder of the computer industry. Figure 1-3 shows the programmer's view of Windows.

What Is Time-sharing?

As was stated previously, Windows allows you to run multiple programs simultaneously, thus making each window appear as an individual screen. For example, if you are not using Windows but instead are running three programs on three individual computers, the output would appear as shown in Figure 1-4. With Windows, each of the applications runs on the same computer, dividing the screen into three distinct regions, as shown in Figure 1-5.

Windows works by time-sharing the central processing unit (CPU). Each time a program runs, the CPU finds the instructions for the program in memory and executes them, as shown in Figure 1-6.

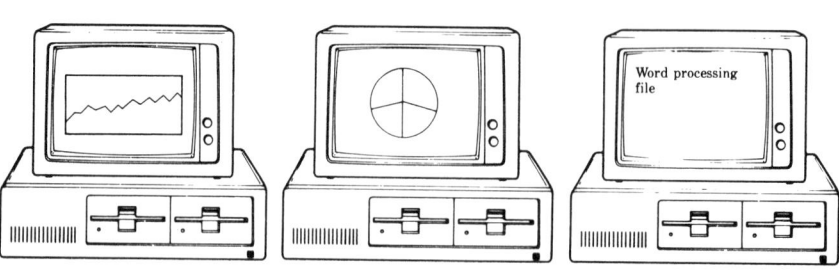

Figure 1-4. Result of running three programs on three computers

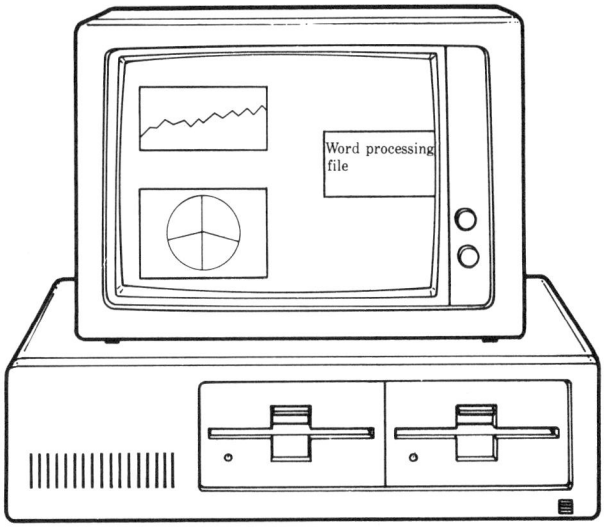

Figure 1-5. Result of running three programs on one computer

Because of the tremendous speed of today's computers, the CPU actually spends the majority of its time idle, waiting to perform additional processing. For example, if you consider a word processing program, the CPU spends the majority of its time waiting for you to type in characters at the keyboard. During a one-second time period, the CPU may be processing only 25% of the time (see Figure 1-7).

Windows exploits CPU idle time by allowing several programs to share the CPU. Given the previous example of three simultaneous programs, you can visualize CPU utilization as shown in Figure 1-8. The first application will receive control of the CPU for a given period of time. When this interval of time (known as a *time slice*) expires, control of the CPU is passed to the second application, which has control of the CPU for its time slice. Next, the third application

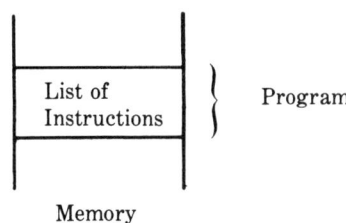

Figure 1-6. List of instructions in memory

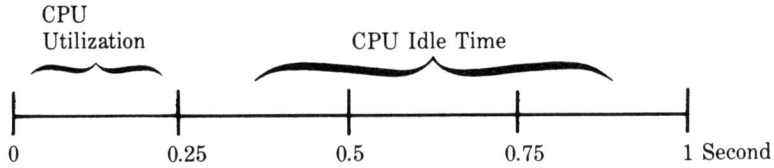

Figure 1-7. Processing time of CPU

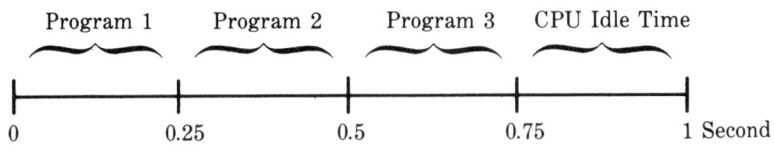

Figure 1-8. CPU utilization in time-sharing system

will receive control of the CPU, and the process then repeats itself. As the number of concurrent applications increases, Windows simply shares the CPU among them by decreasing the time slice given to each application.

Operating systems that share the CPU processing time in this fashion are called *time-sharing systems*. Windows, therefore, is a *time-sharing environment*. When multiple programs are executed simultaneously, each program gets a section of the CPU's processing time. Because this transition is so fast, it appears as though the applications were executing simultaneously.

It is important to note that the processing capability of the personal computer is not unlimited. As the number of concurrent programs increases, the amount of CPU processing time available for each program decreases. This, in turn, decreases the execution speed for each program (see Figure 1-9).

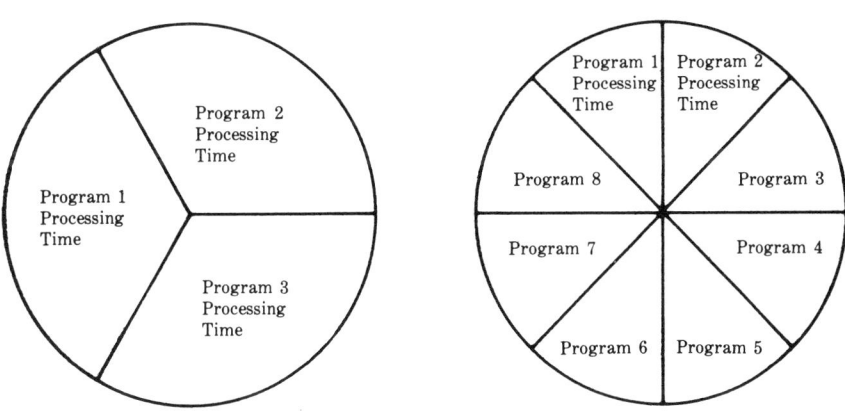

Figure 1-9.   Effects of time-slice allocation on multiple programs

A major factor influencing the speed of your applications is the amount of available memory. As was illustrated previously, each time DOS executes a program, it must first load the program into memory. When you are executing multiple programs with Windows, it will place as many of the programs into memory as possible (see Figure 1-10). Unfortunately, the amount of memory in the system is limited. If you load several large programs under Windows, the majority of your system memory may be allocated, as can be seen in Figure 1-11.

If you invoke an additional program, Windows must make space for the program in memory by temporarily swapping another program out of memory and onto a disk (see Figure 1-12). As the number of programs executing becomes very large, the amount of swapping that Windows must perform increases proportionately. Because of their mechanical nature, disk drives are slower than the electronic circuits that make up the CPU. As a result, disk I/Os (input/output operations) are one of the largest causes of delays in computer processing. Because of the additional overhead of disk I/Os, as swapping increases, the execution speed of your applications decreases.

Windows Requirements

The system requirements for Windows and the Windows Software Development Kit are not identical. Because most of you will be developing applications for end users who will be running a complete Windows system (with the desktop applications), it is important to discuss the requirements for configuring complete systems.

Any system on which you install Windows must meet the following minimum requirements:

☐ A personal computer with two disk drives or a fixed disk

☐ 320K of memory (512K is recommended)

☐ DOS version 2.0 or greater

☐ A monochrome or color monitor with a graphics card

```
┌──────────────┐
│     DOS      │
├──────────────┤
│   Windows    │
├──────────────┤
│  Program 1   │
├──────────────┤
│  Program 2   │
├──────────────┤
│  Program 3   │
└──────────────┘
     Memory
```

Figure 1-10. Multiple programs simultaneously in memory

```
┌──────────────┐
│     DOS      │
├──────────────┤
│   Windows    │
├──────────────┤
│  Program 1   │
├──────────────┤
│  Program 2   │
├──────────────┤
│  Program 3   │
├──────────────┤
│ Free Memory  │
└──────────────┘
     Memory
```

Figure 1-11. Memory allocation after loading Windows

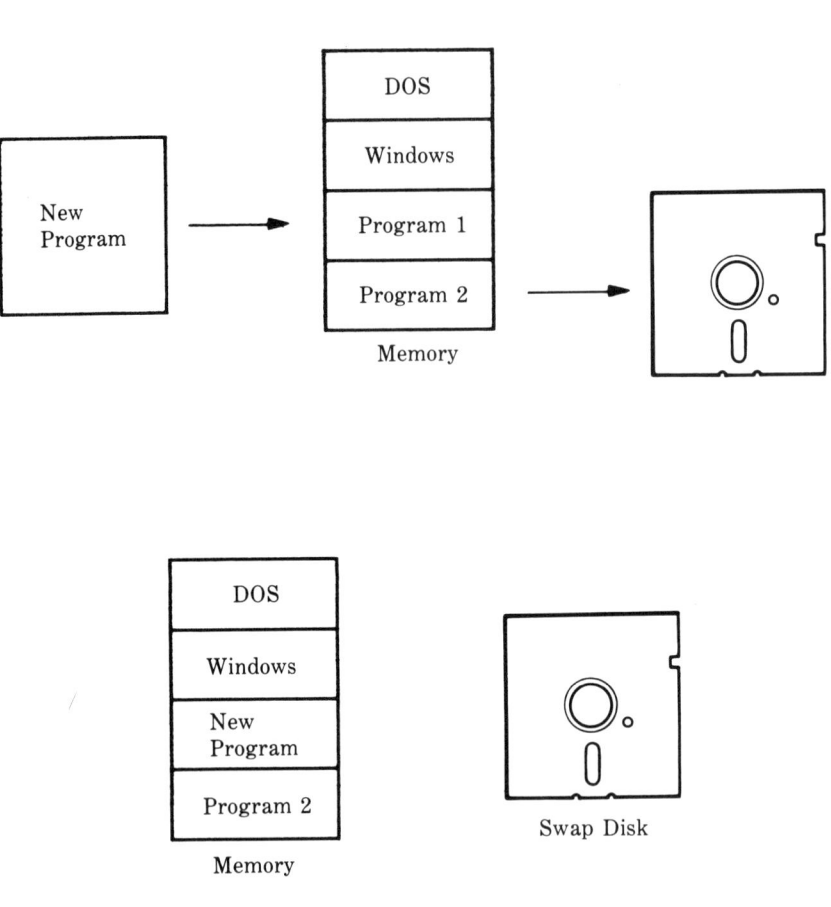

Figure 1-12. Swapping a program out of memory

In addition, you should purchase a mouse. If you are simply using Windows, rather than writing programs for it, a mouse provides a very nice interface. If, however, you are developing applications to run under Windows, a mouse is necessary because you must thoroughly test the user interface. The Logitech mouse shown in Figure 1-13 is an excellent choice.

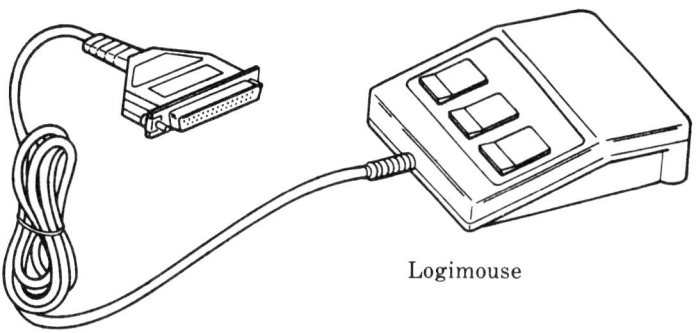

Logimouse

Courtesy of Logitech, Inc.

Figure 1-13. Logitech's Bus Mouse

The Windows Software Development Kit requires the following system configuration:

☐ An IBM Personal Computer XT or AT

☐ A floppy disk drive configured as drive A

☐ A fixed disk drive configured as drive C

☐ 512K of RAM (640K is recommended)

☐ A monochrome or color monitor with a graphics card

☐ DOS version 2.0 or greater

☐ A Microsoft C or Pascal compiler, or macro assembler

Before examining the Windows Software Development Kit, its contents, and installation, let's first examine Windows.

Installing Windows

If you have not already installed Windows on your system, select the Windows "Setup" disk and place it in drive A. As you will see during the installation, you can configure Windows to run from either a floppy disk drive or a fixed disk drive. Simply enter the following:

```
A> SETUP
```

The Windows installation will begin. See Appendix G for Windows installation procedures.

A Quick Review of Windows

This section provides a quick review of the traversal of the Windows screens, menus, and icons. In addition, it examines the manipulation of concurrent processes and the Windows Spooler.

Invoke Windows at the DOS prompt by entering

```
C> WIN
```

Windows will display the following screen:

```
≡                          MS-DOS Executive                          ⌐
  File  View  Special
  A ═■═  B ═■═  C ═■═  D ═■═  C:DOSDISK \WINDOWS2

  PIF              HELVD.FON      TMSRC.FON
  ABC.TXT          KAJ.CAL        TMSRD.FON
  CALC.EXE         KAJ.MSP        VV.CAL
  CALENDAR.EXE     LL.CAL         WIN.BAK
  CARDFILE.EXE     MODERN.FON     WIN.COM
  CLIPBRD.EXE      MSDOS.EXE      WIN.INI
  CLOCK.EXE        NOTEPAD.EXE    WIN100.BIN
  CONTROL.EXE      PAINT.EXE      WIN100.OVL
  COURA.FON        PRACTICE.WRI   WINOLDAP.GRB
  COURC.FON        README.TXT     WINOLDAP.MOD
  COURD.FON        REVERSI.EXE    WRITE.EXE
  DOS.CRD          ROMAN.FON
  DOTHIS.TXT       SCRIPT.FON
  EPSON.DRV        SPOOLER.EXE
  HELVA.FON        TERMINAL.EXE
  HELVC.FON        TMSRA.FON
```

The most obvious items displayed on the screen are the disk drive icons and identifications across the top of the window, the names of the files contained in the current directory, the name of the current directory, and the name MS-DOS Executive within the title bar. Because the MS-DOS Executive allows you to exercise each of the Windows features, and because most users will at one time or another have to utilize its capabilities, it is important to examine this feature in detail. Figure 1-14 shows the components of the Windows screen.

As you will see, many of the commands in Windows can easily be executed with either a mouse or the keyboard. This chapter will present both methods for each example.

To get a feel for how to move around in the MS-DOS Executive, change the current default drive. If you are using a mouse, simply direct the mouse pointer to the desired drive identification, and press the mouse select button (normally the leftmost button). If you are using the keyboard, simultaneously press the CTRL key and the letter

WINDOWS PROGRAMMING SECRETS

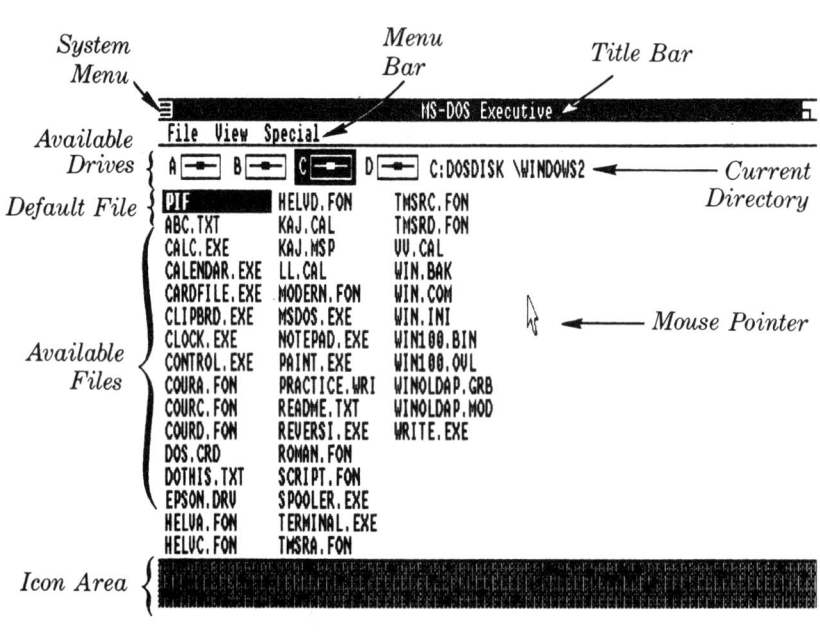

Figure 1-14. Components of Windows screen

of the desired drive. Toggle through all of the disk drives with either method. Note how the file names change as you cycle through the available disk drives.

If you select a disk drive that does not contain a disk, Windows will display the following:

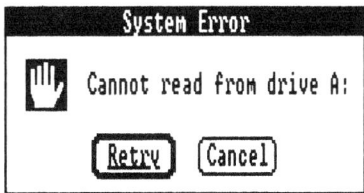

This is a *dialog box*. When Windows applications need to converse with the user, they do so via dialog boxes. In this case, Windows displays the source of the message and the possible user options. Select the Cancel option by pressing the TAB key and then the SPACEBAR or by pointing to the option and pressing the mouse select button.

Keyboard Selection of Dialog Box Option

Press the TAB key until the object desired is selected. Then press the SPACEBAR.

Mouse Selection of Dialog Box Option

Direct the mouse pointer to the option desired and press the mouse select button.

Chapter 4 will describe how to create dialog boxes with the dialog box editor provided with the development kit.

Next, look at the list of files on the screen. The MS-DOS Executive highlights one file by placing it in reverse video. This file is the default for file-manipulation commands. If you are using the keyboard, select files with the cursor arrow keys. If you are using a mouse, simply point to the file desired, and then press the mouse select button.

Keyboard Selection of Windows Default File

Use the cursor arrow keys to move the file selection highlight to the file desired.

Mouse Selection of Windows Default File

Direct the mouse pointer to the file desired and press the mouse select button.

The MS-DOS Executive defines several pull-down menus that allow you to perform additional processing. In general, a *pull-down menu* is simply a menu of options that is displayed on top of the current window. Consider the following partial screen display. The section labeled "Menu Bar" contains the list of available pull-down menus.

```
≡                        MS-DOS Executive                      ⌐
File  View  Special
```

Menu Bar

If you are using a mouse, point to the File menu. If you are using the keyboard, press the ALT key while pressing the key corresponding to the first letter of the menu desired.

Keyboard Selection of a Windows Menu

Simultaneously press the ALT key and the key matching the first letter of
the menu name desired.

Mouse Selection of a Windows Menu

Direct the mouse pointer to the menu desired and press the mouse select
button.

In this case, press ALT-F. The File menu allows you to perform the
following:

If you are using the keyboard, you can select an option from a
pull-down menu by using the cursor arrow keys or by pressing the
first letter of the option desired. Once the option is in reverse video,
press ENTER. If you are using a mouse, simply point to the option
desired and release the select button.

Keyboard Menu-Option Selection

Use the cursor arrow keys to select the option desired, or press the key of the letter matching the first letter of the option desired.

Mouse Menu-Option Selection

With the mouse select button depressed, direct the mouse pointer to the option desired and then release the select button.

If you select the Run option, the MS-DOS Executive will prompt you for the program to execute, as follows:

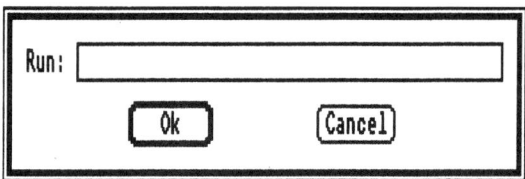

Type in the name of the program that you want to execute, and then press ENTER. To cancel the command, simply press ENTER without typing a file name, or press the ESC key. Pressing the ESC key also allows you to exit dialog boxes and Windows menus.

The Load option makes a program available as an icon. Later, this chapter will examine how to select an application from a list of icons. In this case, load the program CLOCK.EXE as an icon, as shown here:

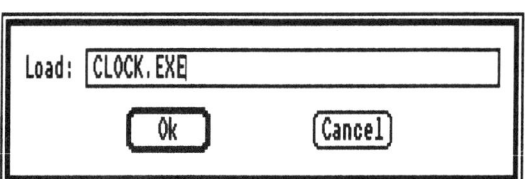

Windows will display the following at the bottom of the screen:

There are two ways of selecting CLOCK.EXE as the program to load. First, you can select the file CLOCK.EXE as the default file with the cursor arrow keys or the mouse. Once you have done this, invoking the File menu and the Load option will display CLOCK .EXE by default. The second method is simply to invoke the File menu and, at the Load option, type the name CLOCK.EXE in the dialog box.

The Copy option allows you to copy one or more files to a new location. By default, Copy will display the current default file as the source file, as in the following example:

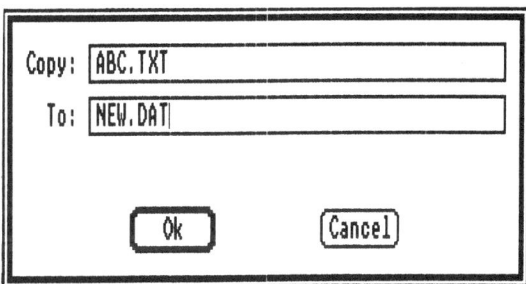

Here, Windows would copy the default source file to a target file named NEW.DAT.

The Get Info option simply displays the name, extension, size, and creation date and time for the default file, as shown here:

☰	Get Info				
ABC	.TXT	42	6-04-85	9:07AM	

The Delete option is similar to the DOS DEL command. By default, the MS-DOS Executive displays the default file as the file to be deleted. If you want to delete this file, simply press ENTER. Otherwise, type in the name of the file to delete, as shown here:

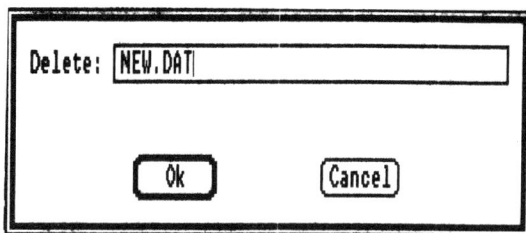

The MS-DOS Executive will delete the specified file. Remember that the ESC key allows you to terminate the command.

The Print option is similar to the DOS PRINT command in that it places a file in a queue (the Windows Spooler) for printing. The command uses the default file, as follows:

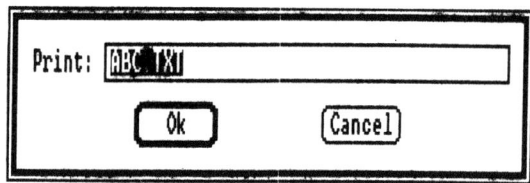

If you want to print a different file, simply type in the name of that file. When you press ENTER, the MS-DOS Executive will display the following:

The Windows Spooler is conceptually similar to the DOS PRINT queue. Once installed, the Spooler displays the following icon:

The complete capabilities of the Spooler will be discussed later in this chapter.

The Rename option allows you to rename the default file. Upon invocation, this option will prompt you for the target file name with the following dialog box:

Rename: ABC.TXT

To:

Ok   Cancel

Simply type in the new file name and press ENTER.

The View menu allows you to specify how the MS-DOS Executive is to display the files contained in the current directory. Select the View menu by pressing ALT-V or by pointing to View with your mouse while depressing its select button. The View menu allows you to select from the following options:

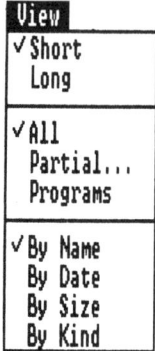

Again, you select options by using the cursor arrow keys, by typing the first letter of the option, or by pointing to the option with your mouse. The Short option directs the MS-DOS Executive simply to display the name and extension of each file in the current directory, as follows:

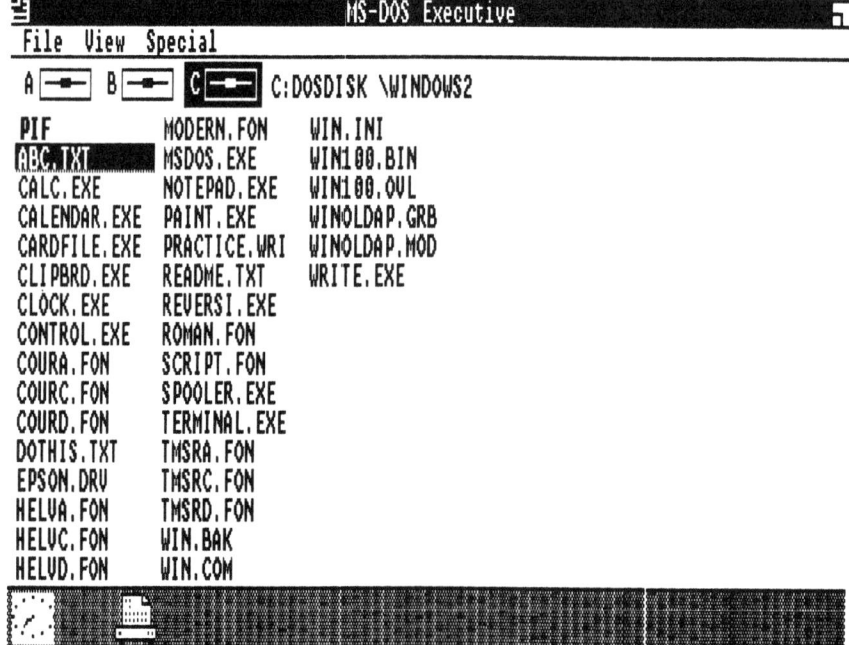

The Long option displays the name, extension, size, and creation date and time of each file:

```
≡                        MS-DOS Executive                           ⌐
  File  View  Special                                               |
  A ═  B ═  C ═    C:DOSDISK \WINDOWS2                               |
 PIF          <DIR>                                               ▲
 ABC      .TXT       42   6-04-85    9:07AM
 CALC     .EXE    25008   5-22-86    4:33AM
 CALENDAR .EXE    37552   5-22-86    7:55AM
 CARDFILE .EXE    36992   5-22-86    4:23AM
 CLIPBRD  .EXE     9712   5-22-86    6:17AM
 CLOCK    .EXE     7984   5-22-86    6:08AM
 CONTROL  .EXE    52704   8-14-86    4:13PM
 COURA    .FON     8720   7-29-86    4:43PM
 COURC    .FON     8784   7-29-86    4:43PM
 COURD    .FON    15136   7-29-86    4:43PM
 DOTHIS   .TXT      493  10-25-85    1:02PM
 EPSON    .DRV    14352   5-22-86   11:07AM
 HELVA    .FON    27056   7-29-86    4:44PM
 HELVC    .FON    26624   7-29-86    4:45PM
 HELVD    .FON    45600   7-29-86    4:45PM            ▼
```

The All option directs the MS-DOS Executive to list all of the files contained in the current directory. The Partial option directs the MS-DOS Executive to display the following dialog box:

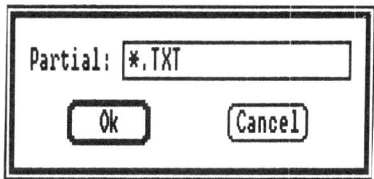

Simply type in the file specification of the file(s) that you want to list. DOS wildcard characters are valid. To display only files having the extension TXT, enter *.TXT.

The options By Name, By Date, By Size, and By Kind specify how you want the directory listing to be sorted. The check marks next to the View options display the current default values. Later chapters will discuss how Windows menus provide check mark capabilities.

The Special menu provides the following options:

The first option, End Session, allows you to terminate the current Windows session and return to DOS. Upon invocation of this option, Windows will display the following:

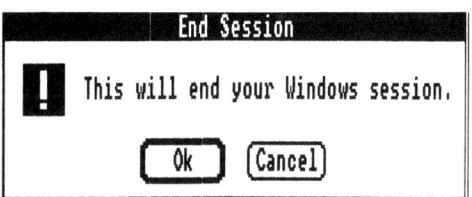

To terminate Windows, simply press ENTER. Otherwise, press the TAB key to select Cancel and then press the SPACEBAR, or select the Cancel option with your mouse.

The Create Directory option displays the following dialog box, which allows you to create DOS subdirectories:

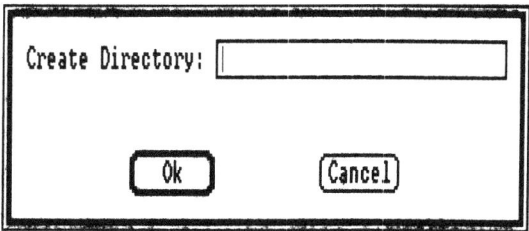

Similarly, the Change Directory option prompts you for the desired directory with the following dialog box:

Type in the name of the desired directory and press ENTER. In addition, you can set the default directory to a subdirectory that appears in the list of files displayed on the screen simply by selecting it as the default file and pressing ENTER or by double-clicking the select button on your mouse. Likewise, pressing the BACKSPACE key moves you one level up in the directory structure.

The Format Data Disk option allows you to format a disk contained in either drive A or drive B, as follows:

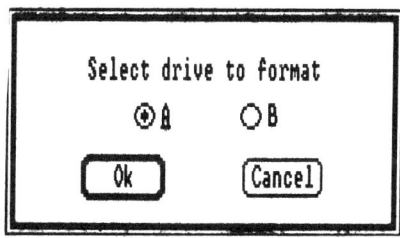

Simply select the desired drive (with the TAB key) and press ENTER. If you do not want to format a disk, press the ESC key to exit the dialog box.

The Make System Disk option executes the DOS SYS command, copying the system to the specified drive, as follows:

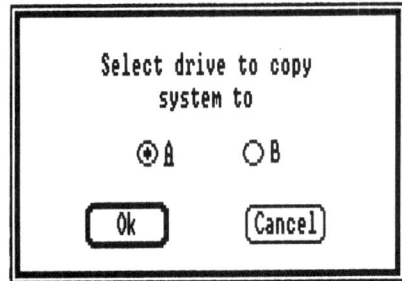

Select the desired drive by pressing the TAB key and then the SPACE-BAR, or by pointing to the drive with your mouse and pressing the select button. Upon completion, the disk selected will be bootable.

The Set Volume Name option allows you to specify the volume label for the current default disk as follows:

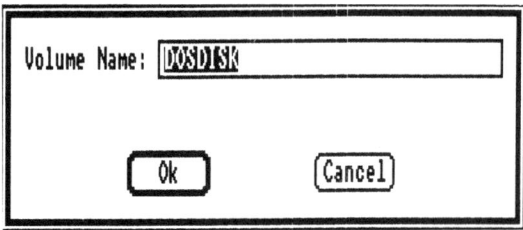

Type in the desired volume label (11 characters maximum) and press ENTER. If you do not want to specify a volume label, press the ESC key.

The System Menu

Every window has a System menu associated with it. You select this menu by pressing the ALT key and the SPACEBAR simultaneously or by pointing the mouse to the System menu box in the upper left-hand corner, as shown here:

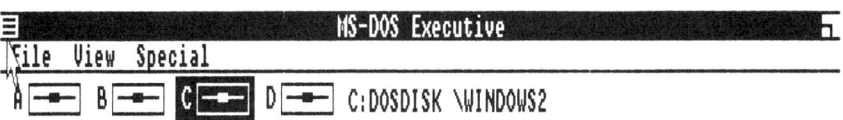

The System menu provides the following capabilities:

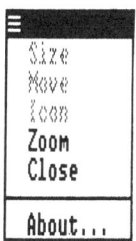

One or more of the options may be gray rather than black. This means that the option is not available for the current window. The Size option allows you to change the size of a window. Most applications support a size box. The Size option is discussed later in this chapter. The ability to modify the size of a window is built into Windows, making it virtually transparent to the applications developed in later chapters.

The Move option allows you to relocate a window on the screen or to move an icon to a window. The Icon option makes the current window an icon and places it in the lower left-hand corner of the screen. The Zoom option expands a window to the full size of the screen, covering up any icons in the lower left corner. The Zoom option works as a toggle—selecting it again shrinks the size of the window. The Close option terminates the application running in the current window and removes it from memory. If you are closing the MS-DOS Executive, Windows will display the following:

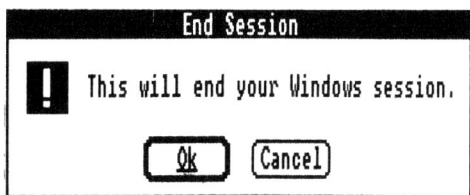

The About option displays information about the application. For the MS-DOS Executive, selecting the About option displays the following:

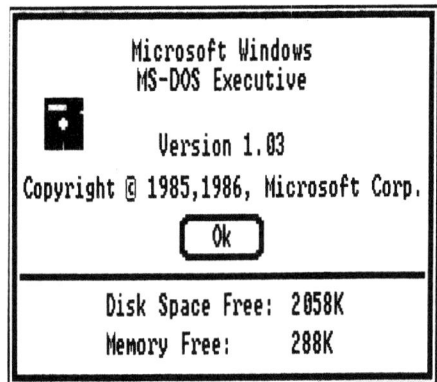

As you will see, application programs require you to define data structures that specify the information that the About option will display.

Selecting Programs from Icons

To fully exploit the true power of Windows, you must invoke several programs simultaneously and switch from one program to the next as your needs require. Windows allows you to load programs into memory as icons and select them for execution at a later time. Windows will display the icon for the program at the bottom of the screen, as follows:

You have already seen how the Spooler creates an icon. If you load a program, it, too, becomes available as an icon. Assume that you have no programs loaded and, therefore, no icons are displayed. Using the File menu, load the program CLOCK.EXE as an icon:

☐ Press ALT-F.

☐ Select Load.

☐ Type in CLOCK.EXE and press ENTER.

Windows will display the following:

Next, load the program CALC.EXE in the same fashion. Your screen should now display the following:

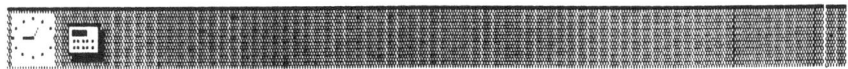

To select an icon with a mouse, simply point to the icon and press the select button on your mouse. If you are using the keyboard, use the ALT-TAB key combination to display the names of the icons. Once the icon that you desire is highlighted, use the ALT-SPACEBAR combination to display the System menu and select the Icon command, or double-click the select button on the mouse.

Keyboard Icon Selection

Press the ALT and TAB keys to toggle through the icons displayed.

Mouse Icon Selection

Direct the mouse pointer to the icon desired and press the mouse select button.

In this case, select and open the Clock icon. Windows will display an analog clock on the screen as follows:

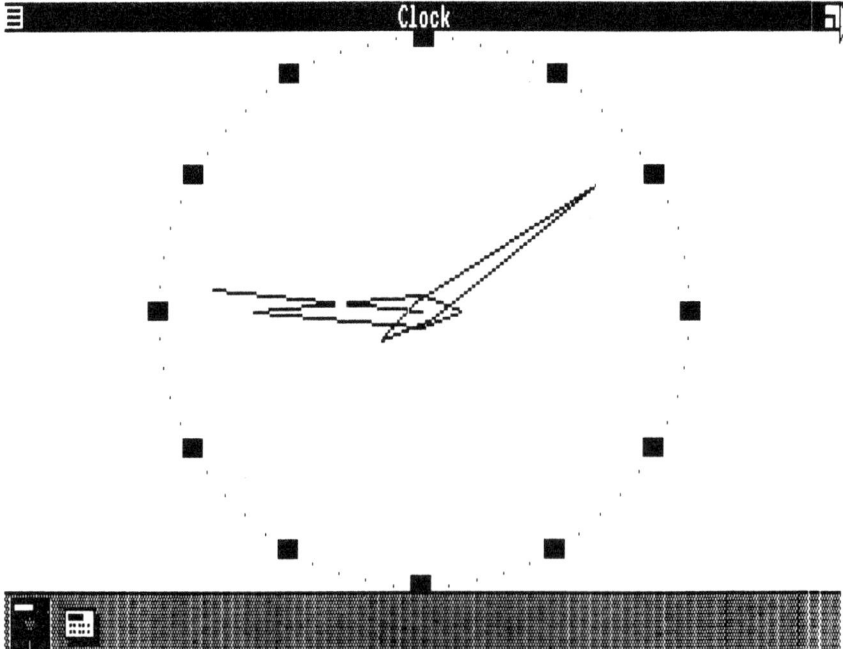

When you grow tired of watching this clock, select the Windows System menu box by pressing the ALT-SPACEBAR key combination, or by pointing your mouse to the System menu box in the upper left corner. Windows will display the following:

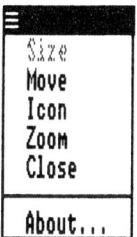

You have several choices. In this case, you want to return to the MS-DOS Executive, so you can either close the clock program (this removes it from memory), or you can select the Icon option, which places the Clock icon back at the lower left-hand corner of the screen. Save the clock program as an icon. Now, because there are multiple icons available, you must select the one that you desire. The icon that looks like a floppy disk represents the MS-DOS Executive. Select and open it; Windows will display the following:

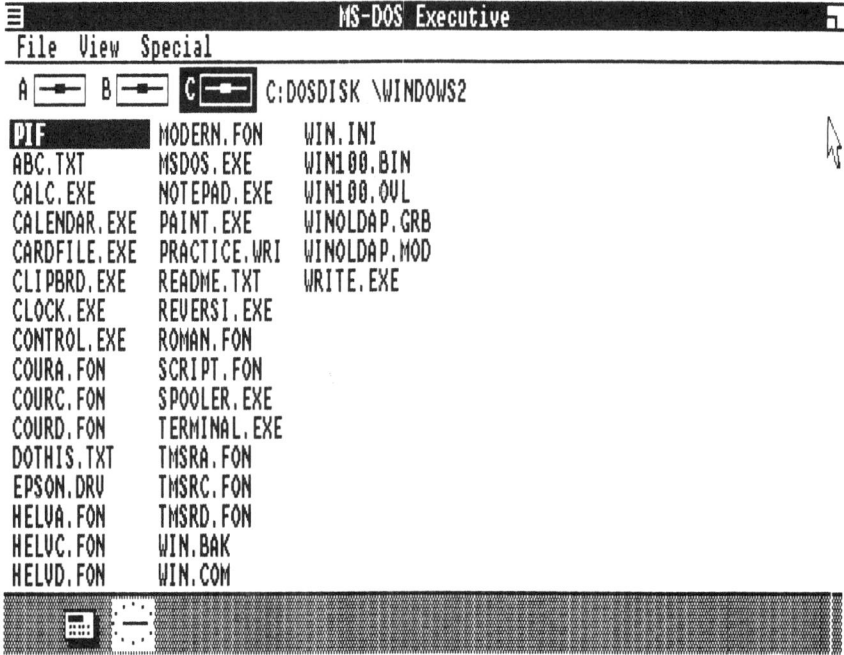

The Windows Spooler

Each time you print a file from within Windows, the file is written to the Spooler. You can gain additional control over the printer via the Spooler icon. Select the Spooler icon. (If it is not available as an icon, simply run SPOOLER.EXE.) Windows will display the following:

If files reside in the Spooler, their names will be displayed on the screen. Select the Priority menu by pointing to the option with your mouse or by pressing ALT-P. The Priority menu gives you the following options:

The High option allows you to print faster by causing the Windows Spooler to release the CPU less frequently. Likewise, the Low command directs Windows to print more slowly by causing the Spooler to use less CPU time.

The Controls menu gives you direct control over the files in the Spooler, as shown here:

The Pause option allows you to suspend printing temporarily, which allows other programs to use the CPU time normally used by the Spooler. The Resume option restarts printing by the Windows Spooler. The Terminate option allows you to remove files from the Spooler. The Spooler will confirm the file to be removed via a dialog box.

Periodically, the Spooler will have messages that it must display. If the Spooler is not the active window, the Spooler icon will flash when it has a message. To display the message, select the Spooler icon as the active window.

What Is the Clipboard?

Windows allows you to exchange information between applications with the Windows Clipboard. In general, the Clipboard is simply a location on which you can store text or graphics that other Windows applications can access, as seen here:

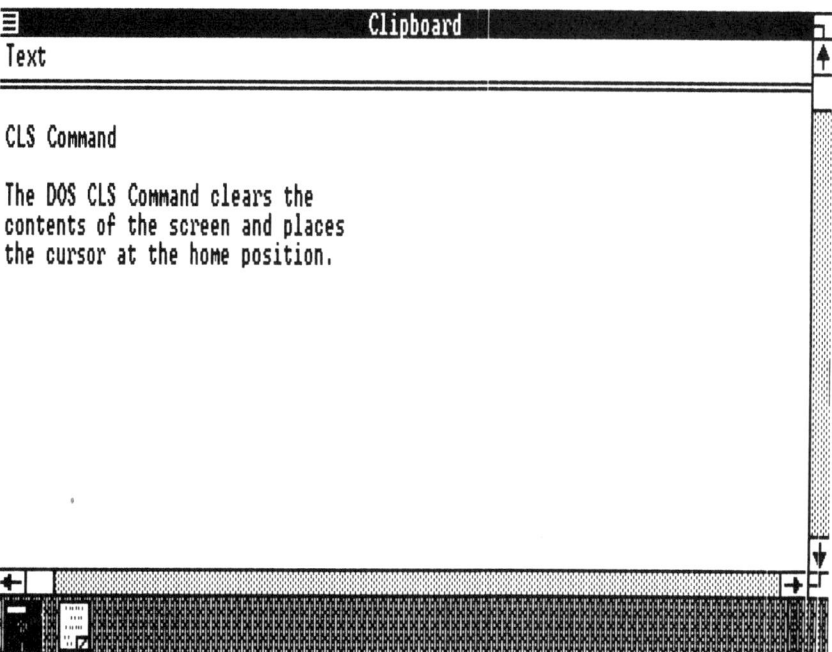

The following scenario assumes that you are conversant with the Windows desktop applications Notepad and Cardfile. If you are not, simply ignore the processing details and note the functional aspects of the Clipboard. Create the following memo with the Notepad:

Pull down the Edit menu from Notepad and choose the Select All option. All of the text should now be displayed in reverse video, shown here:

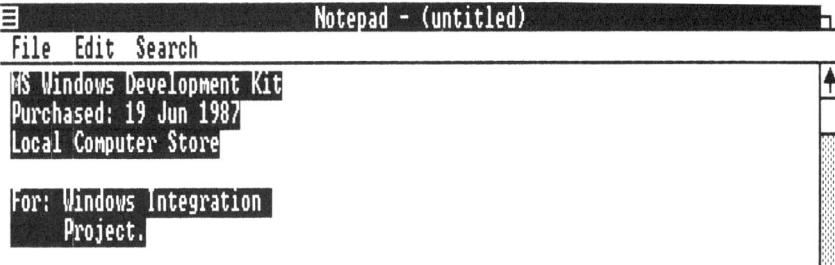

Pull down the Edit menu and select the Copy option. All of the text in reverse video has now been copied to the Windows Clipboard. Next, save Notepad as an icon and invoke the program CLIPBRD.EXE from the MS-DOS Executive. Windows will display the following:

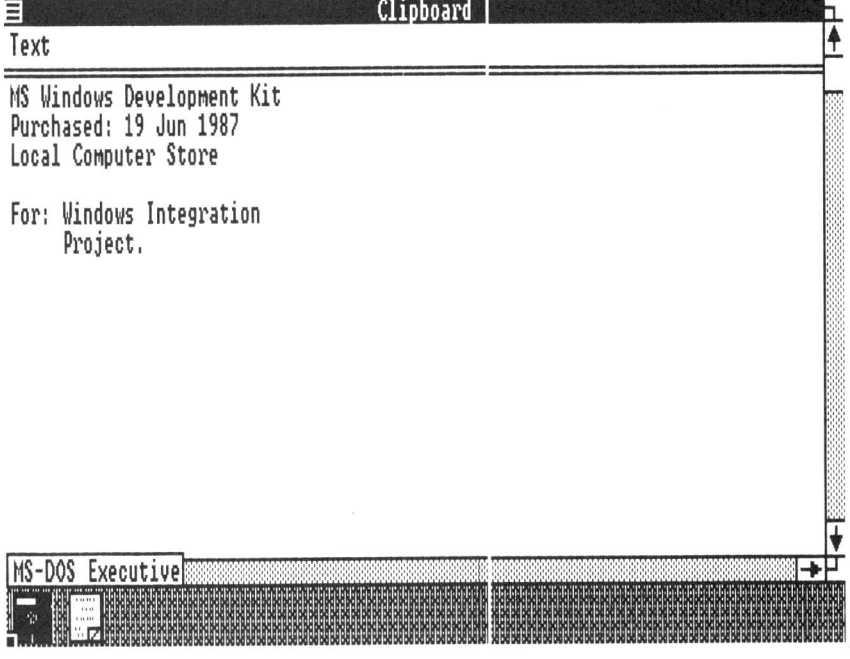

CLIPBRD.EXE allows you to view the information contained in the Windows Clipboard. As you can see, the information that you just selected from your Notepad is displayed. When other applications perform Paste operations, the information that they paste is what is currently contained in the Clipboard.

Save CLIPBRD.EXE as an icon. From the MS-DOS Executive, invoke CARDFILE.EXE. Next, pull down the Edit menu and select the Paste option. Your card should now contain the following:

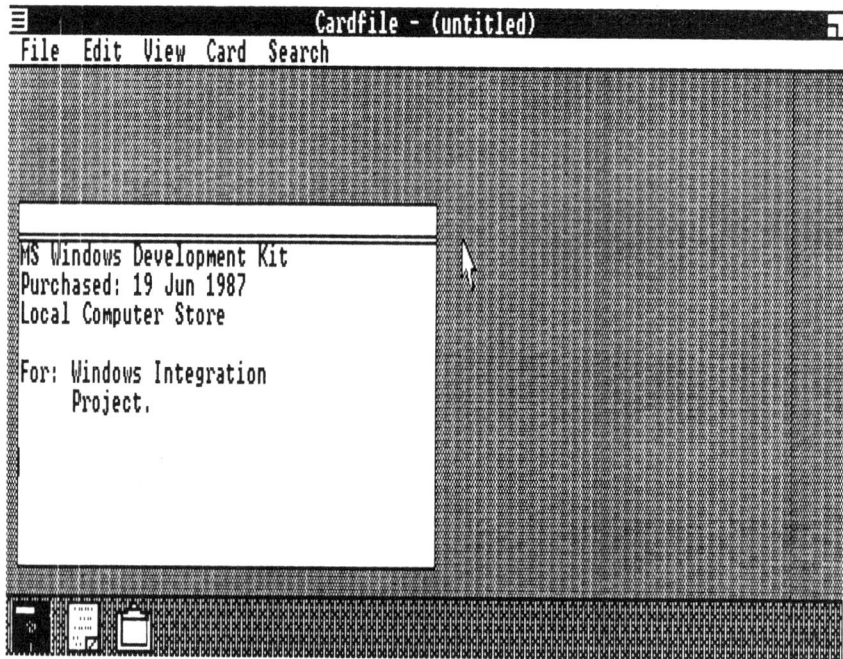

You have just exchanged information between two Windows applications. It is possible to exchange information between all of the Windows applications in this fashion. Chapter 14 will describe the interface to the Windows Clipboard for applications programs.

Running Multiple Applications
Simultaneously

Throughout this chapter, the multiprogramming capabilities of Windows have been discussed. In this section you will invoke several programs simultaneously, move the programs around on the screen, and see that the System menu for each program becomes very powerful when multiple applications are running simultaneously.

From the MS-DOS Executive, load the Clock, Calculator, Notepad, and Calendar as icons. Your screen should contain the following:

Next, select the Clock icon. Invoke the System menu for the clock, and select the Move option. With the mouse or the keyboard arrow keys, move the Clock icon to the title bar of the MS-DOS Executive, as shown here:

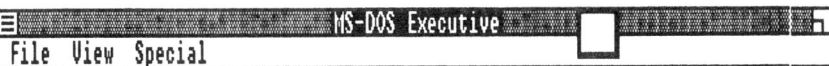

Next, press the ENTER key or your mouse select button. You should now have two applications on your screen. Select the Calculator icon. Move it to the title bar of the analog clock, and expand it in the same fashion. Your screen should now contain the following:

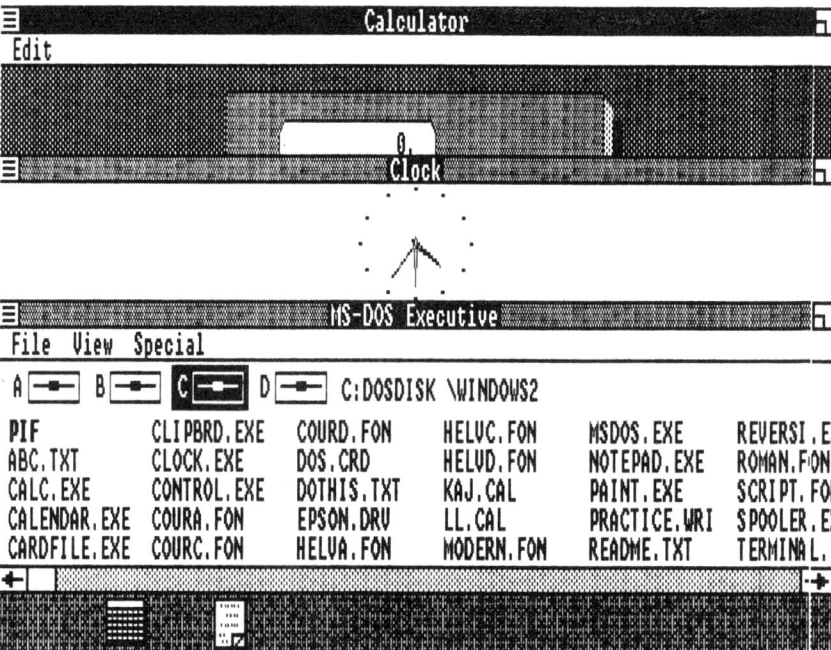

By pressing ALT-TAB, you move first through the applications windows on the screen and then through the available icons. Use ALT-TAB to select the Clock window. When the title bar is displayed in reverse video, the window is the current window. Now select the System menu for Clock. Choose the Size option. With either your mouse or the keyboard arrow keys, move the small size box beyond the borders of the current Clock window, as shown next:

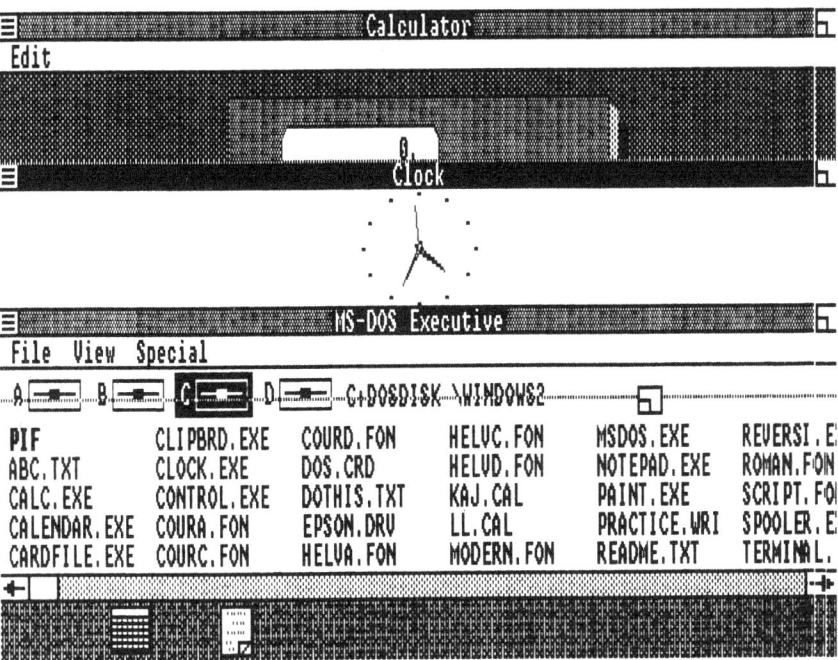

You should now have a movable frame. Move the frame in both directions. It is possible to shrink and expand a window with the Size option. In this case, make the Clock window smaller, as shown next:

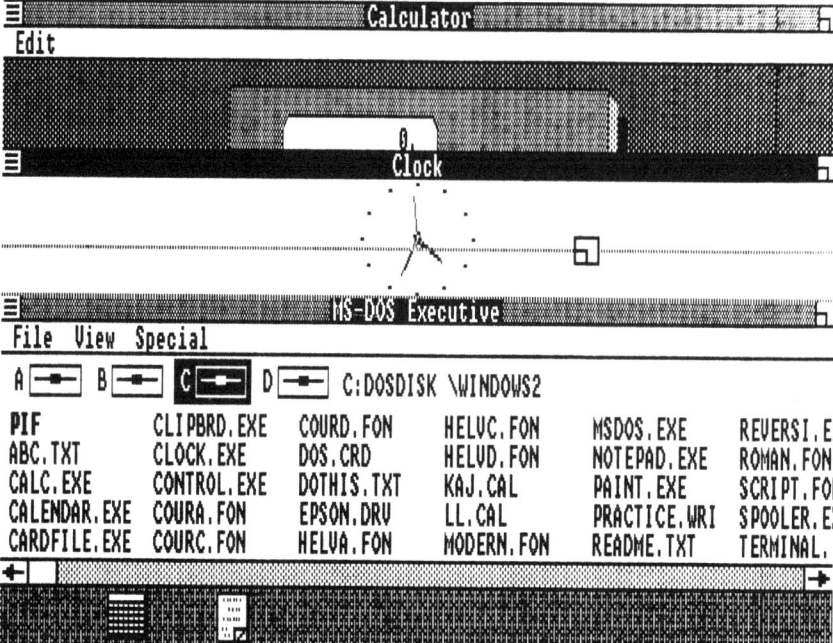

When you press the ENTER key or mouse select button, your screen will contain the following:

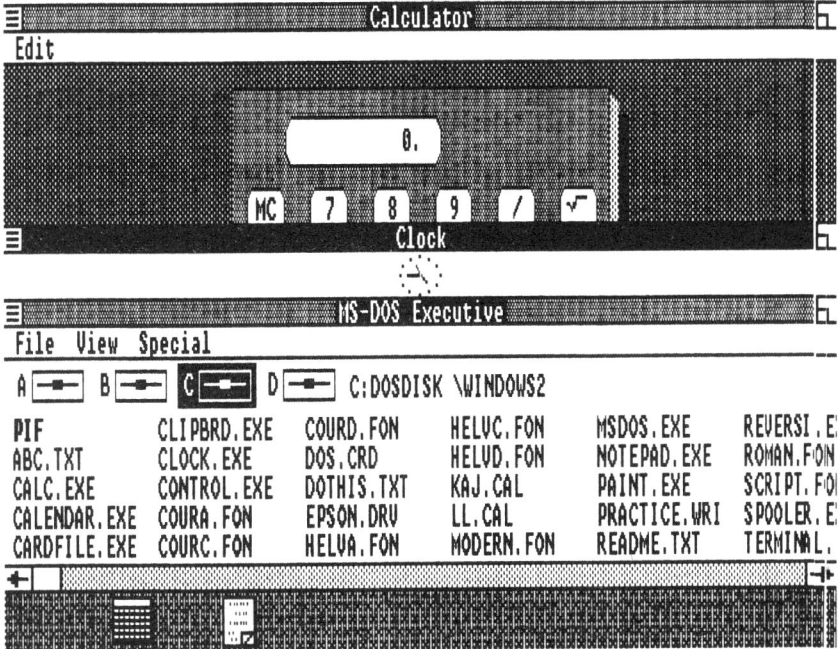

Select the Notepad icon. Move it to the screen, as shown next:

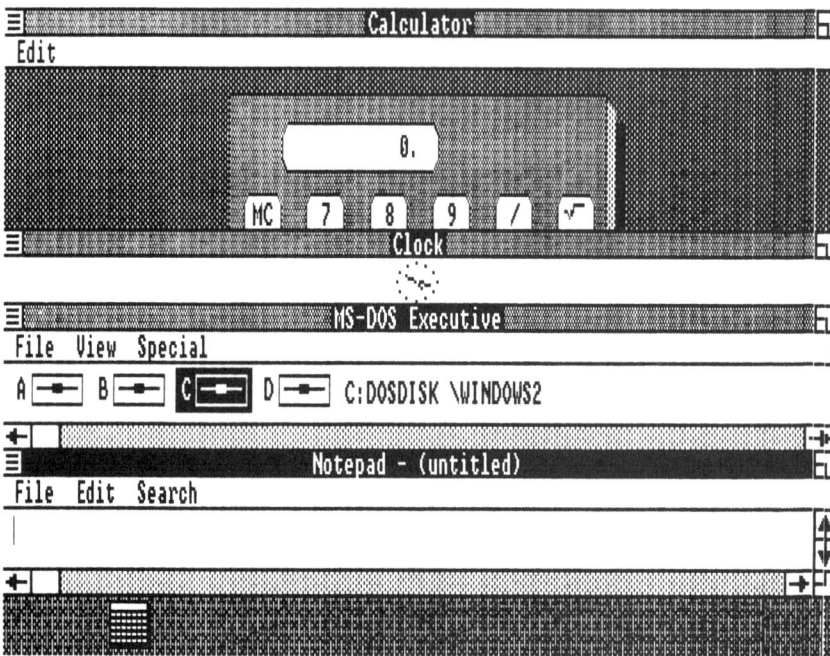

Now move the Clock window. To do this, select the Clock System menu and make it an icon. Next, move the icon to the right-hand border of the Notepad window, as shown here:

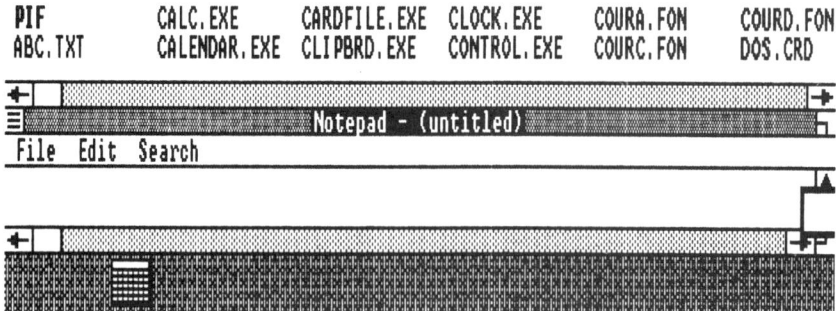

Press ENTER or the select button on your mouse; your screen will
contain the following:

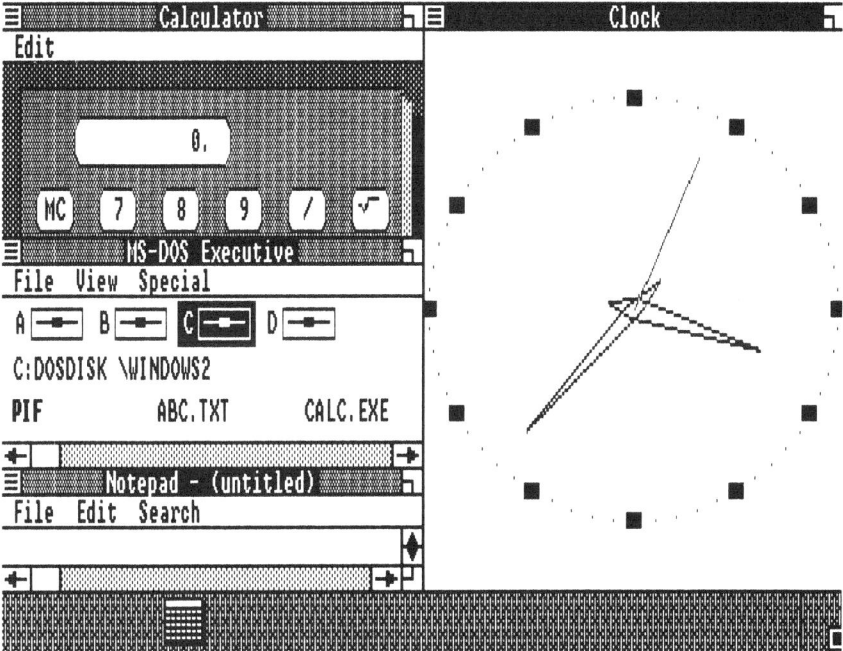

Next, load a second copy of the clock program from the MS-DOS
Executive, and place it on the screen as follows:

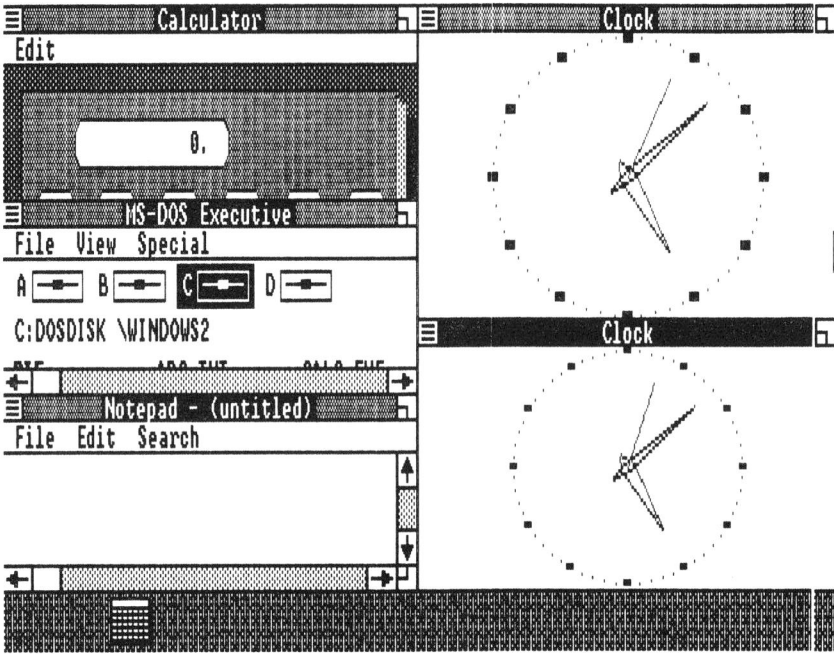

You can now actually watch your system time-share. The two clocks appear to be running simultaneously. If you were to print a file to the Spooler, the file would print in the background, making the computer appear to be performing even more tasks at the same time. With Windows, CPU idle time is soon used to its fullest capacity.

Guidelines for Windows Display

In the previous example you invoked several applications simultaneously, filling the screen with multiple windows. Each time Windows places a window on your screen, it uses the following guidelines:

☐ If no other windows exist on the screen, the window fills the entire screen minus the icon area at the bottom.

☐ If you place an icon within an existing window, the existing window becomes an icon, and the icon that you have selected replaces it.

☐ If you place an icon on an existing window border, the icon you have selected becomes a window along with the windows currently displayed on the screen.

☐ Placing the icon on a horizontal border expands the new window above or below the existing window.

☐ Placing the icon on a vertical border expands the new window beside the existing window.

☐ The existing windows are resized in a manner that minimizes the effects on the current screen display.

Scrolling Within Windows

Often, when several windows are displayed simultaneously on the screen, the application is unable to display all of the information that would normally appear. In such cases, many Windows applications provide scroll bars like the one shown here that you can access with your mouse to scroll the information contained in the window.

```
☰                          MS-DOS Executive                          ⬛
 File  View  Special
   A⬛─⬛  B⬛─⬛  C⬛─⬛  D⬛─⬛  C:DOSDISK \WINDOWS2
  PIF            <DIR>                                                 ▲
  ABC       .TXT        42   6-04-85    9:07AM
  CALC      .EXE     25008   5-22-86    4:33AM
  CALENDAR  .EXE     37552   5-22-86    7:55AM
  CARDFILE  .EXE     36992   5-22-86    4:23AM
  CLIPBRD   .EXE      9712   5-22-86    6:17AM
  CLOCK     .EXE      7984   5-22-86    6:08AM
  CONTROL   .EXE     52704   8-14-86    4:13PM
  COURA     .FON      8720   7-29-86    4:43PM
  COURC     .FON      8784   7-29-86    4:43PM
  COURD     .FON     15136   7-29-86    4:43PM
  DOS       .CRD       772   1-25-87    1:47PM
  DOTHIS    .TXT       493  10-25-85    1:02PM
  EPSON     .DRV     14352   5-22-86   11:07AM
  HELVA     .FON     27056   7-29-86    4:44PM
  HELVC     .FON     26624   7-29-86    4:45PM           ▼
```

If you are using the keyboard, the cursor arrow keys and the PGUP and PGDN keys allow you to scroll information.

Use the bar as follows to scroll information:

☐ To move up or down one line, simply select the scroll arrows at either end of the scroll bar.

☐ To move up or down a window at a time, depress the mouse select button while the arrow is within the gray area of the scroll bar.

☐ The small white box is called the scroll box. Raising it places you closer to the top of the information. Lowering it places you near the end of the information.

The Windows Control Panel

The CONTROL.EXE program allows you to configure new printers, modify port communications parameters, set the color for systems using the Enhanced Graphics Adapter (EGA), set the system date and time, modify the cursor blink rate, and modify mouse double-click delay time. From the MS-DOS Executive, invoke CONTROL .EXE. Windows will display the following:

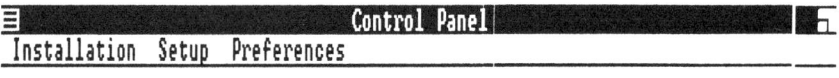

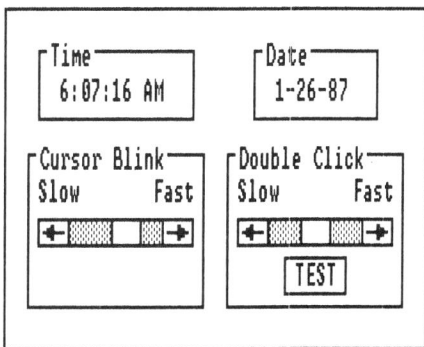

This is your Control Panel. To modify the system date or time, simply select the Time or Date field you wish to change and use the UP ARROW or DOWN ARROW to increment or decrement the value. To modify the cursor blink rate, use the TAB key or the mouse to select the Cursor Blink box, and use the cursor arrow keys or mouse to either speed up or slow down the blink rate.

Each time you press the mouse select button, Windows delays a short period of time to see if you are double-clicking. The Double Click box allows you to increase or decrease this period of time. This allows you to configure your mouse to your own touch.

Now select the Installation menu. The Control Panel will display the following:

Select the Add New Printer option. The Control Panel will prompt you for the location of the printer device-driver file with the following dialog box:

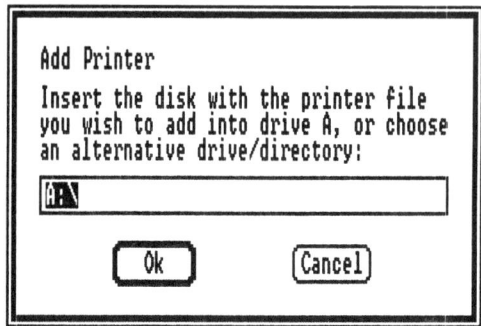

Later you will see how to associate the new printer with a port.

If you select the Delete Printer option, you are prompted for the printer to be removed, as follows:

Select the printer you wish to delete. The printer will become unavailable to Windows.

The Add New Font option allows you to make additional fonts available to Windows applications programs. The Control Panel will prompt you for the font as follows:

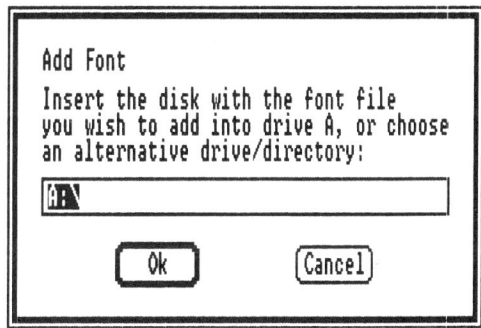

Similarly, the Delete Font option prompts you for the font to be removed from Windows, as follows:

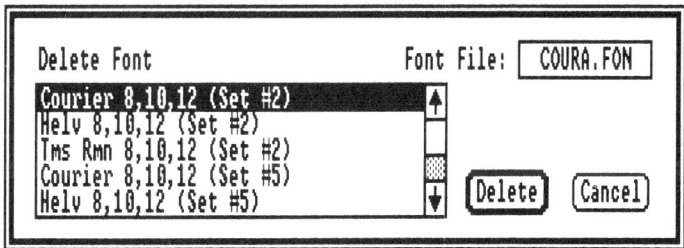

Select the font to be removed with the keyboard cursor keys or the mouse.

Next, invoke the Setup menu. The Control Panel will display the following:

Choose the Connections option. The Control Panel allows you to specify which printer is connected to each port, as follows:

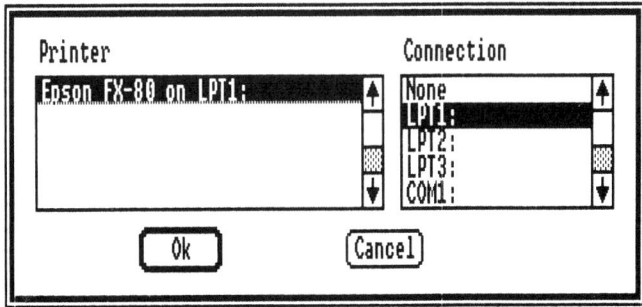

The Printer option defines the current Windows default printer, as follows:

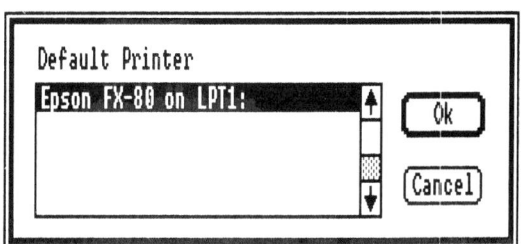

The Communications Port option allows you to specify the communications parameters for a specific port, as follows:

```
┌──────────────────────────────────────────┐
│  Communications Settings                   │
│  Port          ⦿ COM1:      ○ COM2:        │
│  Baud Rate:    │1200│                      │
│  Word Length   ○4 ○5  ○6  ○7 ⦿8            │
│  Parity        ○ Even  ○ Odd  ⦿ None       │
│  Stop Bits     ⦿1     ○1.5   ○2            │
│  Handshake     ○ Hardware  ⦿ None          │
│            [   Ok   ]      [Cancel]         │
└──────────────────────────────────────────┘
```

The Control Panel Preferences menu displays the following options:

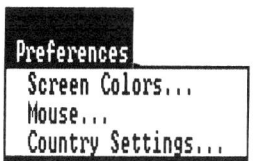

The Screen Colors option allows you to define the colors on the screen for the EGA, as follows:

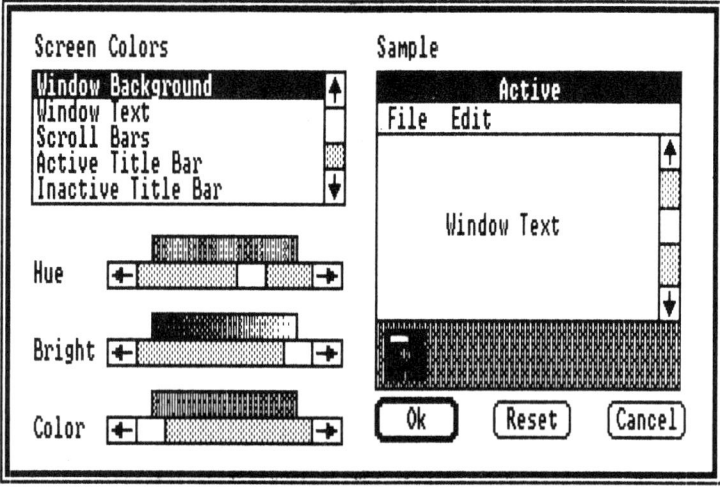

The Mouse option allows you to change the mouse select button from the left to the right button, as shown here:

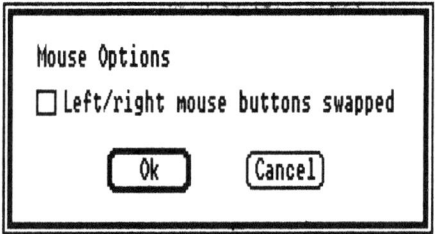

Country Settings allows you to change the date, time, number, and currency formats, as shown here:

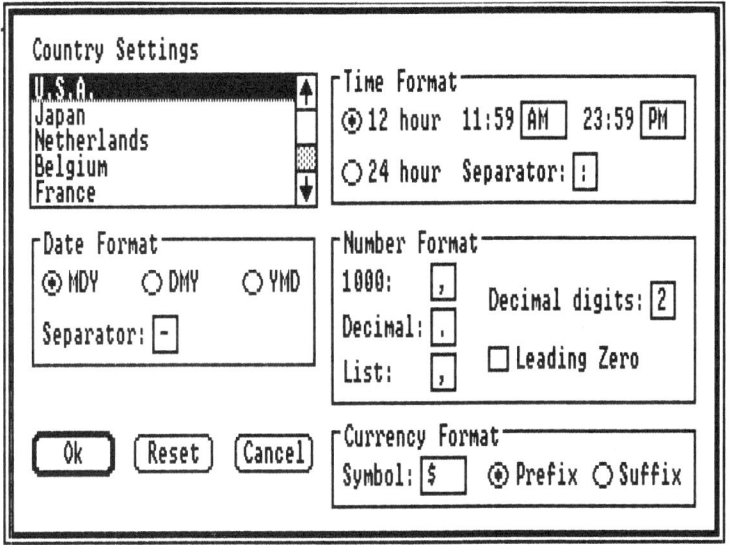

Most users will never invoke the Control Panel. However, once you are confident with Windows, you may want to modify some of the default parameters. Each entry modified via the Control Panel will be updated in the file WIN.INI, the Windows initialization file that Windows uses to configure itself each time it starts. Chapter 6 examines the file WIN.INI in detail.

Windows Software Development Kit

The Microsoft Windows Software Development Kit provides a collection of utility programs, libraries, include files, and debugging tools that allow you to develop programs to execute in the Windows environment. In addition, the kit provides several sample programs with which you can experiment to increase your understanding of programming for Windows.

The Windows Software Development Kit comes with the following documentation:

□ The *Microsoft Windows Software Development Kit Programmer's Guide* (provides an overview of the development process for Windows applications, along with a complete description of the development utilities)

□ The *Microsoft Windows Style Guidelines*

□ The *Microsoft Windows Software Development Kit Programmer's Reference* (provides the calling sequence and description for each of the Windows callable routines)

□ The *Microsoft Windows Programmer's Quick Reference*

Getting Started

Before you begin your Windows application development, write-protect each of the original disks provided with the development kit. Next, use the DOS DISKCOPY command as follows to make a backup copy of each disk provided:

```
A> DISKCOPY A: B:
```

Installing the Windows
Software Development Kit

If you have not already installed Windows on your fixed disk, do so now by entering

```
C> SETUP
```

Either use the INSTALL.BAT procedure provided with the development kit, or use the DOS COPY command to ensure that the following directories contain the files listed.

The subdirectory \WINDOWS\BIN will contain the following executable utility programs:

☐ RC.EXE compiles resource script files and adds them to Windows applications programs.

☐ RCPP.EXE is the preprocessor for Windows resource script files.

☐ IMPLIB.EXE creates user-defined linkable libraries for Windows applications.

☐ LINK4.EXE links Windows applications into executable programs.

☐ SYMDEB.EXE is the Windows symbolic debugger.

☐ MAPSYM.EXE creates symbol files for symbolic debugging.

☐ EXEHDR.EXE decodes and displays the file header of an executable Windows application.

☐ LIB.EXE contains the Microsoft librarian.

☐ MAKE.EXE is the program maintenance aid.

☐ PATCHDBG.EXE modifies the debugging kernel (KERNEL.EXE) of Windows to disable global memory movement.

☐ PATCHRTL.EXE patches the retail version of the kernel to disable global memory movement.

☐ WINSTUB.EXE contains a stub that displays the following warning message:

```
C> CLOCK
This program requires Microsoft Windows.
```

when a user attempts to execute a Windows application outside of Windows.

The subdirectory \WINDOWS\INCLUDE should contain the following files:

☐ WINDOWS.H is the C include file for Windows applications.

☐ CMACROS.INC is the Microsoft Macro Assembler include file for Windows applications.

☐ PASCAL.INC is the include file for the PASLIBW interface.

☐ WINDOWS.INC is the include file for Pascal Windows applications.

☐ STYLE.H is the subset of WINDOWS.H containing just Windows styles. This is useful in creating dialog boxes with the resource compiler.

☐ WINNAMES.INC is the list of Pascal entry point names. When you use this file and delete those entries not used in Pascal applications, the symbol table size will be generated by the first pass of the Pascal compiler.

The subdirectory \WINDOWS\LIB should contain the following files:

☐ CLIBW.LIB is the standard Windows compact-memory model.

☐ CWINLIBC.LIB is the standard C library for Windows libraries for compact-memory-model applications.

☐ SLIBW.LIB is the standard Windows small-memory model.

☐ SWINLIBC.LIB is the standard C library for Windows libraries for small-memory-model applications.

☐ MLIBW.LIB is the standard Windows medium-memory model.

☐ MWINLIBC.LIB is the standard C library for Windows libraries for medium-memory-model applications.

☐ LLIBW.LIB is the standard Windows large-memory model.

☐ LWINLIBC.LIB is the standard C library for Windows libraries for large-memory-model applications.

☐ PASCALW.LIB is the Windows library for Pascal applications.

☐ PASCAL.LIB is the Pascal library for Windows applications.

The subdirectory \WINDOWS should contain the following files:

☐ ATRM1111.FNT is the sample font to use with the font editor.

☐ DLGEDIT.EXE creates dialog boxes for Windows applications.

☐ FONTEDIT.EXE creates fonts for Windows applications.

☐ HEAPWALK.EXE lists the owners and sizes of memory locations in the heap.

☐ ICONEDIT.EXE creates icons, cursors, and bitmaps for Windows applications.

☐ SHAKER.EXE forces memory movement in the heap by randomly allocating free space.

☐ GDI.SYM contains the symbols for use with the symbolic debugger (SYMDEB) for the graphics device interface (GDI) portion of Windows.

☐ KERNEL.SYM contains the symbols for use with the symbolic debugger (SYMDEB) for the operating system extensions (KERNEL) portion of Windows.

☐ USER.SYM contains the symbols for use with the symbolic debugger (SYMDEB) for the Windows manager (USER) portion of Windows.

The subdirectory \WINDOWS\C will contain the C, icon (ICO), resource script (RC), and definition files (DEF) for the sample C programs. The subdirectory \WINDOWS\PASCAL should contain the files required to create the sample Pascal Windows applications. The Software Development Kit provides the complete source code for the Windows Cardfile application.

Next, create a directory called \TEMP in your root directory by executing the command shown here. Periodically, Windows applications require temporary files. In such instances, the files will be created in this subdirectory.

```
C> MKDIR \TEMP
```

You may have noticed that you ignored the files required for the Windows symbolic debugger. The debugger will be examined in an appendix at the end of this book.

Now you must modify the file CONFIG.SYS to ensure that it has the following entries:

FILES=20
BUFFERS=25

For practice, use the Notepad desktop application to modify this file.

```
≡                                     Notepad - CONFIG.SYS
 File  Edit  Search
 files=20
 buffers=25
 device=\dos\ansi.sys
 device=\dos\vdisk.sys 192 512 12
```

Finally, you must define the Windows environment by placing the following entries in the AUTOEXEC.BAT file in the root directory:

SET LIB=C:\WINDOWS\LIB
SET INCLUDE=C:\WINDOWS\INCLUDE
SET TMP=C:\TEMP
SET TEMP=C:\TEMP
SET PATH=C:\WINDOWS\BIN;C:\WINDOWS\PIF;C:\WINDOWS
    \LIB

If you have already defined a path, simply append the Windows references to it. Again, use the Notepad to update the file. Once these changes are complete, reboot your system.

2

CREATING ICONS, CURSORS, AND BITMAPS

Most Windows applications have a unique icon associated with them. In addition, each can have an individual cursor. This chapter examines how to create icons and cursors, as well as bitmaps, for your Windows applications. You will create an icon and a cursor to be used in later applications in this text; bitmaps will be covered in more detail in Chapter 16 when we discuss GDI functions. The creation of each of these is a very important step in the process of developing your Windows applications.

If you have installed your Windows Software Development Kit as described in Chapter 1, invoke the program ICONEDIT.EXE, the Windows icon editor. Your screen will contain the following:

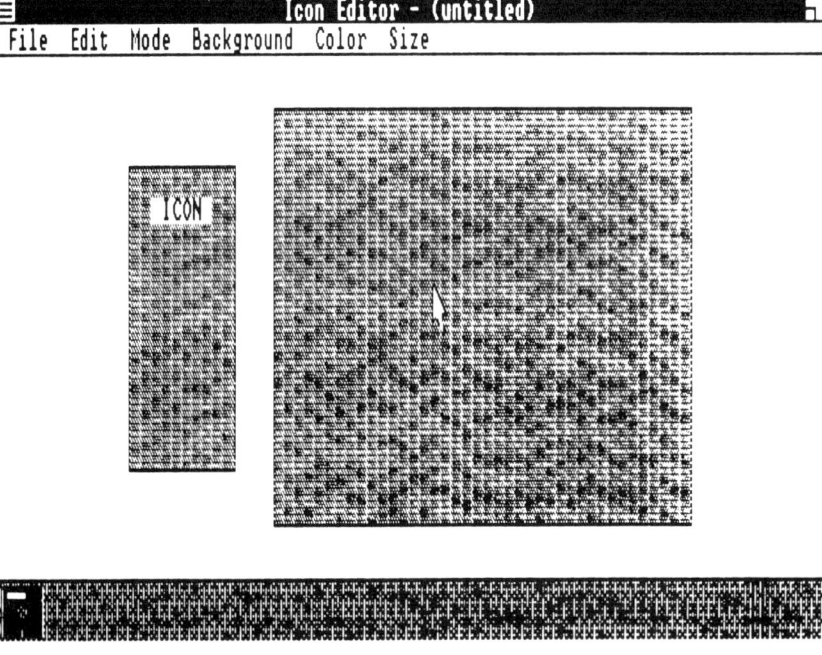

The window displayed is a standard Windows screen that contains a System menu, title bar, icon area, display area, and menu bar. In addition, Iconedit adds a drawing box and a display box (see Figure 2-1). The drawing box is the region in which you create icons, cursors, and bitmaps. The image in this box is oversized to simplify your artwork. The display box will contain a scale replica of the icon, cursor, or bitmap that you are editing.

Drawing an Object

Before you create an actual icon and cursor pair for an application, simply move your mouse around the drawing box with the left mouse

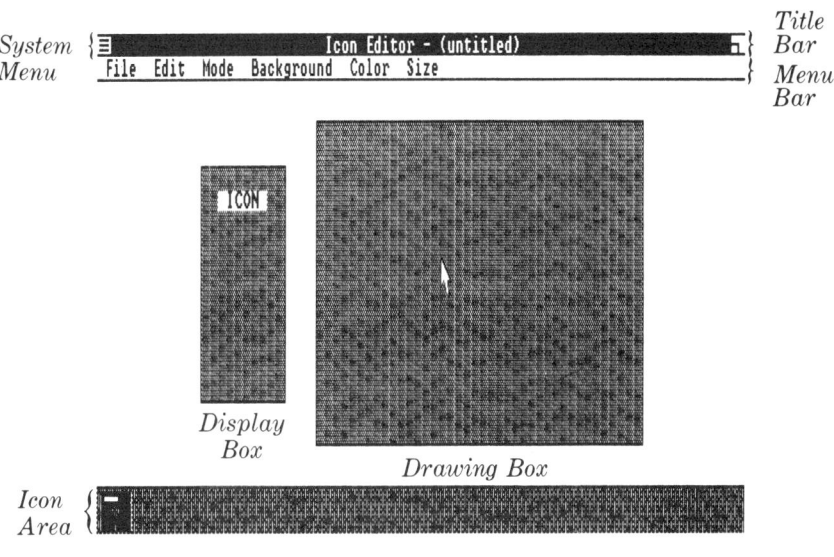

Figure 2-1. Components of the Icon Editor screen

select button depressed, as shown here:

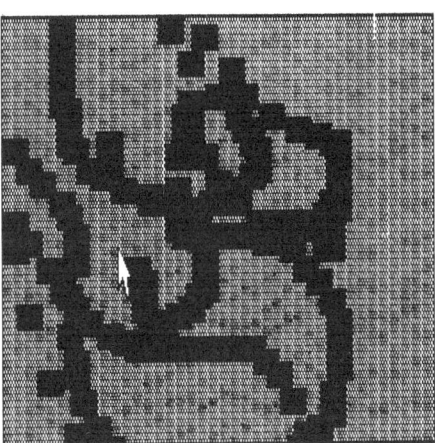

Next, note that the right mouse select button works as an eraser. Erase a portion of the contents of the drawing box. As you manipulate the drawing box, watch the effect on the contents of the display box, as shown here:

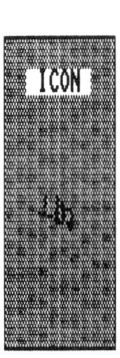 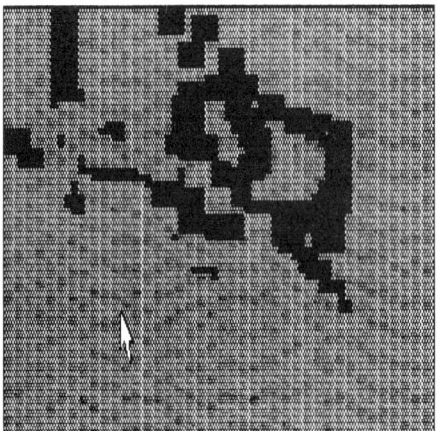

Working Through the Iconedit Menu Bar

Iconedit provides several commands in the menu bar. This section examines each in detail.

Select the File menu; the following will appear:

The New option gives you a clean slate with which to begin your development work. Assuming that the drawing box still contains your previous artwork,

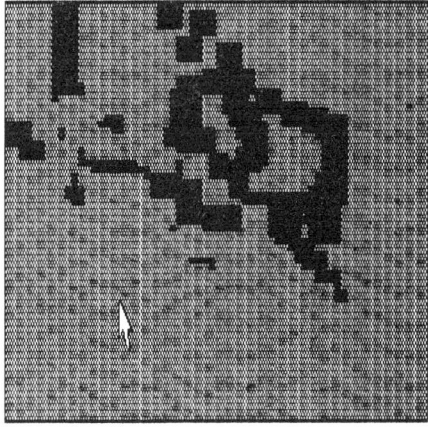

selecting the New option results in the following dialog box:

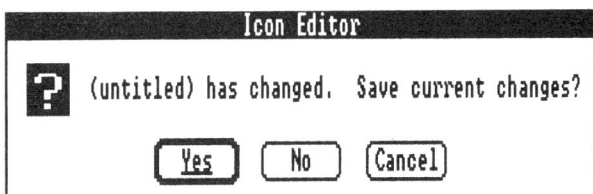

Once you select the No option, you will have a clean slate, as follows:

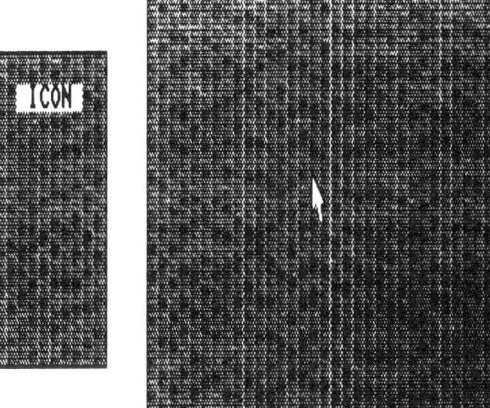

The Open option allows you to modify a currently existing icon, cursor, or bitmap. Upon invocation, it will prompt you for the file you wish to open, as follows:

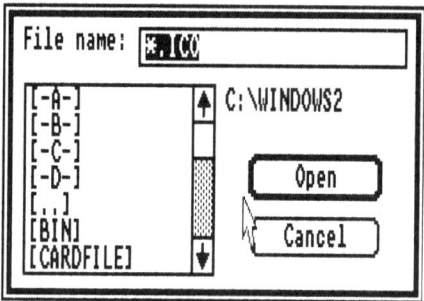

Type in the name of the file, or select the file by pointing to its name and double-clicking the mouse select button. Likewise, the Save and Save as options allow you to save the current icon, cursor, or bitmap to a file, as follows:

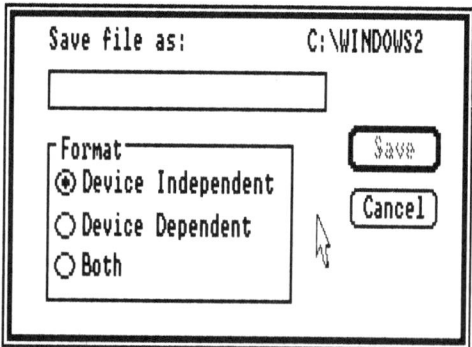

You can save your work in either a device-dependent or device-independent form. You should use the device-dependent form only if your application will query the device resolution and handle the proper display of the item. The device-independent option allows Windows to scale the image for the device automatically and is the preferred format. Enter the name of the desired file. If the file already exists, Iconedit will display the following dialog box:

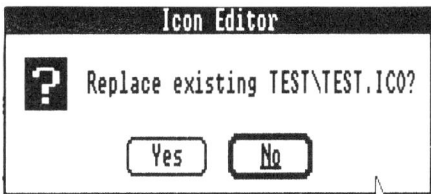

The Edit menu provides the following capabilities:

Redraw redisplays the object on the screen. The Grid option works as a toggle. The first time you select this option, Iconedit places a grid on the drawing box to assist in your design, as shown here:

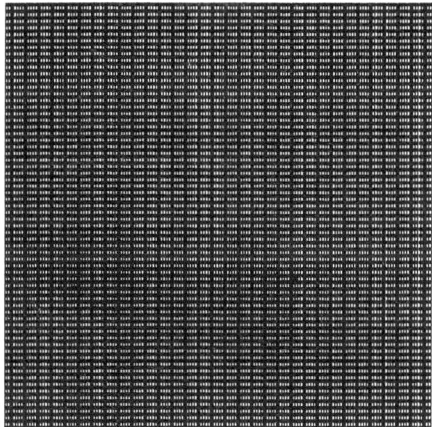

Many users first develop their icons by hand on graph paper and then use the grid to translate the handwritten form of the object into an icon or cursor.

The Mode menu allows you to specify whether you are working on an icon, cursor, or bitmap. Upon invocation, Mode displays the following:

Notice the effect on the screen as you select each mode. First, select Icon:

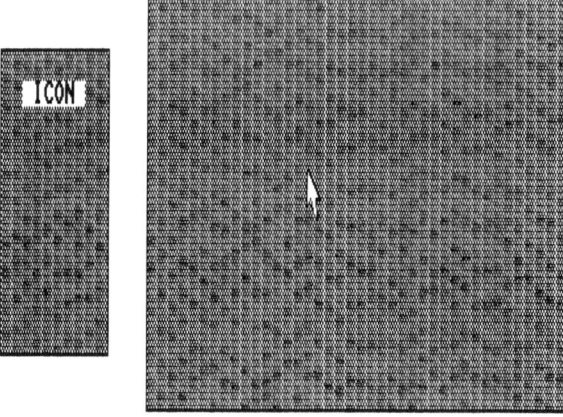

In this mode, the drawing box represents a 64×64 block of pixels. Next, select the Cursor option; the following will be displayed:

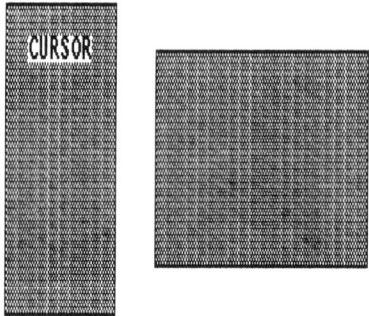

In Cursor edit mode, the drawing box represents a block that measures 32 × 32 pixels.

The Bitmap mode allows you to specify a drawing box ranging from a 64 × 64 block of pixels down to a 1 × 1 block. Upon invocation, the Bitmap option displays the following dialog box:

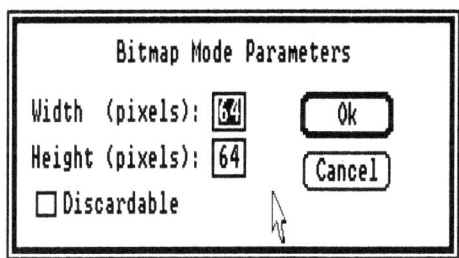

Enter the width and height, in pixels, of the bitmap. The Discardable option allows you to indicate that Windows can discard the object during memory-compression operations. These operations will be examined in Appendix E.

The last option of the Mode menu allows you to specify a hotspot. With the Hotspot option, you can specify the following:

☐ *Icon*   The hotspot specifies the pixel from which Windows determines the location of the icon on the screen. This location is used to determine the row or column into which a window dragged onto the screen will be placed. By default, the hotspot is the center of the icon.

☐ *Cursor*   The hotspot specifies the pixel from which Windows will take the cursor's current screen coordinates. By default, the hotspot is the center of the cursor.

Select the Hotspot option; the following will be displayed:

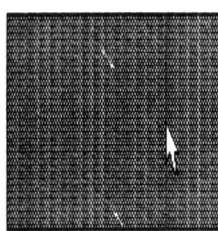

Note the current x and y coordinate indicators below the display box. These values show the current location of the hotspot. If you want to change hotspot values, simply use your mouse pointer to select the desired pixel.

The Background menu allows you to set the background color of the drawing box, as follows:

Note the effect on the drawing box as you toggle through the available background colors. The first background color is black, as shown here:

The second available color is white, as follows:

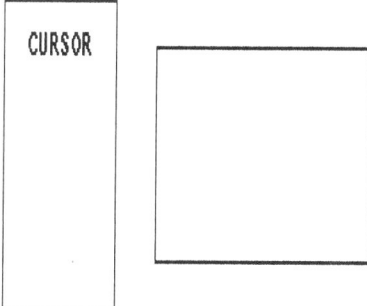

Iconedit supports two shades of gray: normal gray

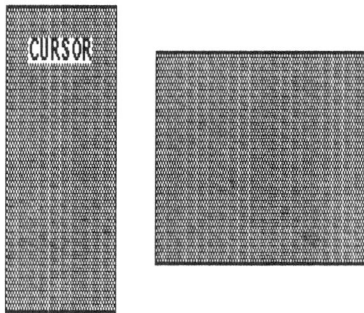

and light gray.

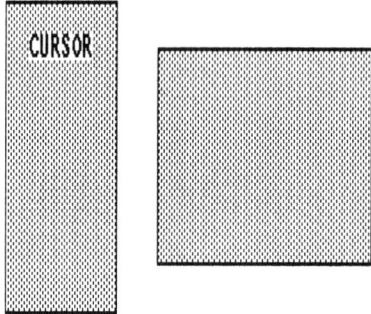

The Iconedit Color menu allows you to specify one of the following four colors for the drawing pen:

The first two colors are straightforward: black and white. The Screen option changes the pen to the same color as the screen that underlies the current image. The −Screen color selects the inverse of the screen display color. In other words, if the screen is white, −Screen results in a black pen color.

The Size menu allows you to control the width (in pixels) of each stroke of the pen. The following pen sizes are supported:

The Small pen size manipulates a pixel at a time and is best used for detailing. The Medium pen increases the number of pixels used, whereas Large uses a significant number of pixels, as shown here:

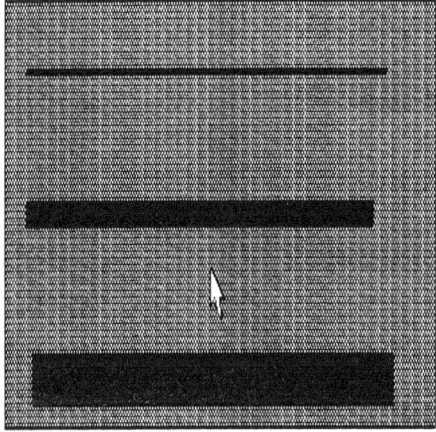

A Complete Application

The following instructions create a cursor and icon for a Windows application. Before drawing them on the screen, you should develop the cursor and icon on graph paper, as shown in Figure 2-2.

To create the icon, select the Mode menu and the Icon option. Draw the following icon:

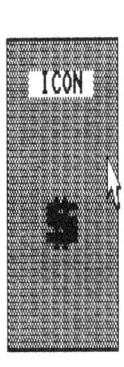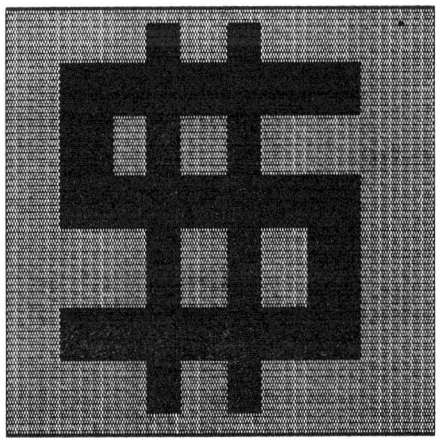

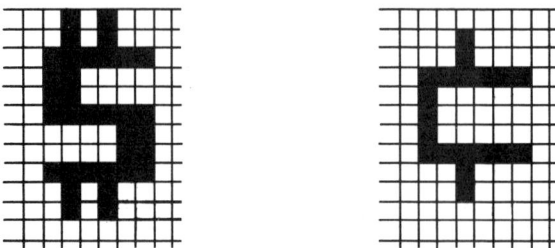

Figure 2-2. Sample rough draft of art on graph paper

Save the icon under the name DOLLAR.ICO, as follows:

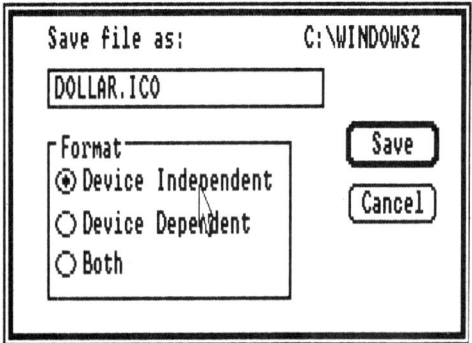

Next, select the Cursor mode option and create the following cursor:

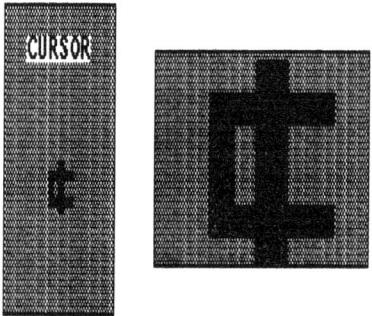

Save the cursor under the name CENTS.CUR, as follows:

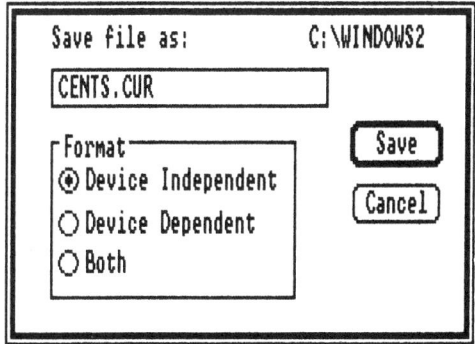

The following chapters will develop several Windows applications. The ability to create unique icons and cursors will be essential to the success of those applications.

3

CREATING FONTS

In addition to specialized icons and cursors, many applications require unique fonts either for screen displays or for printed reports. This chapter teaches you how to create custom fonts specific to your Windows applications. Before you get started with Fontedit, the Windows Software Development Kit's font editor, examine the standard fonts provided with Windows. Invoke Write to display each font, as follows:

Most fonts fall into one of several categories. These categories are listed in Table 3-1.

Invoke the program FONTEDIT.EXE. Fontedit will prompt you for the name of the font file that you want to edit, as follows:

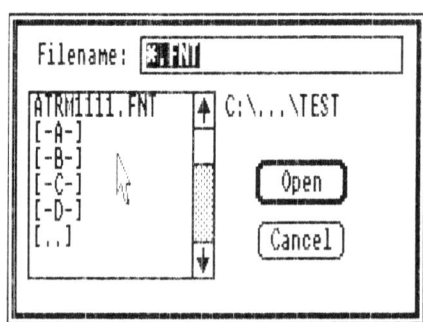

Name	Description
Decorative	Novelty font
Italic	Italic (slanted) font
Roman	Proportionally spaced font containing serifs (a line projecting from the main portion of the character)
Script	Cursive font
Strikeout	Font in which the characters have a strikeout line typed through them
Swiss	Proportionally spaced font with no serifs
Typewriter	Fixed-pitch font
Underline	Font in which the characters are all underlined
Unknown	User-defined font

Table 3-1. Categories of Fonts

Fontedit does not allow you to develop a font from scratch. Instead you must begin with a defined font file and modify it to your specifications. Simply type in the name of the file you wish to edit, or scroll through the files displayed on the screen, selecting the desired file by double-clicking the mouse select button. For now, use the default file supplied by Fontedit. Your screen should now contain all of the components shown in Figure 3-1.

The *character window* is your drawing board for custom fonts. The cells in the character window represent the pixels that make up the character font. Each cell can be turned on or off to reproduce the character font that you desire.

The *character viewing window* contains two scale replicas of the character that you are editing. Fontedit displays two characters to provide a better illustration of how your fonts will appear on the screen in relation to other characters.

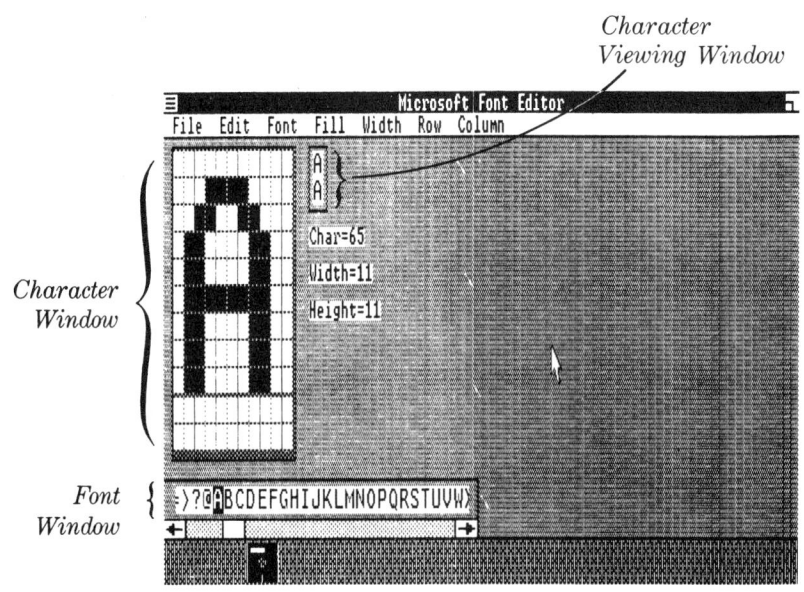

Figure 3-1. Components of the Fontedit screen

The *font window* displays copies of each of the characters contained in the font file. The scroll bar at the bottom of the window provides easy access to individual characters.

Note the Char, Width, and Height boxes beside the character that you are editing. Char specifies the ASCII code associated with the characters. Width defines the number of pixels (number of columns) in the width of the character. Similarly, Height specifies the height (number of rows) of the character in pixels. For fun, toggle through several of the characters available for editing, as shown in the following examples:

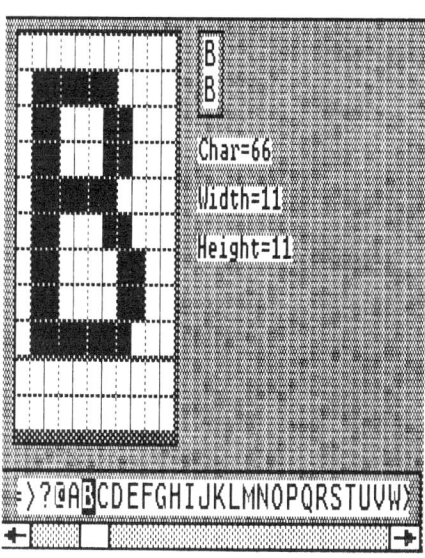

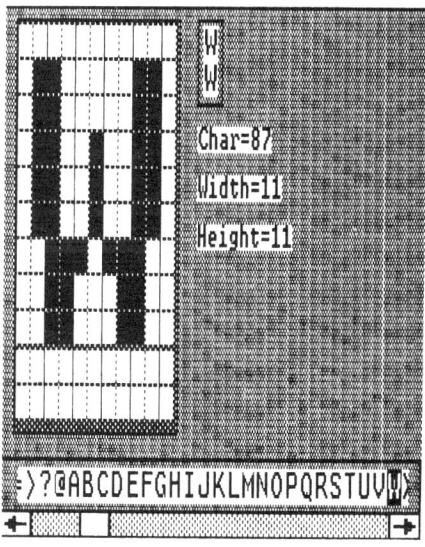

Next, modify the current font by using your mouse. Direct the mouse pointer to the pixel (cell) you wish to change and press the mouse select button. In this case, modify the font for the letter A as shown here:

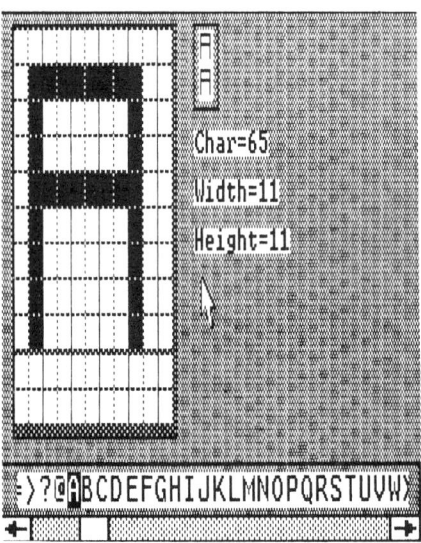

The Fontedit screen is a standard Windows display. If you examine the menu bar, you will see that Fontedit provides the following capabilities:

```
≡                    Microsoft Font Editor                    ⊓
File  Edit  Font  Fill  Width  Row  Column
```

The File Menu

The File menu allows you to specify the name of the file that you want to edit or the name of the file to which you want to save your new font. Upon invocation, this menu displays the following:

As was stated previously, you must create font files by first modifying the fonts contained in an existing file. To select a file, choose the Open option. Fontedit will respond with the following:

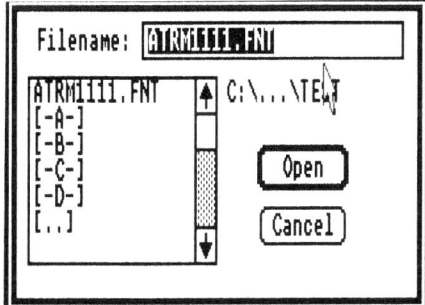

Type in the file name containing the desired font, or scroll through the list of available files and select a file by double-clicking the mouse select button. If you specify a file that is not a valid font file, Fontedit will display the following dialog box:

The Save as option allows you to specify the name of the file to contain your newly created font. When you invoke this option, Fontedit will display the following:

Type in the name of the file, or press ENTER to use the default file name provided.

The Edit Menu

The Fontedit Edit menu allows you to perform the following:

The Copy option works in conjunction with the Windows Clipboard. If you copy the current character to the Clipboard, the letter is placed in the Clipboard, as follows:

Similarly, the Paste option places the character currently contained in the Clipboard into the character window. If the Clipboard does not contain a font character, Fontedit will display the following dialog box:

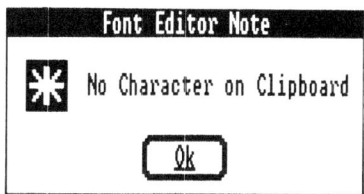

The Undo option allows you to reverse the previous Fontedit instruction. The Refresh option restores the current font in the character window with the character referenced in the font window.

The Font Menu

The Font menu provides the following capabilities:

When you select the Size option, Fontedit displays the following:

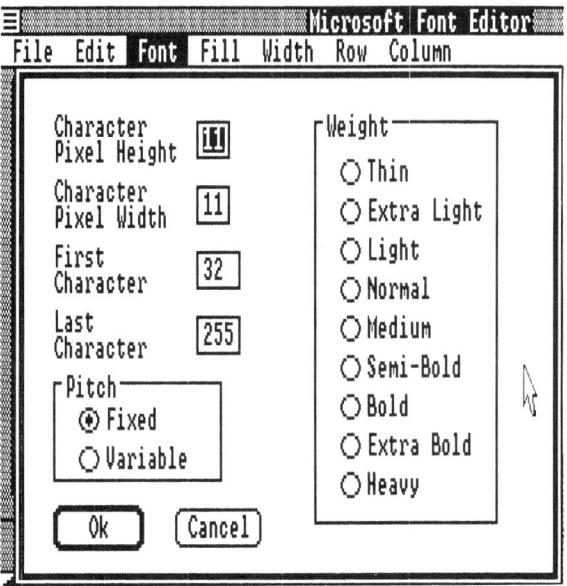

The Size option allows you to specify the size of a font. Character Pixel Height specifies the maximum number of pixels (rows) in the character height, and it must be an integer value in the range 1 to 32. Similarly, Character Pixel Width specifies the maximum number of pixel columns in a character and must be an integer value in the range 1 to 32. The First Character and Last Character fields allow you to specify the ASCII values for the first and last characters that you want in the font file. These must be integer values in the range 0 to 255.

The Weight values allow you to specify a level of darkness for a font. The Pitch field indicates whether the *pitch* (number of pixels per inch) is fixed for each character, or if it can vary. It is important to note that you can change a fixed-pitch font to one with a variable pitch, but not vice versa.

When you select the Header option from the Font menu, Fontedit displays the following:

```
┌─────────────────────────────────────────────────────────────────────┐
│ Face Name  [terminal                        ]           ⌐  Ok  ⌐      │
│                                                   ╲                    │
│ File Name  [ATRM1111.FNT    ]                     ▶    (Cancel)        │
│ Copyright:                                                             │
│ [(c) Copyright Bitstream Inc. 1984. All rights reserved.      ]        │
│                                                                        │
│ Nominal Point [29]  Height of    [9]   ⊙ANSI  ○OEM     [0]             │
│ Size                Ascent                                             │
│ Nominal Vert. [27]  Nominal Horiz. [65]  ┌Font Family────────────┐    │
│ Resolution          Resolution           │ ○ Roman   ⊙Typewriter  │    │
│ External      [0]   Internal      [0]    │ ○ Swiss   ○Decorative  │    │
│ Leading             Leading              │ ○ Script  ○Unknown     │    │
│ Default       [96]  Break         [0]    └───────────────────────┘    │
│ Character           Character                                         │
│ □Italic        □Underline      □Strikeout                             │
└─────────────────────────────────────────────────────────────────────┘
```

The Face Name is a unique name that allows you to distinguish one font from another. It is a character string containing up to 32 characters. File Name is the name of the font file that you are creating.

The Copyright field allows you to copyright your custom fonts. Enter a character string containing up to 60 characters. Nominal Point Size defines the size of the characters in the font. A point is 1/72 inch. A 36-point font, therefore, is 1/2 inch high.

Height of Ascent specifies the number of pixels from the top of the character to the baseline. This value gives a truer measure of the size of the characters than Nominal Point Size. Nominal Vertical Resolution and Nominal Horizontal Resolution define the resolution along the y and x axes at which the font was digitized.

External Leading defines the suggested number of rows (pixels) to insert between rows of characters. Internal Leading specifies the number of rows at the top of the font that contain no foreground pixels.

Default Character specifies the ASCII character to be used if you attempt to display a character outside of the range of First Character or Last Character. Break Character defines the ASCII character to be used to pad lines that have been justified. The default value for the break character is ASCII 32 (space). The ANSI/OEM options allow you to specify the default Windows character set, ANSI, or a machine-dependent OEM character set. The value to the right can range from 0 to 255; however, only the character sets 0 and 255 are defined.

Font Family allows you to specify the family into which the font you are creating falls. See the previous discussion of font types to determine the correct font category.

The Fill Menu

The Fontedit Fill menu helps you create your fonts by providing the following capabilities:

The Clear option allows you to clear a block of pixels contained in the character. Select the Clear option and point the mouse to one of the corners of the block you want to clear. Press the select button; the selected pixel should now be highlighted in gray. Without releasing the mouse select button, point to the pixel representing the opposite diagonal corner of the block to be cleared. Pressing the mouse select button will set to white the block you have selected.

The Solid option on the Fill menu works in a manner similar to Clear. Select the Solid option and highlight one of the corner pixels.

Point to the pixel in the opposite corner and release the select button. The block of text will become black, as shown here:

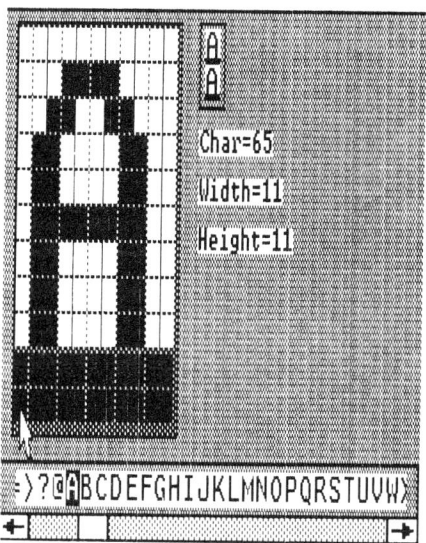

The Hatched option creates a checkerboard pattern in the specified block of pixels, as shown here:

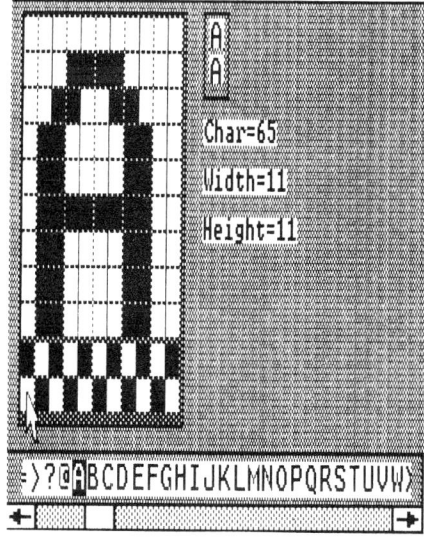

Follow the same steps as before to select the block of pixels.

The Inverted option changes all of the light pixels in a specified block to dark and all of the dark pixels to light. Selecting all of the pixels in the character window for the letter A results in the following:

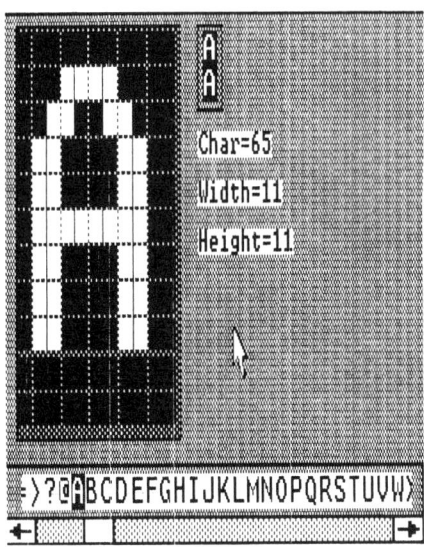

The Left=Right option flip-flops columns in the selected block of pixels. Likewise, the Top=Bottom option exchanges rows within the selected block of pixels. The Copy and Paste options allow you to move blocks of pixels around the character window. In the following example, the top half of the window has been copied and pasted to the lower half:

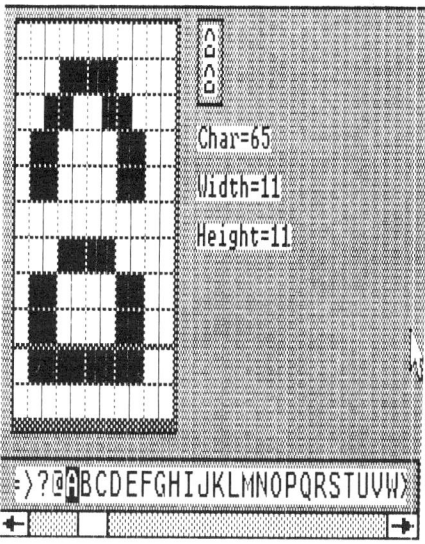

The Width Menu

The Width menu allows you to change the width (in pixels) of characters in a variable-pitch font. As was stated previously, pitch indicates the number of pixels per inch. Variable-pitch fonts allow the number of pixels in each character to differ. The characters in a fixed-pitch font, however, are all the same width. If you attempt to widen a fixed-pitch font, Fontedit will display the following dialog box:

Upon invocation, the Width menu displays the following options:

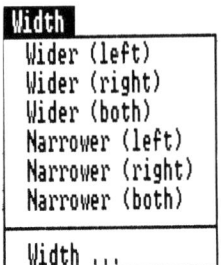

The Wider (left) option adds a column of pixels to the left of the character. Similarly, the Wider (right) option adds a column to the right of the character. The Wider (both) option adds a column of pixels to both sides of the character. The Narrower options work in the same fashion, removing columns of pixels as specified. Finally, if you select the Width... option, Fontedit will display the following dialog box:

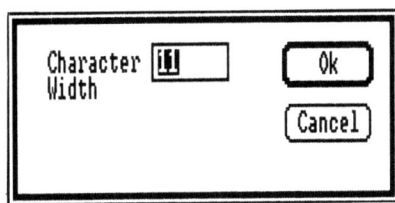

This allows you to specify the width of the font in pixels. The value must be between 1 and 64.

The Row Menu

The Row menu allows you to add a row of pixels to or delete a row of pixels from the character window:

   The Add option works like a copy. Select the Add option from the Row menu. Next, direct the mouse pointer to the location where you want the new row of pixels placed, and press the mouse select button. The row of pixels will be inserted at th specified location, and all of the rows of pixels below that point will be moved down one level. If you want to copy only a portion of a given row, direct the mouse pointer to the desired rightmost pixel in the row and press the select button. The row will be added, and the pixels to the left of the selected pixel will be white.
   The Delete option works in a similar manner. Select the Delete option from the Row menu, direct the mouse pointer to the row to be deleted, and press the select button. Fontedit will delete the selected row of pixels.

The Column Menu

The Column menu allows you to add and delete columns of pixels, as shown here:

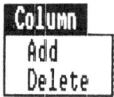

The Add option copies a column of pixels to the location referenced by the mouse pointer. The columns to the right of the desired column are moved to the right. It is also possible to copy only a portion of the column. To delete a column of pixels, simply select the Delete option from the Column menu, point to the column to be removed, and press the mouse select button.

The creation and use of custom fonts can make your applications programs very appealing to the end user. Later chapters examine a complete application that deals strictly with fonts.

CHAPTER

4

THE DIALOG EDITOR

Besides giving you the ability to produce your own cursors and icons, the Windows Software Development Kit provides a dialog box editor in a file called DIALOG.EXE. To simplify the user interface (and to improve consistency), most Windows applications use dialog boxes to communicate with the user. For example, each time you terminate Windows, the following message box is displayed:

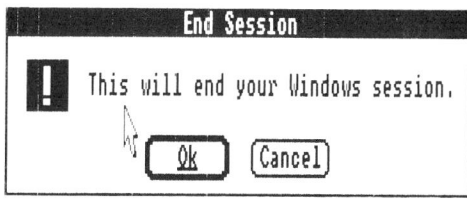

Likewise, the Control Panel uses a number of controls within its dialog box, as shown here:

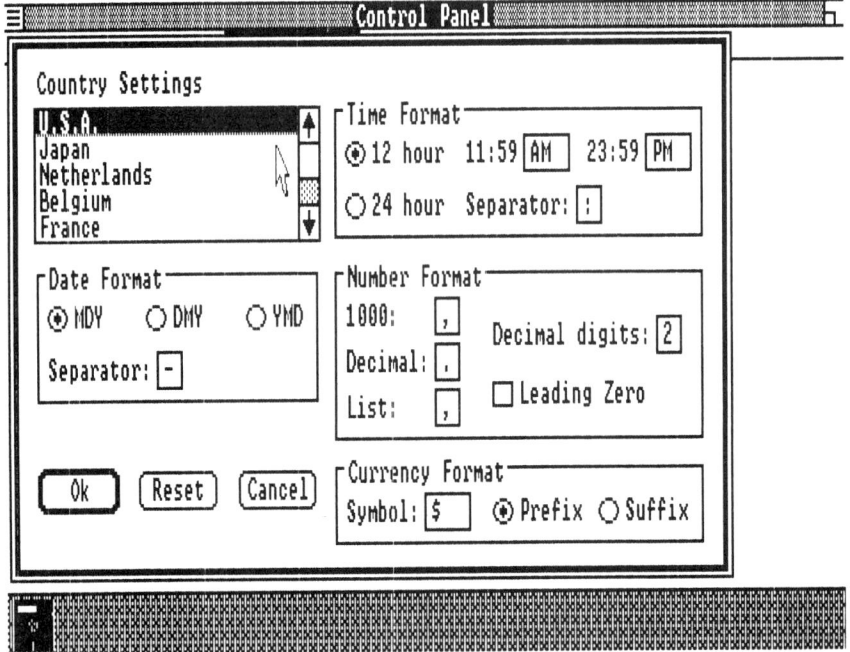

From Windows, invoke DIALOG.EXE. Your screen will contain the following:

```
 ≡        Dialog Editor - sample                      ⌐
  File  Edit  Styles  Control  Include  Options
```

```
                                          ▓▓▓▓Size▓▓▓▓
                                          x =0
                                          y =0
                                          cx =0
                                          cy =0
                                          ──────────
                                          Work Mode
                                          Decimal Mode
```

The Dialog Editor allows you to design and create dialog boxes to be used within your applications programs. You can also modify previously created dialog boxes. Note the menu bar at the top of the screen:

```
 ≡        Dialog Editor - sample                      ⌐
  File  Edit  Styles  Control  Include  Options
```

In addition, the Dialog Editor provides the following Size window in the lower right-hand corner of the screen:

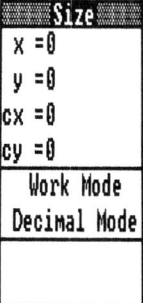

This window provides you with information about the current dialog box or one of its entries. This information is described in Table 4-1. All of your changes to the dialog box are reflected in the Size window. Each of the entries in the window is specified in dialog box

Entry	Description
x	The x coordinate of the upper left corner of the dialog box or selected control
y	The y coordinate of the upper left corner of the dialog box or selected control
cx	The height of the dialog box or selected control
cy	The width of the dialog box or selected control
Work/Test Mode	Specifies whether the editor is in Work mode (which allows editing) or Test mode (which allows testing of the controls in the dialog box)
Decimal/Hex Mode	Specifies whether identification control values are displayed in hex or decimal
Control Type	Specifies the type of the selected control

Table 4-1. Entries in the Size Window

units. Four horizontal dialog box units are equivalent to the *width* of a character in the standard system font, and eight vertical dialog box units are equivalent to the *height* of a character in the font.

Select the File menu. You will see the following:

The New option allows you to clear your slate and begin working on a new dialog box. The Dialog Editor uses a default file called SAMPLE to store the box you are developing. Notice that the File menu lists several keyboard accelerator combinations. Pressing CTRL-N from the keyboard, for example, is equivalent to selecting the New option from this menu.

The Open option allows you to modify a previously created dialog box. Upon selection it displays the following:

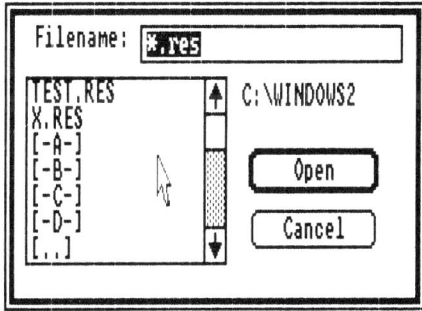

Type in the name of the file you want to open, or double-click the mouse select button on the desired file.

Once you have created a dialog box, Save and Save As allow you to place the contents of the dialog box into a file, as follows:

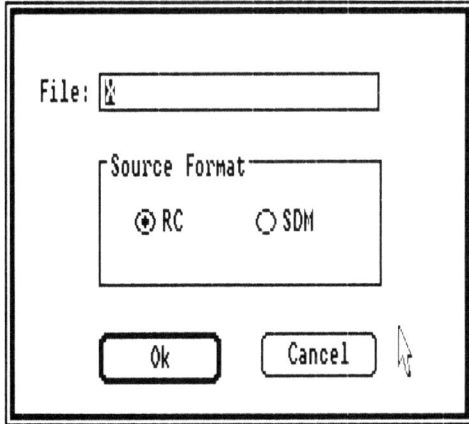

Finally, the View Dialog option allows you to list the current dialog box files. Upon selection the option displays the following:

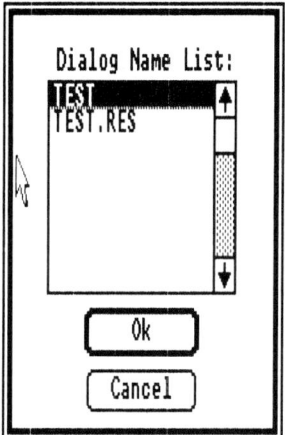

Select the Edit menu; the following will be displayed:

Edit	
Restore dialog	Sh Esc
Cut Dialog	Del
Copy Dialog	F2
Paste Dialog...	Ins
Clear	
New Dialog...	**^D**
Rename Dialog...	^R
Grid...	

The New Dialog option allows you to begin work on a new dialog box. Upon selection it prompts you for the name of the dialog box. In this case simply type the name TEST and select the Ok button, as follows:

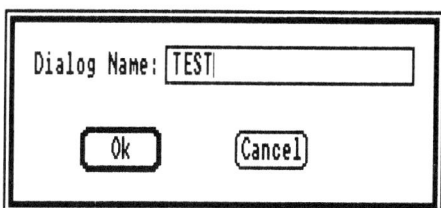

The Dialog Editor displays a frame that surrounds your dialog box definition, as follows:

To modify the size of the box, select one of the handles on the edge of the frame, and use your mouse to expand the frame, as shown here:

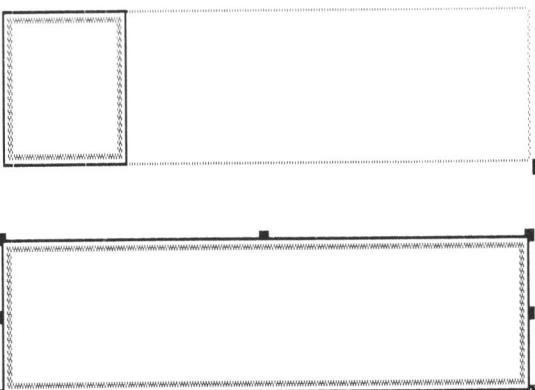

Next, increase the vertical height of the frame by selecting the handle in the lower corner, as follows:

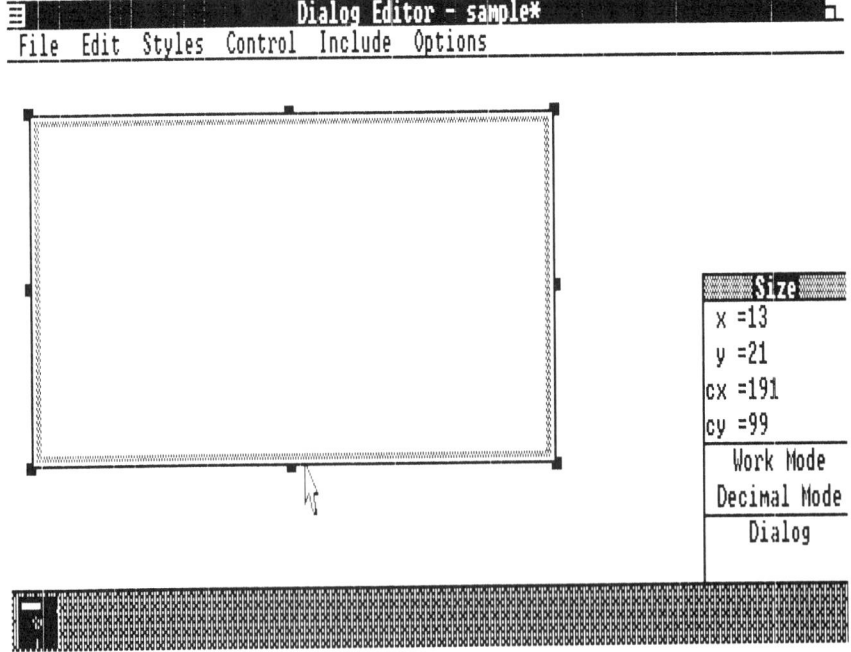

Notice that the Size window reflects the change in your dialog box:

```
░░░░░Size░░░░░
 x =13
 y =21
cx =191
cy =99
   Work Mode
  Decimal Mode
     Dialog
```

Now select the Control menu.

```
Control
   Check Box
   Radio Button
   Push Button
   Group Box
   Horz, Scroll
   Vert, Scroll
   List Box
   Edit
   Text
   Frame
   Rect
   Icon
```

The options in the Control menu are summarized in Table 4-2.

Option	Description
Check Box	Creates a small, square box with text to the right. Groups of check boxes allow the user to select one or more of several choices
Radio Button	Creates a small circle with text to the right. Groups of radio buttons allow the user to select *one* of a group of choices
Push Button	Creates a small, rounded rectangle that contains text. Push buttons allow the user to respond to immediate prompts
Group Box	Creates a rectangle with text in the upper left that is used to group two or more related controls
Horizontal Scroll Bar	Creates a scroll bar that the user can use to scroll through data horizontally
Vertical Scroll Bar	Creates a vertical scroll bar
List Box	Creates a rectangle that contains a vertical scroll bar on its right edge
Edit	Creates an edit control within which the user can enter and edit text
Text	Creates a static control that often serves as a label
Frame	Creates a rectangle that can be used to frame other controls
Rectangle	Creates a filled rectangle
Icon	Creates a space in which the user can place an icon

Table 4-2. Options of the Control Menu

Select the Check Box option. The Dialog Editor displays a cross on your screen, as follows:

Move the cross to the desired location and press the mouse select button. You will see the following:

Use the handles to adjust the size of the frame, as follows:

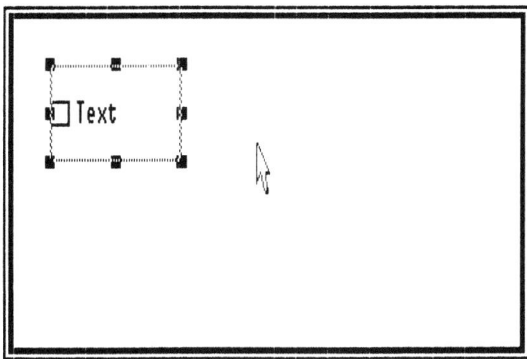

Next, select the Styles menu; the following will be displayed:

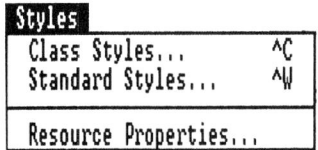

The first option, Class Styles, allows you to specify the following:

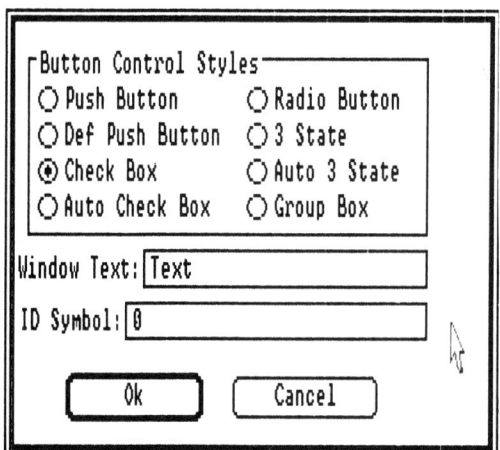

Select the Window Text edit field and type in CHECK BOX, as shown here:

```
┌─────────────────────────────────────┐
│ ┌Button Control Styles───────────┐   │
│ │ ○ Push Button      ○ Radio Button │ │
│ │ ○ Def Push Button  ○ 3 State      │ │
│ │ ◉ Check Box        ○ Auto 3 State │ │
│ │ ○ Auto Check Box   ○ Group Box    │ │
│ └───────────────────────────────────┘ │
│ Window Text:│CHECK BOX              │ │
│ ID Symbol:│0                        │ │
│      ┌─────────┐   ┌─────────┐       │
│      │   Ok    │   │ Cancel  │       │
│      └─────────┘   └─────────┘       │
└─────────────────────────────────────┘
```

Select the Ok button; your screen will contain the following:

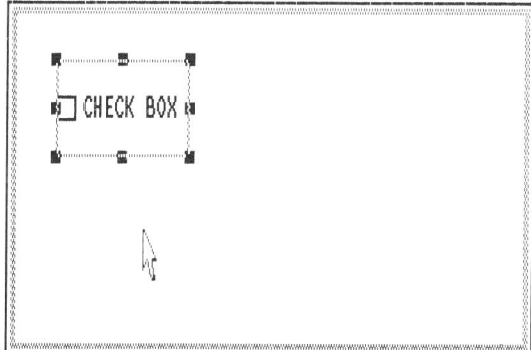

The Standard Styles option of the Styles menu allows you to specify the following:

```
┌─────────────────────────────────────────┐
│ ┌Global Window Styles────────────────┐   │
│ │ ☐ Close Box / Sys Menu Box  ☐ Border  │
│ │ ☐ Horz Scroll Style         ☐ Caption │
│ │ ☐ Vert Scroll Style         ☐ Group Bit │
│ │ ☐ Dialog Frame              ☒ Tab Stop Bit │
│ │ ☐ Size box                  ☐ Visible Bit │
│ └───────────────────────────────────┘   │
│                                           │
│      Window Text: │CHECK BOX         │    │
│                                           │
│        [    Ok    ]    [  Cancel  ]  ↖    │
└─────────────────────────────────────────┘
```

Take time to experiment with these options to see how each affects the dialog box.

The Resource Properties option of the Styles menu allows you to specify how the Memory Manager will treat the control that you have selected, as shown here:

```
┌─────────────────────────────┐
│ ┌Memory Manager Flags┐      │
│ │   ☒ Moveable        │     │
│ │   ☐ Preload         │     │
│ │   ☒ Discard         │     │
│ └───────────────────┘       │
│     [ Ok ]  [Cancel]        │
└─────────────────────────────┘
```

For now, it is important only that you be aware of these capabilities and know how to integrate them into your dialog boxes. Later chapters will examine each in greater detail.

Moving a Control

Once you have placed a control in the dialog box on the screen, you may decide to move it to a new location. With your mouse pointer, simply select the control that you want to move, as illustrated here:

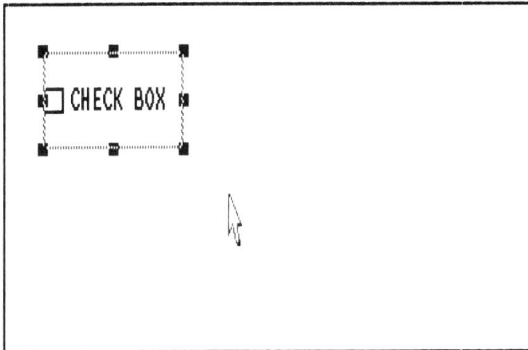

With the mouse select button depressed, drag the control to its new location.

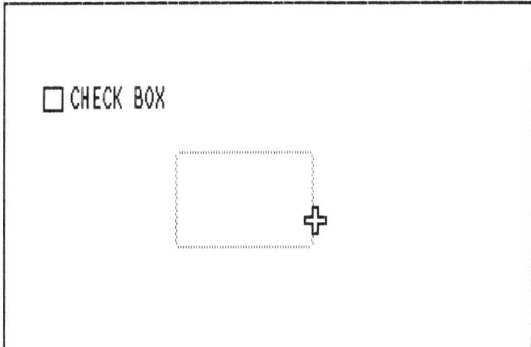

When you release the mouse select button, the control will be in the location desired.

Create the additional controls shown here:

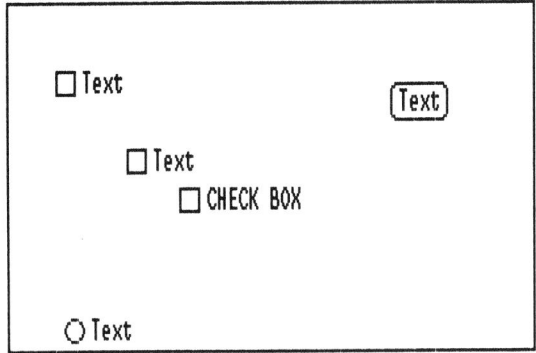

To move several controls at once, press the CTRL key and point with the mouse to each control you wish to move, pressing and releasing the mouse select button on each, as shown here:

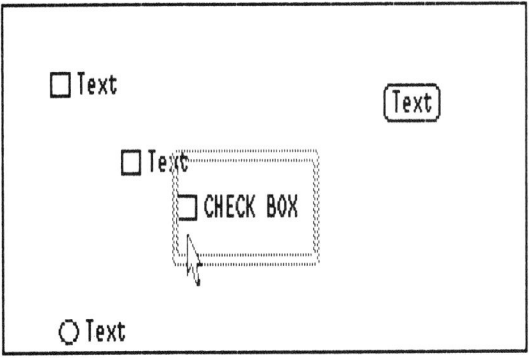

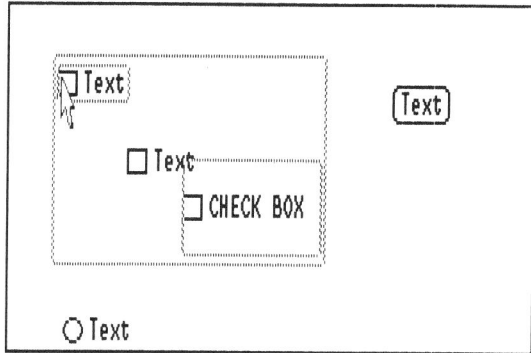

After selecting the controls to be moved, press the mouse select button within the group of controls and drag them to the new location, as follows:

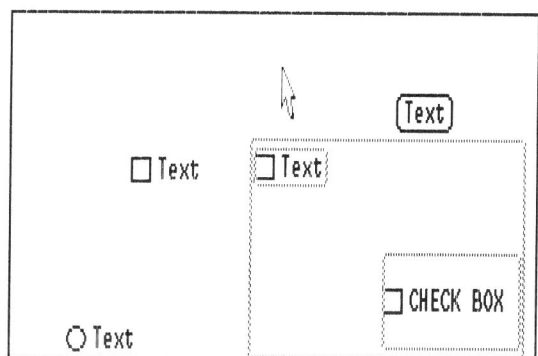

Release the mouse select button to complete the move.

Deleting a Control

The Dialog Editor allows you to remove controls in a similar manner. Simply select the control to be removed with your mouse pointer, as follows:

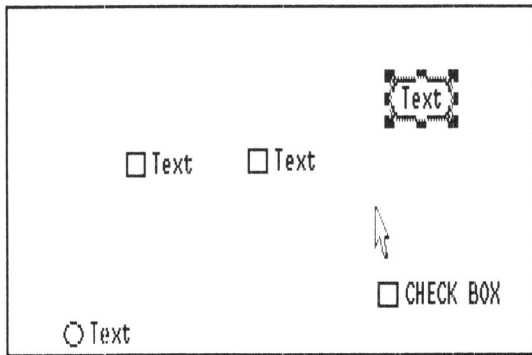

Next, select the Clear option from the Edit menu.

Edit	
Restore dialog	Sh Esc
Cut Dialog	Del
Copy Dialog	F2
Paste Dialog...	Ins
Clear	
New Dialog...	^D
Rename Dialog...	^R
Grid...	

Your screen should now contain the following:

```
≡        Dialog Editor - sample*                    ⌐
 File  Edit  Styles  Control  Include  Options
```

```
                 ↖  ☐ Text      ☐ Text



                                    ☐ CHECK BOX
               ○ Text
```

```
▨▨▨Size▨▨▨
 x =0
 y =0
cx =0
cy =0
───────────
  Work Mode
  Decimal Mode
```

Editing Controls in the Dialog Box

Select the Edit menu, as follows:

```
 Edit
 Restore dialog   Sh Esc
 Cut Dialog       Del
 Copy Dialog      F2
 Paste Dialog...  Ins
 Clear
─────────────────────────
 New Dialog...    ^D
 Rename Dialog... ^R
─────────────────────────
 Grid...
```

The options in this menu allow you to create or modify dialog boxes. The Restore dialog option restores the current dialog box to its previously saved state. If, for example, you decide that you do not like the changes you have made to the dialog box, you can use the Restore dialog option to return to the previously saved version. The Cut Dialog option places the current dialog box into the Clipboard. For example, if your dialog box contains

selecting the Cut Dialog option places the following in the Clipboard:

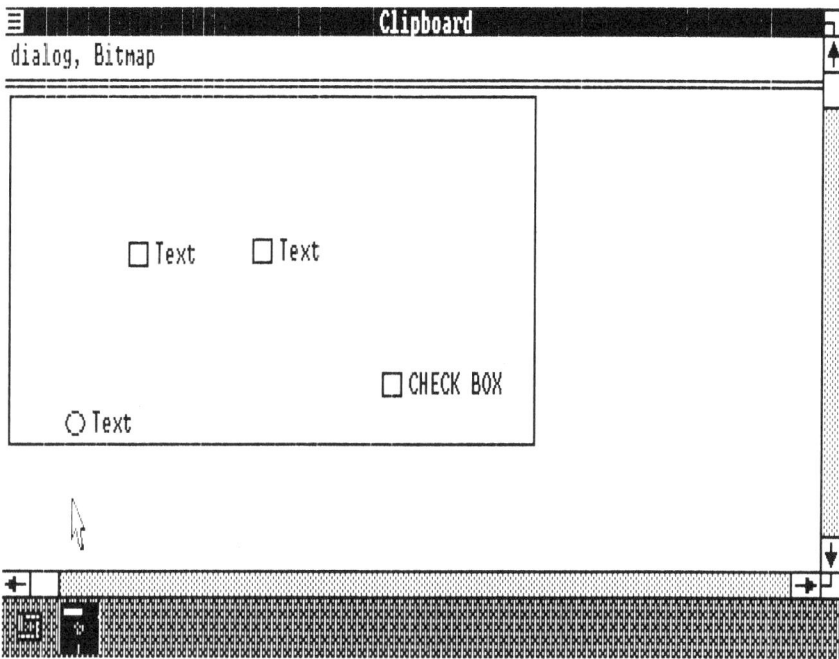

The items placed in the Clipboard will be removed from the dialog box.

The Copy Dialog option places a copy of the contents of your dialog box into the Clipboard. The contents of the Dialog box will remain unchanged. Both the text and bitmap formats are available in the Clipboard. The Paste Dialog option restores the contents of the Clipboard to the current dialog box. The Clear option, which removes a control from the box, was discussed previously. The Rename Dialog option allows you to rename the current dialog box, as shown here:

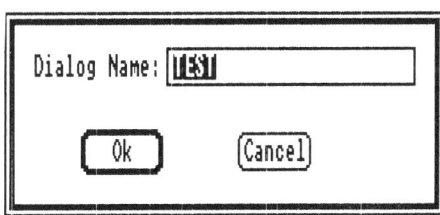

The Grid option helps you define the upper left-hand corner of the dialog box. The coordinates are defined in multiples of dialog box units (by default, the multiple is 1). These values in turn affect the values displayed for cx and cy in the Size window. Most programmers simply use the default values.

Specifying the Control Access Order

Select the Options menu.

```
Options
Test Mode        ^T
Order Groups... ^G
```

The Dialog Editor allows you to test your dialog box during its development. To do this, select the Test Mode option. Note the change to the mode in the Size Window when you do this. In Test mode, the Dialog Editor is ready for you to access the controls in the dialog box in the same manner as the application user.

By default, controls in the dialog box are accessed in the order in which you placed them on the screen. That is, the first control you place in the box will be the first one the user accesses. Likewise, the last control in the box will be the last control accessed. If this access order is not acceptable, select the Order Groups option from the Options menu, as follows:

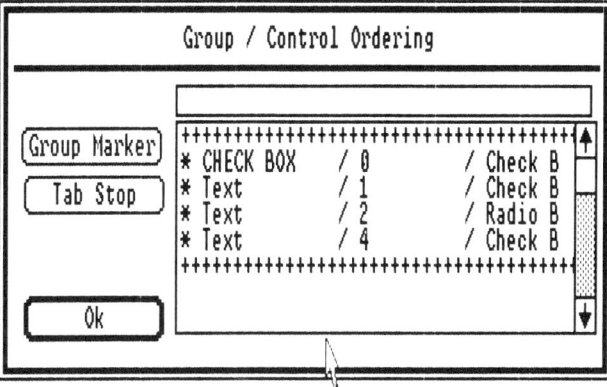

This option allows you to specify the sequence in which the user accesses the controls in the box. In this case, use your mouse pointer to select the last control on the list.

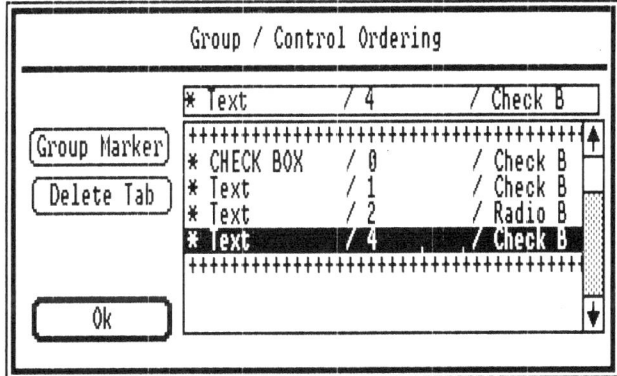

Now move the control to the top of the access list. As you move the mouse pointer up the list, a small horizontal bar will appear, as shown here:

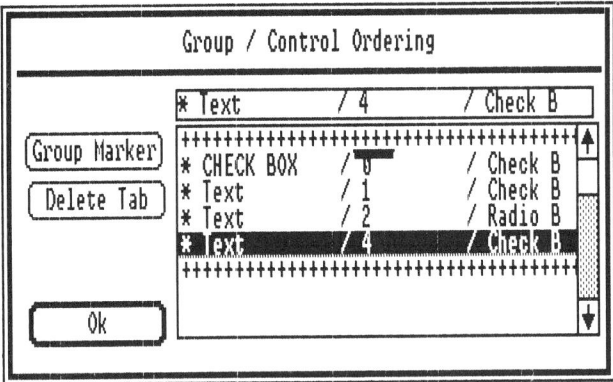

Once this bar is over the desired control location, press your mouse select button; the following will be displayed:

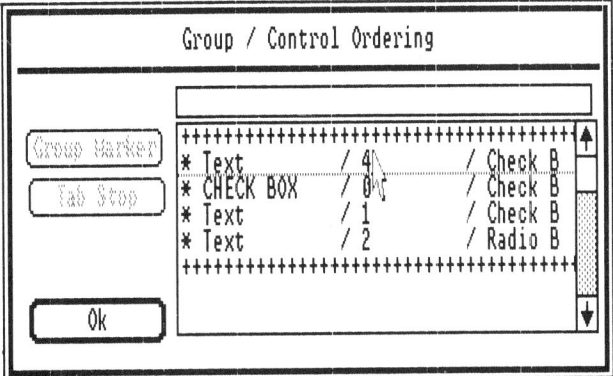

The Group Marker option allows you to define groups of controls. Control groups allow the user to step through many options with the keyboard arrow keys. To define a group, you must highlight the first control to be contained in the group, as shown here:

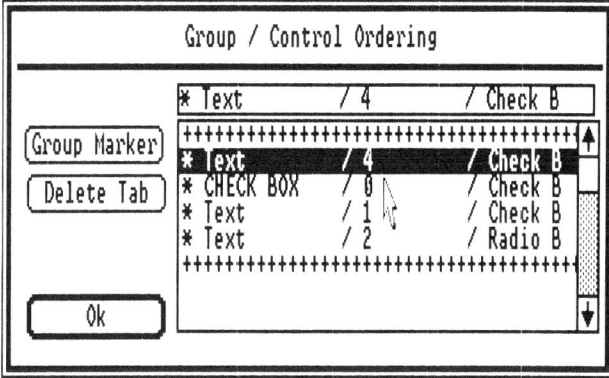

Select the Group Marker button. A dashed line should appear, indicating the top of the group.

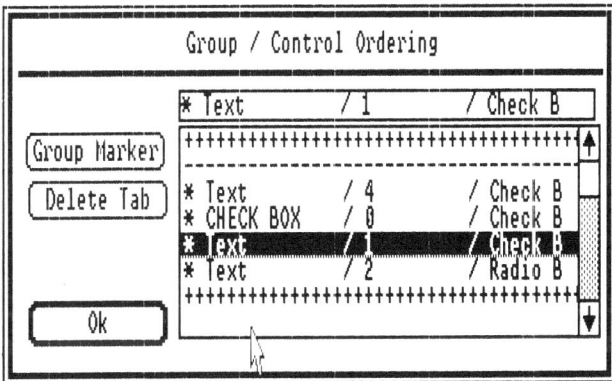

Next, select the control immediately below the last control to be contained in the group, as shown here:

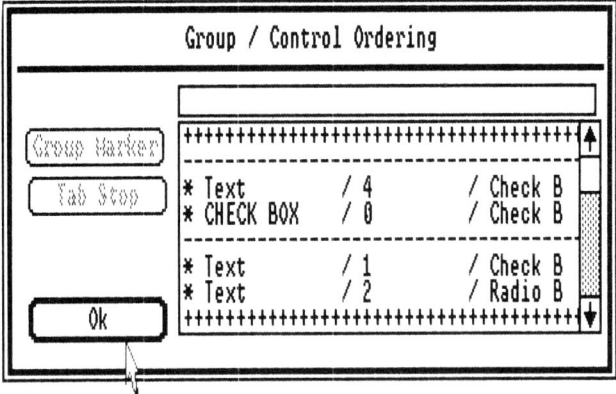

Select the Group Marker button again. You have now created a group of dialog box controls. If you later decide that you do not want control groups, simply select the Group Marker button and choose the Delete Group option.

Tab stops allow you to specify where the cursor will be placed when the user presses the TAB key. Look at the list of controls. If a control has an asterisk next to it, it has a tab stop. Remove the tab stop for the current control by toggling the Tab Stop option.

Tab stops and control groups are convenient when you have multiple groups (lists) of options from which the user may want to choose. In such cases, set a tab stop for the first control in each group and then allow the user to step through the controls within the group via the keyboard arrow keys. This will increase the user's ability to traverse your dialog boxes while using the keyboard.

Include Files

Each dialog box has associated with it an include file that contains the definitions for each of the controls used within your applications programs. By default, include files have a .H extension. The include file contains #define statements that define the constants your programs will reference, thus simplifying your programming efforts.

These definitions will be examined in detail in later chapters when we examine programming applications. Therefore, the definition of your dialog box controls is a critical step in the creation of your dialog boxes. The Include menu allows you to perform the following functions:

The New option creates a new file for your definitions. The Open option allows you to modify an existing .H file, as follows:

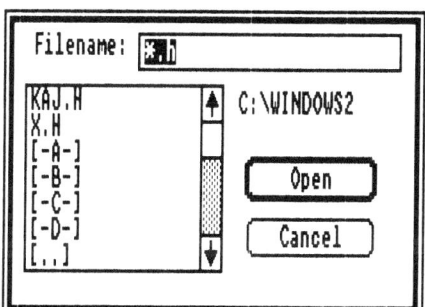

Type in the name of the file you wish to open, or double-click your mouse select button on the desired file. The Save and Save As options allow you to store your definitions in a .H file. When selected, these options both display the following:

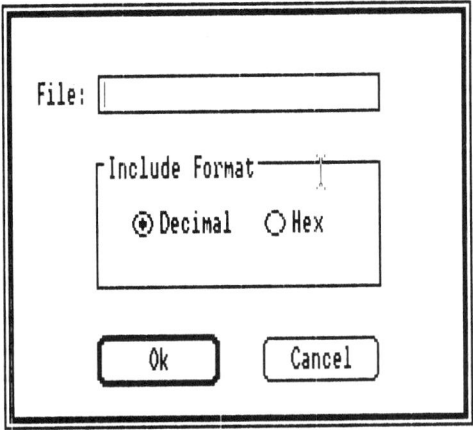

The Hex mode option of the Include menu allows you to toggle between Hexadecimal and Decimal mode. In Hexadecimal mode, your constant values are written to the file in hex. In Decimal mode, the constant values are in decimal form.

The View include option allows you to display or modify your current control definitions. To see how this works, select one of the controls in your dialog box, as follows:

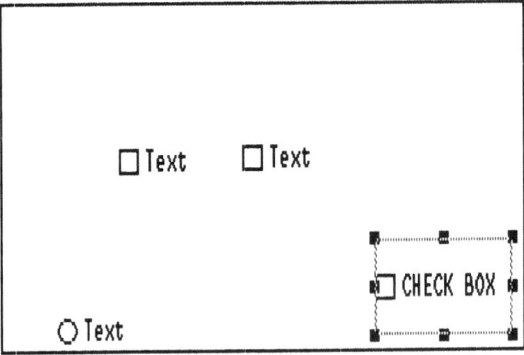

Next, select the View include option from the Include menu; the following will be displayed:

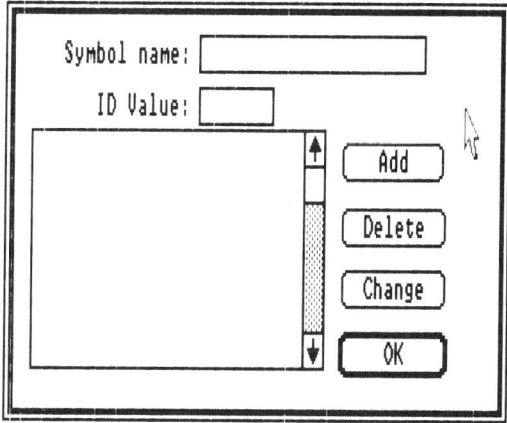

In the Symbol name field type the name you want to use to refer to the control within your programs.

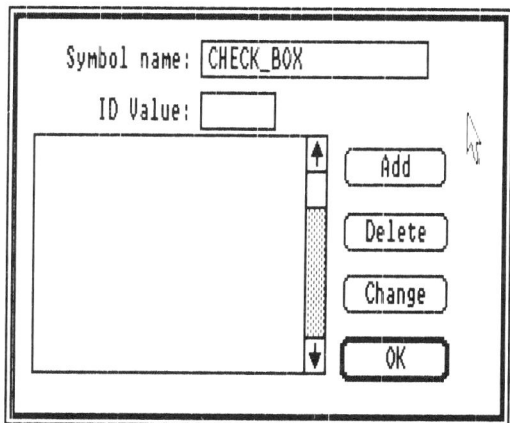

In the ID Value field type the numeric value that you want assigned to the constant. The numeric value is the actual value that the programs will use to reference a control.

Note that Windows predefines actions for the values 1 and 2. The value 1 should be used for your default button (an Ok button, for example). When the ENTER or ESC key is pressed, Windows automatically sends a response message to the dialog input function, along with the identification value of 1. Therefore, you should assign your default control the value 1. Likewise, the value 2 should be used for Cancel buttons. When the ESC key is pressed, Windows automatically sends a message and the identification value of 2. Be sure you have assigned these two values to the intended controls.

Select the Ok button. Next, invoke the Save option to place the definition into a .H file. The Dialog Editor will prompt you to specify the .H file to which you want the definitions saved, as follows:

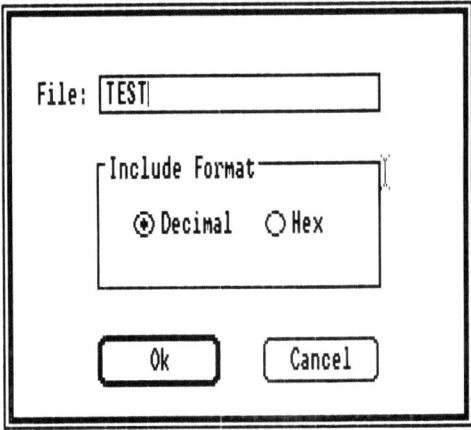

If you later examine the .H file you created, it will contain the following entry for the symbol definition:

#define CHECK—BOX 3

Complete dialog boxes are critical to the overall success of your applications programs. The Dialog Editor provides you with tremendous flexibility in designing a powerful user interface.

CHAPTER

5

PROGRAM INFORMATION FILES (PIFs)

Although the purpose of this text is to teach you how to develop applications programs that run in the Windows environment, it is important to remember that Windows will execute programs that were not designed to be run under Windows, as long as you have created a *program information file* (PIF) for the application. These files provide Windows with an application's memory and system resource requirements and information about their utilization.

127

Creating PIFs

The standard Windows environment provides a utility program called PIFEDIT.EXE, which is the program information file editor. To create a PIF, set your current working directory to \WINDOWS\PIF, as follows:

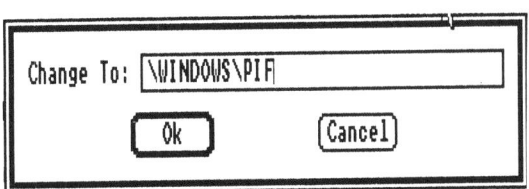

Invoke the program PIFEDIT.EXE; your screen will contain the following:

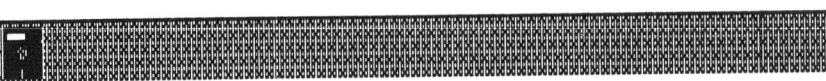

Select the File menu to display the following options:

The File menu allows you to start a new PIF description, edit a previously defined PIF, or save the current PIF description to a file. If you select the Open option, Pifedit will display the available PIFs, as follows:

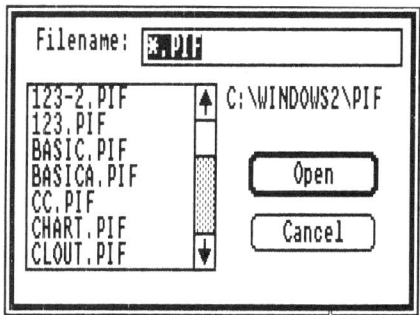

Either type in the name of the desired file, or select the PIF from the list of available files by double-clicking your mouse select button once the file is highlighted in reverse video. When you have completed the PIF description, select the Save option. Pifedit will prompt you for the name of the file to contain the description, as follows:

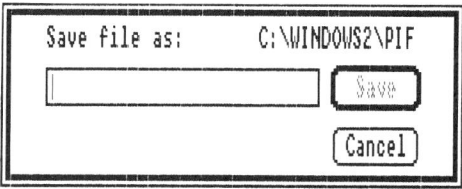

Type in the name under which you wish to save the file. If a file with the same name already exists, Pifedit will display the following dialog box:

You create or edit a PIF by entering information into a number of different fields on the screen. The Program Name field is the name of the program for which you are creating the PIF. For example, if you have a C program called LS.EXE that displays a directory of files, you would enter the following:

Program Title is the program description that Windows will place in the title bar of a window. You may want to make it more descriptive than the program name, as follows:

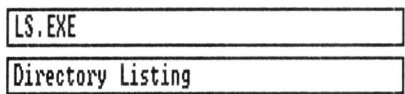

If the application requires command-line parameters, the Program Parameters field allows you to specify them. For example, if LS performs a global file listing when the wildcard characters *.* are used, you would enter the following:

```
┌─────────────────────────────────────┐
│ LS.EXE                               │
├─────────────────────────────────────┤
│ Directory Listing                    │
├─────────────────────────────────────┤
│ *.*                                  │
└─────────────────────────────────────┘
```

If, instead of the asterisks, you enter a question mark,

```
┌─────────────────────────────────────┐
│ LS.EXE                               │
├─────────────────────────────────────┤
│ Directory Listing                    │
├─────────────────────────────────────┤
│ ?                                    │
└─────────────────────────────────────┘
```

Windows will prompt you to enter the command-line arguments each time the program executes, as follows:

```
┌─────────────────────────────────────┐
│          Directory Listing           │
│                                       │
│ Parameters ┌──────────────────────┐  │
│            └──────────────────────┘  │
│              ┌────────────┐           │
│              │     Ok     │           │
│              └────────────┘           │
└─────────────────────────────────────┘
```

The Initial Directory field allows you to specify a directory name that Windows will automatically set as the default each time the application is invoked. This field is left blank for most applications.

The KB Required field of the Memory Requirements section allows you to specify in kilobytes the amount of memory that an application requires to execute. If Windows cannot allocate the specified amount of memory, it will attempt to remove itself from memory temporarily so that the application can run. If Windows is successful, the application will run to completion. Otherwise, Windows will display the following message:

For most applications 52K is sufficient.

The KB Desired field of the Memory Requirements section allows you to specify the amount of memory that an application would like to have. Many applications become more efficient as the amount of memory available to them increases. Again, 52K of memory is sufficient for most applications.

The Directly Modifies section allows you to specify whether the application accesses resources in a manner that prevents the resources from being shared. For example, many older word processors require direct memory-mapped access to the video memory to display output. Direct manipulation of the screen in this fashion prevents Windows from allowing the screen to be shared with other applications. If the application accesses the screen display directly, or if you are not sure, select the Screen option. Likewise, if the program accesses the keyboard hardware or keyboard buffer directly, select the Keyboard option. Selecting either of these options prevents Windows from executing the application in a window. If the program directly accesses either the COM1 or COM2 communications port, select these options. If these ports are allocated to another program and the application requires access to them, Windows will not allow the program to start.

Select the Memory option if the application program terminates while resident in DOS or if it disregards the available system memory. Programs running in this mode have the lowest level of Windows compatibility. This option should be left blank for most applications.

The Program Switch section specifies how Windows treats applications that cannot execute within a window but that allow you to switch back to Windows by pressing ALT-TAB. The Prevent option disables ALT-TAB switching for the application. If this option is selected, Windows will ignore the ALT-TAB key combination. The Text option specifies that Windows will allow the application to switch back to Windows only when it is in text mode. Selecting this option causes Windows to allocate an additional 4K of memory each time the application is invoked. The Graphics/Multiple Text option enables program switching when the program is in graphics mode. Depending upon the graphics card contained in the target computer, this option causes Windows to allocate 16K to 32K of memory each time the application is invoked.

The Screen Exchange section allows you to specify how an application exchanges information with Windows. While an application is executing, Windows allows you to take snapshots of the screen that can be shared by other programs. To take a snapshot, you press the ALT and PRTSC keys simultaneously. Windows then captures the current screen contents and places them in the Clipboard. For example, consider a screen that contains the following:

```
WINOLDAP.MOD     19824 bytes   08/01/1986   03:16:58   ARCHIVE
WINOLDAP.GRB      1403 bytes   07/16/1986   23:07:08   ARCHIVE
MSDOS.EXE            1 bytes   11/23/1986   20:34:20   ARCHIVE
WIN.COM           4873 bytes   08/06/1986   14:59:44   ARCHIVE
WIN100.BIN      180512 bytes   08/06/1986   14:59:44   ARCHIVE
EPSON.DRV        14352 bytes   05/22/1986   11:07:52   ARCHIVE
COURA.FON         8720 bytes   07/29/1986   16:43:18   ARCHIVE
HELVA.FON        27056 bytes   07/29/1986   16:44:48   ARCHIVE
TMSRA.FON        26256 bytes   07/29/1986   16:46:32   ARCHIVE
COURD.FON        15136 bytes   07/29/1986   16:43:54   ARCHIVE
HELVD.FON        45600 bytes   07/29/1986   16:45:38   ARCHIVE
TMSRD.FON        45200 bytes   07/29/1986   16:47:24   ARCHIVE
COURC.FON         8784 bytes   07/29/1986   16:43:40   ARCHIVE
HELVC.FON        26624 bytes   07/29/1986   16:45:20   ARCHIVE
TMSRC.FON        25824 bytes   07/29/1986   16:47:06   ARCHIVE
ROMAN.FON        11120 bytes   07/09/1986   17:19:14   ARCHIVE
SCRIPT.FON       10304 bytes   07/09/1986   17:18:44   ARCHIVE
MODERN.FON        7584 bytes   07/09/1986   17:18:12   ARCHIVE
CALC.EXE         25008 bytes   05/22/1986   04:33:36   ARCHIVE
CALENDAR.EXE     37552 bytes   05/22/1986   07:55:48   ARCHIVE
CARDFILE.EXE     36992 bytes   05/22/1986   04:23:40   ARCHIVE
CLIPBRD.EXE       9712 bytes   05/22/1986   06:17:52   ARCHIVE
CLOCK.EXE         7984 bytes   05/22/1986   06:08:08   ARCHIVE
CONTROL.EXE      52704 bytes   08/14/1986   16:13:12   ARCHIVE
NOTEPAD.EXE      18736 bytes   05/22/1986   06:28:22   ARCHIVE
```

Pressing the ALT-PRTSC key combination causes the following to be placed in the Clipboard:

```
┌─────────────────────────────── Clipboard ───────────────────────────┐
│ Text                                                               ▲ │
├═══════════════════════════════════════════════════════════════════╤═┤
│                                                                    ▓ │
│  WINOLDAP.MOD   19824 bytes  08/01/1986  03:16:58   ARCHIVE        ▓ │
│  WINOLDAP.GRB    1403 bytes  07/16/1986  23:07:08   ARCHIVE        ▓ │
│  MSDOS.EXE          1 bytes  11/23/1986  20:34:20   ARCHIVE          │
│  WIN.COM         4873 bytes  08/06/1986  14:59:44   ARCHIVE          │
│  WIN100.BIN    180512 bytes  08/06/1986  14:59:44   ARCHIVE          │
│  EPSON.DRV      14352 bytes  05/22/1986  11:07:52   ARCHIVE          │
│  COURA.FON       8720 bytes  07/29/1986  16:43:18   ARCHIVE          │
│  HELVA.FON      27056 bytes  07/29/1986  16:44:48   ARCHIVE          │
│  TMSRA.FON      26256 bytes  07/29/1986  16:46:32   ARCHIVE          │
│  COURD.FON      15136 bytes  07/29/1986  16:43:54   ARCHIVE          │
│  HELVD.FON      45600 bytes  07/29/1986  16:45:38   ARCHIVE          │
│  TMSRD.FON      45200 bytes  07/29/1986  16:47:24   ARCHIVE          │
│  COURC.FON       8784 bytes  07/29/1986  16:43:40   ARCHIVE          │
│  HELVC.FON      26624 bytes  07/29/1986  16:45:20   ARCHIVE          │
│  TMSRC.FON      25824 bytes  07/29/1986  16:47:06   ARCHIVE        ▼ │
├───────────────────────────────────────────────────────────────────┬─┤
│ ←  █                                                              → │
└─────────────────────────────────────────────────────────────────────┘
```

When the None option is selected, no screen exchanges are allowed; this is often done to conserve memory for the application. The Text option allows screen exchanges to occur only when the application is in text mode, and the Graphics/Text option supports screen exchanges while the application is in graphics mode. The Text and Graphics/Text options cause Windows to allocate an additional 4K to 32K of memory for the application.

The Close Window on exit option directs Windows to close the standard application window when the program terminates.

The Default PIF

If Windows cannot find a PIF for a specific application, it attempts to execute the program with the default values shown in Table 5-1. If these parameters are sufficient, Windows will execute the program.

Windows also allows you to specify memory requirements for specific applications in the Windows initialization file, WIN.INI (see Chapter 6), as follows:

```
[pif]
  command.com=32
  chkdsk.com=52
  ls.exe=52
  hello.exe=25
```

If Windows does not find a PIF for an application, it will check the list of applications defined in WIN.INI. If it finds a reference to the file, Windows will use the default values shown in Table 5-2. This eliminates the need for multitudes of PIFs.

Field	Default Value
Program Title	Ignored
Initial Directory	Ignored
Memory Required	52K
Memory Desired	All available memory
Directly Modifies	Screen
Program Switch	Prevent

Table 5-1. Default Values for Execution by PIF

Field	Default Value
Program Title	File name (no extension)
Initial Directory	Ignored
Parameters	Ignored
Memory Required	Value from WIN.INI
Memory Desired	Same as memory required
Directly Modifies	None
Program Switch	Ignored
Screen Exchange	Ignored

Table 5-2. Default Values for File References

Executing an Application
Within a Window

If Windows can execute an application within a window, it will. The window will function as a standard window with a System menu and other Windows components. Simply treat the application as a standard Windows application.

CHAPTER

6

UTILIZING
WIN.INI

Each time Windows begins execution, it uses the contents of the file WIN.INI to configure itself in memory. WIN.INI contains values for default file extensions, font information, device settings, applications to be automatically loaded as icons (or executed), color settings for the EGA, country settings for international users, and PIF memory requirements (see Chapter 5). Before you get started with this chapter, print the file WIN.INI, as follows:

137

Most users will never directly modify the contents of WIN.INI. Instead, they will use the Control Panel discussed in Chapter 1, as shown here:

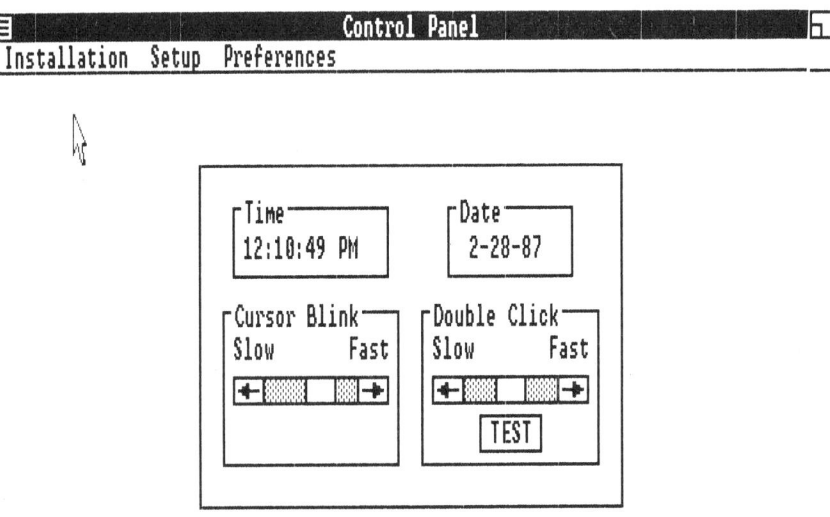

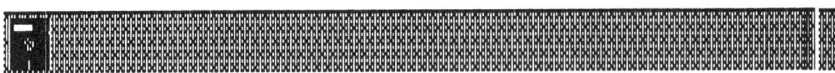

The most common instance requiring the modification of WIN.INI is when you want to have Windows automatically load applications as icons or execute certain applications immediately upon Windows invocation. Once you modify the contents of WIN.INI, you must reinvoke Windows for the changes to take effect. Use the desktop application Notepad to modify the contents of WIN.INI, as follows:

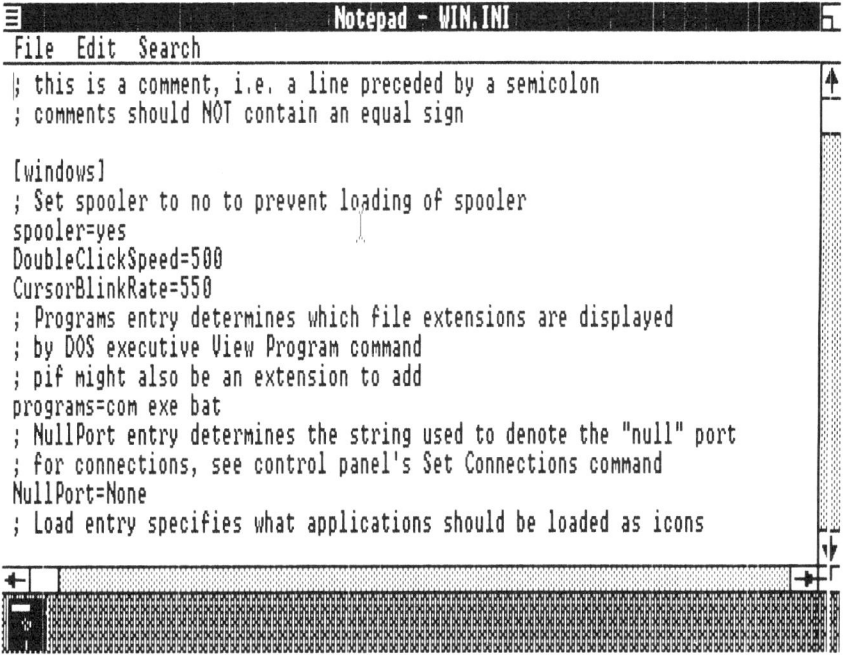

```
≡                    Notepad - WIN.INI                        ⌐
 File  Edit  Search
; this is a comment, i.e. a line preceded by a semicolon      ▲
; comments should NOT contain an equal sign

[windows]
; Set spooler to no to prevent loading of spooler
spooler=yes
DoubleClickSpeed=500
CursorBlinkRate=550
; Programs entry determines which file extensions are displayed
; by DOS executive View Program command
; pif might also be an extension to add
programs=com exe bat
; NullPort entry determines the string used to denote the "null" port
; for connections, see control panel's Set Connections command
NullPort=None
; Load entry specifies what applications should be loaded as icons   ▼
```

Functional Sections of WIN.INI

Examine your hard-copy listing of WIN.INI. As you will see, WIN.INI is divided into functional sections.

[windows]

This section specifies settings for the cursor blink rate, the mouse double-click delay, the default printer, and applications to be loaded upon Windows invocation. In addition, this section allows you to enable or disable spooling and specify the file extensions for executable programs. Entries are made as follows:

```
[windows]
    DoubleClickSpeed=600
    CursorBlinkRate=500
    Device=Epson FX-80,epson,LPT1:
    Load=calendar.exe
    Run=calc.exe
    Spooler=yes
    Programs=com exe bat
```

[extensions]

This section specifies the default file-name extensions to be used with each Windows application. Entries are specified as follows:

```
[extensions]
    cal=calendar.exe^.cal
    txt=notepad.exe^.txt
```

[pif]

This section provides memory requirements for applications programs that were not developed to support the Windows environment but that you wish to run under Windows. In addition, this section allows you to specify the swapsize and swapdisk that Windows will use when it runs multiple applications simultaneously. Memory requirements are specified in kilobytes as follows:

```
[pif]
    chkdsk.com=52
    ls.exe=32
    swapdisk=?
    ; ? directs Windows to use the first hard disk
    swapsize=0
    ; minimum swap size
```

[intl]

This section provides country symbols for international users as follows:

```
[intl]
  iCountry=1
  iDate=0
  iCurrency=0
  iDigits=2
  iTime=0
  iLzero=0
  s1159=AM
  s2359=PM
  sCurrency=$
  sThousand=,
  sDecimal=.
  sDate=-
  sTime=:
  sList=,
  dialog=yes
```

[colors]

This section specifies the colors for the EGA. Most users choose to set
these via the Control Panel (see Chapter 1). Colors are specified as
follows:

```
[colors]
  Window=255 255 255
  WindowText=0 0 0
  Scrollbar=192 192 192
  ActiveTitle=0 0 0
  InactiveTitle=128 128 128
  TitleText=255 255 255
  WindowFrame=0 0 0
  Menu=255 255 255
  MenuText=0 0 0
  Background=159 53 53
```

[fonts]

This section provides information on each of the available fonts. Most
users choose to add fonts via the Control Panel (see Chapter 1). Fonts
are specified as follows:

```
[fonts]
  Courier 8,10,12 (Set #2)=COURA
  Helv 8,10,12 (Set #2)=HELVA
  Tms Rmn 8,10,12 (Set #2)=TMSRA
```

```
Courier 8,10,12 (Set #5)=COURD
Helv 8,10,12 (Set #5)=HELVD
Tms Rmn 8,10,12 (Set #5)=TMSRD
Courier 8,10,12 (Set #4)=COURC
Helv 8,10,12 (Set #4)=HELVC
Tms Rmn 8,10,12 (Set #4)=TMSRC
Roman (Set #1)=ROMAN
Script (Set #1)=SCRIPT
Modern (Set #1)=MODERN
```

[ports]

This section specifies the data communications parameters for the serial and parallel ports on the system. Entries are made as follows:

```
[ports]
   LPT1:=
   LPT2:=
   LPT3:=
   COM1:=1200,n,8,1
   COM2:=1200,n,8,1
```

[devices]

This section specifies the printing devices available on the system and the associated printer device files. Entries are made as follows:

```
[devices]
   Epson FX-80=EPSON,LPT1:
```

Modifying WIN.INI

It is important to note that most users will never directly modify the file WIN.INI. The most common reason for modifying the file is to load or execute a program immediately each time Windows is invoked. For example, the following entry

```
Load=CALC.EXE
```

causes Windows to load the Calculator desktop application each time it begins, as follows:

```
┌─────────────────────── MS-DOS Executive ──────────────────┐ 6
│ File  View  Special                                        │
│────────────────────────────────────────────────────────── │
│ A ─■─  B ─■─  │C ─■─│ D ─■─  C:DOSDISK \WINDOWS2           │
│ BIN          COURA.FON      LL.CAL        THSRD.FON         │
│ C            COURC.FON      MODERN.FON    USER.SYM          │
│ CARDFILE     COURD.FON      MSDOS.EXE     VV`.CAL           │
│ INCLUDE      DIALOG.EXE     NOTEPAD.EXE   WIN.BAK           │
│ LIB          DOS.CRD        PAINT.EXE     WIN.COM           │
│ PASCAL       DOTHIS.TXT     PRACTICE.WRI  WIN.INI           │
│ PIF          EPSON.DRV      README.TXT    WIN100.BIN        │
│ TEST         FONTDEMO.WRI   ROMAN.FON     WIN100.OVL        │
│ ABC.TXT      FONTEDIT.EXE   SCRIPT.FON    WINOLDAP.GRB      │
│ ATRM1111.FNT GDI.SYM        SHAKER.EXE    WINOLDAP.MOD      │
│ │CALC.EXE│   HEAPWALK.EXE   SLAPJR.EXE    WRITE.EXE         │
│ CALENDAR.EXE HELVA.FON      SPOOLER.EXE                     │
│ CARDFILE.EXE HELVC.FON      TARGET.DAT                      │
│ CLIPBRD.EXE  HELVD.FON      TEMP.ART                        │
│ CLOCK.EXE    ICONEDIT.EXE   THSRA.FON                       │
│ CONTROL.EXE  KERNEL.SYM     THSRC.FON                       │
└────────────────────────────────────────────────────────────┘
```

Likewise, if you have a personal calendar that you would like Windows to use each time the program is invoked, you could specify

```
Load=MY.CAL
```

Windows will load the Calendar desktop program using MY.CAL for the default file, as follows:

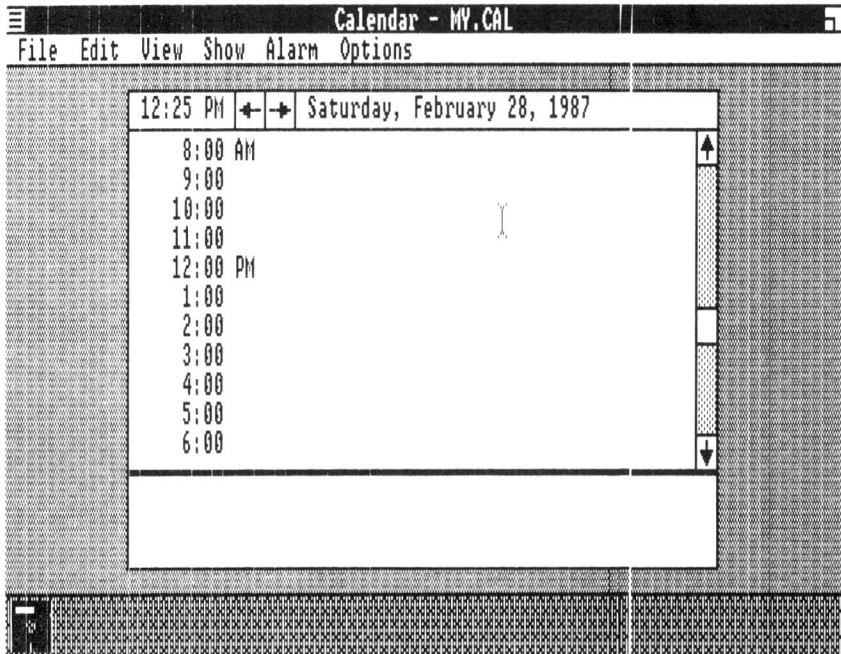

Finally, if you want an application to run immediately when Windows is invoked, use the Run entry, as follows:

```
Run=NOTEPAD
```

Instead of displaying the MS-DOS Executive each time Windows begins, the desktop application Notepad will execute, as follows:

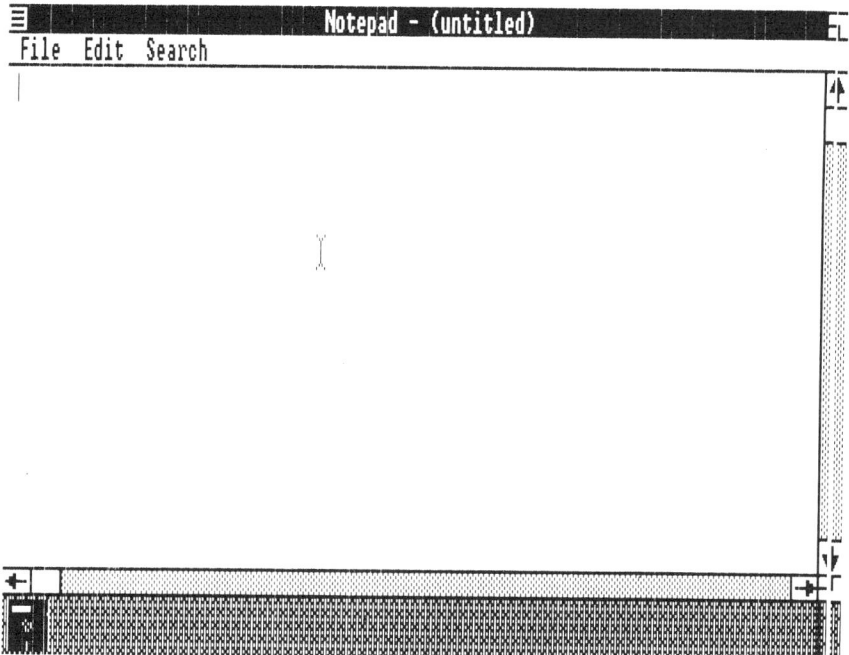

Experiment with a few of these combinations before proceeding to later chapters; this will give you an appreciation of the varied functions provided by WIN.INI.

7

COMPLETING
THE TOOLBOX

Before beginning an examination of Windows programming applications, it is important to examine the last few pieces of the application development toolbox. This chapter discusses the steps required to produce an executable Windows application. They are as follows:

1. Create a C, Pascal, or assembly language program with a standard text editor.

2. Compile or assemble the applications program with the Microsoft C compiler, Pascal compiler, or Microsoft Macro Assembler.

3. Create application resources with the icon, font, and dialog editors.

4. Create a resource script file that defines the application resources with a standard text editor.

5. Compile the resource script file with RC.EXE, the resource compiler, thus producing a .RES file.

6. Create a module definition file for the application with a standard text editor.

7. Link the applications program, run-time, and Windows libraries to the module definition file with LINK4.EXE, thus producing an .EXE file.

8. Use the resource compiler, RC.EXE, to bind the .RES file to the .EXE file, thus producing an executable Windows application.

Compilation and Assembly

To create an application that runs in the Windows environment, you must use the Microsoft C or Pascal compiler or the Microsoft Macro Assembler. Because most Windows applications are written in C, the Microsoft C compiler is examined first.

Once you have created your C Windows application, use the following command line to compile the program:

```
cl -c -AS -Gsw -Os -Zdp filename.c
```

This example compiles a program for the small memory model. The -c option ensures that the compiler generates code that is executable under Windows. The -AS option specifies the small memory model. The -Gsw option directs the compiler to include the Windows prolog and epilog, along with stack probes. (A *stack probe* is code that ensures that sufficient space is available for local variables each time a function is invoked. If insufficient space is available, the stack probe code invokes the FatalExit function.) The -*Os* option directs the compiler to optimize for size over speed. If you do not want this optimization, use the -*Od* option instead. Finally, the -*Zdp* option directs the compiler to include line-number information in the object code for debugging and to pack bytes in structures. The program CL will automatically invoke each pass of the C compiler.

If instead you develop your Windows application in Pascal, simply invoke pass one and pass two of the compiler as follows:

```
PAS1 filename.pas
PAS2
```

Chapter 9 describes several *metacommands* (compiler directives) that you should include in your Pascal source code to achieve effects similar to switches specified in the C command line presented previously.

If your application was developed using the Microsoft Macro Assembler, use the following command line to assemble the program:

```
MASM filename;
```

Script Files

You must define the resources (icon, cursor, menus, and dialog boxes) used by your application during the development of your Windows application. Define them in a resource script file (a file having the extension RC), for example, SAMPLE.RC.

Once you have completed your resource script file, you use the resource compiler, RC.EXE, to compile its contents. The resource script file contains the names and attributes of each of the application's resources. This file consists of one or more resource statements, which are categorized as shown in Table 7-1.

A single-line resource statement defines a resource that is contained in a single file, such as an icon or cursor. The format for a single-line statement is resource—name   type [load—attr] [memory—attr] filename

The values are defined as follows:

resource—name   A unique name that identifies the resource. The resource compiler supports integer values for names. For fonts, the name must be an integer value.

type   Specifies the kind of resource; must be one of the following keywords:

BITMAP
CURSOR
FONT
ICON

General Resources

Single-line statements	BITMAP CURSOR FONT ICON

User-defined Resources

Multiple-line statements	ACCELERATORS DIALOG MENU STRINGTABLE
Directives	#define #elif #else #endif #if #ifdef #ifndef #include #rcinclude #undef

---

Table 7-1. Categories of Resource Statements

load—attr
: Specifies when the resource is loaded into memory. If present, the load—attr must be one of the following: PRELOAD (load into memory immediately) or LOADONCALL (load into memory when called).

memory—attr
: Specifies the resource memory attributes. If present, memory—attr must be any combination of the following keywords:

DISCARDABLE
FIXED
MOVEABLE

Table 7-2 lists the default memory attributes for standard Windows resources.

filename
: Specifies the name of the file containing the resource. Complete DOS pathnames are supported.

The following are examples of valid single-line resource statements:

```
csr        CURSOR      TEST.CUR
ticon      ICON        TEST.ICO
map        BITMAP      TEST.BMP
font1      FONT        TEST.FNT
```

Resource	Load Option	Memory Option
Bitmap	LOADONCALL	MOVEABLE
Cursor	LOADONCALL	MOVEABLE, DISCARDABLE
Font	LOADONCALL	MOVEABLE, DISCARDABLE
Icon	LOADONCALL	MOVEABLE, DISCARDABLE

Table 7-2. Default Memory Attributes

Windows applications can also define their own resources. In such cases the resource is simply any data that the application intends to use. The general format for user-defined resources is

resource_name   type [load_attr] [memory_attr] filename

The only field in this statement that differs from the fields in the single-line resource statements is the type field, which must be a unique name or integer value. If an integer is used, it must exceed 255. (0 to 255 are reserved for Windows.) The following are valid user-defined statements:

size   256   TEST.SZE   PRELOAD
K   1024   TEST.K

The STRINGTABLE resource is simply a table that contains one or more ASCIIZ (null-terminated) strings accessible by the Windows application. The general format for the string table is

```
STRINGTABLE [load_attr] [memory_attr]
BEGIN
    definitions
END
```

The load_attr and memory_attr fields are identical to those specified in the single-line statements. The default values are LOAD-ONCALL and MOVEABLE, DISCARDABLE, respectively. The following example shows a valid string table definition:

```
STRINGTABLE
  BEGIN
        program  "WINDOWS"
        op_sys   "MSDOS"
        computer "IBM AT"
  END
```

Accelerators are predefined keystrokes that provide the user with a quick means of executing a task. For example, several of the following options can be selected by using a predefined control-key combination.

```
┌─────┐
│ Edit│
├──────────────────┐
│ Undo Editing  Sh Esc │
├──────────────────┤
│ Cut           Del    │
│ Copy          F2     │
│ Paste         Ins    │
├──────────────────┤
│ Move Picture         │
│ Size Picture         │
└──────────────────┘
```

To define an accelerator, use the following format:

table_name   ACCELERATORS
BEGIN
    event_type, id_value, [,type][,NOINVERT][,SHIFT][,CONTROL]
END

The values are defined as follows:

table_name   A unique name that specifies the accelerator table.

event_type   A keystroke that invokes the accelerator.

event_type must be one of the following:

"character"   A single character enclosed by double quotation marks. If the character is preceded by a caret (^), it is a control key combination.

ASCII value   An integer value representing an ASCII character.

Virtual key character An integer value representing a virtual key. (See Appendix F for a description of a virtual key.)

id—value	An integer value that uniquely identifies the accelerator.
type	Used only for the ASCII event—type; must be either the keyword ASCII or the word VIRTKEY.
NOINVERT	If present, directs Windows to suppress the display of the high-level menu option each time the accelerator is used.
SHIFT	Causes the accelerator to be performed only when the SHIFT key is depressed.
CONTROL	Causes the accelerator to be performed only when the CONTROL key is depressed.

The following are valid accelerator definitions:

```
ACC_TABLE       ACCELERATORS
  BEGIN
        "^X", FILE_SAVE
        "^Q", FILE_DEL, NOINVERT
        "q",  FILE_DEL, NOINVERT, CONTROL
  END
```

The resource script MENU statement allows you to define menu resources for your application. The general format is

menu—name MENU [load—attr] [memory—attr]
BEGIN
    menu—definitions
END

The menu—name field is a unique name or number used to identify the menu resource.

The load—attr and memory—attr fields are identical to those described previously for single-line statements. The default values for menu resources are LOADONCALL and MOVEABLE, DISCARDABLE.

The menu—definitions section uses the keywords MENUITEM and POPUP. The format for MENUITEM is as follows:

MENUITEM "string" result—value, options

The values are defined as follows:

string
: A character-string prompt that appears for the menu option.

result—value
: An integer value returned when the menu item is selected.

options
: A list of comma-separated options that specifies how the item appears. The following keywords are supported:

CHECKED
GRAYED
INACTIVE
MENUBREAK

The following examples illustrate the use of the MENUITEM keyword:

```
TEST      MENU
  BEGIN
        MENUITEM "Version", 1
        MENUITEM "Time", 2
        MENUITEM "Space", 3
        MENUITEM "Volume", 4, CHECKED
  END
```

A *pop-up* is the most commonly used type of menu and is displayed when the specified menu item is selected. The general format for a pop-up menu is

POPUP "string" options

The values are defined as follows:

string   A character-string prompt that appears for the menu item.

options   Specifies the appearance of the items in the pop-up menu.

The options can be any of the following:

CHECKED   A check mark appears next to the option

GRAYED   Item appears in a light gray shade

INACTIVE   Menu option not available under current menu

MENUBREAK   The item is in a new column

MENUBARBREAK   The item is in a new column and old items are separated by a bar

These options can be combined via the C bitwise or operator.

The following illustrates a pop-up menu definition:

```
TEST  MENU
  BEGIN
        MENUITEM "Less"  ,  100
        POPUP "More"
          BEGIN
            MENUITEM "Age", 200
            MENUITEM "Sex", 300
          END
  END
```

Note that pop-up menus cannot be nested.
    Finally, the directive

MENUITEM SEPARATOR

can be used within the element definitions to place a dividing bar between two options.

Some users use the DIALOG statement to create dialog boxes for their applications. The general format is

dialog—box—name DIALOG [load—attr] [memory—attr] x, y,
      width, height

The complete description of the dialog statement is presented in Chapter 13, which discusses the dialog box interface to Windows applications.

The load—attr and memory—attr fields are the same as those for single-line statements. For dialog boxes the default values are LOAD-ONCALL and MOVEABLE.

The other values are defined as follows:

x	Specifies the X coordinate of the upper left corner of the dialog box.
y	Specifies the Y coordinate of the upper left corner of the dialog box.
width	Specifies the width of the dialog box. Four width units are equivalent to the width of the Windows default character.
height	Specifies the height of the dialog box. Eight height units are equivalent to the height of the Windows default character.

Dialog option statements specify the attributes of the dialog box. If present, they can use the following keywords:

STYLE style—value	An integer value specifying a window style. For predefined names, see the file WINDOWS.H.
CAPTION "string"	Specifies the text to appear in the caption bar of the dialog box.
MENU menu—name	Specifies the name of dialog box menu (normally empty).
CLASS "string"	Defines the dialog box class.

Dialog control statements define the attributes of the control items that appear in the dialog box. Their general form is

control_type "string",control_id, x, y, width, height [,control_style]

The values are defined as follows:

control_type	Specifies the type of control; must be one of the following keywords: CHECKBOX CONTROL CTEXT DEFPUSHBUTTON EDITTEXT GROUPBOX ICON LISTBOX LTEXT PUSHBUTTON RADIOBUTTON RTEXT
string	Gives the text to be displayed within the control.
control_id	Specifies a unique number that identifies the control.
x	Specifies the X coordinate of the upper left corner of the control.
y	Specifies the Y coordinate of the upper left corner of the control.
width	Specifies the width of the control. Four width units are equivalent to the width of a Window default character.

height   Specifies the height of the control. Eight height units are equivalent to the height of a Window default character.

control—style   Specifies the style of the control. See the file WINDOWS.H for predefined styles.

The following is an example of the use of the DIALOG statement:

```
#include "windows.h"

drive   DIALOG 10, 10, 300, 200
STYLE   WS_BORDER | WS_POPUP
CAPTION "Disk Drive"
  BEGIN
    CTEXT "Select drive:", 1, 10, 10, 280, 12
    RADIOBUTTON "A", 2, 75, 30, 60, 12
    RADIOBUTTON "B", 3, 75, 50, 60, 12
    RADIOBUTTON "C", 4, 75, 80, 60, 12

  END
```

Most users will instead use the Dialog Editor presented in Chapter 4.

Finally, the resource compiler supports the following directives normally associated with the C preprocessor:

#define
#elif
#else
#endif
#if
#ifdef
#ifndef
#include
#rcinclude
#undef

The #define directive assigns a value to a given name. For example, the statement

#define MAX 5

assigns the value 5 to the constant name MAX.

The #include statement specifies a file name, the contents of which the resource compiler is to read and place into the current list of resources. Its format is

#include "filename"

For example, the statement

#include "windows.h"

directs the resource compiler to include the file WINDOWS.H.

The #undef statement undefines a constant starting from that specific point in the file. The format for #undef is

#undef name

For example, the statement

#undef NAME—KIND

undefines the constant NAME—KIND throughout the remainder of the file.

The #if, #ifdef, #ifndef, #elif, #else, and #endif statements are used for conditional processing. Their use is illustrated in the following examples:

```
#ifdef NULL
#undef NULL
#endif
```

```
#ifndef SIZE
#define SIZE 255
#else
#undef SIZE
#define SIZE 255
#endif
```

In addition to the #include statement, the resource compiler supports the #rcinclude statement. Its general form is as follows:

#rcinclude filename

The processing of an #rcinclude statement differs from that of an #include statement in that the resource compiler will process everything in the specified file when the #rcinclude directive is used. If you instead use the #include statement, only #define statements contained within the file are processed. You should, therefore, use the #rcinclude statement whenever you are including resource files.

The Resource Compiler

Once your application resource script file is complete, compile it with the resource compiler using the command

rc [-r] script_filename [executable_filename]

The -r option directs the resource compiler to produce a .RES file that contains the resources in binary form. The script filename is the name of the file that contains the application's resources. The executable_filename option is the name of the file containing the executable application.

Consider the following example:

rc -r TEST

This command instructs the resource compiler to process the file TEST.RC and produce the binary file TEST.RES. The command

rc TEST.RES TEST.EXE

causes the compiler to link the binary file TEST.RES to the executable program file TEST.EXE. This is the last step in the Windows program-development cycle.

Module Definition File

All Windows applications must have a module definition file that you create with a text editor. This file specifies an application's attributes (such as the number of segments or the module names imported and exported by the application). The module definition file name must have the extension .DEF. Module definition files are composed of statements that utilize the following keywords:

NAME executable—name	Specifies the name of the executable program.
LIBRARY library—name	Specifies the name of a nonexecutable library file.
DESCRIPTION 'string'	Specifies a text string contained in single quotation marks for documentation.
HEAPSIZE num—bytes	Specifies the size of the local heap. The value of num—bytes must be in the range 0 to 65,356; 4096 is recommended.
STACKSIZE num—bytes	Specifies the size of the local stack. The value of num—bytes must be in the range 0 to 65,356; 4096 is recommended.

CODE memory__attr
load__attr pure__attr

pure__attr specifies whether the segment contains only code (pure) or code and data (impure).

DATA memory__attr
instance__attr

instance__attr specifies the number of data segments that can be created for the module: NONE, SINGLE, or MULTIPLE (default).

SEGMENT segment__
name memory__attr
pure__attr load__attr
min__size

min__size specifies the minimum number of bytes allocated for the segment.

EXPORTS function__
name ordinal__value
[RESIDENTNAME]
[NODATA] [num__words]

function__name specifies the name of the function. If the name is not the actual name of the function, you can use the following statement form:

exportname=actualname

ordinal__value is an integer value in the form @value that uniquely references the function within the application.

RESIDENTNAME indicates that the function is memory resident at all times.

NODATA indicates that the function is not bound to a specific data segment. Each time the function is invoked, it uses the current data segment.

num__words is an integer value that specifies the number of 16-bit words that the function expects to receive as parameters.

IMPORTS internal__
name module__name
function__reference

internal__name specifies the name by which the function will be referenced.

module__name gives the name of the module containing the function.

function—reference is either the name of the function or its ordinal reference within the module.

STUB filename supplies the name of the file to place in the Windows application to produce a warning when the application is not run with the Windows environment.

The following module definition file illustrates these statements:

```
NAME     TEST

DESCRIPTION 'Simple Windows Application'

STUB      'WINSTUB.EXE'

CODE      MOVEABLE
DATA      MOVEABLE MULTIPLE

HEAPSIZE  128
STACKSIZE 4096

EXPORTS
    TestWndProc @1
```

LINK4

Once you have created and compiled your program text, built your application resources, created and compiled your resource script file, and built your module definition file, you are ready to link all of the pieces together to create an executable file. Use the LINK4.EXE program to link files together. The command format is

LINK4 [options] object—files, [executable—file], [map—file], [library—files], definition—file

where the following is true:

options	Specifies LINK4 options; these consist of one or more of the following keywords:
/alignment:boundary_size	Aligns segment data on boundaries of the size specified. boundary_size must be a power of 2. A boundary size of 16 is recommended. The default value is 512.
/help	Directs LINK4 to display a list of the available options.
/linenumbers	Directs LINK4 to include line-number information in the executable file for debugging.
/map	Directs LINK4 to place information in the map file about each symbol referenced.
/nofarcalltrans	Directs LINK4 to prevent the translation of far calls in the current segment.
/noignorecase	Directs LINK4 to preserve the case of all symbols referenced.
/packcode[:segment_size]	Directs LINK4 to pack contiguous segments into one physical segment. The segment_size can range from 0 to 65,536. The default is 65,536.
/pause	Directs LINK4 to pause and display a prompt before writing the executable file to disk.
/segments:max_segments	Specifies the maximum number of segments that LINK4 will process.
/stack:stack_size	Specifies the program's stack size in bytes.
/warnfixup	Directs LINK4 to display error messages each time an offset is outside of the current physical segment.
object_files	Specifies the .OBJ input files for linking.

executable_file	Specifies the name of the .EXE file produced.
map_file	Specifies the name of the file containing the linker map.
library_files	Specifies the name of the .LIB files used for run-time or Windows references.
definition_file	Specifies the name of the module definition file.

The following is a typical Windows application LINK4 command:

LINK4 TEST,/ALIGN:16,/MAP,SLIBW,TEST.DEF

The Make Application Manager

Obviously, the process of building executable Windows applications is not a simple task. To simplify your program maintenance, Microsoft provides a utility program called Make that helps you update your programs following a code change. Make is an intelligent application manager that recompiles, reassembles, or links only the files affected by a source code change. It does this by analyzing the date and time stamps associated with every file in the application.

To begin, you must create a Make description file (using a standard text editor) that consists of one or more descriptions in the following format:

```
target_file: dependent_file [,dependent_file...]
    command
    [command...]
```

The values are defined as follows:

target_file	Specifies the name of a file that may or may not need to be updated based on a change in a source file.

dependent—file   Specifies the name of a file from which
                      the target file is built. If the date stamp
                      on a dependent file is newer than that on
                      the target file, the commands that follow
                      are executed. If the number of depen-
                      dent files exceeds one line, place a back-
                      slash at the end of the line and continue
                      listing the names on the following line.

command   Specifies a DOS command to be exe-
                      cuted when the dependent file has
                      changed.

Think of the Make description file as a series of IF-THEN statements. **If** the dependent file is newer than the target file, or **if** the
target file does not exist, **then** the series of DOS commands that follow are executed. For example,

TEST.EXE: TEST1.OBJ, TEST2.OBJ
    LINK TEST1+TEST2,TEST;

In this case, if TEST.EXE is older than either .OBJ file, or if
TEST.EXE does not exist, Make will execute the LINK command.

You invoke Make as follows:

MAKE [options] [macro—definitions] filename

The options field specifies the following options:

/d   Directs Make to display the date of each
                      file as it is examined.

/i   Directs Make to ignore error code values
                      returned by the programs it executes.

/n   Directs Make to display each command
                      that it would normally execute instead of
                      actually executing the command.

/s   Directs Make to suppress the display of
                                files as they are processed.

Make supports embedded macros that are later substituted during the Make execution. The format of a Make macro is as follows:

$(macro_name)

For example, consider the following:

$(NAME).EXE: $(NAME).OBJ
    LINK $(NAME);

When you later execute Make, simply invoke the program as follows:

MAKE name=TEST

Make will substitute the macro and process the following:

TEST.EXE: TEST.OBJ
    LINK TEST;

In addition, Make defines three additional macros as follows:

$*   Target file name without extension
$@   Complete target file name
$**   Complete list of dependent files

Make also allows you to specify inference rules that tell Make how to convert from a file of one extension to another. The format for inference rules is as follows:

.dependent_extension.target_extension
    command

For example, to convert from a C program to an .OBJ file, you would use the following:

.OBJ.C
    CL $*.C

The following is a complete Make description file for a Windows application program called test:

```
test.obj: test.c
    cl -d -c -AS -Gsw -Oas -Zpe -FPa -Fo test.c

test.res: test.rc test.ico
  rc -r test.rc

test.exe: test.obj test.def test.res
    link4 test, /ALIGN:16,/map,slibw,test.def
    rc test.res test.exe
```

Make is a very powerful and convenient programming utility. Many of you will find it useful for applications outside of Windows.

CHAPTER

8

WINDOWS DATA TYPES

To begin an examination of programs written to run in the Windows environment, let's first take a look at the many data types and structures permitted within Windows applications. A data type specifies the set of values that a variable can contain along with the set of operations that can be performed on that variable. For example, the C language utilizes the data types int, float, and char. Certain operations can be performed on variables of types int and float, such as addition and subtraction. However, these operations are not allowed on character strings.

171

Data Type	Description
BOOL	A 16-bit Boolean (True or False) value
BYTE	An 8-bit unsigned integer
char	An ASCII character
DWORD	A 32-bit unsigned integer. Normally used for segment /offset combinations
int	A 16-bit signed integer
long	A 32-bit signed integer
short	A 16-bit signed integer
VOID	An empty value. Normally associated with functions that do not return a value
WORD	A 16-bit unsigned integer

Table 8-1. Basic Data Types

Windows programming applications use a myriad of data types. Do not let them intimidate you. Instead, take the time now to familiarize yourself with each available type.

Basic Data Types

The collection of basic data types used in Windows applications should be familiar to C and Pascal programmers. These data types are shown in Table 8-1. Many of the data types presented in this chapter simply build upon these basic data types to produce records or structures.

Pointer Type	Description
FAR	A data type attribute used to create a long pointer
FARPROC	A long pointer to a function
LPINT	A long pointer to a 16-bit integer
LPMSG	A long pointer to a MSG data structure
LPRECT	A long pointer to a RECT data structure
LPSTR	A long pointer to a character string
NEAR	A data type attribute used to create a short pointer
POINT	A pointer to a 16-bit integer
PSTR	A pointer to a character string

Table 8-2.   Predefined Pointer Types

Pointer Data Types

Because Windows is very C oriented, it makes extensive use of pointers. If you are not yet conversant with pointers, a good source of information is the Osborne/McGraw Hill text *C: The Complete Reference* by Herbert Schildt (Berkeley, Calif.: Osborne/McGraw Hill, 1987).

The pointer types used in Windows applications have the following naming conventions:

Ptype—name Pointer to the type specified by type—name
LPtype—name Long (32-bit segment/offset) pointer to the type specified by type—name

Examine the predefined pointer types shown in Table 8-2. Do not be concerned with the RECT and MSG data structures; they will be examined in detail later in this chapter.

Handles

Windows allows you to keep many resources loaded in memory. Windows applications use handles to locate each resource within the internally maintained Windows tables. A handle, therefore, should be viewed simply as an index. Several of the more commonly used Windows handle types are shown in Table 8-3. If you view handles as indexes into Windows' internally maintained tables, they will be much less threatening.

Handle Type	Description
GLOBALHANDLE	A 16-bit index into the system heap for global objects
HANDLE	A 16-bit index into a table identifying program data
HBITMAP	A 16-bit index into the GDI objects for a bitmap
HBRUSH	A 16-bit index into the GDI objects for a brush
HCURSOR	A 16-bit index into a resource table for a cursor
HDC	A 16-bit index into the GDI device context tables
HFONT	A 16-bit index into the GDI objects for a font
HICON	A 16-bit index into a resource table for an icon
HMENU	A 16-bit index into a resource table for a menu
HPEN	A 16-bit index into the GDI objects for a pen
HRGN	A 16-bit index into the GDI objects for a region
HSTR	A 16-bit index into a resource table for a string
HWND	A handle to a specific window
LOCALHANDLE	A 16-bit index into the local heap

Table 8-3. Common Windows Handle Types

Compound Windows Data Structures

This section presents several of the more commonly used Windows
data structures. These structures simply combine the data types
already examined to create logical records containing related fields
of information. If you can understand the function of each of the
fields contained within the following data types, you are well on your
way to becoming a successful Windows application developer.

WNDCLASS

The WNDCLASS data structure defines a window's attributes. Each
window is defined via a WNDCLASS variable. Its fields include the
following:

WORD	style
FARPROC	lpfnWndProc
int	cbClsExtra
int	csWndExtra
HANDLE	hInstance
HCURSOR	hCursor
HICON	hIcon
HBRUSH	hbrBackground
LPSTR	lpszMenuName
LPSTR	lpszClassName

The fields are defined as follows:

style   Specifies the window's class style. Style can be a
combination of the following:

CS_VREDRAW Redraw entire window if vertical
size changes.

CS_HREDRAW Redraw entire window if horizontal size changes.

CS_KEYCVTWINDOW Reserves space for a key conversion window at bottom of the screen.

CS_DBLCLKS Window receives double-click messages.

CS_OEMCHARS Performs OEM character translation.

CS_OWNDC Gives each window instance its own context.

CS_CLASSDC Window receives its own device context.

lpfnWndProc	Serves as a long pointer to the function that serves as the window message-processing procedure.
cbClsExtra	Specifies the number of bytes to allocate after the window's class data structure (normally 0).
cbWndExtra	Specifies the number of bytes to allocate after the window's instance data structure (normally 0).
hInstance	Specifies the handle to the class module.
hCursor	Specifies the handle to the application cursor.
hIcon	Specifies the handle to the application icon.
hbrBackground	Specifies the window class background brush. The value specified can be either a handle to the brush used for painting the background or a color value. If a color value is used, the value must be one of the following:

COLOR_ACTIVECAPTION

COLOR_BACKGROUND

COLOR_CAPTIONTEXT

COLOR_INACTIVECAPTION

COLOR_MENU

COLOR_MENUTEXT

COLOR_SCROLLBAR

COLOR_WINDOW

COLOR_WINDOWFRAME

COLOR_WINDOWTEXT

	Add the value 1 to the color and convert it to the type HBRUSH.
lpszMenuName	Serves as a long pointer to the resource name containing the class menu. The name must be an ASCIIZ string. If an integer value identifies the resource, use the MAKEINTRESOURCE macro. If this field is null, windows of this class will have no default menu.
lpszClassName	Serves as a long pointer to the name of the window class. The name must be an ASCIIZ string.

MSG

The MSG data structure defines the template used for all messages passed by applications to windows. Its format is as follows:

HWND	hwnd
WORD	message
WORD	wParam
LONG	lParam
DWORD	time
POINT	pt

The fields are defined as follows:

hwnd	Specifies a handle to the window receiving the message.

message	Specifies the message number.
wParam	Specifies additional information about the message.
lParam	Specifies additional information about the message.
time	Specifies the time that Windows posted the message.
pt	Specifies the position of the mouse pointer in screen coordinates at the time of the message.

The MSG structure is used extensively throughout the remainder of this text.

PAINTSTRUCT

Windows uses the PAINTSTRUCT type to specify how the client area of an application is painted. Its fields include the following:

```
HDC        hdc
BOOL       fErase
RECT       rcPaint
BOOL       fRestore
BOOL       fIncUpdate
BYTE       rgbReserved[16]
```

Each field is defined as follows:

hdc	Specifies the device context to be used for drawing.
fErase	Specifies whether the background of the window has been redrawn. Nonzero (TRUE) values indicate that the background has been redrawn.
rcPaint	Contains the upper left and lower right corners of the rectangle to be painted.
fRestore, fIncUpdate, rgbReserved	Used internally by Windows.

CREATESTRUCT

Windows uses the CREATESTRUCT type to specify the initialization parameters for a window. Its fields are as follows:

LPSTR	lpCreateParams
HANDLE	hInstance
HANDLE	hMenu
HWND	hwndParent
int	cy
int	cx
int	y
int	x
long	style
LPSTR	lpszName
LPSTR	lpszClass

The fields are defined as follows:

lpCreateParams	Serves as a long pointer to the window-creation parameters.
hInstance	Specifies the module instance handle for the module owning the window.
hMenu	Specifies the handle of the menu for the new window.
hwndParent	Specifies the handle of the window owning the new window.
cy	Specifies the height of the new window.
cx	Specifies the width of the new window.
y	Specifies the y coordinate of the upper left corner of the new window.
x	Specifies the x coordinate of the upper left corner of the new window.
style	Specifies the class style of the new window.

lpszName   Serves as a long pointer to the name of the new
                  window. The name must be an ASCIIZ string.

lpszClass   Serves as a long pointer to the class name of the
                  new window. The class name must be an ASCIIZ
                  string.

GDI Structures

Later chapters examine the Windows graphics device interface (GDI)
functions that provide Windows graphics capabilities. The following
structures are used extensively by the GDI functions.

LOGPEN

The LOGPEN structure is used to define the attributes of a pen. Its
fields include the following:

```
WORD          lopnStyle
POINT         lopnWidth
DWORD         lopnColor
```

The fields are used as follows:

lopnStyle   Specifies the pen type; must be one of the follow-
                  ing:

                  0 Solid
                  1 Dashed
                  2 Dotted
                  3 Dash-dotted
                  4 Dash-dot-dotted
                  5 Null

| lopnWidth | Specifies the width of the pen in logical units. (Normally, 0 is used.) |
| lopnColor | Specifies the pen color. (See the RGB color definitions.) |

LOGBRUSH

The GDI functions use the LOGBRUSH type to define the attributes of the paintbrush. Its fields include the following:

WORD	lbStyle
DWORD	lbColor
short	lbHatch

Each field is defined as follows:

| lbStyle | Specifies the brush style; must be one of the following: |

BS_SOLID
BS_HOLLOW
BS_HATCHED
BS_PATTERN

| lbColor | Specifies the brush color. (See the RGB color definitions.) |
| lbHatch | Specifies the hatch style. If lbStyle is BS_HATCHED, lbHatch specifies the line orientation used to create the hatch. It must be one of the following: |

HS_HORIZONTAL
HS_VERTICAL
HS_FDIAGNOL (left-to-right diagonal)
HS_BDIAGNOL (right-to-left diagonal)

HS_CROSS
HS_DIAGCROSS

LOGFONT

Windows applications use the LOGFONT data type to define the attributes of a font. The fields of the structure include the following:

short	lfHeight
short	lfWidth
short	lfEscapement
short	lfOrientation
short	lfWeight
BYTE	lfItalic
BYTE	lfUnderline
BYTE	lfStrikeOut
BYTE	lfCharSet
BYTE	lfOutPrecision
BYTE	lfClipPrecision
BYTE	lfQuality
BYTE	lfPitchAndFamily
BYTE	lfFaceName[LF_FACESIZE]

The fields are defined as follows:

lfHeight   Specifies the height of the font in user units. The following translations are made based upon the value of lfHeight:

If lfHeight > 0 the units are transformed into device units and matched against available fonts.

If lfHeight $= 0$ a default size is used.

If lfHeight < 0 the units are transformed into device units, and the absolute value is matched against available fonts.

lfWidth	Specifies the width of the font in user units. If lfWidth is 0, the aspect ratio of the device is matched against the digitization aspect ratio of available fonts, and the closest match is selected.
lfEscapement	Specifies the angle (in tenths of degrees) between the X axis of the display and the first and last characters on a line.
lfOrientation	Specifies the angle (in tenths of degrees) between the X axis of the display and the baseline of a character.
lfWeight	Specifies the font weight. The value can range from 0 to 1000 (400 is considered normal, and 700 is considered bold).
lfItalic	If nonzero, indicates that the font is italic.
lfUnderline	If nonzero, indicates that the font is an underlined font.
lfStrikeOut	If nonzero, indicates that the font is a strikeout font.
lfCharSet	Specifies the font's character set. It must be either ANSI_CHARSET or OEM_CHARSET.
lfOutPrecision	Specifies the font's output precision. The value indicates how closely the output font must match the font's height, width, orientation, and so forth. Set this value to OUT_DEFAULT_PRECIS.
lfClipPrecision	Specifies the font's clipping precision. The value indicates how Windows will clip characters that fall outside of the clipping region. Set this value to CLIP_DEFAULT_PRECIS.
lfQuality	Specifies the font's output quality. This value indicates how closely the GDI must match the font's attributes to a physical font. The value must be PROOF_QUALITY, DRAFT_QUALITY, or DEFAULT_QUALITY.

lfPitchAnd Family	Specifies the font pitch and family. The two low-order bits specify the font pitch and must be DEFAULT_PITCH, FIXED_PITCH, or VARIABLE_PITCH. The four high-order bits specify the font family and must be one of the following:

FF_DECORATIVE
FF_DONTCARE
FF_MODERN
FF_ROMAN
FF_SWISS
FF_SCRIPT

lfFaceName	Specifies the font's typeface. The value must be an ASCIIZ string. If the value is null, a default face is used.

BITMAP

The BITMAP data type is used to define a logical bitmap. Its fields include the following:

short	bmType
short	bmWidth
short	bmHeight
short	bmWidthBytes
BYTE	bmPlanes
BYTE	bmBitsPixel
LPSTR	bmBits

Each of the fields is used as follows:

bmType	Specifies the bitmap type. Logical bitmaps use the value 0.
bmWidth	Specifies the width (in pixels) of the bitmap.
bmHeight	Specifies the height (in raster lines) of the bitmap.

bmWidthBytes	Specifies the number of bytes in each raster line. The value must be an even number.
bmPlanes	Specifies the number of bitmap color planes.
bmBitsPixel	Specifies the number of color bits required to define a pixel.
bmBits	Serves as a long pointer to the bit values for the bitmap.

POINT

Windows uses the POINT data type to define x and y coordinates for a given point. Its two fields include the following:

```
int          x
int          y
```

The meanings of the two fields are as follows:

x	Specifies the x coordinate of the point.
y	Specifies the y coordinate of the point.

RECT

The RECT data type describes the four corners of a rectangle as follows:

```
int          left
int          top
int          right
int          bottom
```

The fields are defined as follows:

left	Specifies the x coordinate of the upper left corner.
top	Specifies the y coordinate of the upper left corner.
right	Specifies the x coordinate of the lower right corner.
bottom	Specifies the y coordinate of the lower right corner.

The width of the rectangle (right to left) cannot exceed 32K units.

RGB

The RGB data structure defines the intensity of the red, green, and blue color fields. The type is a 32-bit integer. Windows uses the low-order byte to define the intensity for red. The second byte defines the intensity for green, and the third low-order byte defines the intensity for blue. Intensities range from 0 to 255.

TEXTMETRIC

The TEXTMETRIC data type defines the basic measurements of a physical font. It consists of the following fields:

short	tmHeight
short	tmAscent
short	tmDescent
short	tmInternalLeading
short	tmExternalLeading
short	tmAveCharWidth
short	tmMaxCharWidth
short	tmWeight
BYTE	tmItalic
BYTE	tmUnderlined
BYTE	tmStruckOut

BYTE	
BYTE	tmLastChar
BYTE	tmDefaultChar
BYTE	tmBreakChar
BYTE	tmPitchAndFamily
BYTE	tmCharSet
short	tmOverhang
short	tmDigitizedAspectX
short	tmDigitizedAspectY

These fields are defined as follows:

tmHeight
Specifies the character height.

tmAscent
Specifies the character ascent (units above the baseline).

tmDescent
Specifies the character descent (units below the baseline).

tmInternal Leading
Specifies the amount of additional space, including the value specified by tmHeight. This space typically is above the character and is where the designed font may place accent marks.

tmExternal Leading
Specifies the suggested amount of additional space to be placed between rows of characters for proper display.

tmAveChar Width
Specifies the average width of characters in the font.

tmMaxChar Width
Specifies the maximum width of characters in the font.

tmWeight
Specifies the font's weight.

tmItalic
If nonzero, indicates that the font is italic.

tmUnderlined	If nonzero, indicates that the font is underlined.
tmStruckOut	If nonzero, indicates that the font is struck out.
tmFirstChar	Specifies the ASCII value of the first character in the font.
tmLastChar	Specifies the ASCII value of the last character in the font.
tmDefaultChar	Specifies the ASCII value of the font character to use when a character outside of the font range is specified.
tmBreakChar	Specifies the ASCII value of the font character to use for breaks during text justification.
tmPitchAnd Family	Specifies the font's pitch and family. (Refer to LOG-FONT.)
tmCharSet	Specifies the font's character set.
tmOverhang	Specifies the extra width that can be added to synthesized fonts.
tmDigitized AspectX	Specifies the X aspect ratio of the device for which the font was defined.
tmDigitized AspectY	Specifies the Y aspect ratio of the device for which the font was defined.

METAFILEPICT

The METAFILEPICT data type specifies the metafile picture format used to exchange information through the Clipboard. Its fields include the following:

int	mm
int	xExt

int	yExt
HANDLE	hMF

The fields are defined as follows:

mm	Specifies the mapping mode for which the picture was drawn
xExt	Specifies the X coordinate of the rectangle within which the picture was drawn
yExt	Specifies the Y coordinate of the rectangle within which the picture was drawn
hMF	Specifies the handle to the metafile

Communications Data Structures

This section describes the data types that Windows uses for data communications.

DCB

The DCB data type defines the serial communications parameters for the PC serial ports. Its fields contain the following:

BYTE	id
WORD	BaudRate
BYTE	ByteSize
BYTE	Parity
BYTE	StopBits
WORD	RlsTimeout
WORD	CtsTimeout
WORD	DsrTimeout
BYTE	fBinary:1

BYTE	fRtsDisable:1
BYTE	fParity:1
BYTE	fOutxCtsFlow:1
BYTE	fOutxDsrFlow:1
BYTE	fDummy:2
BYTE	fDtrDisable:1
BYTE	fOutX:1
BYTE	fInX:1
BYTE	fPeChar:1
BYTE	fNull:1
BYTE	fChEvt:1
BYTE	fDtrFlow:1
BYTE	fRtsFlow:1
BYTE	fDummy2:1
char	XonChar
char	XoffChar
WORD	XonLim
WORD	XoffLim
char	PeChar
char	EofChar
char	EvtChar
WORD	TxDelay

Each field is defined as follows:

id	Specifies the communications device. If the most significant bit is set, the DCB is for a parallel device.
BaudRate	Specifies the communications baud rate.
ByteSize	Specifies the number of bits in a byte (4 to 8).
Parity	Specifies the type of parity used. The value must be one of the following:

EVENPARITY
MARKPARITY
NOPARITY

ODDPARITY

SPACEPARITY

StopBits	Specifies the number of stop bits. One of the following values should be used:

ONESTOPBIT

ONE5STOPBITS (one and a half)

TWOSTOPBITS

RlsTimeout	Specifies the maximum number of milliseconds that the device should wait for carrier-detect.
CtsTimeout	Specifies the maximum number of milliseconds that the device should wait for clear-to-send.
DsrTimeout	Specifies the maximum number of milliseconds that the device should wait for data-set-ready.
fBinary	Specifies binary data transmission mode.
fRtsDisable	If set, indicates that request-to-send is disabled.
fParity	If set, indicates that parity checking is enabled.
fOutxCtsFlow	If set, indicates that clear-to-send is enabled.
fOutxDsrFlow	If set, indicates that data-set-ready is enabled.
fDummy:2	Reserved
fDtrDisable	If set, indicates that data-terminal-ready is disabled.
fOutX	If set, indicates that XON/XOFF is enabled for transmission.
fInX	If set, indicates that XON/XOFF is enabled for reception.
fPeChar	Specifies that characters received with parity errors are to be replaced by the character contained in PeChar.
fNull	Specifies that NULL characters are to be discarded.
fChEvt	Specifies that the reception of EvtChar is to be flagged as an event.

fDtrFlow	Specifies that DTR is to be used for flow control.
fRtsFlow	Specifies that RTS is to be used for flow control.
fDummy2:1	Reserved
XonChar	Specifies the ASCII character serving as the XON character.
XoffChar	Specifies the ASCII character serving as the XOFF character.
XonLim	Specifies the minimum number of characters that must be in the receive queue before XON is sent.
XoffLim	Specifies the number of characters that must be in the receive queue before XOFF is sent.
PeChar	Specifies the ASCII character to replace any characters that contained a parity error.
EofChar	Specifies the ASCII character used to signal an end-of-file.
EvtChar	Specifies the ASCII character used to signal an event.
TxDelay	Specifies the minimum number of milliseconds that must occur between the transmission of characters.

COMSTAT

The COMSTAT data structure is used to store information about a communications device. Its fields are the following:

BYTE	fCtsHold:1
BYTE	fDsrHold:1
BYTE	fRlsdHold:1
BYTE	fXoffHold:1
BYTE	fXoffSent:1
BYTE	fEof:1
BYTE	fTxim:1
WORD	cbInQue
WORD	cbOutQue

The fields are defined as follows:

fCtsHold	If set, indicates that transmission is holding for a clear-to-send.
fDsrHold	If sct, indicates that transmission is holding for a data-set-ready signal.
fRlsdHold	If set, indicates that transmission is holding for receive-line signal detect.
fXoffHold	If set, indicates that transmission is holding because of XOFF.
fXoffSent	If set, indicates that transmission is holding because of XOFF being sent.
fEof	If set, indicates that end-of-file has been received.
fTxim	If set, indicates that a character is waiting to be transmitted immediately.
cbInQue	Specifies the number of characters in the receive queue.
cbOutQue	Specifies the number of characters in the transmit queue.

Open File Structure

The following section describes the structure for open files.

OFSTRUCT

The OFSTRUCT data type defines the attributes of an open file. Its fields consist of the following:

```
BYTE        cbytes
BYTE        nFixedDisk
WORD        nErrCode
```

BYTE	reserved[4]
BYTE	szPathName[128]

Each field is defined as:

cbytes	Specifies the length of the structure in bytes.
nFixedDisk	If nonzero, indicates that the file is located on a fixed disk.
nErrCode	Specifies the DOS error code if the routine Open-File failed.
reserved	Reserved for future Windows enhancements.
szPathName	Specifies the complete pathname of the file.

Although you will not immediately be using, within your Windows applications, many of the data types presented in this chapter, become familiar with them and your understanding of the inner workings of Windows will increase.

CHAPTER

9

A SIMPLE
EXAMPLE

This chapter presents your first complete Windows programming application. The program TEST.EXE will illustrate the use of all of the Windows program-development utilities. It is presented in both C and Pascal. The steps you will take to create the executable program are as follows:

1. Create a C or Pascal application named TEST.C or TEST.PAS with a standard text editor.

2. Compile the source code into an .OBJ object file.

3. Create an application icon with the icon editor.

4. Create a resource script file named TEST.RC with a text editor.

5. Compile the resource script file with RC.EXE, the resource compiler.

6. Create the module definition file for the application with a text editor.

7. Link the application and module definition file with LINK4.EXE.

8. Bind the binary resource script file TEST.RES to the executable file TEST.EXE with the resource compiler, RC.EXE.

Application Structure

All Windows applications have the same basic structure. The first routine required is the function WinMain. This function serves as the entry point for Windows applications. Its calling sequence is as follows:

int PASCAL WinMain (hInstance, hPrevInstance, lpszCmdLine,
                    cmdShow);

HANDLE   hInstance, hPrevInstance;

LPSTR   lpszCmdLine;

int   cmdShow;

The hInstance argument is the instance handle for a new instance; hPrevInstance is the instance handle for the previous module instance. lpszCmdLine is a long pointer to the ASCIIZ command line, and cmdShow is a short integer specifying how the window is initially displayed.

Within this function, the code will invoke a routine that defines and registers the window class that is used for the application. Generally, the definition of a window specifies the window's class name; the cursor, menu, and icon associated with the window; and the background color and style of the window. Registering the window places its definition in the internal Windows tables so that it can be used by other applications. Once the window is registered, the application will create its copy of the window via the built-in function CreateWindow.

Finally, the WinMain function processes all messages to and from Windows. The remainder of the routines in the Windows application are user defined. These routines function identically for the C and Pascal implementations.

In general, a Windows application must perform the following steps:

1. See whether the window class specified has already been defined. If not, define and register the window class.

2. Create and display a window of the defined class.

3. Manage the messages to and from Windows.

Windows Messages

Applications running under Windows are message driven. Windows obtains and distributes messages from and to all of the applications that appear to be running simultaneously. Later chapters will examine in detail the messages processed by Windows. For now, however, it is important that you understand the following message functions:

GetMessage	Obtains a message from the application message queue. If no message is present, this function yields control to the other applications.
TranslateMessage	Translates virtual keystroke messages into character messages.
DispatchMessage	Passes the message to the message-handling function defined for the window.
PostQuitMessage	Tells Windows that the application is ready to terminate execution.

The most important point is that messages are the factors that drive programs in the Windows environment.

Application Overview

Before examining the implementation of TEST.EXE, let's first see what the program will do when executed. When the executable program is invoked from the MS-DOS Executive, as follows:

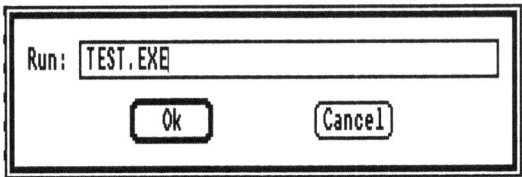

the program will display the following message:

Successful WINDOWS Program!

Note that the application supports a system menu:

You will be able to move the object to an icon, as follows:

Later in this chapter, the creation of the icon shown will be discussed. Admittedly, the processing performed by TEST.EXE is very simple. However, the program lays the foundation for the programs that will be presented throughout the remainder of the text.

The C Application

The following program presents the C implementation of TEST.EXE:

```
#include "windows.h"

#define APPLICATION_NAME "TEST"
#define ICON_NAME "TEST"

long FAR PASCAL TestWndProc(HWND, unsigned, WORD, LONG);

void TestPaint(hWnd, hDC)
HWND hWnd;
HDC hDC;
{
   char message[255];

   TextOut(hDC, 0, 10, (LPSTR) message,
        sprintf(message, "Successful WINDOWS Program!"));
}


BOOL TestInit(hInstance)
HANDLE hInstance;
{
    NPWNDCLASS  pClass;

    pClass = (NPWNDCLASS) LocalAlloc(LPTR, sizeof(WNDCLASS));
```

```
     pClass->hCursor          = LoadCursor(NULL, IDC_ARROW);
     pClass->hIcon            = LoadIcon(hInstance, (LPSTR) ICON_NAME);
     pClass->lpszClassName    = (LPSTR) APPLICATION_NAME;
     pClass->hbrBackground    = (HBRUSH) GetStockObject(WHITE_BRUSH);
     pClass->hInstance        = hInstance;
     pClass->style            = CS_HREDRAW | CS_VREDRAW;
     pClass->lpfnWndProc      = TestWndProc;

     if (!RegisterClass((LPWNDCLASS)pClass))
         return FALSE;

     LocalFree((HANDLE) pClass); /* return space to heap */
     return TRUE;                /* registration successful */
}


int PASCAL WinMain(hInstance, hPrevInstance, lpszCmdLine, cmdShow)
HANDLE hInstance, hPrevInstance;
LPSTR lpszCmdLine;
int cmdShow;
{
  MSG    message;
  HWND   hWnd;

  if (!hPrevInstance)   /* initialize if this is the first instance */
    if (!TestInit(hInstance))
        return FALSE;    /* failure to initialize -- return to Windows */
  hWnd =  CreateWindow((LPSTR) APPLICATION_NAME,
                       (LPSTR) APPLICATION_NAME,
                       WS_TILEDWINDOW,
                       0,               /* x - ignored for tiled
                                           windows */
                       0,               /* y - ignored for tiled
                                           windows */
                       0,               /* cx - ignored for tiled
                                           windows */
                       0,               /* cy - ignored for tiled
                                           windows */
                       (HWND) NULL,      /* no parent */
                       (HMENU) NULL,     /* use class menu */
                       (HANDLE) hInstance, /* handle to window
                                            instance */
                       (LPSTR) NULL      /* no parameters to pass
                                           on */

                       );

     ShowWindow(hWnd, cmdShow);              /* Make window visible */
     UpdateWindow(hWnd);

     /* Poll messages from the event queue and dispatch them */
     while (GetMessage((LPMSG) &message, NULL, 0, 0)) {
         TranslateMessage((LPMSG) &message);
         DispatchMessage((LPMSG) &message);
         }

     return (int) message.wParam; /* return control to Windows */
}
```

```
long FAR PASCAL TestWndProc(hWnd, message, wParam, lParam)
HWND hWnd;
unsigned message;
WORD wParam;
LONG lParam;
{
  PAINTSTRUCT ps;

  switch (message) {
    case WM_DESTROY:
        PostQuitMessage(0);  /* tell Windows ready to terminate */
        break;

    case WM_PAINT:
        BeginPaint(hWnd, (LPPAINTSTRUCT) &ps);
        TestPaint(hWnd, ps.hdc);
        EndPaint(hWnd, (LPPAINTSTRUCT) &ps);
        break;

    default:  /* let Windows process message */
        return DefWindowProc(hWnd, message, wParam, lParam);
        break;
  }
  return (0L);
}
```

The file WINDOWS.H contains all of the predefined constant values used by Windows applications. Take time right now to print the file and examine the defined values.

Next, the statement

long FAR PASCAL TestWndProc (HWND, unsigned, WORD, LONG);

defines the function that receives and processes all of the messages received from Windows. The long keyword specifies the type of value returned by the function. The FAR keyword states that the function requires a segment and offset address combination. PASCAL specifies the calling sequence for the function. Pascal, unlike C, places arguments on the stack from left to right. C routines utilizing this function must do the same. Finally, the argument types for the routine are illustrated.

The function TestPaint is responsible for displaying the message

Successful WINDOWS Program!

Each time the window changes, this function is called to update the screen display.

The function TestInit specifies the window attributes for the class of window used by the application. It defines the icon, cursor, background color, and style. Once defined, this information is registered in the internal Windows table by the call to RegisterClass.

As was mentioned previously, every Windows application must have a function called WinMain. This function is the entry point for the Windows application. The first thing this function does is to register the window class used by the application. Once the class is registered, the window is created by the call to CreateWindow.

Once the window has been created, the calls to ShowWindow and UpdateWindow display the Window on the screen.

Next, the statements

```
/* Poll messages from the event queue and dispatch them */
while (GetMessage((LPMSG) &message, NULL, 0, 0)) {
    TranslateMessage((LPMSG) &message);
    DispatchMessage((LPMSG) &message);
    }
```

obtain and distribute all of the messages received by the application from Windows.

The routine TestWndProc processes specific messages received by the routine. Later chapters will examine more complex message processing.

The statements

```
case WM_PAINT:
    BeginPaint(hWnd, (LPPAINTSTRUCT) &ps);
    TestPaint(hWnd, ps.hdc);
    EndPaint(hWnd, (LPPAINTSTRUCT) &ps);
    break;
```

perform the screen updates. TestPaint, again, is the user-defined routine that displays the application message. BeginPaint and EndPaint inform Windows that the application is ready to paint a portion of the screen. The argument hWnd is the window to be updated, and the structure ps defines how Windows is to display the screen portion.

Finally, the routine DefWindowProc handles all of the messages not explicitly processed by the application. Its arguments include the handle of the window receiving the message (hWnd), the message received (message), and two parameters that contain additional information about the message (wParam and lParam).

The Pascal Application

The following is the Pascal implementation of TEST.EXE:

```
{$windows+}
{$stackseg+ $debug, $symtab,}

INTERFACE;
    UNIT paslibw (
        {$INCLUDE : 'test.inc'}
    );

{$INCLUDE:'windows.inc'}                    { Get WINDOWS definitions. }

MODULE test[];
  USES paslibw (
    {$INCLUDE : 'test.inc'}
  );


PROCEDURE begxqq; EXTERN;

PROCEDURE endxqq; EXTERN;

PROCEDURE ENTGQQ [ PUBLIC ];
BEGIN
      {dummy routine for link4}
END;

PROCEDURE TestPaint (hWindow : HWND;
                     hDC_    : HDC) [ PUBLIC ];

BEGIN
  EVAL(TextOut(hDC_, 0, 10, RETYPE(LPSTR,
    ADS 'Successful WINDOWS Program!'), 27));
END;



FUNCTION TestWndProc(hWindow : HWND;
                     message : UNSIGNED;
```

```
                          wParam  : WORD;
                          lParam  : LONG ) : LONG [ PUBLIC, WINDOWS ];

VAR
  ps : PAINTSTRUCT;

BEGIN

    CASE message OF
        WM_DESTROY:
            PostQuitMessage(0);

        WM_PAINT:
            BEGIN
              EVAL(BeginPaint(hWindow, RETYPE(LPPAINTSTRUCT, ADS ps)));
              TestPaint(hWindow, ps.hdc_);
              EndPaint(hWindow, RETYPE(LPPAINTSTRUCT, ADS ps));
            END;

        OTHERWISE       { Let Windows handle all the other messages }
          BEGIN
            TestWndProc := DefWindowProc(hWindow, message, wParam,
                           lParam);
            RETURN;
          END;

    END;

    TestWndProc := RETYPE(LONG, BYLONG(0,0));
END;

FUNCTION TestInit(hInstance : HANDLE) : BOOL;

VAR
  pClass : WNDCLASS;

BEGIN

    begxqq;

    pClass.lpszClassName := RETYPE(LPSTR, ADS 'TEST' * CHR(0));
    pClass.hIcon_          := LoadIcon( hInstance, RETYPE(LPSTR, ADS
                           'TEST' * CHR(0)));
    pClass.hCursor_        := LoadCursor( RETYPE(HWND, NULL_), IDC_ARROW);
    pClass.hbrBackground := RETYPE(HBRUSH, GetStockObject(WHITE_BRUSH));

    pClass.lpfnWndProc   := ADS TestWndProc;
    pClass.hInstance     := hInstance;
    pClass.style         := CS_VREDRAW OR CS_HREDRAW;
    pClass.cbClsExtra    := 0;
    pClass.cbWndExtra    := 0;

    { register this new class with WINDOWS }
```

A SIMPLE EXAMPLE

```
    IF (RegisterClass(RETYPE(LPWNDCLASS, ADS pClass)) <> TRUE_) THEN
        BEGIN
          TestInit := FALSE_;
          RETURN;
        END;

    TestInit := TRUE_;
END;



FUNCTION WinMain(hInstance     : HANDLE;
                 hPrevInstance : HANDLE;
                 lpszCmdline   : LPSTR;
                 cmdShow       : INT) : BOOL [ PUBLIC ];
VAR
    hWindow : HWND;
    msg_    : MSG;

BEGIN
    IF (hPrevInstance = 0) THEN  { Call initialization routine }
        BEGIN
          IF (TestInit(hInstance) = FALSE_) THEN { Return to Windows }
             BEGIN
                WinMain := FALSE_;
                RETURN;
             END;
        END;

    { Create a window instance of class 'TEST' }

    hWindow := CreateWindow(
        RETYPE(LPSTR, ADS 'TEST' * CHR(0)),   { Class name               }
        RETYPE(LPSTR, ADS 'TEST' * CHR(0)),   { Instance name            }
        WS_TILEDWINDOW,                       { Window style             }
        0,                                    { Desired column           }
        0,                                    { cy: not used             }
        0,                                    { cx: not used             }
        100,                                  { Desired height: pixel    }
        RETYPE(HWND, NULL_),                  { No parent window         }
        RETYPE(HMENU, NULL_),                 { Use default menu         }
        hInstance,                            { Instance handle          }
        RETYPE(LPSTR, BYLONG(0,NULL_)));      { No additional
                                                parameter }

    EVAL(ShowWindow(hWindow, cmdShow)); { Send message to update
                                          window }
    UpdateWindow(hWindow);

    WHILE (GetMessage(RETYPE(LPMSG, ADS msg_), NULL_, 0, 0) <> 0) DO
        BEGIN
          EVAL(TranslateMessage(RETYPE(LPMSG, ADS msg_)));
          EVAL(DispatchMessage(RETYPE(LPMSG, ADS msg_)));
        END;
```

```
endxqq;

END;

END.
```

The routines TestWndProc, TestPaint, TestInit, and WinMain are
functionally identical to their counterparts in the C implementation.
The only differences are the procedure calls to begxqq and endxqq,
which function as follows:

begxqq   Specifies the defined entry point for the load
                module.

endxqq   Specifies the overall termination routine for Pas-
                cal applications.

Note the following metacommands (compiler directives):

{$windows+}

{$stackseg+ $debug- $symtab-}

The first, {$windows+}, instructs the compiler to include the Win-
dows subroutine prolog and epilog code sequences.

In the second directive, $stagseg+ specifies that the stack seg-
ment should be the same as the data segment; $debug- specifies that
all debug options should be turned off; and $symtab- specifies that the
symbol table information should be excluded from the listing file.

The INTERFACE and MODULE sections reduce the number of
symbols that Pascal needs to keep track of during compilation. The
WINDOWS.INC file contains every variable, data type, and subroutine declaration available from Windows, but few programs use every
option. When you define a UNIT that contains the symbols needed,
more compiler symbol table space is available for your application.

The following is the symbol table include file used for TEST.PAS:

```
int,
short;
long,
unsigned,
FALSE_,
TRUE_,
NULL_,
BYTE,
WORD,
DWORD,
BOOL,
PSTR,
LPSTR,
LPINT,
HANDLE,
HSTR,
HICON,
HDC,
HMENU,
HPEN,
HBRUSH,
HCURSOR,
WNDCLASS,
PWNDCLASS,
LPWNDCLASS,
HWND,
MSG,
PMSG,
LPMSG,
WM_DESTROY,
WM_PAINT,
CS_VREDRAW,
CS_HREDRAW,
WS_TILEDWINDOW,
PAINTSTRUCT,
LPPAINTSTRUCT,
CREATESTRUCT,
WHITE_BRUSH,
GetMessage,
TranslateMessage,
DispatchMessage,
DefWindowProc,
PostQuitMessage,
RegisterClass,
```

```
CreateWindow,
DestroyWindow,
ShowWindow,
UpdateWindow,
BeginPaint,
EndPaint,
TextOut,
GetStockObject,
LoadCursor,
IDC_ARROW,
LoadIcon,
LoadMenu
```

The Icon

From the MS-DOS Executive, invoke the icon editor and create the following icon for TEST.EXE:

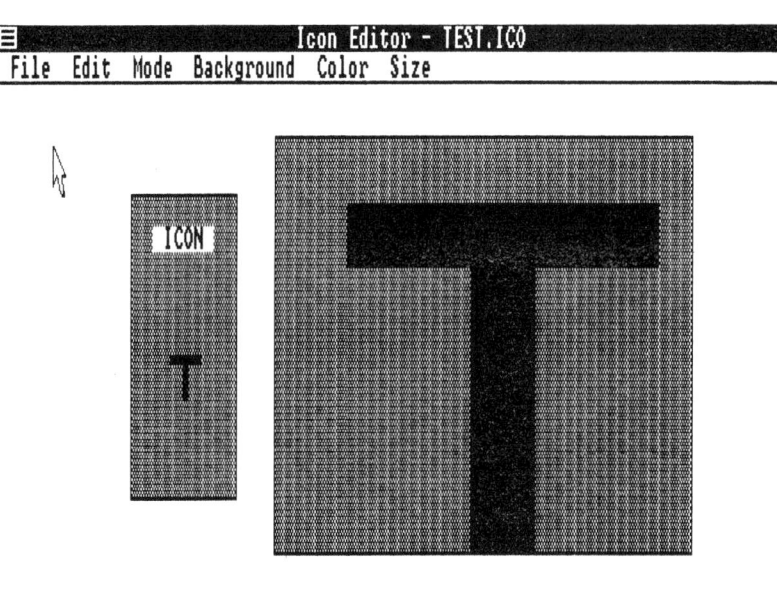

Save the file as TEST.ICO.

The Resource Script File

The contents of TEST.RC, the resource script file for the application,
are as follows:

```
#include "windows.h"

TEST   ICON    TEST.ICO
```

Once you have created this file, compile it with the resource compiler, RC.EXE, as follows:

RC -r TEST.RC

The Module Definition File

Now create the following module definition file TEST.DEF for the
program TEST.EXE:

```
NAME      Test
DESCRIPTION 'Microsoft Windows Pascal Application'

CODE      MOVEABLE
DATA      MOVEABLE MULTIPLE PRELOAD

STUB      'WINSTUB.EXE'

HEAPSIZE     2048
STACKSIZE    4096

EXPORTS
    TestWndProc
```

Once you have successfully compiled your application, created your icon, created and compiled your resource script file, and created your module definition file, link the application with LINK4, as follows:

LINK4 TEST,/a:16,,library—files,TEST.DEF

Then, bind the binary resource script file to the executable file, as follows:

RC TEST.RES TEST.EXE

Your first Windows application is now ready to be executed.

10

WINDOWS MESSAGES

Windows applications are message driven. The TEST.EXE example program presented in Chapter 9 illustrated the use of several of the Windows message-handling functions. This chapter examines each of the messages exchanged between Windows and the applications that run in the Windows environment. It is important for you to have a general understanding of the message types exchanged during different Windows events before you examine the programs that are presented in later chapters. As you will see, each of the messages examined falls into a general category. The message classes presented in this chapter include the following:

☐ Window management messages

☐ Initialization messages

☐ Input messages

☐ System messages

☐ Clipboard messages

☐ System information messages

☐ Control window messages

☐ Edit control messages

☐ List box messages

☐ Notification messages codes

☐ Nonclient area messages

Although it is not necessary to memorize the format of each of these messages, you should remember the basic functions that are provided by each.

Messages in Windows consist of the following three parts:

☐ A message number (predefined names)

☐ A word parameter (wParam)

☐ A long parameter (lParam)

The message number identifies the message. The word parameter (wParam) stores a word of information about the message. If the message does not require additional information, wParam is NULL. The long parameter (lParam) is used for pointers or compound data structures that contain several pieces of information relative to the message. You should use the predefined routines HIWORD and LOWORD to extract the information contained in each parameter. Complete explanations of the contents of the parameters are provided for each Windows message.

Window Management Messages

Windows sends the following messages to your application each time a change occurs in window state.

WM—ACTIVATE

Function   Occurs when Windows activates or deactivates a window.

wParam   Zero if the window has become inactive. Otherwise, it is one of the following values:

1. The window became active by some means other than a mouse click.

2. The window became active by a user mouse click.

lParam   If wParam is 0, the low-order word of lParam is a handle to a window becoming active. Otherwise, the low-order word of lParam is a handle to the window becoming inactive. If the high-order word of lParam is nonzero, the window is iconic.

Default Action   If the new active window is not iconic, DefWindow-Proc assigns the input focus to the window.

WM—ACTIVATEAPP

Function   Occurs when the window being made active is from an application other than the application that was previously active.

wParam   Zero if the window is becoming inactive; otherwise, it is nonzero.

lParam   If wParam is 0, the low-order word of lParam contains a handle to the task of the previous application. Otherwise, the low-order word contains a handle to the application becoming active.

Default Action   None.

WM ─ CLOSE

Function   Received when the window is closed.

wParam   Not used.

lParam   Not used.

Default Action   DefWindowProc invokes DestroyWindow to destroy the window.

WM ─ CREATE

Function   Received when the function CreateWindow is called. Windows sends WM ─ CREATE before the window is made visible and control returns from CreateWindow. Upon receipt of WM ─ CREATE, the application should perform its initialization.

wParam   Not used.

lParam   A long pointer to a CREATESTRUCT data structure whose fields contain values equivalent to the parameters passed to the CreateWindow function.

Default Action   None.

WM—CTLCOLOR

Function   Received by a parent window when a control or message box is to be displayed. This allows the application to set the text and background color for the control or message box.

wParam   The handle to the device context for the control or message box.

lParam   The low-order word contains the handle to the control or message box. The high-order word specifies the type of control, as follows:

CTLCOLOR—BTN	Button control
CTLCOLOR—DLG	Dialog box control
CTLCOLOR—EDIT	Edit box control
CTLCOLOR—LISTBOX	List box control
CTLCOLOR—MSGBOX	Message box control
CTLCOLOR—SCROLLBAR	Scroll bar control
CTLCOLOR—STATIC	Static control

Default Action   DefWindowProc selects the system default colors.

WM—DESTROY

Function   Received once DestroyWindow has removed the window from the screen. If the window is in the Clipboard chain, its first action must be to remove itself from the chain via ChangeClipboard-Chain.

wParam   Not used.

lParam   Not used.

Default Action None.

WM — ENABLE

Function Received when a window is enabled or disabled.

wParam Zero if the window has been disabled; otherwise, it is nonzero.

lParam Not used.

Default Action None.

WM — ENDSESSION

Function Received when the application responds to a WM — QUERYENDSESSION message with a nonzero value. It specifies whether or not the Windows session will actually terminate.

wParam Zero if the session will continue; otherwise, it is nonzero.

lParam Not used.

Default Action None.

WM — ERASEBKGND

Function Received when the window background needs to be erased. If the application processes this message, it must return one of the following values:

☐ Nonzero if the background was erased.

☐ Zero if the background was not erased.

wParam The handle to the device context.

lParam Not used.

Default Action DefWindowProc erases the background with the class background brush.

WM—GETDLGCODE

Function Sent to a control by the dialog manager to allow the control to process input. The program can specify what type of inputs it would like to process, as follows:

DLGC—HASSETSEL	Process EM—SETSEL messages
DLGC—WANTALLKEYS	Process all key input
DLGC—WANTARROWS	Process arrow keys
DLGC—WANTTAB	Process TAB key

wParam Not used.

lParam Not used.

Default Action DefWindowProc returns 0, specifying that the application will not process special inputs.

WM—GET—TEXT

Function Specifies that the text of a window is to be copied.

wParam An integer value specifying the maximum number of bytes to be copied.

lParam A long pointer to the buffer to store the text.

Default Action None.

WM — GETTEXTLENGTH

Function Requests the number of bytes of text associated with a window, minus the NULL terminator.

wParam Not used.

lParam Not used.

Default Action None.

WM — KILLFOCUS

Function Occurs immediately before the application loses the input focus.

wParam The handle to the window obtaining the input focus.

lParam Not used.

Default Action None.

WM — MOVE

Function Received when a window is moved.

wParam Not used.

lParam The low-order word contains the y coordinate of the window. The high-order word contains the new x coordinate.

Default Action None.

WM—PAINT

Function Received when Windows (or an application) requests that a portion of a window be repainted.

wParam Not used.

lParam A long pointer to a PAINTSTRUCT structure that contains information about the screen area to be painted.

Default Action None.

WM—QUERYENDSESSION

Function Occurs when the user selects the End Session option. If the application does not want to shut down, it must return 0; otherwise, it returns a nonzero value.

wParam Not used.

lParam Not used.

Default Action DefWindowProc returns a nonzero value, allowing the application to be shut down.

WM—QUERYOPEN

Function Sent to an icon when the user is attempting to expand it into a window. A return of 0 indicates that it wants to prevent the icon expansion; otherwise, a nonzero value is returned.

wParam Not used.

lParam Not used.

Default Action DefWindowProc returns a nonzero value, permitting the icon expansion.

WM—QUIT

Function Generated by the PostQuitMessage function when the application wishes to terminate.

wParam The exit status code provided to PostQuitMessage.

lParam Not used.

Default Action None.

WM—SETFOCUS

Function Occurs when the application has obtained the input focus.

wParam The handle to the window losing the input focus. This value is null if no previous application held the input focus.

lParam Not used.

Default Action None.

WM—SETREDRAW

Function Sets or clears the redraw flag that specifies whether updates to controls are displayed. When set, updates are displayed.

wParam Zero if the redraw flag is cleared; otherwise, it is nonzero.

lParam   Not used.

Default Action   None.

WM — SETTEXT

Function   Specifies the text of a window to be set.

wParam   Not used.

lParam   A long pointer to the buffer containing the text to set.

Default Action   None.

WM — SETVISIBLE

Function   Sent immediately before a window is made visible or invisible.

wParam   Zero if the window will be invisible; otherwise, it is nonzero.

lParam   Not used.

Default Action   None.

WM — SHOWWINDOW

Function   Received when Windows hides or shows a window as a result of one of the following:

☐ A call made to ShowWindow

☐ A tiled window being zoomed

☐ A tiled window being opened or closed

wParam Zero if the window is being hidden; otherwise, it is nonzero.

lParam Zero if ShowWindow was called; otherwise, one of the following values:

SW_OTHERZOOM	The window was zoomed.
SW_OTHERRUNZOOM	Another window was zoomed.
SW_PARENTCLOSING	The window was closed.
SW_PARENTOPENING	The window was opened.

Default Action DefWindowProc hides or shows the specified window.

WM_SIZE

Function Received when the size of a window has changed.

wParam Defines the new size, as follows:

SIZEFULLSCREEN	The window consumes the full screen.
SIZEICONIC	The window has become iconic.
SIZENORMAL	The window size has changed.
SIZEZOOMHIDE	Another window has zoomed to full-screen size.
SIZEZOOMSHOW	Another window has zoomed to its normal size.

lParam The low-order word contains the width of the client area of the window. The high-order word contains the height.

Default Action None.

Windows Initialization Messages

Windows sends the following messages to your application when a menu or dialog box is created for the first time.

WM—INITDIALOG

Function   Received before Windows displays a dialog box; allows the application to modify the dialog box before it is shown.

wParam   The handle to the first item in the dialog box that can be given the input focus. If the application returns 0, the input focus is given to the first item. Otherwise, the dialog box will set the input focus itself.

lParam   Not used.

Default Action   DefWindowProc returns 0, allowing the first item to receive the input focus.

WM—INITMENU

Function   Received before Windows displays a menu; allows the application to modify a menu before it is shown.

wParam   The handle of the menu to be initialized.

lParam   Not used.

Default Action   None.

WM—INITMENUPOPUP

Function   Received immediately before a pop-up menu is displayed.

wParam The handle to the pop-up menu.

lParam The low-order word is the index of the pop-up menu in the main menu. If the high-order word is nonzero, the pop-up menu is the System menu.

Default Action None.

Input Messages

The following messages are generated by Windows each time the application receives input from the keyboard, mouse, scroll bars, or system timer.

WM—CHAR

Function Result of a WM—KEYUP or WM—KEYDOWN translation; contains the ASCII value of the key pressed or released.

wParam The ASCII value of the keyboard key.

lParam A bitmap used as follows:

Bits 1-16	Repeat count (number of times key is repeated)
Bits 17-25	Scan code (OEM-dependent value)
Bit 30	Context code (1 if ALT key is pressed; otherwise, 0)
Bit 31	Previous state key (1 if key was pressed prior to message; otherwise, 0)
Bit 32	Transition state (0 if key is being pressed; 1 if key is being released)

Default Action None.

WM—COMMAND

Function   Received when the user selects an item from a menu or presses an accelerator combination, or when a control message is passed to a parent window.

wParam   The menu item value, the accelerator identification, or the control identification.

lParam   Defines the message source, as follows:

0	Menu message
1 in high-order word of window handle	Accelerator message
Handle in high-order word	Control message (low-order word contains the control identification)

Default Action   None.

WM—DEADCHAR

Function   Result of WM—KEYUP or WM—KEYDOWN translation; specifies that the key selected is a dead key. Dead keys are keys used to form composite characters.

wParam   The value of the dead key.

lParam   A bitmap used as follows:

Bits 1-16	Repeat count (number of times key is repeated)
Bits 17-25	Scan code (OEM-dependent value)
Bit 30	Context code (1 if ALT key is pressed; otherwise, 0)
Bit 31	Previous state key (0 if key was pressed prior to message; otherwise, 0)

Bit 32   Transition state (0 if key is being pressed; 1 if key
                        is being released)

Default Action None.

WM—HSCROLL

Function Received when the user clicks the mouse on a horizontal
scroll bar.

wParam A scrolling request, as follows:

SB—BOTTOM	Scroll to far right
SB—ENDSCROLL	Terminate scroll
SB—LINEDOWN	Scroll right one line
SB—LINEUP	Scroll left one line
SB—PAGEDOWN	Scroll right one page
SB—PAGEUP	Scroll left one page
SB—THUMBPOSITION	Scroll to absolute position
SB—THUMBTRACK	Scroll with thumb
SB—TOP	Scroll to far left

lParam The low-order word contains the thumb position.

Default Action None.

WM—KEYDOWN

Function Received when a nonsystem key is pressed.

wParam An integer value specifying the virtual key code of the
given key.

lParam A bitmap used as follows:

Bits 1-16	Repeat count (number of times key is repeated)
Bits 17-25	Scan code (OEM-dependent value)
Bit 30	Context code (1 if ALT key is pressed; otherwise, 0)
Bit 31	Previous state key (1 if key was pressed prior to message; otherwise, 0)
Bit 32	Transition state (0 if key is being pressed; 1 if key is being released)

Default Action None.

WM—KEYUP

Function Received when a nonsystem key is released.

wParam An integer value specifying the virtual key code of the given key.

lParam A bitmap used as follows:

Bits 1-16	Repeat count (number of times key is repeated)
Bits 17-25	Scan code (OEM-dependent value)
Bit 30	Context code (1 if ALT key is pressed; otherwise, 0)
Bit 31	Previous state key (1 if key was pressed prior to message; otherwise, 0)
Bit 32	Transition state (0 if key is being pressed; 1 if key is being released)

Default Action None.

WM—LBUTTON

Function Received when the user presses the left mouse button.

wParam A value indicating which virtual keys are pressed. It can be a combination of the following:

MK_CONTROL	CTRL key
MK_MBUTTON	Middle mouse button
MK_RBUTTON	Right mouse button
MK_SHIFT	SHIFT key

lParam The low-order word contains the x coordinate of the mouse cursor. The high-order word contains the y coordinate.

Default Action None.

WM_LBUTTONDBLCLK

Function Received when the user double-clicks the left mouse button.

wParam A value indicating which virtual keys are pressed. It can be a combination of the following:

MK_CONTROL	CTRL key
MK_MBUTTON	Middle mouse button
MK_RBUTTON	Right mouse button
MK_SHIFT	SHIFT key

lParam The low-order word contains the x coordinate of the mouse cursor. The high-order word contains the y coordinate.

Default Action None.

WM—LBUTTONUP

Function   Received when the user releases the left mouse button.

wParam   A value indicating which virtual keys are pressed. It can be a combination of the following:

MK—CONTROL	CTRL key
MK—MBUTTON	Middle mouse button
MK—RBUTTON	Right mouse button
MK—SHIFT	SHIFT key

lParam   The low-order word contains the x coordinate of the mouse cursor. The high-order word contains the y coordinate.

Default Action   None.

WM—MBUTTON

Function   Received when the user presses the middle mouse button.

wParam   A value indicating which virtual keys are pressed. It can be a combination of the following:

MK—CONTROL	CTRL key
MK—LBUTTON	Left mouse button
MK—RBUTTON	Right mouse button
MK—SHIFT	SHIFT key

lParam   The low-order word contains the x coordinate of the mouse cursor. The high-order word contains the y coordinate.

Default Action   None.

WM—MBUTTONDBLCLK

Function   Received when the user double-clicks the middle mouse button.

wParam   A value indicating which virtual keys are pressed. It can be a combination of the following:

MK—CONTROL	CTRL key
MK—LBUTTON	Left mouse button
MK—RBUTTON	Right mouse button
MK—SHIFT	SHIFT key

lParam   The low-order word contains the x coordinate of the mouse cursor. The high-order word contains the y coordinate.

Default Action   None.

WM—MBUTTONUP

Function   Received when the user releases the middle mouse button.

wParam   A value indicating which virtual keys are pressed. It can be a combination of the following:

MK—CONTROL	CTRL key
MK—LBUTTON	Left mouse button
MK—RBUTTON	Right mouse button
MK—SHIFT	SHIFT key

lParam The low-order word contains the x coordinate of the mouse cursor. The high-order word contains the y coordinate.

Default Action None.

WM—MOUSEMOVE

Function Received when the user moves the mouse.

wParam A value indicating which virtual keys are pressed. It can be a combination of the following:

MK—CONTROL	CTRL key
MK—LBUTTON	Left mouse button
MK—MBUTTON	Middle mouse button
MK—RBUTTON	Right mouse button
MK—SHIFT	SHIFT key

lParam The low-order word contains the x coordinate of the mouse cursor. The high-order word contains the y coordinate.

Default Action None.

WM—RBUTTON

Function Received when the user presses the right mouse button.

wParam A value indicating which virtual keys are pressed. It can be a combination of the following:

MK—CONTROL	CTRL key
MK—LBUTTON	Left mouse button

MK_MBUTTON   Middle mouse button

MK_SHIFT   SHIFT key

lParam   The low-order word contains the x coordinate of the mouse cursor. The high-order word contains the y coordinate.

Default Action   None.

WM_RBUTTONDBLCLK

Function   Received when the user double-clicks the right mouse button.

wParam   A value indicating which virtual keys are pressed. It can be a combination of the following:

MK_CONTROL   CTRL key

MK_LBUTTON   Left mouse button

MK_MBUTTON   Middle mouse button

MK_SHIFT   SHIFT key

lParam   The low-order word contains the x coordinate of the mouse cursor. The high-order word contains the y coordinate.

Default Action   None.

WM_RBUTTONUP

Function   Received when the user releases the right mouse button.

wParam   A value indicating which virtual keys are pressed. It can be a combination of the following:

MK__CONTROL	CTRL key
MK__LBUTTON	Left mouse button
MK__MBUTTON	Middle mouse button
MK__SHIFT	SHIFT key

lParam The low-order word contains the x coordinate of the mouse cursor. The high-order word contains the y coordinate.

Default Action None.

WM__TIMER

Function Received when a time limit for a specific timer has elapsed.

wParam An integer value that uniquely identifies the timer.

lParam A long pointer to the function passed to the routine Set-Timer when the timer was created.

Default Action None.

WM__VSCROLL

Function Received when the user clicks the mouse on a vertical scroll bar.

wParam A scrolling request, as follows:

SB__BOTTOM	Scroll to bottom
SB__ENDSCROLL	Terminate scroll
SB__LINEDOWN	Scroll down one line

SB_LINEUP	Scroll up one line
SB_PAGEDOWN	Scroll down one page
SB_PAGEUP	Scroll up one page
SB_THUMBPOSITION	Scroll to absolute position
SB_THUMBTRACK	Scroll with thumb
SB_TOP	Scroll to top

lParam   The low-order word contains the thumb position.

Default Action   None.

System Messages

Windows sends the following messages to an application each time the user accesses the System menu, scroll bars, or size box. Most applications programs ignore these messages, allowing DefWindow-Proc to perform the required processing.

WM_SYSCHAR

Function   Result of a WM_SYSKEYUP or WM_SYSKEYDOWN translation; specifies the virtual key code of the menu key.

wParam   The virtual key code of the menu key selected.

lParam   A bitmap used as follows:

Bits 1-16	Repeat count (number of times key is repeated)
Bits 17-25	Scan code (OEM-dependent value)
Bit 30	Context code (1 if ALT key is pressed; otherwise, 0. If 0, message is because no window owns the input focus)

Bit 31	Previous state key (1 if key was pressed prior to message; otherwise, 0)
Bit 32	Transition state (0 if key is being pressed; 1 if key is being released)

Default Action None.

WM—SYSCOMMAND

Function Received when the user selects a command from the System menu.

wParam An integer value specifying the system command selected:

SC—CLOSE	Close the window
SC—HSCROLL	Horizontally scroll window contents
SC—ICON	Make the window iconic
SC—KEYMENU	Request a menu via the keyboard
SC—MOUSEMENU	Request a menu via the mouse
SC—MOVE	Move the window
SC—NEXTWINDOW	Move to next window
SC—PREVWINDOW	Move to previous window
SC—SIZE	Change window size
SC—VSCROLL	Vertically scroll window contents
SC—ZOOM	Zoom the window

lParam Not used.

Default Action DefWindowProc carries out the System menu request.

WM—SYSDEADCHAR

Function   Result of a WM—SYSKEYUP or WM—SYSKEYDOWN translation; specifies the value of a dead key.

wParam   The character value of the dead key.

lParam   The low-order word contains the repeat count. The high-order word contains the auto-repeat count.

Default Action   None.

WM—SYSKEYDOWN

Function   Received either when the user holds down the ALT key and presses any other key, or when no window has the input focus.

wParam   The virtual key code of the key being pressed.

lParam   A bitmap used as follows:

Bits 1-16	Repeat count (number of times key is repeated)
Bits 17-25	Scan code (OEM-dependent value)
Bit 30	Context code (1 if ALT key is pressed; otherwise, 0 If 0, message is because no window owns the input focus)
Bit 31	Previous state key (1 if key was pressed prior to message; otherwise, 0)
Bit 32	Transition state (0 if key is being pressed; 1 if key is being released)

Default Action   None.

WM—SYSKEYUP

Function   Received either when the user releases a key that was pressed while the ALT key was held down or when no window owns the input focus.

wParam   The virtual key code of the key being released.

lParam   A bitmap used as follows:

Bits 1-16	Repeat count (number of times key is repeated)
Bits 17-25	Scan code (OEM-dependent value)
Bit 30	Context code (1 if ALT key is pressed; otherwise, 0 If 0, message is because no window owns the input focus)
Bit 31	Previous state key (1 if key was pressed prior to message; otherwise, 0)
Bit 32	Transition state (0 if key is being pressed; 1 if key is being released)

Default Action   None.

Clipboard Messages

The following messages are sent to an application when other applications attempt to access the Windows Clipboard. Later chapters examine the use of the Windows Clipboard in detail.

WM—ASKCBFORMATNAME

Function   Sent to the owner of the Clipboard to request a copy of the format name.

wParam An integer value specifying the maximum number of bytes to copy.

lParam A long pointer to the buffer to store the copy of the format name.

Default Action None.

WM—CHANGECBCHAIN

Function Sent to the first window in the Clipboard viewer chain each time a window is removed from the chain. Each window is responsible for notifying the succeeding window in the viewer chain via SendMessage.

wParam The handle to the window being removed from the Clipboard viewer chain.

lParam The low-order word contains the handle to the window immediately following the window removed from the viewer chain.

Default Action None.

WM—DESTROYCLIPBOARD

Function Sent to the owner of the Clipboard when the Clipboard is emptied by way of a call to the EmptyClipboard routine.

wParam Not used.

lParam Not used.

Default Action None.

WM—DRAWCLIPBOARD

Function   Sent to the first window in the Clipboard viewer chain each time the Clipboard contents are changed. The window should notify other windows in the viewer chain via SendMessage.

wParam   Not used.

lParam   Not used.

Default Action   None.

WM—HSCROLLCLIPBOARD

Function   Sent to the Clipboard owner to specify that an event has occurred in the Clipboard horizontal scroll bar.

wParam   The handle to the Clipboard application window.

lParam   The low-order word specifies the scroll-bar code, as follows:

SB—BOTTOM	Scroll to far right
SB—ENDSCROLL	Terminate scroll
SB—LINEDOWN	Scroll right one line
SB—LINEUP	Scroll left one line
SB—PAGEDOWN	Scroll right one page
SB—PAGEUP	Scroll left one page
SB—THUMBPOSITION	Scroll to absolute position
SB—THUMBTRACK	Scroll with thumb
SB—TOP	Scroll to far left

The high-order word contains the thumb position.

Default Action   None.

WM — PAINTCLIPBOARD

Function   Sent to the owner of the Clipboard to request that all or a portion of the Clipboard be repainted.

wParam   The handle to the Clipboard application window.

IParam   A long pointer to a PAINTSTRUCT structure that specifies the region of the Clipboard to repaint.

Default Action   None.

WM — RENDERALLFORMATS

Function   Requests that the owner of the Clipboard format the Clipboard data in all of the possible formats and pass handles to the routine SetClipboardData before the owner application is destroyed.

wParam   Not used.

IParam   Not used.

Default Action   None.

WM — RENDERFORMAT

Function   Requests that the owner of the Clipboard format the Clipboard data in the specified format and return a handle to the Clipboard data.

wParam Specifies the Clipboard data format desired. See the routine SetClipboardData in Chapter 14.

lParam Not used.

Default Action None.

WM — SIZECLIPBOARD

Function Sent to the owner of the Clipboard to inform it that the Clipboard application window has changed size.

wParam The handle to the Clipboard application window.

lParam The low-order word is a pointer to a RECT structure, which specifies the size of the Clipboard application window.

Default Action None.

WM — VSCROLLCLIPBOARD

Function Sent to the Clipboard owner to specify that an event has occurred in the Clipboard vertical scroll bar.

wParam The handle to the Clipboard application window.

lParam The low-order word specifies the scroll-bar code, as follows:

SB — BOTTOM	Scroll to bottom
SB — ENDSCROLL	Terminate scroll
SB — LINEDOWN	Scroll down one line
SB — LINEUP	Scroll up one line
SB — PAGEDOWN	Scroll down one page

SB_PAGEUP	Scroll up one page
SB_THUMBPOSITION	Scroll to absolute position
SB_THUMBTRACK	Scroll with thumb
SB_TOP	Scroll to top

The high-order word contains the thumb position.

Default Action   None.

System Information Messages

The following messages are sent to an application each time system-wide resources are changed. The changes may occur as the result of a user action or an application action.

WM_DEVMODECHANGE

Function   Sent to all top-level windows when the user changes a device mode setting.

wParam   Not used.

lParam   A long pointer to the device name.

Default Action   None.

WM_FONTCHANGE

Function   Sent to all top-level windows by an application that changes the font resources available by adding or removing a font.

wParam   Not used.

lParam   Not used.

Default Action   None.

WM—SYSCOLORCHANGE

Function   Sent to all top-level windows when the system color changes.

wParam   Not used.

lParam   Not used.

Default Action   DefWindowProc will paint the portions of the screen affected by the color change.

WM—SYSTEMERROR

Function   Sent to all top-level windows when an out-of-memory condition occurs.

wParam   The value 8, indicating an out-of-memory condition.

lParam   Not used.

Default Action   The user is notified of the out-of-memory condition.

WM—TIMECHANGE

Function   Sent to all top-level windows by an application that changes the system time.

wParam Not used.

lParam Not used.

Default Action None.

WM—WININICHANGE

Function Sent to all top-level windows by an application that changes the Windows initialization file, WIN.INI.

wParam Not used.

lParam A long pointer specifying the name of the section of WIN .INI that has changed. If lParam is 0, multiple sections have changed, and each application must determine what the sections are.

Default Action None.

Control Window Messages

The following messages are sent from an application to control windows via the SendMessage function. The control accomplishes the task required and returns a value to the calling routine.

BM—GETCHECK

Function Used to determine if a check box or radio button is checked. A nonzero return value indicates a check.

wParam Not used.

lParam Not used.

BM—GETSTATE

Function   Used to determine whether the cursor is over a button and the user has pressed the mouse select button or SPACEBAR. A nonzero return value indicates that the specified state has occurred.

wParam   Not used.

IParam   Not used.

BM—SETCHECK

Function   Places or removes a check for a radio button or check box.

wParam   Zero removes a check; nonzero inserts a check.

IParam   None.

BM—SETSTATE

Function   Enables or disables the highlight of a button or check box.

wParam   Zero removes the highlight. A nonzero value produces a frame around the button or highlights the check box.

IParam   Not used.

Edit Control Messages

The following messages are sent from an application to an edit control window. Each message requests that the control window perform a specific task.

EM—CANUNDO

Function Determines whether or not an edit control window can respond to an EM—UNDO message. A nonzero return value indicates that the control can handle the EM—UNDO message.

wParam Not used.

lParam Not used.

EM—FMTLINES

Function Places or removes end-of-line characters on word-wrapped lines.

wParam Zero removes end-of-line characters. Nonzero places end-of-line characters on each line of word-wrapped text.

lParam Not used.

EM—GETHANDLE

Function Obtains the local handle to a text buffer used to store the contents of a control window.

wParam Not used.

lParam Not used.

EM—GETLINE

Function Copies data from the specified line number from the control window into a buffer.

wParam The desired line number. The first line is offset 0.

lParam A far pointer to the storage buffer.

EM — GETLINECOUNT

Function Obtains the number of lines of text in the edit control window.

wParam Not used.

lParam Not used.

EM — GETRECT

Function Obtains the formatting rectangle for a control window.

wParam Not used.

lParam A long pointer to a RECT structure that contains the rectangle of the current control window.

EM — GETSEL

Function Returns the starting and ending positions of the current solution in the edit control window. The value returned is a long word in which the low-order word contains the starting position and the high-order word contains the ending position.

wParam Not used.

lParam Not used.

EM—LIMITTEXT

Function   Specifies the maximum number of bytes the user can enter.

wParam   The maximum number of bytes allowed. Zero implies no limit.

lParam   Not used.

EM—LINEINDEX

Function   Obtains the number of character positions that occur before the first character in a given line.

wParam   The line number of interest (-1 is the current line).

lParam   Not used.

EM—LINELENGTH

Function   Returns the number of bytes in the line specified within the control window.

wParam   The character index of a character in the desired line.

lParam   Not used.

EM—LINESCROLL

Function   Requests that the control window scroll its contents the specified number of lines or character positions.

wParam Not used.

lParam The low-order word contains the number of character positions to scroll horizontally. The high-order word contains the number of lines to scroll vertically.

EM—REPLACESEL

Function Replaces the selected text with new text.

wParam Not used.

lParam A far pointer to an ASCIIZ (null-terminated) string containing the new text.

EM—SCROLL

Function Directs the control window to scroll its contents as specified by the contents of wParam. The current thumb position is returned.

wParam Specifies the scrolling action, as follows:

EM—GETTHUMB	Return the current thumb position
SB—LINEDOWN	Scroll down one line
SB—LINEUP	Scroll up one line
SB—PAGEDOWN	Scroll down one page
SB—PAGEUP	Scroll up one page
SB—THUMBPOSITION	Scroll to absolute position

lParam Not used.

EM—SETFONT

Function Sets the font to be used within the edit control window.

wParam A fixed-pitch font identification.

lParam Not used.

EM—SETHANDLE

Function Specifies the text buffer to store the contents of the control window.

wParam The local handle to the storage buffer.

lParam Not used.

EM—SETRECT

Function Sets the formatting rectangle for a control window.

wParam Not used.

lParam A structure of type RECT that specifies the new formatting rectangle.

EM—SETRECTNP

Function Similar to EM—SETRECT except that the specified control window is not repainted.

wParam Not used.

lParam A structure of type RECT that specifies the new formatting rectangle.

EM—SETSEL

Function   Selects the characters in the current edit control text that are within the range specified by lParam.

wParam   Not used.

lParam   The low-order word contains the starting character position, and the high-order word contains the ending position. The range must fall into the range 0 to 32,676.

EM—UNDO

Function   Undoes the last edit to the edit control window.

wParam   Not used.

lParam   Not used.

WM—CLEAR

Function   Erases the current selection.

wParam   Not used.

lParam   Not used.

WM—COPY

Function   Places a copy of the current selection in the Clipboard in CF—TEXT format.

wParam   Not used.

lParam   Not used.

WM—CUT

Function Places the current selection in the Clipboard and then removes the selection from the control window.

wParam Not used.

lParam Not used.

WM—PASTE

Function Inserts the contents of the Clipboard at the current cursor position. The Clipboard must contain data in CF—TEXT format.

wParam Not used.

lParam Not used.

List Box Messages

The following messages are sent from your application to list box controls to request specific functions.

LB—ADDSTRING

Function Adds a string to a list box. If the list is sorted, the string is placed in the proper location. Otherwise, the string is appended to the list. The index of the string in the box is returned.

wParam Not used.

lParam A long pointer to the ASCIIZ string to be placed into the list box.

LB—DELETESTRING

Function   Deletes a string from a list box.

wParam   The index of the string to be deleted.

lParam   Not used.

LB—DIR

Function   Adds strings to a list box containing files from the current directory. These files contain the attributes specified by wParam.

wParam   The desired MS-DOS file attribute as follows:

1	Read-only
2	Hidden
4	System
8	Volume label
16	Directory
32	Archive

lParam   A long pointer to an ASCIIZ file specification. The DOS wildcard characters *.* can be used to obtain all file names.

Default Action   None.

LB—GETCOUNT

Function   Returns a count of the number of strings in the list box.

wParam   Not used.

lParam   Not used.

LB — GETCURSEL

Function   Returns the index of the currently selected string.

wParam   Not used.

lParam   Not used.

LB — GETSEL

Function   Returns the selection state of a string. Zero indicates that the string is currently selected.

wParam   The index of the desired string.

lParam   Not used.

LB — GETTEXT

Function   Copies the currently selected text into a buffer.

wParam   The index of the string to be copied.

lParam   A long pointer to the buffer to store the copied text.

LB — GETTEXTLEN

Function   Returns the number of bytes in the currently selected string.

wParam   The index of the desired string.

lParam   Not used.

LB—INSERTSTRING

Function Inserts a message into a list box with no sorting performed.

wParam The index in the list box indicating where the string is to be placed (−1 specifies the end of the list).

lParam A long pointer to the ASCIIZ string to be placed into the list box.

LB—SELECTSTRING

Function Selects as the current string the first string having the specified prefix. LB—ERR is returned if the prefix is not found.

wParam The index of the starting point for the search. A −1 specifies the beginning of the list as the starting point.

lParam A long pointer to the ASCIIZ string containing the prefix to be matched.

LB—SETCURSEL

Function Selects a string from a list box and scrolls it into view. Previous highlights are turned off.

wParam The index of the string to be selected.

lParam A −1 specifies that the list box is set to have no selection.

LB—SETSEL

Function Sets the selection state of a string.

wParam   Zero removes a highlight. A nonzero value highlights the selected string.

lParam   The low-order word contains the index of the string to be set (−1 sets the entire list).

Notification Messages

When edit controls and button controls return a WM—COMMAND message to the parent window, they normally use wParam to specify the action that occurred within the control. The following notification codes are returned to parent windows in wParam.

Button Notification Codes

BN—CLICKED	Button has been clicked
BN—DISABLE	Disable button
BN—HILITE	Highlight button
BN—PAINT	Repaint button
BN—UNHILITE	Remove button highlight

Edit Control Notification Codes

EN—CHANGE	User may have modified control text
EN—ERRSPACE	Edit control is out of space
EN—HSCROLL	User has clicked mouse in the edit control's horizontal scroll bar
EN—KILLFOCUS	Edit control has lost input focus
EN—SETFOCUS	Edit control has input focus
EN—VSCROLL	User has clicked mouse in the edit control's vertical scroll bar

List Box Notification Codes

LB_NDBLCLK	User has double-clicked selection
LB_NERRSPACE	List box is out of space
LB_NSELCHANGE	Selection has changed

Nonclient Area Messages

The following messages are sent by Windows to an application when the nonclient area of a window is affected by user actions. The nonclient area includes such regions as the caption bar and window frame.

WM_NCACTIVATE

Function   Sent to a window when its caption bar or icon needs to be changed to indicate active or inactive status.

wParam   Zero for inactive, nonzero for active.

lParam   Not used.

Default Action   DefWindowProc makes the active caption bar black and others gray, or it places a white border around the active icon.

WM_NCCALCSIZE

Function   Requests that the size of the client area be calculated.

wParam   Not used.

lParam   A long pointer to a RECT structure that contains the coordinates of the window.

Default Action DefWindowProc returns the size of the window in the RECT structure.

WM—NCCREATE

Function Sent prior to the WM—CREATE message to initialize the nonclient portion of the window to be created.

wParam The handle to the window being created.

lParam A long pointer to a CREATESTRUCT structure for the window to be created.

Default Action Memory is allocated to maintain the window internally. Window scroll bars are initialized.

WM—NCDESTROY

Function Sent following the WM—DESTROY message to destroy the internal memory block allocated to maintain the window.

wParam Not used.

lParam A long pointer to a RECT structure that contains the coordinates of the window being destroyed.

Default Action All memory associated with the window is freed.

WM—NCHITTEST

Function Sent each time the mouse cursor is moved.

wParam Not used.

lParam   The low-order word contains the x coordinate. The high-order word contains the y coordinate.

Default Action   DefWindowProc returns one of the following:

HTCAPTION	In caption area
HTCLIENT	In client area
HTERROR	On screen background or in between windows (DefWindowProc beeps to signal an error)
HTGROWBOX	In size box
HTHSCROLL	In horizontal scroll bar
HTMENU	In menu area
HTNOWHERE	On screen background or in between windows
HTSYSMENU	In System menu area
HTTRANSPARENT	On a currently covered window
HTVSCROLL	In vertical scroll bar

WM—NCLBUTTONDBLCLK

Function   Sent to a window when the mouse cursor is in the non-client area of the window and the left mouse select button is double-clicked.

wParam   The code returned from the WM—NCHITTEST message.

lParam   A POINT structure containing the x and y coordinates of the mouse cursor.

Default Action   If necessary, WM—SYSCOMMAND messages are sent to the window.

WM—NCLBUTTONDOWN

Function   Sent to a window when the mouse cursor is in the non-client area of the window and the mouse select button is pressed.

wParam   The code returned from the WM—NCHITTEST message.

lParam   A POINT structure containing the x and y coordinates of the mouse cursor.

Default Action   If necessary, WM—SYSCOMMAND messages are sent to the window.

WM—NCLBUTTONUP

Function   Sent to a window when the mouse cursor is in the non-client area of the window and the mouse select button is released.

wParam   The code returned from the WM—NCHITTEST message.

lParam   A POINT structure containing the x and y coordinates of the mouse cursor.

Default Action   If necessary, WM—SYSCOMMAND messages are sent to the window.

WM—NCMBUTTONDBLCLK

Function   Sent to a window when the mouse cursor is in the non-client area of the window and the middle mouse select button is double-clicked.

wParam   The code returned from the WM—NCHITTEST message.

lParam   A POINT structure containing the x and y coordinates of the mouse cursor.

Default Action   None.

WM—NCMBUTTONDOWN

Function   Sent to a window when the mouse cursor is in the non-client area of the window and the middle mouse select button is pressed.

wParam   The code returned from the WM—NCHITTEST message.

lParam   A POINT structure containing the x and y coordinates of the mouse cursor.

Default Action   None.

WM—NCMBUTTONUP

Function   Sent to a window when the mouse cursor is in the non-client area of the window and the middle mouse select button is released.

wParam   The code returned from the WM—NCHITTEST message.

lParam   A POINT structure containing the x and y coordinates of the mouse cursor.

Default Action   None.

WM—NCMOUSEMOVE

Function   Sent to a window whenever the mouse cursor is placed in the window's nonclient area.

wParam   The code returned from the WM—NCHITTEST message.

lParam   A POINT structure containing the x and y coordinates of the mouse cursor.

Default Action   If necessary, WM—SYSCOMMAND messages are sent to the window.

WM—NCPAINT

Function   Sent to a window when its frame needs repainting.

wParam   Not used.

lParam   Not used.

Default Action   DefWindowProc repaints the frame.

WM—NCRBUTTONDBLCLK

Function   Sent to a window when the mouse cursor is in the non-client area of the window and the right mouse select button is double-clicked.

wParam   The code returned from the WM—NCHITTEST message.

lParam   A POINT structure containing the x and y coordinates of the mouse cursor.

Default Action   None.

WM—NCRBUTTONDOWN

Function   Sent to a window when the mouse cursor is in the non-client area of the window and the right mouse select button is pressed.

wParam   The code returned from the WM—NCHITTEST message.

lParam   A POINT structure containing the x and y coordinates of the mouse cursor.

Default Action   None.

WM—NCRBUTTONUP

Function   Sent to a window when the mouse cursor is in the non-client area of the window and the right mouse select button is released.

wParam   The code returned from the WM—NCHITTEST message.

lParam   A POINT structure containing the x and y coordinates of the mouse cursor.

Default Action   None.

11

USING MENUS AND ACCELERATORS

Most Windows applications make use of menus. Menus play a critical role in the success of your Windows programming applications. This chapter examines how to utilize standard and pop-up menus within applications. It concludes with a thorough examination of menu accelerators and their implementation within your applications.

The program to implement the following menu bar will illustrate the creation of standard menus:

The menu resource definition for this menu bar appears in the application's resource script file as follows:

```
#include "windows.h"

MENU ICON     MENU.ICO

MENU menu
begin
    MENUITEM "Windows Version!", 1
    MENUITEM "DOS Version!", 2
    MENUITEM "System Time", 3
end
```

If you select the Windows Version option, the application displays the following message:

Windows Version 1.3!

Likewise, if you choose the DOS Version option, the application displays the following:

DOS Version 3.0!

The System Time option produces the following:

```
≣                              MENU                                    ⌐
Windows Version  DOS Version  System Time
```

System Time 0:12:22

The following C program, MENU.C, implements the menu bar:

```c
#include "windows.h"
#include <dos.h>         /* needed to interface with DOS */

#define APPLICATION_NAME "MENU"
#define ICON_NAME "MENU"

long FAR PASCAL MenuWndProc(HWND, unsigned, WORD, LONG);

MenuChoice (hWnd, selection)
HWND hWnd;
WORD selection;
{
  HDC hdc;
  char msg[255];
  int major, minor, hours, minutes, seconds;
  union REGS inregs;
  union REGS outregs;

  hdc = GetDC (hWnd);

  switch (selection) {
    case 1: major = GetVersion();    /* Display Windows Version */
            minor = major >> 8;
            major = major & 255;
            TextOut(hdc, 0, 10, (LPSTR) msg,
              sprintf(msg, "Windows Version %d.%d  ", major, minor));
            break;

    case 2: inregs.h.ah = 0x30;      /* Display DOS Version */
            intdos (&inregs, &outregs);
            major = outregs.h.al;
            minor = outregs.h.ah;
            TextOut(hdc, 0, 10, (LPSTR) msg,
              sprintf(msg, "DOS Version  %d.%d    ", major, minor));
            break;

    case 3: inregs.h.ah = 0x2C;      /* Display system time */
            intdos (&inregs, &outregs);
            hours = outregs.h.ch;
            minutes = outregs.h.cl;
            seconds = outregs.h.dh;
            TextOut(hdc, 0, 10, (LPSTR) msg,
              sprintf(msg, "System Time  %d:%d:%d  ",
                      hours, minutes, seconds));
            break;
  }
}


BOOL MenuInit(hInstance)
HANDLE hInstance;
{
```

```
        NPWNDCLASS  pClass;

        pClass = (NPWNDCLASS) LocalAlloc(LPTR, sizeof(WNDCLASS));

        pClass->hCursor        = LoadCursor(NULL, IDC_ARROW);
        pClass->hIcon          = LoadIcon(hInstance, (LPSTR) ICON_NAME);
        pClass->lpszMenuName   = (LPSTR) APPLICATION_NAME;
        pClass->lpszClassName  = (LPSTR) APPLICATION_NAME;
        pClass->hbrBackground  = (HBRUSH) GetStockObject(WHITE_BRUSH);
        pClass->hInstance      = hInstance;
        pClass->style          = CS_HREDRAW | CS_VREDRAW;
        pClass->lpfnWndProc    = MenuWndProc;

        if (!RegisterClass((LPWNDCLASS)pClass))
            return FALSE;

        LocalFree((HANDLE) pClass); /* return space to heap */
        return TRUE;                /* registration successful */
}


int PASCAL WinMain(hInstance, hPrevInstance, lpszCmdLine, cmdShow)
HANDLE hInstance, hPrevInstance;
LPSTR lpszCmdLine;
int cmdShow;
{
  MSG   message;
  HWND  hWnd;

  if (!hPrevInstance)   /* initialize if this is the first instance */
    if (!MenuInit(hInstance))
        return FALSE;    /* failure to initialize -- return to Windows */

  hWnd = CreateWindow((LPSTR) APPLICATION_NAME,
                      (LPSTR) APPLICATION_NAME,
                      WS_TILEDWINDOW,
                      0,               /* x - ignored for tiled
                                             windows */
                      0,               /* y - ignored for tiled
                                             windows */
                      0,               /* cx - ignored for tiled
                                             windows */
                      0,               /* cy - ignored for tiled
                                             windows */
                      (HWND) NULL,     /* no parent */
                      (HMENU) NULL,    /* use class menu */
                      (HANDLE) hInstance, /* handle to window
                                             instance */
                      (LPSTR) NULL     /* no parameters to pass
                                             on */
                      );

    ShowWindow(hWnd, cmdShow);              /* Make window visible */
    UpdateWindow(hWnd);

        /* Poll messages from the event queue and dispatch them */
        while (GetMessage((LPMSG) &message, NULL, 0, 0)) {
            TranslateMessage((LPMSG) &message);
            DispatchMessage((LPMSG) &message);
            }

        return (int) message.wParam; /* return control to Windows */
    }
```

```
long FAR PASCAL MenuWndProc(hWnd, message, wParam, lParam)
HWND hWnd;
unsigned message;
WORD wParam;
LONG lParam;
{
  PAINTSTRUCT ps;
  switch (message) {
    case WM_COMMAND:
          MenuChoice (hWnd, wParam); /* Process menu choice */
          break;

    case WM_DESTROY:
          PostQuitMessage(0);  /* tell Windows ready to terminate */
          break;

    default:                   /* let Windows process message */
          return DefWindowProc(hWnd, message, wParam, lParam);
          break;
    }

  return (0L);
}
```

Note that the program is very similar to the application presented in Chapter 9. In this case, however, each time the user interacts with the menu, Windows passes a WM—COMMAND message to the application message-processing function. The wParam field of the message contains the value associated with the selected menu option. Remember that you must assign each menu option a unique value within the resource script file. These values allow your application to determine which menu option was selected.

The module definition file, MENU.DEF, is very similar to the other module definition files presented thus far:

```
NAME    MENU

DESCRIPTION 'Simple Windows Menu Application'

STUB    'WINSTUB.EXE'

CODE    MOVEABLE
DATA    MOVEABLE MULTIPLE

HEAPSIZE 512
STACKSIZE 4096

EXPORTS
    MenuWndProc @1
```

Perform the following processing steps to create the executable version of the program, MENU.EXE:

```
cl -d -c -AS -Gsw -Oas -Zpe -FPa -F.menu.obj menu.c

rc -r menu.rc

link4 menu,/align:16,,slibw,menu.def

rc menu.res menu.exe
```

Pop-Up Menus

Pop-up menus like the following are the menu form most commonly used by Windows applications:

The resource script file associated with this menu would contain the following:

```
#include "windows.h"

name MENU
begin
  POPUP "File"
    begin
      MENUITEM "Run...", 1
      MENUITEM "Load...", 2
      MENUITEM "Copy...", 3
      MENUITEM "Get Info...", 4
      MENUITEM "Delete...", 5
      MENUITEM "Print...", 6
      MENUITEM "Rename...", 7
    end
end
```

This section presents a program called POPUP.EXE that illustrates the use of pop-up menus within Windows applications. The program provides the following menu bar:

Each menu option displays a pop-up menu. For example, the Disk option produces the following menu:

The Version option results in the following:

Finally, the Date/Time option allows you to set the system date or time, as follows:

The resource script file used in this application consists of the following:

```
#include "windows.h"

POPUP   ICON    POPUP.ICO

POPUP MENU
begin
  POPUP "Disk"
    begin
      MENUITEM "Disk Space", 1
      MENUITEM "Default Drive", 2
    end
  POPUP "Version"
    begin
      MENUITEM "DOS Version", 3
      MENUITEM "Windows Version", 4
    end
  POPUP "Date/Time"
    begin
      MENUITEM "Date", 5
      MENUITEM "Time", 6
    end
end
```

Pop-up menus are conceptually no different from the simple menu bar presented in the previous section. Assign each menu option a unique value that the application program can evaluate. Although POPUP.EXE simply displays text messages when each menu option is chosen, the program provides a foundation from which you can develop your own pop-up applications.

The Pascal program to implement the pop-up menus is as follows:

```
{$windows+}
{$stackseg+ $debug- $symtab-}

INTERFACE;
    UNIT paslibw (
        {$INCLUDE : 'popup.inc'}
    );

{$INCLUDE:'windows.inc'}                   { Get WINDOWS definitions. }

MODULE popup[];
  USES paslibw (
    {$INCLUDE : 'popup.inc'}
  );


PROCEDURE begxqq; EXTERN;
```

```
PROCEDURE endxqq; EXTERN;

PROCEDURE ENTGQQ [ PUBLIC ];
BEGIN
      {dummy routine for link4}
END;

PROCEDURE PopupChoice (hWindow : HWND;
                       choice  : WORD) [ PUBLIC ];

var
  hDC_ : HDC;

BEGIN
  hDC_ := GetDC (hWindow);

  case choice of
    1:  EVAL(TextOut(hDC_, 0, 10, RETYPE(LPSTR,
          ADS 'Disk space procedure called here   '), 35));

    2:  EVAL(TextOut(hDC_, 0, 10, RETYPE(LPSTR,
          ADS 'Default drive procedure called here'), 35));

    3:  EVAL(TextOut(hDC_, 0, 10, RETYPE(LPSTR,
          ADS 'DOS Version number displayed here  '), 35));

    4:  EVAL(TextOut(hDC_, 0, 10, RETYPE(LPSTR,
          ADS 'Windows Version number shown here  '), 35));

    5:  EVAL(TextOut(hDC_, 0, 10, RETYPE(LPSTR,
          ADS 'Date setting routine here          '), 35));

    6:  EVAL(TextOut(hDC_, 0, 10, RETYPE(LPSTR,
          ADS 'Time setting routine here          '), 35));
  end;

END;




FUNCTION PopupWndProc(hWindow : HWND;
                      message : UNSIGNED;
                      wParam  : WORD;
                      lParam  : LONG ) : LONG [ PUBLIC, WINDOWS ];

VAR
  ps : PAINTSTRUCT;

BEGIN

    CASE message OF
        WM_DESTROY:
            PostQuitMessage(0);

        WM_COMMAND:
            PopupChoice (hwindow, wParam);

        OTHERWISE    { Let Windows handle all the other messages }
          BEGIN
            PopupWndProc := DefWindowProc(hWindow, message, wParam,
                            lParam);

            RETURN;
          END;

    END;
```

```
      PopupWndProc := RETYPE(LONG, BYLONG(0,0));
END;


FUNCTION PopupInit(hInstance : HANDLE) : BOOL;

VAR
  pClass : WNDCLASS;

BEGIN

    begxqq;

    pClass.lpszClassName := RETYPE(LPSTR, ADS 'PopUp' * CHR(0));
    pClass.hIcon_        := LoadIcon( hInstance, RETYPE(LPSTR, ADS
                            'POPUP' * CHR(0)));
    pClass.hCursor_      := LoadCursor( RETYPE(HWND, NULL_), IDC_ARROW);
    pClass.lpszMenuName  := RETYPE(LPSTR, ADS 'POPUP' * Chr(0));
    pClass.hbrBackground := RETYPE(HBRUSH, GetStockObject(WHITE_BRUSH));

    pClass.lpfnWndProc   := ADS PopupWndProc;
    pClass.hInstance     := hInstance;
    pClass.style         := CS_VREDRAW OR CS_HREDRAW;
    pClass.cbClsExtra    := 0;
    pClass.cbWndExtra    := 0;

    { register this new class with WINDOWS }

    IF (RegisterClass(RETYPE(LPWNDCLASS, ADS pClass)) <> TRUE_) THEN
       BEGIN
         PopupInit := FALSE_;
         RETURN;
       END;

    PopupInit := TRUE_;
END;



FUNCTION WinMain(hInstance     : HANDLE;
                 hPrevInstance : HANDLE;
                 lpszCmdline   : LPSTR;
                 cmdShow       : INT) : BOOL [ PUBLIC ];

VAR
   hWindow : HWND;
   msg_    : MSG;

BEGIN
    IF (hPrevInstance = 0) THEN  { Call initialization routine }
       BEGIN
         IF (PopupInit(hInstance) = FALSE_) THEN { Return to Windows }
            BEGIN
               WinMain := FALSE_;
               RETURN;
            END;
       END;

    { Create a window instance of class 'PopUp' }

    hWindow := CreateWindow(
        RETYPE(LPSTR, ADS 'POPUP' * CHR(0)),    { Class name     }
        RETYPE(LPSTR, ADS 'POPUP' * CHR(0)),    { Instance name  }
        WS_TILEDWINDOW,                         { Window style   }
        0,                                      { Desired column }
```

```
        0,                                  { cy: not used        }
        0,                                  { cx: not used        }
        100,                                { Desired height: pixel }
        RETYPE(HWND, NULL_),                { No parent window    }
        RETYPE(HMENU, NULL_),               { Use default menu    }
        hInstance,                          { Instance handle     }
        RETYPE(LPSTR, BYLONG(0,NULL_)));    { No additional
                                              parameter }

    EVAL(ShowWindow(hWindow, cmdShow)); { Send message to update
                                          window }
    UpdateWindow(hWindow);

    WHILE (GetMessage(RETYPE(LPMSG, ADS msg_), NULL_, 0, 0) <> 0) DO
        BEGIN
            EVAL(TranslateMessage(RETYPE(LPMSG, ADS msg_)));
            EVAL(DispatchMessage(RETYPE(LPMSG, ADS msg_)));
        END;

    endxqq;

END;

END.
```

POPUP.PAS uses the following POPUP.INC file:

```
int,
short,
long,
unsigned,
FALSE_,
TRUE_,
NULL_,
BYTE,
WORD,
DWORD,
BOOL,
PSTR,
LPSTR,
LPINT,
HANDLE,
HSTR,
HICON,
HDC,
HMENU,
HPEN,
HBRUSH,
HCURSOR,
WNDCLASS,
PWNDCLASS,
LPWNDCLASS,
HWND,
MSG,
PMSG,
LPMSG,
```

```
WM_DESTROY,
WM_COMMAND,
WM_PAINT,
CS_VREDRAW,
CS_HREDRAW,
WS_TILEDWINDOW,
PAINTSTRUCT,
LPPAINTSTRUCT,
CREATESTRUCT,
WHITE_BRUSH,
GetMessage,
TranslateMessage,
DispatchMessage,
DefWindowProc,
PostQuitMessage,
RegisterClass,
CreateWindow,
DestroyWindow,
ShowWindow,
UpdateWindow,
BeginPaint,
EndPaint,
TextOut,
GetStockObject,
LoadCursor,
IDC_ARROW,
LoadIcon,
LoadMenu,
GetDC
```

The module definition file for the program contains the following:

```
NAME    Popup
DESCRIPTION 'Microsoft Windows Pascal Application'

CODE     MOVEABLE
DATA     MOVEABLE MULTIPLE PRELOAD

STUB     'WINSTUB.EXE'

HEAPSIZE    2048
STACKSIZE   4096

EXPORTS
    PopupWndProc
```

Perform the following steps to create the executable version, POPUP.EXE:

```
PAS1 POPUP;

PAS2

RC -R POPUP.RC

LINK4 POPUP, /a:16,, PASLIBW, POPUP.DEF

RC POPUP.RES POPUP.EXE
```

Accelerators

An accelerator is an application-defined series of keystrokes that allows the user to perform a specific task in a fast, convenient manner. For example, consider the following menu:

The user can select the Date/Time pop-up menu and then choose the Set Time option by using the keyboard or mouse. If you examine the Set Time option, however, you will note that it has an accelerator, ^T. Instead of requiring the user to point to the Set Time option in order to invoke it, the application provides the CTRL-T keyboard combination as an accelerator to the function. Accelerators are also provided for the Disk Space option of the Disk menu and for the DOS Version option of the Version menu. The following resource script file defines the accelerators for this application:

```
#include "windows.h"

ACCEL  ICON    ACCEL.ICO

ACCEL MENU
```

```
begin
  POPUP "Disk"
    begin
      MENUITEM "Disk Space   ^D", 1
      MENUITEM "Default Drive", 2
    end
  POPUP "Version"
    begin
      MENUITEM "DOS Version   ^V", 3
      MENUITEM "Windows Version", 4
    end
  POPUP "Date/Time"
    begin
      MENUITEM "Set Date", 5
      MENUITEM "Set Time   ^T", 6
    end
end

ACCEL ACCELERATORS
begin
  "^D", 1
  "^V", 3
  "^T", 6
end
```

The use of accelerators has little impact upon the complexity of your program code. In fact, to provide accelerators, you need only insert the following lines of code within your program:

```
hAccelTable := LoadAccelerators (hInstance, RETYPE(LPSTR,
                               ADS 'ACCEL' * Chr(0)));

if (TranslateAccelerator (hWindow, hAccelTable, RETYPE (
                      LPMSG, ADS msg_)) = 0) then
  BEGIN
    EVAL(TranslateMessage(RETYPE(LPMSG, ADS msg_)));
    EVAL(DispatchMessage(RETYPE(LPMSG, ADS msg_)));
  END;
```

The first statement simply makes the table of accelerators (defined in the resource script file) available to the application. The second statement performs the meat of the processing. Each time the Windows application receives a message, it will compare the contents of the message to a predefined accelerator to see whether they match. If they do not match, the routine TranslateAccelerator returns the value 0, and the message can be processed normally. If they do match, the message is an accelerator, and the routine converts the message into a WM—COMMAND message. The value assigned to the accelerator within the resource script file is placed into the wParam field. This method of processing eliminates any need to modify other portions of your applications when you implement accelerators.

The following Pascal program, ACCEL.PAS, implements the example application:

```
{$windows+}
{$stackseg+ $debug- $symtab-}

INTERFACE;
    UNIT paslibw (
        {$INCLUDE : 'accel.inc'}
    );

{$INCLUDE:'windows.inc'}                      { Get WINDOWS definitions. }

MODULE popup[];
  USES paslibw (
    {$INCLUDE : 'accel.inc'}
  );


PROCEDURE begxqq; EXTERN;

PROCEDURE endxqq; EXTERN;

PROCEDURE ENTGQQ [ PUBLIC ];
BEGIN
      {dummy routine for link4}
END;

PROCEDURE AccelChoice (hWindow : HWND;
                       choice  : WORD) [ PUBLIC ];

var
  hDC_ : HDC;

BEGIN
  hDC_ := GetDC (hWindow);

  case choice of
    1:    EVAL(TextOut(hDC_, 0, 10, RETYPE(LPSTR,
            ADS 'Disk space procedure called here    '), 35));

    2:    EVAL(TextOut(hDC_, 0, 10, RETYPE(LPSTR,
            ADS 'Default drive procedure called here'), 35));

    3:    EVAL(TextOut(hDC_, 0, 10, RETYPE(LPSTR,
            ADS 'DOS Version number displayed here   '), 35));

    4:    EVAL(TextOut(hDC_, 0, 10, RETYPE(LPSTR,
            ADS 'Windows Version number shown here   '), 35));

    5:    EVAL(TextOut(hDC_, 0, 10, RETYPE(LPSTR,
            ADS 'Date setting routine here           '), 35));
```

```
    6:    EVAL(TextOut(hDC_, 0, 10, RETYPE(LPSTR,
          ADS 'Time setting routine here            '), 35));
otherwise:


      EVAL(TextOut(hDC_, 0, 10, RETYPE(LPSTR,
          ADS 'Wierd value                          '), 35));

    end;

END;




FUNCTION AccelWndProc(hWindow : HWND;
                      message : UNSIGNED;
                      wParam  : WORD;
                      lParam  : LONG ) : LONG [ PUBLIC, WINDOWS ];

VAR
  ps : PAINTSTRUCT;

BEGIN

    CASE message OF
        WM_DESTROY:
            PostQuitMessage(0);

        WM_COMMAND:
            AccelChoice (hwindow, wParam);

        OTHERWISE      { Let Windows handle all the other messages }
            BEGIN
              AccelWndProc := DefWindowProc(hWindow, message, wParam,
                              lParam);
              RETURN;
            END;

    END;

    AccelWndProc := RETYPE(LONG, BYLONG(0,0));
END;


FUNCTION AccelInit(hInstance : HANDLE) : BOOL;

VAR
  pClass : WNDCLASS;

BEGIN

    begxqq;

    pClass.lpszClassName := RETYPE(LPSTR, ADS 'Accel' * CHR(0));
    pClass.hIcon_        := LoadIcon( hInstance, RETYPE(LPSTR, ADS
                            'ACCEL' * CHR(0)));
    pClass.hCursor_      := LoadCursor( RETYPE(HWND, NULL_), IDC_ARROW);
    pClass.lpszMenuName  := RETYPE(LPSTR, ADS 'ACCEL' * Chr(0));
    pClass.hbrBackground := RETYPE(HBRUSH, GetStockObject(WHITE_BRUSH));
    pClass.lpfnWndProc   := ADS AccelWndProc;
    pClass.hInstance     := hInstance;
    pClass.style         := CS_VREDRAW OR CS_HREDRAW;
    pClass.cbClsExtra    := 0;
    pClass.cbWndExtra    := 0;
```

```
    { register this new class with WINDOWS }

    IF (RegisterClass(RETYPE(LPWNDCLASS, ADS pClass)) <> TRUE_) THEN
        BEGIN
          AccelInit := FALSE_;
          RETURN;
        END;

    AccelInit := TRUE_;
END;



FUNCTION WinMain(hInstance      : HANDLE;
                 hPrevInstance : HANDLE;
                 lpszCmdLine   : LPSTR;
                 cmdShow       : INT) : BOOL [ PUBLIC ];

VAR
    hWindow : HWND;
    msg_    : MSG;
    hAccelTable: HANDLE;

BEGIN
    IF (hPrevInstance = 0) THEN   { Call initialization routine }
        BEGIN
          IF (AccelInit(hInstance) = FALSE_) THEN { Return to Windows }
              BEGIN
                WinMain := FALSE_;
                RETURN;
              END;
        END;

    { Create a window instance of class 'Accel' }

    hWindow := CreateWindow(
        RETYPE(LPSTR, ADS 'ACCEL' * CHR(0)),    { Class name            }
        RETYPE(LPSTR, ADS 'ACCEL' * CHR(0)),    { Instance name         }
        WS_TILEDWINDOW,                         { Window style          }
        0,                                      { Desired column        }
        0,                                      { cy: not used          }
        0,                                      { cx: not used          }
        100,                                    { Desired height: pixel }
        RETYPE(HWND, NULL_),                    { No parent window      }
        RETYPE(HMENU, NULL_),                   { Use default menu      }
        hInstance,                              { Instance handle       }
        RETYPE(LPSTR, BYLONG(0,NULL_)));        { No additional
                                                  parameter }

        EVAL(ShowWindow(hWindow, cmdShow)); { Send message to update
                                              window }

        UpdateWindow(hWindow);

        { load the accelerator table }

        hAccelTable := LoadAccelerators (hInstance, RETYPE(LPSTR,
                                 ADS 'ACCEL' * Chr(0)));

        WHILE (GetMessage(RETYPE(LPMSG, ADS msg_), NULL_, 0, 0) <> 0) DO
            BEGIN
              if (TranslateAccelerator (hWindow, hAccelTable, RETYPE (
                  LPMSG, ADS msg_)) = 0) then
                  BEGIN
                    EVAL(TranslateMessage(RETYPE(LPMSG, ADS msg_)));
                    EVAL(DispatchMessage(RETYPE(LPMSG, ADS msg_)));
                  END;
```

```
        END;

    endxqq;

END;

END.
```

The module definition file for this program contains the following:

```
NAME    Accel
DESCRIPTION 'Microsoft Windows Pascal Application'

CODE    MOVEABLE
DATA    MOVEABLE MULTIPLE PRELOAD

STUB    'WINSTUB.EXE'

HEAPSIZE    2048
STACKSIZE   4096

EXPORTS
    AccelWndProc
```

The file ACCEL.INC contains the following definitions:

```
int,
short,
long,
unsigned,
FALSE_,
TRUE_,
NULL_,
BYTE,
WORD,
DWORD,
BOOL,
PSTR,
LPSTR,
LPINT,
HANDLE,
HSTR,
HICON,
HDC,
HMENU,
HPEN,
HBRUSH,
HCURSOR,
WNDCLASS,
PWNDCLASS,
```

```
LPWNDCLASS,
HWND,
MSG,
PMSG,
LPMSG,
WM_DESTROY,
WM_COMMAND,
WM_PAINT,
CS_VREDRAW,
CS_HREDRAW,
WS_TILEDWINDOW,
PAINTSTRUCT,
LPPAINTSTRUCT,
CREATESTRUCT,
WHITE_BRUSH,
GetMessage,
TranslateMessage,
DispatchMessage,
DefWindowProc,
PostQuitMessage,
RegisterClass,
CreateWindow,
DestroyWindow,
ShowWindow,
UpdateWindow,
BeginPaint,
EndPaint,
TextOut,
GetStockObject,
LoadCursor,
IDC_ARROW,
LoadIcon,
LoadMenu,
GetDC,
TranslateAccelerator,
LoadAccelerators
```

The only aspect of menu processing still to be discussed is the modification of menu options. Later chapters show in detail how to modify the System menu. For now, simply experiment with the menu concepts presented in this chapter.

PART

II

ADVANCED TECHNIQUES

12

USER INPUT
AND STRING LOADING

All of the applications presented thus far have either simply displayed information on the screen or relied upon the user to make a menu selection. This chapter presents keyboard input in the Windows environment, something that greatly expands the user's ability to interact with Windows applications. It concludes by demonstrating how you can use the resource script file STRINGTABLE statement within your applications.

Keyboard Input

Because of its concurrent nature, Windows must maintain strict control over the input and output of each application. For example, while one window is active, you do not want another window displaying new output or capturing keystrokes entered by the user. Windows specifies which application is to receive keystrokes entered by the user by defining an *input focus*. In general, the input focus is the ownership of the keyboard.

An application must acquire the input focus from Windows. When Windows makes a window active, that window obtains the input focus. Only one Windows application can have the input focus at any given time. Each of the input routines is dependent upon the application having control of the input focus.

The following program is a very simplistic file generator. Upon invocation, the program displays the following:

You can simply start typing text into this window as follows:

```
≣▌                            FILE                            ▐
Simply type in text and the
file generator will echo each line
to the screen,
```

The program echoes each line of text that you enter. If you do not press the ENTER key, the application will wrap the text for you when it reaches column 79 on the screen, as follows:

```
≣▌                            FILE                            ▐
Simply type in text and the
file generator will echo each line
to the screen,

aaaaaaaaaaaaaaaaaaaaaaaaaaaaaaaaaaaaaaaaaaaaaaaaaaaaaaaaaaaaaaaaaaaaaaaaaaaa
aaaaaaa
```

When you reach the bottom of the display screen, the application
scrolls the window up one row, as follows:

When you exit the application by way of the System menu, each line
that you have entered is written to the file TEMP.NTS. The following
C program implements FILE.EXE:

```c
#include "windows.h"
#include <stdio.h>
#include <malloc.h>
#include <string.h>

#define APPLICATION_NAME "FILE"
#define ICON_NAME "FILE"
#define is_printable(x) ((((x) >= 32) && ((x) < 127))  ? 1: 0)
#define BACKSPACE '\b'
#define CARRIAGERETURN '\r'

char string[85];        /* current line buffer */
char *buffer[25];       /* screen contents buffer */
WORD StringIndex;       /* current character index */
WORD FontHeight;
WORD FontWidth;
WORD CurrentLine;       /* current line number */
FILE *fp;               /* file pointer to TEMP.NTS */
RECT wBox;              /* window coordinates */
```

```
long FAR PASCAL FileWndProc(HWND, unsigned, WORD, LONG);

CantOpenFile (hWnd, filename)
 HWND hWnd;
 char filename[];
{
 HDC hDC;
 long int i;

 hDC = GetDC (hWnd);

 TextOut(hDC, 0, 10, (LPSTR) string,
         sprintf(string, "Cannot open file %s", filename));

 for (i = 1; i < 96000; i++) ;  /* delay for message */

 ReleaseDC (hWnd, hDC);
}


GetLen (str)
 char *str;
{
 int count = 0;

 while (is_printable(*str) || *str == '\t')
  {
    str++;
    count++;
  }

 return (count);
}


RedisplayScreen (hWnd)
 HWND hWnd;
{
 HDC hDC;
 WORD i;
 int length;

 hDC = GetDC (hWnd);

  for (i = 0; i <= CurrentLine; i++)
    {
      length = GetLen (buffer[i]);
      TextOut(hDC, 0, i * FontHeight, (LPSTR) buffer[i], length);
    }

 ReleaseDC (hWnd, hDC);
}


void FileCharInfo (hWnd)
 HWND hWnd;
{
 HDC hDC;
 TEXTMETRIC TM;     /* get font sizes */

 hDC = GetDC (hWnd);
 GetTextMetrics (hDC, (TEXTMETRIC FAR *) &TM);
 FontWidth = TM.tmAveCharWidth;
 FontHeight = TM.tmHeight + TM.tmExternalLeading;
 ReleaseDC (hWnd, hDC);
}
```

```
ShuffleBuffer ()
{
 int i, j;

 for (i = 0, j = i + 1; j <= CurrentLine; i++, j++)
    strcpy (buffer[i], buffer[j]);

 *buffer[j] = NULL;
}



PutInString (hWnd, letter)
 HWND hWnd;
 char letter;
{
 HDC hDC;
 char OutLetter[2];

WORD ScreenHeight;

hDC = GetDC (hWnd);

OutLetter[0] = letter;
OutLetter[1] = NULL;

GetWindowRect (hWnd, (LPRECT) &wBox);

if (is_printable(letter))
  {
    string[StringIndex++] = letter;
    TextOut (hDC, FontWidth * (StringIndex - 1),
             (CurrentLine * FontHeight), OutLetter, 1);

    if (StringIndex == 79)
      {
        string[79] = '\n';
        string[80] = NULL;
        StringIndex = 0;
        fputs (string, fp);
        strcpy (buffer[CurrentLine++], string);

        if (CurrentLine*FontHeight > (wBox.bottom - 2 * FontHeight))
          {
            CurrentLine--;
            ShuffleBuffer ();
            ScrollWindow (hWnd, 0, -FontHeight, (LPRECT) NULL, (LPRECT)
              NULL);
            UpdateWindow(hWnd);
          }
      }
    else
      {
        string[StringIndex] = NULL;
        strcpy (buffer[CurrentLine], string);
      }
  }
else if ((letter == BACKSPACE) && (StringIndex > 0))
  {
    OutLetter[0] = ' ';
    StringIndex--;
    TextOut (hDC, FontWidth * StringIndex,
             CurrentLine * FontHeight, OutLetter, 1);
    string[StringIndex] = NULL;
    strcpy (buffer[CurrentLine], string);
  }
```

```
     else if (letter == CARRIAGERETURN)
       {
        string[StringIndex++] = '\n';
        string[StringIndex] = NULL;
        StringIndex = 0;
        fputs (string, fp);
        strcpy (buffer[CurrentLine++], string);

        if (CurrentLine*FontHeight > (wBox.bottom - 2 * FontHeight))
          {
            CurrentLine--;
            ShuffleBuffer ();
            ScrollWindow (hWnd, 0, -FontHeight, (LPRECT) NULL, (LPRECT)
              NULL);
            UpdateWindow(hWnd);
          }
       }

  ReleaseDC (hWnd, hDC);
}


BOOL FileInit(hInstance)
HANDLE hInstance;
{
    NPWNDCLASS  pClass;
    int i;
    char *calloc();

    pClass = (NPWNDCLASS) LocalAlloc(LPTR, sizeof(WNDCLASS));

    pClass->hCursor         = LoadCursor(NULL, IDC_ARROW);
    pClass->hIcon           = LoadIcon(hInstance, (LPSTR) ICON_NAME);
    pClass->lpszClassName   = (LPSTR) APPLICATION_NAME;
    pClass->hbrBackground   = (HBRUSH) GetStockObject(WHITE_BRUSH);
    pClass->hInstance       = hInstance;
    pClass->style           = CS_HREDRAW | CS_VREDRAW;
    pClass->lpfnWndProc     = FileWndProc;

    if (!RegisterClass((LPWNDCLASS)pClass))
        return FALSE;

    LocalFree((HANDLE) pClass); /* return space to heap */

    for (i = 0; i < 25; i++)
      if ((buffer[i] = calloc (85, sizeof(char))) == NULL)
        return FALSE;

    return TRUE;                 /* registration successful */
}


int PASCAL WinMain(hInstance, hPrevInstance, lpszCmdLine, cmdShow)
HANDLE hInstance, hPrevInstance;
LPSTR lpszCmdLine;
int cmdShow;
{
  MSG    message;
  HWND   hWnd;
  HBITMAP hBitmap;
  FILE *fopen();

  if (!hPrevInstance)    /* initialize if this is the first instance */

    {
```

```
   if (!FileInit(hInstance))
      return FALSE;    /* failure to initialize -- return to Windows */
   }
 else
   return FALSE;       /* only allow one version */


 hWnd  =  CreateWindow((LPSTR) APPLICATION_NAME,
                       (LPSTR) APPLICATION_NAME,
                       WS_TILEDWINDOW,
                       0,                   /*  x - ignored for tiled
                                                windows */
                       0,                   /*  y - ignored for tiled
                                                windows */
                       0,                   /*  cx - ignored for tiled
                                                windows */
                       0,                   /*  cy - ignored for tiled
                                                windows */
                       (HWND) NULL,         /* no parent */
                       (HMENU) NULL,        /* use class menu */
                       (HANDLE) hInstance,  /* handle to window
                                                instance */
                       (LPSTR) NULL         /* no parameters to pass
                                                on */

                       );

    ShowWindow(hWnd, cmdShow);              /* Make window visible */
    UpdateWindow(hWnd);

    if ((fp = fopen ("TEMP.NTS", "w")) == NULL)
       CantOpenFile (hWnd, "TEMP.NTS");
    else
       {
       FileCharInfo (hWnd);
       CurrentLine = 0;
       StringIndex = 0;

       /* Poll messages from the event queue and dispatch them */
       while (GetMessage((LPMSG) &message, NULL, 0, 0)) {
           TranslateMessage((LPMSG) &message);
           DispatchMessage((LPMSG) &message);
           }
       if (StringIndex != 0)
        {
         string[StringIndex] = NULL;
         fputs (string, fp);
        }

       fclose (fp);
       }

    return (int) message.wParam; /* return control to Windows */
}

long FAR PASCAL FileWndProc(hWnd, message, wParam, lParam)
HWND hWnd;
unsigned message;
WORD wParam;
LONG lParam;
{
  PAINTSTRUCT ps;

  switch (message) {
    case WM_SYSCOMMAND:          /* disable zoom */
        if (wParam != SC_ZOOM)
          return DefWindowProc(hWnd, message, wParam, lParam);
        break;
```

```
case WM_DESTROY:
    PostQuitMessage(0);   /* tell Windows ready to terminate */
    break;

case WM_CHAR:
  PutInString (hWnd, wParam);
  SetCaretPos (FontWidth * StringIndex, (CurrentLine+1) *
      FontHeight);
  break;

case WM_SETFOCUS:
  RedisplayScreen (hWnd);
  CreateCaret (hWnd, 0, 4, 2);
  SetCaretPos (FontWidth * StringIndex, (CurrentLine+1) *
      FontHeight);
  ShowCaret (hWnd);
  break;

case WM_ACTIVATE:
  SetFocus (hWnd);
  ShowCaret (hWnd);
  break;

case WM_SIZE:
  RedisplayScreen (hWnd);
  break;

case WM_KILLFOCUS:
  HideCaret (hWnd);
  DestroyCaret ();
  break;

default:  /* let Windows process message */
    return DefWindowProc(hWnd, message, wParam, lParam);
    break;
}

return (0L);
}
```

Compared to the programs presented earlier in this text, this one is rather complex. It is important, therefore, to examine each routine in detail. The first, CantOpenFile, is called if the application cannot open the TEMP.NTS file.

```
CantOpenFile (hWnd, filename)
 HWND hWnd;
 char filename[];
{
 HDC hDC;
 long int i;

 hDC = GetDC (hWnd);

 TextOut(hDC, 0, 10, (LPSTR) string,
        sprintf(string, "Cannot open file %s", filename));

 for (i = 1; i < 96000; i++) ;  /* delay for message */

 ReleaseDC (hWnd, hDC);
}
```

This routine simply displays an error message and delays long enough to ensure that the user has read it. Later chapters examine how to use dialog boxes in this scenario.

The second routine, GetLen, returns the length of the string it receives. GetLen was used instead of the library function strlen to count only characters up to a NULL, carriage return, or line feed.

```
GetLen (str)
 char *str;
{
 int count = 0;

 while (is_printable(*str) || *str == '\t')
  {
    str++;
    count++;
  }

 return (count);
}
```

The RedisplayScreen routine is called each time the window obtains the input focus or changes in size. This is done because when the previous application gained control of the screen, it erased the window contents. To ensure that the contents of the window are restored, each character typed by the user is placed in a buffer, an array of 25 character strings capable of storing a screen of information. When the window needs to be restored, the contents of this buffer are displayed on the screen.

```
RedisplayScreen (hWnd)
 HWND hWnd;
{
 HDC hDC;
 WORD i;
 int length;

 hDC = GetDC (hWnd);

  for (i = 0; i <= CurrentLine; i++)
   {
     length = GetLen (buffer[i]);
     TextOut(hDC, 0, i * FontHeight, (LPSTR) buffer[i], length);
   }

 ReleaseDC (hWnd, hDC);
}
```

The routine FileCharInfo is called once to establish the size of the character font being used by FILE.EXE. This information is stored in the global variables FontHeight and FontWidth.

```
void FileCharInfo (hWnd)
 HWND hWnd;
{
 HDC hDC;
 TEXTMETRIC TM;      /* get font sizes */

 hDC = GetDC (hWnd);
 GetTextMetrics (hDC, (TEXTMETRIC FAR *) &TM);
 FontWidth = TM.tmAveCharWidth;
 FontHeight = TM.tmHeight + TM.tmExternalLeading;
 ReleaseDC (hWnd, hDC);
}
```

The next routine, ShuffleBuffer, is called each time the screen is scrolled up one line. This ensures that the screen buffer always contains the lines currently displayed in the window.

```
ShuffleBuffer ()
{
 int i, j;

 for (i = 0, j = i + 1; j <= CurrentLine; i++, j++)
   strcpy (buffer[i], buffer[j]);

 *buffer[j] = NULL;
}
```

Upon examination, the routine appears to have a significant amount of overhead in the series of array copies. However, in the text editor environment, the copies are completed fast enough to be transparent to the user.

The routine PutInString is called each time the user presses a key. If the key represents a displayable character, it is written to the screen and placed into the current line buffer (string). If the character is the seventy-ninth in the current row, the string wraps and the routine writes the previous line to the file TEMP.NTS. Likewise, if the character is a carriage return, the routine writes the line to the file and places the cursor at the start of the next line. Note that the routine checks to see whether the cursor has reached the bottom of the screen. If it has, the routine scrolls the window contents up one line and modifies the screen buffer.

```c
PutInString (hWnd, letter)
 HWND hWnd;
 char letter;
{
 HDC hDC;
 char OutLetter[2];

 WORD ScreenHeight;

 hDC = GetDC (hWnd);

 OutLetter[0] = letter;
 OutLetter[1] = NULL;

 GetWindowRect (hWnd, (LPRECT) &wBox);

 if (is_printable(letter))
   {
     string[StringIndex++] = letter;
     TextOut (hDC, FontWidth * (StringIndex - 1),
             (CurrentLine * FontHeight), OutLetter, 1);

     if (StringIndex == 79)
       {
         string[79] = '\n';
         string[80] = NULL;
         StringIndex = 0;
         fputs (string, fp);
         strcpy (buffer[CurrentLine++], string);

         if (CurrentLine*FontHeight > (wBox.bottom - 2 * FontHeight))
           {
             CurrentLine--;
             ShuffleBuffer ();
             ScrollWindow (hWnd, 0, -FontHeight, (LPRECT) NULL, (LPRECT)
             NULL);
             UpdateWindow(hWnd);
           }
       }
     else
       {
         string[StringIndex] = NULL;
         strcpy (buffer[CurrentLine], string);
       }
   }
 else if ((letter == BACKSPACE) && (StringIndex > 0))
   {
     OutLetter[0] = ' ';
     StringIndex--;
     TextOut (hDC, FontWidth * StringIndex,
             CurrentLine * FontHeight, OutLetter, 1);
     string[StringIndex] = NULL;
     strcpy (buffer[CurrentLine], string);
   }
 else if (letter == CARRIAGERETURN)
   {
     string[StringIndex++] = '\n';
     string[StringIndex] = NULL;
     StringIndex = 0;
     fputs (string, fp);
     strcpy (buffer[CurrentLine++], string);
```

```
  if (CurrentLine*FontHeight > (wBox.bottom - 2 * FontHeight))
    {
      CurrentLine--;
      ShuffleBuffer ();
      ScrollWindow (hWnd, 0, -FontHeight, (LPRECT) NULL, (LPRECT)
        NULL);
      UpdateWindow(hWnd);
    }
  }

 ReleaseDC (hWnd, hDC);
}
```

The FileInit routine performs the window initialization functions
for FILE.EXE. This routine is similar to those presented in previous
chapters. The only difference here is the "for" loop at the bottom of
the routine, which allocates memory for the screen buffer.

```
BOOL FileInit(hInstance)
HANDLE hInstance;
{
    NPWNDCLASS  pClass;
    int i;
    char *calloc();

    pClass = (NPWNDCLASS) LocalAlloc(LPTR, sizeof(WNDCLASS));

    pClass->hCursor        = LoadCursor(NULL, IDC_ARROW);
    pClass->hIcon          = LoadIcon(hInstance, (LPSTR) ICON_NAME);
    pClass->lpszClassName  = (LPSTR) APPLICATION_NAME;
    pClass->hbrBackground  = (HBRUSH) GetStockObject(WHITE_BRUSH);
    pClass->hInstance      = hInstance;
    pClass->style          = CS_HREDRAW | CS_VREDRAW;
    pClass->lpfnWndProc    = FileWndProc;

    if (!RegisterClass((LPWNDCLASS)pClass))
        return FALSE;

    LocalFree((HANDLE) pClass); /* return space to heap */

    for (i = 0; i < 25; i++)
      if ((buffer[i] = calloc (85, sizeof(char))) == NULL)
        return FALSE;

    return TRUE;                /* registration successful */
}
```

The WinMain routine is functionally equivalent to the WinMain
routines presented throughout this text. Note, however, that because
this application opens a file with a specific name, TEMP.NTS, file
corruption could easily occur if a second invocation of the function
were allowed. To disable a second invocation of FILE.EXE, the program simply exits to Windows if a previous instance of the program
exists.

```
int PASCAL WinMain(hInstance, hPrevInstance, lpszCmdLine, cmdShow)
HANDLE hInstance, hPrevInstance;
LPSTR lpszCmdLine;
int cmdShow;
{
  MSG     message;
  HWND    hWnd;
  HBITMAP hBitmap;
  FILE *fopen();

  if (!hPrevInstance)    /* initialize if this is the first instance */
    {
     if (!FileInit(hInstance))
        return FALSE;      /* failure to initialize -- return to Windows */
    }
  else
    return FALSE;         /* only allow one instance */


  hWnd  =  CreateWindow((LPSTR) APPLICATION_NAME,
                        (LPSTR) APPLICATION_NAME,
                        WS_TILEDWINDOW,
                        0,                   /* x - ignored for tiled
                                                windows */
                        0,                   /* y - ignored for tiled
                                                windows */
                        0,                   /* cx - ignored for tiled
                                                windows */
                        0,                   /* cy - ignored for tiled
                                                windows */
                        (HWND) NULL,         /* no parent */
                        (HMENU) NULL,        /* use class menu */
                        (HANDLE) hInstance,  /* handle to window
                                                instance */
                        (LPSTR) NULL         /* no parameters to pass
                                                on */
                        );

    ShowWindow(hWnd, cmdShow);              /* Make window visible */
    UpdateWindow(hWnd);

    if ((fp = fopen ("TEMP.NTS", "w")) == NULL)
        CantOpenFile (hWnd, "TEMP.NTS");
    else
      {
       FileCharInfo (hWnd);
       CurrentLine = 0;
       StringIndex = 0;

       /* Poll messages from the event queue and dispatch them */
       while (GetMessage((LPMSG) &message, NULL, 0, 0)) {
          TranslateMessage((LPMSG) &message);
          DispatchMessage((LPMSG) &message);
          }
       if (StringIndex != 0)
         {
          string[StringIndex] = NULL;
          fputs (string, fp);
         }

       fclose (fp);
      }

    return (int) message.wParam; /* return control to Windows */
}
```

Finally, the routine FileWndProc performs the message processing for FILE.EXE. The messages of specific interest to this application are WM—SETFOCUS and WM—KILLFOCUS, which the window receives when it obtains and loses the input focus, respectively. This routine illustrates the capture of input from the application's System menu. In this case it simply ignores attempts to zoom the window.

```
long FAR PASCAL FileWndProc(hWnd, message, wParam, lParam)
HWND hWnd;
unsigned message;
WORD wParam;
LONG lParam;
{
  PAINTSTRUCT ps;

  switch (message) {
    case WM_SYSCOMMAND:            /* disable zoom */
         if (wParam != SC_ZOOM)
           return DefWindowProc(hWnd, message, wParam, lParam);
         break;

    case WM_DESTROY:
         PostQuitMessage(0);  /* tell Windows ready to terminate */
         break;

    case WM_CHAR:
      PutInString (hWnd, wParam);
      SetCaretPos (FontWidth * StringIndex, (CurrentLine+1) *
         FontHeight);
      break;

    case WM_SETFOCUS:
      RedisplayScreen (hWnd);
      CreateCaret (hWnd, 0, 4, 2);
      SetCaretPos (FontWidth * StringIndex, (CurrentLine+1) *
         FontHeight);
      ShowCaret (hWnd);
      break;

    case WM_ACTIVATE:
      SetFocus (hWnd);
      ShowCaret (hWnd);
      break;

    case WM_SIZE:
      RedisplayScreen (hWnd);
      break;

    case WM_KILLFOCUS:
      HideCaret (hWnd);
      DestroyCaret ();
      break;

    default: /* let Windows process message */
         return DefWindowProc(hWnd, message, wParam, lParam);
         break;
  }

  return (0L);
}
```

The resource script file for the application, FILE.RC, contains the following:

```
#include "windows.h"

FILE BITMAP   file.bmp
FILE ICON     file.ico
```

FILE.DEF, the module definition file, contains the following:

```
NAME     FILE

DESCRIPTION 'Simple Windows Application'

STUB     'WINSTUB.EXE'

CODE     MOVEABLE
DATA     MOVEABLE MULTIPLE

HEAPSIZE  512
STACKSIZE 4096

EXPORTS
    FileWndProc a1
```

Use the following commands to produce FILE.EXE:

```
cl -d -c -AS -Gsw -Oas -Zpe -FPa -FoFILE.OBJ FILE.C

rc -r FILE.RC

link4 FILE,/a:16,,slibw,FILE.DEF

rc FILE.RES
```

Experiment with this program to enhance its functional use; you will become much more conversant with Windows messages and screen updates.

String Loading

Chapter 7 examined the STRINGTABLE statement for resource script files. The general form of this statement is

STRINGTABLE
begin
  definitions
end

Consider the following resource script file, STRLOAD.RC:

```
#include "windows.h"
#include "strload.h"

STRLOAD ICON    strload.ico

STRINGTABLE
begin
  MESSAGE "Successful string load"
  APP_NAME "STRLOAD"
end
```

This file defines two string table entries. The numeric values for each entry are defined in the file STRLOAD.H, as follows:

```
#define MESSAGE 1
#define APP_NAME 2
```

If the application includes the file STRLOAD.H, like this:

```
#include "windows.h"
#include "strload.h"
```

it can later use the LoadString routine to obtain the actual string definitions from the resource script file, as follows:

```
LoadString (hInstance, MESSAGE, (LPSTR) display_message, 255);
LoadString (hInstance, APP_NAME, (LPSTR) application_name, 255);
```

Let's look at another program, STRLOAD.EXE. Upon invocation, the program displays the following:

```
≡  ▇▇▇▇▇▇▇▇▇▇▇▇▇▇▇▇▇▇▇▇ STRLOAD ▇▇▇▇▇▇▇▇▇▇▇▇▇▇▇▇▇▇▇▇  ᴸ
```

Successful string load

The window caption entry and the message displayed in the window are simply the values loaded from the resource script file. The following C program implements STRLOAD.EXE:

```
#include "windows.h"
#include "strload.h"

long FAR PASCAL StrLoadWndProc(HWND, unsigned, WORD, LONG);

char display_message[255];
char application_name[255];

void StrLoadPaint(hDC)
HDC hDC;
{

  TextOut(hDC, 0, 10, (LPSTR) display_message, strlen
    (display_message));

}


BOOL StrLoadInit(hInstance)
HANDLE hInstance;
{
    NPWNDCLASS  pClass;

    pClass = (NPWNDCLASS) LocalAlloc(LPTR, sizeof(WNDCLASS));

    pClass->hCursor       = LoadCursor(NULL, IDC_ARROW);
    pClass->hIcon         = LoadIcon(hInstance, (LPSTR)
                            application_name);
    pClass->lpszClassName = (LPSTR) application_name;
    pClass->hbrBackground = (HBRUSH) GetStockObject(WHITE_BRUSH);
    pClass->hInstance     = hInstance;
    pClass->style         = CS_HREDRAW | CS_VREDRAW;
    pClass->lpfnWndProc   = StrLoadWndProc;

    if (!RegisterClass((LPWNDCLASS)pClass))
        return FALSE;

    LocalFree((HANDLE) pClass); /* return space to heap */
    return TRUE;                /* registration successful */
}
```

```
int PASCAL WinMain(hInstance, hPrevInstance, lpszCmdLine, cmdShow)
HANDLE hInstance, hPrevInstance;
LPSTR lpszCmdLine;
int cmdShow;
{
  MSG    message;
  HWND   hWnd;

  LoadString (hInstance, MESSAGE, (LPSTR) display_message, 255);

  LoadString (hInstance, APP_NAME, (LPSTR) application_name, 255);

  if (!hPrevInstance)    /* initialize if this is the first instance */
    if (!StrLoadInit(hInstance))
       return FALSE;     /* failure to initialize -- return to Windows */

  hWnd = CreateWindow((LPSTR) application_name,
                      (LPSTR) application_name,
                      WS_TILEDWINDOW,
                      0,                    /*  x - ignored for tiled
                                                windows */
                      0,                    /*  y - ignored for tiled
                                                windows */
                      0,                    /*  cx - ignored for tiled
                                                windows */
                      0,                    /*  cy - ignored for tiled
                                                windows */
                      (HWND) NULL,          /* no parent */
                      (HMENU) NULL,         /* use class menu */
                      (HANDLE) hInstance,   /* handle to window
                                               instance */
                      (LPSTR) NULL          /* no parameters to pass
                                               on */
                      );

    ShowWindow(hWnd, cmdShow);                /* Make window visible */
    UpdateWindow(hWnd);

    /* Poll messages from the event queue and dispatch them */
    while (GetMessage((LPMSG) &message, NULL, 0, 0)) {
        TranslateMessage((LPMSG) &message);
        DispatchMessage((LPMSG) &message);
        }

    return (int) message.wParam;  /* return control to Windows */
}


long FAR PASCAL StrLoadWndProc(hWnd, message, wParam, lParam)
HWND hWnd;
unsigned message;
WORD wParam;
LONG lParam;
{
  PAINTSTRUCT ps;

  switch (message) {
    case WM_DESTROY:
        PostQuitMessage(0);  /* tell Windows ready to terminate */
        break;

    case WM_PAINT:
        BeginPaint(hWnd, (LPPAINTSTRUCT) &ps);
        StrLoadPaint(ps.hdc);
        EndPaint(hWnd, (LPPAINTSTRUCT) &ps);
```

```
        break;

    default:  /* let Windows process message */
        return DefWindowProc(hWnd, message, wParam, lParam);
        break;
    }
  return (0L);
}
```

The module definition file for this program, STRLOAD.DEF, contains the following:

```
NAME     TEST

DESCRIPTION 'Simple Windows Application'

STUB     'WINSTUB.EXE'

CODE     MOVEABLE
DATA     MOVEABLE MULTIPLE

HEAPSIZE  512
STACKSIZE 4096

EXPORTS
    StrLoadWndProc a1
```

Compile and link the program as follows:

```
cl -d -c -AS -Gsw -Oas -Zpe -FPa -FoSTRLOAD.OBJ STRLOAD.C

link4 STRLOAD,/a:16,,SLIBW,STRLOAD.DEF

rc -r STRLOAD.RC

rc STRLOAD.RES STRLOAD.EXE
```

When you place string constants within your resource script file, program modification becomes much simpler.

CHAPTER

13

USING
DIALOG BOXES

Chapter 4 examined the dialog box editor and its use in creating dialog boxes for Windows applications. When a Windows application needs to converse with the user, it normally does so by way of a dialog box. The Windows Control Panel dialog is an example.

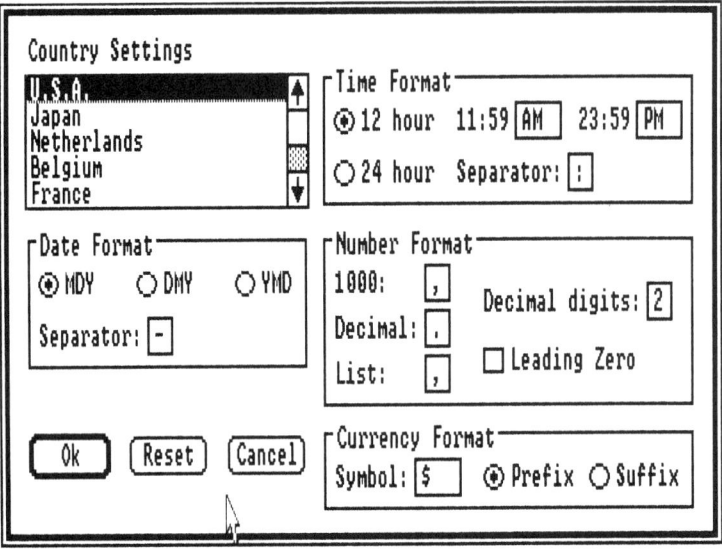

This chapter examines dialog box definitions within your resource script file and tells how to create and display an About dialog box, include an option in the System menu, access button controls from your Windows applications programs, access EDITTEXT controls within the dialog box, and use Windows default messages via the MessageBox function.

Dialog Box Overview

Windows programming applications use dialog boxes to obtain input from or display output to the user. A dialog box can be either modal or modeless. A modal dialog box temporarily suspends execution of the application until the user responds to a message. Such a box requires the user to respond to a prompt or terminate processing. A modeless dialog box, however, allows the user to continue the processing of the current application. Windows allows the user to move modeless dialog boxes out of the way so that processing can continue

unobscured. The style guide in the Windows Software Development
Kit recommends the following characteristics for dialog box display:

☐ Do not use menu bars in dialog boxes.

☐ Indicate unavailable system menu options by graying (or removing) them.

☐ Place a framed border around modal dialog boxes.

☐ Provide a System menu and title bar for all modeless dialog
boxes. Place a caption within the title bar.

☐ For modeless dialog boxes, make all System menu options (except
Move and Close) unavailable.

The following programs illustrate the use of several dialog boxes.

About

The Windows application presented in this section allows you to display the About dialog box shown here:

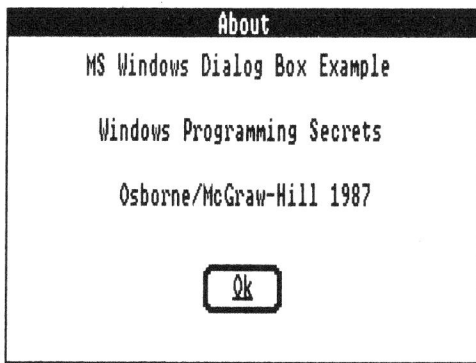

Upon invocation, the System menu for the application displays the following:

Note the About option at the bottom of the menu. The following C program implements ABOUT.EXE:

```
#include "windows.h"
#include "about.h"

#define APPLICATION_NAME "ABOUT"
#define ICON_NAME "ABOUT_ICON"

FARPROC lpprocAbout;

long FAR PASCAL AboutWndProc(HWND, unsigned, WORD, LONG);

static HANDLE hInst;

BOOL FAR PASCAL DlgAboutBox(hDlg, message, wParam, lParam)
 HWND hDlg;
 unsigned message;
 WORD wParam;
 LONG lParam;
{
 switch (message)
   {
   case WM_COMMAND:
      EndDialog (hDlg, TRUE);
      return (TRUE);
      break;

   case WM_INITDIALOG:
      return (TRUE);
      break;

   default:
      return (FALSE);
      break;
   }
}

void AboutPaint(hWnd, hDC)
HWND hWnd;
HDC hDC;
{
   char message[255];
```

```
    TextOut(hDC, 0, 10, (LPSTR) message,
        sprintf(message, "Successful WINDOWS Dialog Box Program!"));
}


BOOL AboutInit(hInstance)
HANDLE hInstance;
{
    NPWNDCLASS  pClass;

    pClass = (NPWNDCLASS) LocalAlloc(LPTR, sizeof(WNDCLASS));
    pClass->hCursor         = LoadCursor(NULL, IDC_ARROW);
    pClass->hIcon           = LoadIcon(hInstance, (LPSTR) ICON_NAME);
    pClass->lpszClassName   = (LPSTR) APPLICATION_NAME;
    pClass->hbrBackground   = (HBRUSH) GetStockObject(WHITE_BRUSH);
    pClass->hInstance       = hInstance;
    pClass->style           = CS_HREDRAW | CS_VREDRAW;
    pClass->lpfnWndProc     = AboutWndProc;

    if (!RegisterClass((LPWNDCLASS)pClass))
        return FALSE;

    LocalFree((HANDLE) pClass); /* return space to heap */
    return TRUE;                /* registration successful */
}


int PASCAL WinMain(hInstance, hPrevInstance, lpszCmdLine, cmdShow)
HANDLE hInstance, hPrevInstance;
LPSTR lpszCmdLine;
int cmdShow;
{
  MSG    message;
  HWND   hWnd;
  HMENU  hMenu;


  if (!hPrevInstance)   /* initialize if this is the first instance */
    if (!AboutInit(hInstance))
        return FALSE;   /* failure to initialize -- return to Windows */

  hWnd = CreateWindow((LPSTR) APPLICATION_NAME,
                        (LPSTR) APPLICATION_NAME,
                        WS_TILEDWINDOW,
                        0,                  /* x - ignored for tiled
                                               windows */
                        0,                  /* y - ignored for tiled
                                               windows */
                        0,                  /* cx - ignored for tiled
                                               windows */
                        0,                  /* cy - ignored for tiled
                                               windows */
                        (HWND) NULL,        /* no parent */
                        (HMENU) NULL,       /* use class menu */
                        (HANDLE) hInstance, /* handle to window
                                               instance */
                        (LPSTR) NULL        /* no parameters to pass
                                               on */
                        );

    lpprocAbout = MakeProcInstance ((FARPROC) DlgAboutBox, hInstance);
    hInst = hInstance;
    hMenu = GetSystemMenu (hWnd, FALSE);
    ChangeMenu (hMenu, 0, (LPSTR) "About", ABOUT, MF_APPEND |
                        MF_STRING);
```

```
     ShowWindow(hWnd, cmdShow);                    /* Make window visible */
     UpdateWindow(hWnd);

     /* Poll messages from the event queue and dispatch them */
     while (GetMessage((LPMSG) &message, NULL, 0, 0)) {
         TranslateMessage((LPMSG) &message);
         DispatchMessage((LPMSG) &message);
         }

     return (int) message.wParam;  /* return control to Windows */
}


long FAR PASCAL AboutWndProc(hWnd, message, wParam, lParam)
HWND hWnd;
unsigned message;
WORD wParam;
LONG lParam;
{
   PAINTSTRUCT ps;

   switch (message) {
     case WM_SYSCOMMAND:
         if (wParam == ABOUT)
           DialogBox (hInst, (LPSTR) "ABOUT_BOX", hWnd, lpprocAbout);
         else
            return DefWindowProc(hWnd, message, wParam, lParam);
         break;

     case WM_DESTROY:
         PostQuitMessage(0);   /* tell Windows ready to terminate */
         break;

     case WM_PAINT:
         BeginPaint(hWnd, (LPPAINTSTRUCT) &ps);
         AboutPaint(hWnd, ps.hdc);
         EndPaint(hWnd, (LPPAINTSTRUCT) &ps);
         break;

     default:  /* let Windows process message */
         return DefWindowProc(hWnd, message, wParam, lParam);
         break;
     }

   return (0L);
}
```

A close examination of the program reveals that it is very similar to the first Windows programming application presented in this text. It is the dialog box message handler. A new function, DlgAboutBox, has been added. Within an application a dialog box is treated as the functional equivalent of a window. Dialog boxes, like windows, require a procedure that handles the messages sent to and from the dialog box. The function of this routine will be examined in detail after an overview of the entire program is given.

The routines AboutPaint, AboutInit, WinMain, and AboutWnd-Proc perform the same functions as their counterparts in other Windows applications. A few differences are examined here. First, note the following statements in the WinMain procedure:

```
hMenu = GetSystemMenu (hWnd, FALSE);
ChangeMenu (hMenu, 0, (LPSTR) "About", ABOUT, MF_APPEND |
                                       MF_STRING);
```

The System menu for ABOUT.EXE contains an option for About. The first statement retrieves a handle to the System menu for the application. The call to ChangeMenu then adds the About option to the menu. In addition, note the following statement:

```
hInst = hInstance;
```

This statement stores the value of the process instance in the global variable hInst, which is used later for dialog box processing. Because of the strictly defined Windows procedure interface, global variables are often required to complete difficult programming applications. Do not, however, forget the rules of structured programming or abuse global variables.

The following statement defines the default procedure for processing dialog box messages:

```
lpprocAbout = MakeProcInstance ((FARPROC) DlgAboutBox, hInstance);
```

Note also the processing of the WM—SYSMESSAGES in AboutWndProc:

```
case WM_SYSCOMMAND:
    if (wParam == ABOUT)
      DialogBox (hInst, (LPSTR) "ABOUT_BOX", hWnd, lpprocAbout);
    else
       return DefWindowProc(hWnd, message, wParam, lParam);
    break;
```

You have already seen that application menus return the WM — COMMAND message. In a similar manner, the System menu for this Windows application returns WM—SYSCOMMAND. In this case, the only concern is the processing of the About option. Other options are simply passed to DefWindowProc.

If the About option is selected, the routine invokes the Windows function DialogBox, which creates a model dialog box based upon the template defined by ABOUT—BOX. The application will later use this dialog box to display the information about the program.

Now for a look at the new routine, DlgAboutBox:

```
BOOL FAR PASCAL DlgAboutBox(hDlg, message, wParam, lParam)
 HWND hDlg;
 unsigned message;
 WORD wParam;
 LONG lParam;
{
 switch (message)
  {
    case WM_COMMAND:
       EndDialog (hDlg, TRUE);
       return (TRUE);
       break;

    case WM_INITDIALOG:
       return (TRUE);
       break;

    default:
       return (FALSE);
       break;
  }
}
```

The routine is simply a message processor. Each time a control is modified within a dialog box, the WM—COMMAND message is returned to the dialog box. At this point you would normally poll the values of each control to see which values have changed and alter your processing accordingly. In this case, however, the only control is an Ok button. Once the user selects it, the application terminates the dialog box and frees up the memory it consumed.

Each time Windows displays a dialog box, it sends a WM — INITDIALOG message to the dialog box. Again, you would normally assign each control its default value at this point. In this case, however, there are no controls to initialize, and so the procedure simply returns control to the calling routine.

The include file ABOUT.H contains the following:

```
#define ABOUT 1
#define DLGOK 2
```

The following resource script file is used for ABOUT.EXE:

```
#include "windows.h"
#include "about.h"

ABOUT_ICON ICON     about.ico

ABOUT_BOX DIALOG 10, 10, 180, 100
STYLE WS_DLGFRAME | WS_POPUP
CAPTION "About'
begin
   CTEXT "MS Windows Dialog Box Example"    -1, 25, 5, 125, 15
   CTEXT "Windows Programming Secrets"      r1, 26, 25, 125, 15
   CTEXT "Osborne/McGraw-Hill 1987"         -1, 28, 45, 125, 15
   DEFPUSHBUTTON  "Ok"                      DLGOK, 75, 70, 30, 15
                                            WS_GROUP
end
```

The module definition file contains the following:

```
NAME      ABOUT

DESCRIPTION 'Windows Dialog Box Application'

STUB      'WINSTUB.EXE'

CODE      MOVEABLE
DATA      MOVEABLE MULTIPLE

HEAPSIZE  512
STACKSIZE 4096

EXPORTS
   AboutWndProc a1
```

Although ABOUT.EXE is functionally correct, the following program, ABOUT2.EXE, dresses up the application. First, the program separates the About option from the default system options on the System menu, as follows:

Next, the program includes the application icon in the dialog box, as follows:

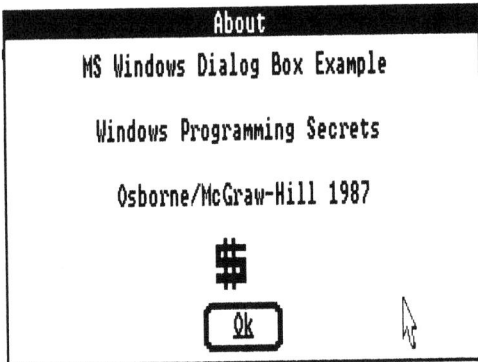

Each of these modifications was simple to implement. The first required an additional statement in WinMain:

```
hMenu = GetSystemMenu (hWnd, FALSE);
ChangeMenu (hMenu, 0, NULL, -1, MF_APPEND | MF_SEPARATOR);
ChangeMenu (hMenu, 0, (LPSTR) "About", ABOUT, MF_APPEND |
                                            MF_STRING);
```

The second was simply the following change to the resource script file:

```
#include "windows.h"
#include "about.h"

ABOUT_ICON ICON     about.ico

ABOUT_BOX DIALOG 10, 10, 180, 100
STYLE WS_DLGFRAME | WS_POPUP
CAPTION "About"
begin
   CTEXT "MS Windows Dialog Box Example"  -1, 25, 5, 125, 15
   CTEXT "Windows Programming Secrets"    -1, 26, 25, 125, 15
   CTEXT "Osborne/McGraw-Hill 1987"       -1, 28, 45, 125, 15
   DEFPUSHBUTTON  "Ok"                    DLGOK, 75, 82, 30, 15,
                                          WS_GROUP

   ICON  "ABOUT_ICON" -1, 78, 62, 0, 0
end
```

The program is compiled and linked as follows:

```
cl -d -c -AS -Gsw -Oas -Zpe -FPa -FoABOUT2.obj ABOUT2.C

link4 ABOUT2,/a:16,,slibw,ABOUT.DEF

rc -r ABOUT.RC

rc ABOUT.RES ABOUT.EXE
```

GETDRIVE

The Windows application program GETDRIVE.EXE displays the
following dialog box:

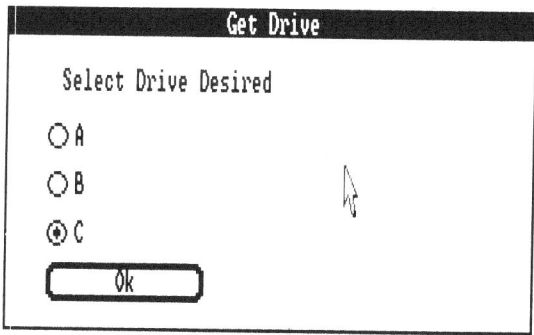

The user selects a disk drive by choosing one of the three radio buttons. By default, each time the dialog box is displayed, drive C is highlighted. The user can toggle through the three available drives to select the desired one. Based upon the user's selection, the variable desired—drive is set to the associated drive number.

The following C program implements GETDRIVE.EXE:

```
#include "windows.h"
#include "getdrive.h"

#define APPLICATION_NAME "GETDRIVE"
#define ICON_NAME "GDR_ICO"

FARPROC lpprocGetDrive;

long FAR PASCAL GetDriveWndProc(HWND, unsigned, WORD, LONG);

static HANDLE hInst;
int desired_drive = 3;

BOOL FAR PASCAL DlgGetDriveBox(hDlg, message, wParam, lParam)
 HWND hDlg;
 unsigned message;
 WORD wParam;
 LONG lParam;
{
 switch (message)
  {
   case WM_COMMAND:
     if (wParam == OK_PUSH)
       EndDialog (hDlg, TRUE);
     else if (wParam == DRIVE_A)
       {
       CheckDlgButton (hDlg, DRIVE_A, 1);
       CheckDlgButton (hDlg, DRIVE_B, 0);
       CheckDlgButton (hDlg, DRIVE_C, 0);
       desired_drive = 0;
       }
     else if (wParam == DRIVE_B)
       {
       CheckDlgButton (hDlg, DRIVE_B, 1);
       CheckDlgButton (hDlg, DRIVE_A, 0);
       CheckDlgButton (hDlg, DRIVE_C, 0);
       desired_drive = 1;
       }
     else if (wParam == DRIVE_C)
       {
       CheckDlgButton (hDlg, DRIVE_C, 1);
       CheckDlgButton (hDlg, DRIVE_A, 0);
       CheckDlgButton (hDlg, DRIVE_B, 0);
       desired_drive = 2;
       }
     return (TRUE);
     break;

   case WM_INITDIALOG:
     CheckDlgButton (hDlg, DRIVE_C, 1);
     return (TRUE);
     break;
```

```
   default:
      return (FALSE);
      break;
  }
}


BOOL GetDriveInit(hInstance)
HANDLE hInstance;
{
    NPWNDCLASS  pClass;

    pClass = (NPWNDCLASS) LocalAlloc(LPTR, sizeof(WNDCLASS));

    pClass->hCursor        = LoadCursor(NULL, IDC_ARROW);
    pClass->hIcon          = LoadIcon(hInstance, (LPSTR) ICON_NAME);
    pClass->lpszClassName  = (LPSTR) APPLICATION_NAME;
    pClass->lpszMenuName   = (LPSTR) "GDR_MENU";
    pClass->hbrBackground  = (HBRUSH) GetStockObject(WHITE_BRUSH);
    pClass->hInstance      = hInstance;
    pClass->style          = CS_HREDRAW | CS_VREDRAW;
    pClass->lpfnWndProc    = GetDriveWndProc;

    if (!RegisterClass((LPWNDCLASS)pClass))
        return FALSE;

    LocalFree((HANDLE) pClass); /* return space to heap */
    return TRUE;                /* registration successful */
}


int PASCAL WinMain(hInstance, hPrevInstance, lpszCmdLine, cmdShow)
HANDLE hInstance, hPrevInstance;
LPSTR lpszCmdLine;
int cmdShow;
{
  MSG    message;
  HWND   hWnd;

  if (!hPrevInstance)   /* initialize if this is the first instance */
    if (!GetDriveInit(hInstance))
       return FALSE;    /* failure to initialize -- return to Windows */

  hWnd  =  CreateWindow((LPSTR) APPLICATION_NAME,
                        (LPSTR) APPLICATION_NAME,
                        WS_TILEDWINDOW,
                        0,              /*  x - ignored for tiled
                                            windows */
                        0,              /*  y - ignored for tiled
                                            windows */
                        0,              /*  cx - ignored for tiled
                                            windows */
                        0,              /*  cy - ignored for tiled
                                            windows */
                        (HWND) NULL,    /* no parent */
                        (HMENU) NULL,   /* use class menu */
                        (HANDLE) hInstance, /* handle to window
                                            instance */
                        (LPSTR) NULL    /* no parameters to pass
                                            on */
                        );

    lpprocGetDrive = MakeProcInstance ((FARPROC) DlgGetDriveBox,
                                        hInstance);
```

```
    hInst = hInstance;

    ShowWindow(hWnd, cmdShow);                    /* Make window visible */
    UpdateWindow(hWnd);

    /* Poll messages from the event queue and dispatch them */
    while (GetMessage((LPMSG) &message, NULL, 0, 0)) {
        TranslateMessage((LPMSG) &message);
        DispatchMessage((LPMSG) &message);
        }

    return (int) message.wParam;  /* return control to Windows */
}


long FAR PASCAL GetDriveWndProc(hWnd, message, wParam, lParam)
HWND hWnd;
unsigned message;
WORD wParam;
LONG lParam;
{
  switch (message) {
    case WM_COMMAND:
         DialogBox (hInst, (LPSTR) "GDR_DLG", hWnd, lpprocGetDrive);
         break;

    case WM_DESTROY:
         PostQuitMessage(0);  /* tell Windows ready to terminate */
         break;

    default: /* let Windows process message */
         return DefWindowProc(hWnd, message, wParam, lParam);
         break;
    }
  return (0L);
}
```

The majority of the processing performed by GETDRIVE.EXE is in the dialog message-processing procedure DlgGetDriveBox, shown here:

```
BOOL FAR PASCAL DlgGetDriveBox(hDlg, message, wParam, lParam)
 HWND hDlg;
 unsigned message;
 WORD wParam;
 LONG lParam;
{
 switch (message)
  {
   case WM_COMMAND:
     if (wParam == OK_PUSH)
       EndDialog (hDlg, TRUE);
     else if (wParam == DRIVE_A)
       {
       CheckDlgButton (hDlg, DRIVE_A, 1);
       CheckDlgButton (hDlg, DRIVE_B, 0);
       CheckDlgButton (hDlg, DRIVE_C, 0);
       desired_drive = 0;
       }
```

```
   else if (wParam == DRIVE_B)
    {
     CheckDlgButton (hDlg, DRIVE_B, 1);
     CheckDlgButton (hDlg, DRIVE_A, 0);
     CheckDlgButton (hDlg, DRIVE_C, 0);
     desired_drive = 1;
    }
   else if (wParam == DRIVE_C)
    {
     CheckDlgButton (hDlg, DRIVE_C, 1);
     CheckDlgButton (hDlg, DRIVE_A, 0);
     CheckDlgButton (hDlg, DRIVE_B, 0);
     desired_drive = 2;
    }
   return (TRUE);
   break;

 case WM_INITDIALOG:
   CheckDlgButton (hDlg, DRIVE_C, 1);
   return (TRUE);
   break;

 default:
   return (FALSE);
   break;
 }
}
```

Each time the user modifies a control on the dialog box, the WM—
COMMAND message is sent to DlgGetDriveBox. The wParam field
of the message contains the control identification value that was
affected. In this case, wParam can contain only one of four possible
values. If wParam is equal to a disk-drive radio button, the routine
sets the variable desired—drive to the selected drive. If the user has
selected the Ok button, the dialog box is removed since the desired
drive has been chosen.

The include file, GETDRIVE.H, contains the following definitions:

```
#define OK_PUSH    1
#define DRIVE_A    10
#define DRIVE_B    20
#define DRIVE_C    30
```

The contents of the resource script file, GETDRIVE.RC, are as
follows:

```
#include "windows.h"
#include "getdrive.h"

GDR_ICO ICON    GETDRIVE.ICO

GDR_MENU menu
begin
   MENUITEM "Select Drive", 1
end

GDR_DLG  DIALOG 10, 10, 200, 90
STYLE WS_POPUP | WS_BORDER
CAPTION "Get Drive"
BEGIN
   CTEXT "Select Drive Desired", 1, 10, 10, 100, 12
   RADIOBUTTON "A", DRIVE_A, 15, 25, 60, 12
   RADIOBUTTON "B", DRIVE_B, 15, 40, 60, 12
   RADIOBUTTON "C", DRIVE_C, 15, 55, 60, 12
   DEFPUSHBUTTON "Ok", OK_PUSH, 15, 70, 60, 12
END
```

GETDRIVE.DEF consists of the following:

```
NAME    GETDRIVE

DESCRIPTION 'Simple Windows Dialog Application'

STUB    'WINSTUB.EXE'

CODE    MOVEABLE
DATA    MOVEABLE MULTIPLE

HEAPSIZE  512
STACKSIZE 4096

EXPORTS
   GetDriveWndProc @1
```

GETNAME

The program presented in this section illustrates the use of an
EDITTEXT control box to obtain the user's name. Upon invocation,
the program displays the following:

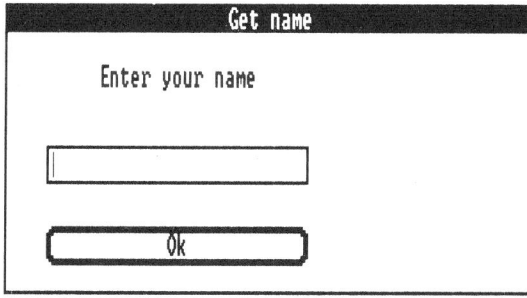

Selection of the Change name menu option causes the following dialog box to be displayed:

The user types in a name and then selects the Ok button.
The following C program implements GETNAME.EXE:

```c
#include "windows.h"
#include "getname.h"

#define APPLICATION_NAME "GETNAME"
#define ICON_NAME "GETNAME_ICO"

FARPROC lpprocGetName;

long FAR PASCAL GetNameWndProc(HWND, unsigned, WORD, LONG);

static HANDLE hInst;
char name_buffer[255];

BOOL FAR PASCAL DlgGetNameBox(hDlg, message, wParam, lParam)
 HWND hDlg;
 unsigned message;
 WORD wParam;
 LONG lParam;
{
 switch (message)
  {
    case WM_COMMAND:
      if (wParam == OK_PUSH)
        {
          GetDlgItemText (hDlg, NAME, (LPSTR) name_buffer, 255);
          EndDialog (hDlg, TRUE);
        }
      return (TRUE);
      break;

    case WM_INITDIALOG:
      SetDlgItemText (hDlg, NAME, (LPSTR) name_buffer);
      return (TRUE);
      break;

    default:
      return (FALSE);
      break;
  }
}


BOOL GetNameInit(hInstance)
HANDLE hInstance;
{
    NPWNDCLASS pClass;

    pClass = (NPWNDCLASS) LocalAlloc(LPTR, sizeof(WNDCLASS));

    pClass->hCursor        = LoadCursor(NULL, IDC_ARROW);
    pClass->hIcon          = LoadIcon(hInstance, (LPSTR) ICON_NAME);
    pClass->lpszClassName  = (LPSTR) APPLICATION_NAME;
    pClass->lpszMenuName   = (LPSTR) "GETNAME_MENU";
    pClass->hbrBackground  = (HBRUSH) GetStockObject(WHITE_BRUSH);
    pClass->hInstance      = hInstance;
    pClass->style          = CS_HREDRAW | CS_VREDRAW;
    pClass->lpfnWndProc    = GetNameWndProc;

    if (!RegisterClass((LPWNDCLASS)pClass))
        return FALSE;
```

```
    LocalFree((HANDLE) pClass); /* return space to heap */
    return TRUE;                 /* registration successful */
}


int PASCAL WinMain(hInstance, hPrevInstance, lpszCmdLine, cmdShow)
HANDLE hInstance, hPrevInstance;
LPSTR lpszCmdLine;
int cmdShow;
{
  MSG    message;
  HWND   hWnd;

  if (!hPrevInstance)    /* initialize if this is the first instance */
    if (!GetNameInit(hInstance))
       return FALSE;      /* failure to initialize -- return to
                             Windows */

  hWnd =  CreateWindow((LPSTR) APPLICATION_NAME,
                       (LPSTR) APPLICATION_NAME,
                       WS_TILEDWINDOW,
                       0,                    /* x - ignored for tiled
                                                windows */
                       0,                    /* y - ignored for tiled
                                                windows */
                       0,                    /* cx - ignored for tiled
                                                windows */
                       0,                    /* cy - ignored for tiled
                                                windows */
                       (HWND) NULL,          /* no parent */
                       (HMENU) NULL,         /* use class menu */
                       (HANDLE) hInstance,   /* handle to window
                                                instance */
                       (LPSTR) NULL          /* no parameters to pass
                                                on */
                       );

    lpprocGetName = MakeProcInstance ((FARPROC) DlgGetNameBox,
                                  hInstance);
    hInst = hInstance;

    ShowWindow(hWnd, cmdShow);                /* Make window visible */
    UpdateWindow(hWnd);


    /* Poll messages from the event queue and dispatch them */
    while (GetMessage((LPMSG) &message, NULL, 0, 0)) {

        TranslateMessage((LPMSG) &message);
        DispatchMessage((LPMSG) &message);
        }


    return (int) message.wParam;  /* return control to Windows */
}


long FAR PASCAL GetNameWndProc(hWnd, message, wParam, lParam)
HWND hWnd;
unsigned message;
WORD wParam;
LONG lParam;
{
  switch (message) {
    case WM_COMMAND:
```

```
        DialogBox (hInst, (LPSTR) "GETNAME_DLG", hWnd,
                  lpprocGetName);
        break;

    case WM_DESTROY:
        PostQuitMessage(0);   /* tell Windows ready to terminate */
        break;

    default:  /* let Windows process message */
        return DefWindowProc(hWnd, message, wParam, lParam);
        break;
    }

  return (0L);
}
```

Two Windows routines are used within the dialog message-processing routine, DlgGetNameBox, to set and retrieve the value contained in the EDITTEXT control.

```
BOOL FAR PASCAL DlgGetNameBox(hDlg, message, wParam, lParam)
HWND hDlg;
unsigned message;
WORD wParam;
LONG lParam;
{
 switch (message)
   {
    case WM_COMMAND:
      if (wParam == OK_PUSH)
        {
          GetDlgItemText (hDlg, NAME, (LPSTR) name_buffer, 255);
          EndDialog (hDlg, TRUE);
        }
      return (TRUE);
      break;

    case WM_INITDIALOG:
      SetDlgItemText (hDlg, NAME, (LPSTR) name_buffer);
      return (TRUE);
      break;

    default:
      return (FALSE);
      break;
   }
}
```

The first, GetDlgItemText, obtains the value currently in the EDIT-TEXT control. The second, SetDlgItemText, assigns a value to the control. EDITTEXT controls are used extensively throughout Windows. As you can see, their use is quite straightforward.

The file GETNAME.H contains the following:

```
#define OK_PUSH 1
#define NAME 2
```

The file GETDRIVE.RC contains

```
#include "windows.h"
#include "getname.h"

GETNAME ICON     GETDRIVE.ICO

GETNAME_MENU menu
begin
    MENUITEM "Change name", 1
end

GETNAME_DLG  DIALOG 10, 10, 200, 80
STYLE WS_POPUP | WS_BORDER
CAPTION "Get name"
BEGIN
  CTEXT "Enter your name", 1, 15, 10, 100, 12
  EDITTEXT NAME, 15, 35, 100, 12
  DEFPUSHBUTTON "Ok", OK_PUSH, 15, 60, 100, 12
END
```

And the contents of GETDRIVE.DEF are as follows:

```
NAME     GETNAME

DESCRIPTION 'Windows Dialog Edit Application'

STUB     'WINSTUB.EXE'

CODE     MOVEABLE
DATA     MOVEABLE MULTIPLE

HEAPSIZE  512
STACKSIZE 4096

EXPORTS
    GetNameWndProc @1
```

Message Box

A message box is a predefined Windows dialog box that an application can use to display critical messages. Message boxes are modal dialog boxes that require the user to respond before processing can continue. Windows applications use the MessageBox procedure as follows:

MessageBox (hWnd, lpMessage, lpCaption, wType): result

where the following is true:

hWnd	The handle to the window that owns the message box.
lpMessage	A long pointer to the message to be displayed within the message box.
lpCaption	A long pointer to the message box caption.
wType	An integer specifying the contents of the message box.

The integer can be a combination of the following values:

MB―OK	Ok button
MB―OKCANCEL	Ok and Cancel buttons
MB―RETRYCANCEL	Retry and Cancel buttons
MB―ABORTRETRYIGNORE	Abort, Retry, Ignore buttons
MB―YESNO	Yes and No buttons
MB―YESNOCANCEL	Yes, No, Cancel buttons
MB―ICONHAND	Hand icon in message box
MB―ICONQUESTION	Question mark icon in message box
MB―ICONEXCLAMATION	Exclamation mark icon in message box
MB―ICONASTERISK	Asterisk icon in message box

MB_DEFBUTTON1	Button 1 is the default
MB_DEFBUTTON2	Button 2 is the default
MB_DEFBUTTON3	Button 3 is the default
MB_APPLMODAL	Other Windows applications are active
MB_SYSTEMMODAL	No applications can continue
result	The result of the user response. It can be one of the following: IDOK IDCANCEL IDABORT IDRETRY IDIGNORE IDYES IDNO

The following message boxes illustrate some of these options:

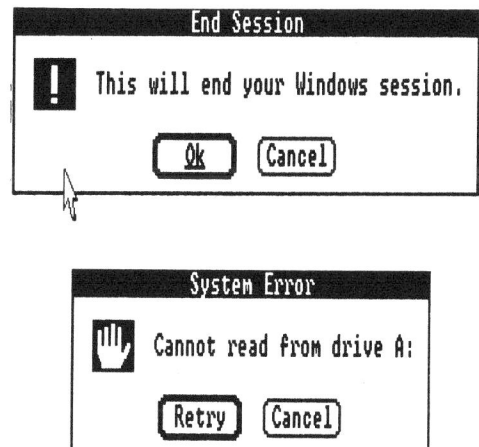

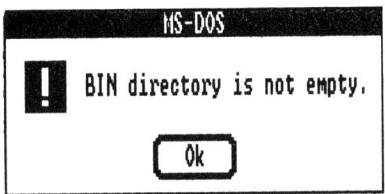

The Windows application presented next displays the following message box:

The C program to display this message box, MESSAGE.C, contains the following:

```
#include "windows.h"

#define APPLICATION_NAME "MESSAGE"
#define ICON_NAME "MESSAGE"

long FAR PASCAL MessageWndProc(HWND, unsigned, WORD, LONG);

BOOL MessageInit(hInstance)
HANDLE hInstance;
{
    NPWNDCLASS pClass;

    pClass = (NPWNDCLASS) LocalAlloc(LPTR, sizeof(WNDCLASS));

    pClass->hCursor         = LoadCursor(NULL, IDC_ARROW);
    pClass->hIcon           = LoadIcon(hInstance, (LPSTR) ICON_NAME);
```

```
    pClass->lpszClassName   = (LPSTR) APPLICATION_NAME;
    pClass->hbrBackground   = (HBRUSH) GetStockObject(WHITE_BRUSH);
    pClass->hInstance       = hInstance;
    pClass->style           = CS_HREDRAW | CS_VREDRAW;
    pClass->lpfnWndProc     = MessageWndProc;

    if (!RegisterClass((LPWNDCLASS)pClass))
        return FALSE;

    LocalFree((HANDLE) pClass); /* return space to heap */
    return TRUE;                /* registration successful */
}


int PASCAL WinMain(hInstance, hPrevInstance, lpszCmdLine, cmdShow)
HANDLE hInstance, hPrevInstance;
LPSTR lpszCmdLine;
int cmdShow;
{
  MSG   message;
  HWND  hWnd;

  if (!hPrevInstance)   /* initialize if this is the first instance */
    if (!MessageInit(hInstance))
        return FALSE;   /* failure to initialize -- return to Windows */

  hWnd  =  CreateWindow((LPSTR) APPLICATION_NAME,
                        (LPSTR) APPLICATION_NAME,
                        WS_TILEDWINDOW,
                        0,                  /*  x - ignored for tiled
                                                windows */
                        0,                  /*  y - ignored for tiled
                                                windows */
                        0,                  /*  cx - ignored for tiled
                                                windows */
                        0,                  /*  cy - ignored for tiled
                                                windows */
                        (HWND) NULL,        /* no parent */
                        (HMENU) NULL,       /* use class menu */
                        (HANDLE) hInstance, /* handle to window
                                                instance */
                        (LPSTR) NULL        /* no parameters to pass
                                                on */
                        );

    ShowWindow(hWnd, cmdShow);              /* Make window visible */
    UpdateWindow(hWnd);

    MessageBox (hWnd, (LPSTR) "Message Box Text", (LPSTR)
               "Message Box", MB_OK | MB_ICONASTERISK);

    /* Poll messages from the event queue and dispatch them */
    while (GetMessage((LPMSG) &message, NULL, 0, 0)) {
        TranslateMessage((LPMSG) &message);
        DispatchMessage((LPMSG) &message);
        }

    return (int) message.wParam;  /* return control to Windows */
}


long FAR PASCAL MessageWndProc(hWnd, message, wParam, lParam)
HWND hWnd;
unsigned message;
WORD wParam;
LONG lParam;
```

```
{
  switch (message) {
    case WM_DESTROY:
        PostQuitMessage(0);  /* tell Windows ready to terminate */
        break;

    default:  /* let Windows process message */
        return DefWindowProc(hWnd, message, wParam, lParam);
        break;
  }

  return (0L);
}
```

MESSAGE.RC contains

```
#include "windows.h"

MESSAGE ICON    MESSAGE.ico
```

And the contents of MESSAGE.DEF are as follows:

```
NAME    MESSAGE

DESCRIPTION 'Windows Message Box Application'

STUB    'WINSTUB.EXE'

CODE    MOVEABLE
DATA    MOVEABLE MULTIPLE

HEAPSIZE  512
STACKSIZE 4096

EXPORTS
    MessageWndProc @1
```

Dialog boxes are critical to the development of successful Windows applications. Modify the programs provided in this chapter to gain a thorough understanding of dialog box processing.

14

ACCESSING
THE CLIPBOARD

The concurrent nature of Windows makes it possible to execute multiple programs simultaneously. One of the most convenient (and most essential) Windows features is its ability to allow these applications to exchange information. The Clipboard is the Windows medium for exchanging data between two applications. This chapter examines two applications. The first places a bitmap into the Clipboard for access by other applications. The second returns the owner and data formats currently available on the Clipboard.

Clipboard Bitmap

Using the Windows icon editor, create the following bitmap:

The program CLIPTEST.EXE loads this bitmap and places it into the Clipboard, as follows:

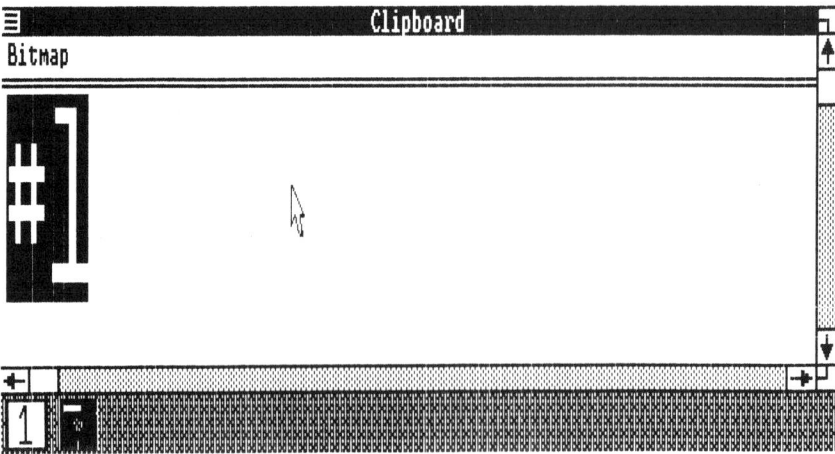

The program then displays the following:

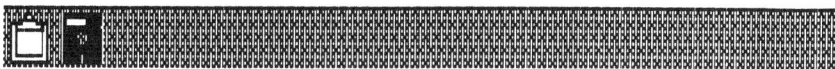

The following Pascal program implements CLIPTEST.EXE:

```
{$windows+}
{$stackseg+ $debug- $symtab-}

INTERFACE;
    UNIT paslibw (
        {$INCLUDE : 'cliptest.inc'}
    );

{$INCLUDE:'windows.inc'}                    { Get WINDOWS definitions. }

MODULE test[];
  USES paslibw (
    {$INCLUDE : 'cliptest.inc'}
  );


PROCEDURE begxqq; EXTERN;

PROCEDURE endxqq; EXTERN;

PROCEDURE ENTGQQ [ PUBLIC ];
BEGIN
     {dummy routine for link4}
END;

PROCEDURE ClipTestPaint (hWindow : HWND;
                    hDC_    : HDC) [ PUBLIC ];
```

```
BEGIN
  EVAL(TextOut(hDC_, 0, 10, RETYPE(LPSTR,
    ADS 'Successful WINDOWS Clipboard Program!'), 37));
END;



FUNCTION ClipTestWndProc(hWindow : HWND;
                         message : UNSIGNED;
                         wParam  : WORD;
                         lParam  : LONG ) : LONG [ PUBLIC, WINDOWS ];


VAR
  ps : PAINTSTRUCT;

BEGIN

    CASE message OF
        WM_DESTROY:
            PostQuitMessage(0);

        WM_PAINT:
            BEGIN
                EVAL(BeginPaint(hWindow, RETYPE(LPPAINTSTRUCT, ADS ps)));
                ClipTestPaint(hWindow, ps.hdc_);
                EndPaint(hWindow, RETYPE(LPPAINTSTRUCT, ADS ps));
            END;

        OTHERWISE      { Let Windows handle all the other messages }
          BEGIN
            ClipTestWndProc := DefWindowProc(hWindow, message, wParam,
                               lParam);
            RETURN;
          END;

    END;

    ClipTestWndProc := RETYPE(LONG, BYLONG(0,0));
END;


FUNCTION ClipTestInit(hInstance : HANDLE) : BOOL;

VAR
  pClass : WNDCLASS;

BEGIN

    begxqq;

    pClass.lpszClassName := RETYPE(LPSTR, ADS 'CLIPTEST' * CHR(0));
    pClass.hIcon_        := LoadIcon( hInstance, RETYPE(LPSTR,
                            ADS 'CLIPTEST' * CHR(0)));
    pClass.hCursor_      := LoadCursor( RETYPE(HWND, NULL_), IDC_ARROW);
    pClass.hbrBackground := RETYPE(HBRUSH, GetStockObject(WHITE_BRUSH));

    pClass.lpfnWndProc   := ADS ClipTestWndProc;
    pClass.hInstance     := hInstance;
    pClass.style         := CS_VREDRAW OR CS_HREDRAW;
    pClass.cbClsExtra    := 0;
    pClass.cbWndExtra    := 0;

    { register this new class with WINDOWS }

    IF (RegisterClass(RETYPE(LPWNDCLASS, ADS pClass)) <> TRUE_) THEN
        BEGIN
```

```
            ClipTestInit := FALSE_;
            RETURN;
         END;

    ClipTestInit := TRUE_;
END;



FUNCTION WinMain(hInstance     : HANDLE;
                 hPrevInstance : HANDLE;
                 lpszCmdline   : LPSTR;
                 cmdShow       : INT) : BOOL [ PUBLIC ];

VAR
   hWindow : HWND;
   msg_    : MSG;
   hBitmap : HANDLE;

BEGIN
   IF (hPrevInstance = 0) THEN  { Call initialization routine }
      BEGIN
         IF (ClipTestInit(hInstance) = FALSE_) THEN { Return to Windows }
            BEGIN
               WinMain := FALSE_;
               RETURN;
            END;
      END;

   { Create a window instance of class 'TEST' }

   hWindow := CreateWindow(
      RETYPE(LPSTR, ADS 'CLIPTEST' * CHR(0)),   { Class name              }
      RETYPE(LPSTR, ADS 'CLIPTEST' * CHR(0)),   { Instance name           }
      WS_TILEDWINDOW,                            { Window style            }
      0,                                         { Desired column          }
      0,                                         { cy: not used            }
      0,                                         { cx: not used            }
      100,                                       { Desired height: pixel   }
      RETYPE(HWND, NULL_),                       { No parent window        }
      RETYPE(HMENU, NULL_),                      { Use default menu        }
      hInstance,                                 { Instance handle         }
      RETYPE(LPSTR, BYLONG(0,NULL_)));           { No additional
                                                   parameter }

   EVAL(ShowWindow(hWindow, cmdShow)); { Send message to update
                                         window }
   UpdateWindow(hWindow);

   { put bitmap in the clipboard }

   EVAL (OpenClipboard (hWindow));
   hBitmap := LoadBitmap (hInstance, RETYPE(LPSTR, ADS
                      'CLIPMAP'* Chr(0)));
   EVAL(SetClipboardData (CF_BITMAP, hBitmap));
   EVAL (CloseClipboard);

   WHILE (GetMessage(RETYPE(LPMSG, ADS msg_), NULL_, 0, 0) <> 0) DO
      BEGIN
         EVAL(TranslateMessage(RETYPE(LPMSG, ADS msg_)));
         EVAL(DispatchMessage(RETYPE(LPMSG, ADS msg_)));
      END;

   endxqq;

END;

END.
```

This program is very similar to the other Windows applications examined thus far. The only new code occurs in WinMain, which loads the bitmap, opens the Clipboard for write access, places the bitmap contents into the Clipboard, and closes the Clipboard:

```
{ put bitmap in the clipboard }

EVAL (OpenClipboard (hWindow));
hBitmap := LoadBitmap (hInstance, RETYPE(LPSTR, ADS
                       'CLIPMAP'* Chr(0)));
EVAL(SetClipboardData (CF_BITMAP, hBitmap));
EVAL (CloseClipboard);
```

For this application, CLIPTEST.INC contains the following:

```
int,
short,
long,
unsigned,
FALSE_,
TRUE_,
NULL_,
BYTE,
WORD,
DWORD,
BOOL,
PSTR,
LPSTR,
LPINT,
HANDLE,
HSTR,
HICON,
HDC,
HMENU,
HPEN,
HBRUSH,
HCURSOR,
WNDCLASS,
PWNDCLASS,
LPWNDCLASS,
HWND,
MSG,
PMSG,
LPMSG,
WM_DESTROY,
WM_PAINT,
CS_VREDRAW,
CS_HREDRAW,
WS_TILEDWINDOW,
PAINTSTRUCT,
LPPAINTSTRUCT,
```

```
CREATESTRUCT,
WHITE_BRUSH,
CF_BITMAP,
GetMessage,
TranslateMessage,
DispatchMessage,
DefWindowProc,
PostQuitMessage,
RegisterClass,
CreateWindow,
DestroyWindow,
ShowWindow,
UpdateWindow,
BeginPaint,
EndPaint,
TextOut,
GetStockObject,
LoadCursor,
IDC_ARROW,
LoadIcon,
LoadMenu,
LoadBitmap,
CloseClipboard,
OpenClipboard,
SetClipboardData
```

The resource script file contains the following:

```
#include "windows.h"

CLIPTEST ICON    cliptest.ico
CLIPMAP  BITMAP  cliptest.bmp
```

The module definition file consists of the following:

```
NAME     CLIPTEST

DESCRIPTION 'Windows Clipboard Application'

STUB     'WINSTUB.EXE'

CODE     MOVEABLE
DATA     MOVEABLE MULTIPLE

HEAPSIZE 1024
STACKSIZE 4096

EXPORTS
    ClipTestWndProc a1
```

Compile and link the application as follows:

```
rc -r cliptest.rc

pas1 cliptest;

pas2

link4 cliptest, /align:16, /map, paslibw, cliptest.def

rc cliptest.res
```

Clipboard Utilization

The following Clipboard program simply displays the current status of the Windows Clipboard. Assuming that another application has opened the Clipboard and placed data into it, CLIPINFO.EXE will display the following upon invocation:

Clipboard Formats

Predefined Windows clipboard format

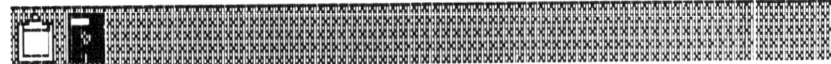

Examine the following C code for CLIPINFO.EXE:

```c
#include "windows.h"

#define APPLICATION_NAME "CLIPINFO"
#define ICON_NAME "CLIPINFO"

long FAR PASCAL ClipInfoWndProc(HWND, unsigned, WORD, LONG);

void ClipInfoPaint(hWnd, hDC)
HWND hWnd;
HDC hDC;
{
  char message[255];
  char fmtstr[255];

  int i, x=0, y=20, format=0;

  TextOut(hDC, x, 0, (LPSTR) message,
          sprintf(message, "Clipboard Formats"));

  for (i = 1; i <= CountClipboardFormats(); i++)
   {
    format = EnumClipboardFormats (format);

    GetClipboardFormatName (format, (LPSTR) fmtstr, 255);

    if (format != 0)
      TextOut(hDC, x, y, (LPSTR) message, sprintf(message, "%s",
                          fmtstr));
    else
      TextOut(hDC, x, y, (LPSTR) message, sprintf(message,
              "Predefined Windows clipboard format"));

    y += 25;
   }
}


BOOL ClipInfoInit(hInstance)
HANDLE hInstance;
{
    NPWNDCLASS  pClass;

    pClass = (NPWNDCLASS) LocalAlloc(LPTR, sizeof(WNDCLASS));

    pClass->hCursor        = LoadCursor(NULL, IDC_ARROW);
    pClass->hIcon          = LoadIcon(hInstance, (LPSTR) ICON_NAME);
    pClass->lpszClassName  = (LPSTR) APPLICATION_NAME;
    pClass->hbrBackground  = (HBRUSH) GetStockObject(WHITE_BRUSH);
    pClass->hInstance      = hInstance;
    pClass->style          = CS_HREDRAW | CS_VREDRAW;
    pClass->lpfnWndProc    = ClipInfoWndProc;

    if (!RegisterClass((LPWNDCLASS)pClass))
        return FALSE;

    LocalFree((HANDLE) pClass); /* return space to heap */
    return TRUE;                /* registration successful */
}


int PASCAL WinMain(hInstance, hPrevInstance, lpszCmdLine, cmdShow)
HANDLE hInstance, hPrevInstance;
LPSTR lpszCmdLine;
```

```
int cmdShow;
{
  MSG   message;
  HWND  hWnd;

  if (!hPrevInstance)   /* initialize if this is the first instance */
    if (!ClipInfoInit(hInstance))
       return FALSE;   /* failure to initialize -- return to Windows */

  hWnd  =  CreateWindow((LPSTR) APPLICATION_NAME,
                        (LPSTR) APPLICATION_NAME,
                        WS_TILEDWINDOW,
                        0,                 /*  x - ignored for tiled
                                                 windows */
                        0,                 /*  y - ignored for tiled
                                                 windows */
                        0,                 /*  cx - ignored for tiled
                                                 windows */
                        0,                 /*  cy - ignored for tiled
                                                 windows */
                        (HWND) NULL,        /* no parent */
                        (HMENU) NULL,       /* use class menu */
                        (HANDLE) hInstance, /* handle to window
                                                 instance */
                        (LPSTR) NULL        /* no parameters to pass
                                                 on */
                        );

    ShowWindow(hWnd, cmdShow);             /* Make window visible */
    UpdateWindow(hWnd);

    /* Poll messages from the event queue and dispatch them */
    while (GetMessage((LPMSG) &message, NULL, 0, 0)) {
        TranslateMessage((LPMSG) &message);
        DispatchMessage((LPMSG) &message);
        }

    return (int) message.wParam;  /* return control to Windows */
}


long FAR PASCAL ClipInfoWndProc(hWnd, message, wParam, lParam)
HWND hWnd;
unsigned message;
WORD wParam;
LONG lParam;
{
  PAINTSTRUCT ps;

  switch (message) {
    case WM_DESTROY:
         PostQuitMessage(0);  /* tell Windows ready to terminate */
         break;

    case WM_PAINT:
         BeginPaint(hWnd, (LPPAINTSTRUCT) &ps);
         ClipInfoPaint(hWnd, ps.hdc);
         EndPaint(hWnd, (LPPAINTSTRUCT) &ps);
         break;

    default: /* let Windows process message */
         return DefWindowProc(hWnd, message, wParam, lParam);
         break;
    }

  return (0L);
}
```

Again, the majority of the program's code is no different from the other code examined in this text. The only new processing is

```
void ClipInfoPaint(hWnd, hDC)
HWND hWnd;
HDC hDC;
{
  char message[255];
  char fmtstr[255];

  int i, x=0, y=20, format=0;

  TextOut(hDC, x, 0, (LPSTR) message,
          sprintf(message, "Clipboard Formats"));

  for (i = 1; i <= CountClipboardFormats(); i++)
    {
    format = EnumClipboardFormats (format);

    GetClipboardFormatName (format, (LPSTR) fmtstr, 255);

    if (format != 0)
      TextOut(hDC, x, y, (LPSTR) message, sprintf(message, "%s",
                          fmtstr));
    else
      TextOut(hDC, x, y, (LPSTR) message, sprintf(message,
              "Predefined Windows clipboard format"));

    y += 25;
  }
}
```

The EnumClipboardFormats routine returns either the next format in the list of available Clipboard data formats or the value 0 if the format is a predefined Windows Clipboard format.

The module definition file for the application contains the following:

```
NAME     CLIPINFO

DESCRIPTION 'Windows Clipboard Application'

STUB     'WINSTUB.EXE'

CODE     MOVEABLE
DATA     MOVEABLE MULTIPLE

HEAPSIZE  1024
STACKSIZE 4096

EXPORTS
    ClipInfoWndProc a1
```

The resource script file consists of the following:

```
#include "windows.h"

CLIPINFO ICON     clipinfo.ico
CLIPMAP  BITMAP   clipinfo.bmp
```

Write a simple C program that uses the routine RegisterClipboard-Format. Note its effect upon the result displayed by CLIPINFO.EXE.

Standard Applications

Many programmers often forget that Windows allows you to place the contents of the current screen in the Clipboard by pressing the ALT-PRTSC key combination. For example, if your screen contains

```
ABOUT            975 bytes  07/18/1986  04:00:06  ARCHIVE
MENU.DEF         256 bytes  04/01/1987  16:40:56  ARCHIVE
ONE.BMP          528 bytes  04/07/1987  16:39:18  ARCHIVE
MENU.ICO        1038 bytes  07/18/1986  04:00:06  ARCHIVE
MENU.RC          256 bytes  04/18/1987  10:08:42  ARCHIVE
WINSTUB.EXE      570 bytes  09/15/1986  11:58:20  ARCHIVE
TEST.ICO        1038 bytes  07/18/1986  04:00:06  ARCHIVE
FILE.BMP         528 bytes  04/03/1987  10:18:32  ARCHIVE
SHELLO.DEF       256 bytes  03/18/1987  22:27:42  ARCHIVE
TYPE.H           264 bytes  09/29/1986  09:42:26  ARCHIVE
TYPE.C          8586 bytes  09/29/1986  09:41:52  ARCHIVE
TYPE.RC          693 bytes  09/29/1986  09:42:30  ARCHIVE
TYPE.DEF         287 bytes  09/29/1986  09:42:22  ARCHIVE
TYPE.ICO        1038 bytes  03/18/1986  20:52:32  ARCHIVE
OUTLIB.LIB      1024 bytes  04/15/1987  19:33:54  ARCHIVE
MENU.RES        1117 bytes  04/18/1987  10:09:38  ARCHIVE
OUT.DEF          256 bytes  04/15/1987  19:16:46  ARCHIVE
COMMAND.PIF      369 bytes  04/01/1987  17:20:56  ARCHIVE
FONTDIG.DEF      256 bytes  04/11/1987  06:31:30  ARCHIVE
ART11.9          256 bytes  04/02/1987  00:56:14  ARCHIVE
CLIPINFO.OBJ    1488 bytes  04/21/1987  09:49:48  ARCHIVE
HELLO.RC         128 bytes  03/25/1987  01:21:08  ARCHIVE
FILE.RC          128 bytes  04/03/1987  10:11:10  ARCHIVE
FILE.RES         588 bytes  04/04/1987  08:33:06  ARCHIVE
HELLO.C         3200 bytes  03/25/1987  02:18:48  ARCHIVE
```

then pressing ALT-PRTSC results in the following Clipboard:

```
≡                              Clipboard                              ⌐
Text                                                                 ▲

ABOUT              975 bytes   07/18/1986   04:00:06   ARCHIVE
MENU.DEF           256 bytes   04/01/1987   16:40:56   ARCHIVE
ONE.BMP            528 bytes   04/07/1987   16:39:18   ARCHIVE
MENU.ICO          1038 bytes   07/18/1986   04:00:06   ARCHIVE
MENU.RC            256 bytes   04/18/1987   10:08:42   ARCHIVE
WINSTUB.EXE        570 bytes   09/15/1986   11:58:20   ARCHIVE
TEST.ICO          1038 bytes   07/18/1986   04:00:06   ARCHIVE
FILE.BMP           528 bytes   04/03/1987   10:18:32   ARCHIVE
SHELLO.DEF         256 bytes   03/18/1987   22:27:42   ARCHIVE
TYPE.H             264 bytes   09/29/1986   09:42:26   ARCHIVE
TYPE.C            8586 bytes   09/29/1986   09:41:52   ARCHIVE
TYPE.RC            693 bytes   09/29/1986   09:42:30   ARCHIVE
TYPE.DEF           287 bytes   09/29/1986   09:42:22   ARCHIVE
TYPE.ICO          1038 bytes   03/18/1986   20:52:32   ARCHIVE
OUTLIB.LIB        1024 bytes   04/15/1987   19:33:54   ARCHIVE
←                                                                    →
```

The Windows Clipboard is a powerful tool. Experiment with the desktop applications that use the Clipboard; you will become much more conversant with Windows data formats.

15

USING FONTS

One of the most attractive features of the Windows desktop applications is the liberal use of font styles. This chapter examines several Windows applications that manipulate and use various fonts. Each of the routines presented makes extensive use of the LOGFONT data structure, whose fields include the following:

```
short  lfHeight
short  lfWidth
short  lfEscapement
short  lfOrientation
short  lfWeight
byte   lfItalic
byte   lfUnderline
```

```
byte    lfStrikeout
byte    lfCharSet
byte    lfOutPrecision
byte    lfClipPrecision
byte    lfQuality
byte    lfPitchAndFamily
byte    lfFaceName[LF_FACESIZE]
```

These fields are defined in Chapter 8.

MAKEFONT

This section presents MAKEFONT, a Windows application that uses
the GDI routine CreateFont to produce the following screen:

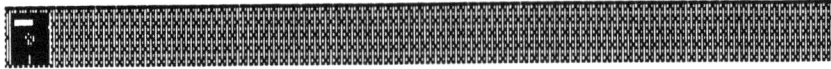

Chapter 16 explains GDI graphics routines in detail.

The calling sequence for CreateFont is

CreateFont (nHeight, nWidth, nEscapement, nOrientation,
          nWeight, cItalic, cStrikeOut, nCharSet,
          nOutputPrecision, nClipPrecision, cQuality,
          cPitchAndFamily, lpFacename);

Each of the arguments to CreateFont relates to a field in the LOG-FONT structure. CreateFont returns a handle to a font that can later be selected as the current font via SelectObject.

The following C program implements MAKEFONT:

```c
#include "windows.h"

#define APPLICATION_NAME "MAKEFONT"
#define ICON_NAME "MAKEFONT"

long FAR PASCAL MakeFontWndProc(HWND, unsigned, WORD, LONG);

LOGFONT lFont;
LPLOGFONT lpFont;

DisplayMessage (hWnd)
  HWND hWnd;
  {
    HDC hDC;
    HANDLE hFont, hOldFont;

    char message[255];

    hDC = GetDC (hWnd);

    hFont = CreateFontIndirect (lpFont);
    hOldFont = SelectObject (hDC, hFont);

    TextOut (hDC, 10, 10, message,
            sprintf (message, "FONT TEST"));

    SelectObject (hDC, hOldFont);
    DeleteObject (hFont);

    ReleaseDC (hWnd, hDC);
  }


BOOL MakeFontInit(hInstance)
HANDLE hInstance;
{
    NPWNDCLASS pClass;
```

```
    pClass = (NPWNDCLASS) LocalAlloc(LPTR, sizeof(WNDCLASS));

    pClass->hCursor        = LoadCursor(NULL, IDC_ARROW);
    pClass->hIcon          = LoadIcon(hInstance, (LPSTR) ICON_NAME);
    pClass->lpszClassName  = (LPSTR) APPLICATION_NAME;
    pClass->hbrBackground  = (HBRUSH) GetStockObject(WHITE_BRUSH);
    pClass->hInstance      = hInstance;
    pClass->style          = CS_HREDRAW | CS_VREDRAW;
    pClass->lpfnWndProc    = MakeFontWndProc;

    if (!RegisterClass((LPWNDCLASS)pClass))
        return FALSE;

    LocalFree((HANDLE) pClass); /* return space to heap */

    lpFont = (LPLOGFONT) &lFont;

    lFont.lfHeight = 32;
    lFont.lfWidth = 64;
    lFont.lfEscapement = 0;
    lFont.lfOrientation = 0;
    lFont.lfWeight = 400;
    lFont.lfItalic = 16;
    lFont.lfUnderLine = 0;
    lFont.lfStrikeOut = 0;
    lFont.lfCharSet = ANSI_CHARSET;
    lFont.lfOutPrecision = OUT_DEFAULT_PRECIS;
    lFont.lfClipPrecision = CLIP_DEFAULT_PRECIS;
    lFont.lfQuality = DRAFT_QUALITY;
    lFont.lfPitchAndFamily = FIXED_PITCH;

    return TRUE;                /* registration successful */
}

int PASCAL WinMain(hInstance, hPrevInstance, lpszCmdLine, cmdShow)
HANDLE hInstance, hPrevInstance;
LPSTR lpszCmdLine;
int cmdShow;
{
  MSG   message;
  HWND  hWnd;

  if (!hPrevInstance)   /* initialize if this is the first instance */
    if (!MakeFontInit(hInstance))
        return FALSE;   /* failure to initialize -- return to Windows */

  hWnd =  CreateWindow((LPSTR) APPLICATION_NAME,
                       (LPSTR) APPLICATION_NAME,
                       WS_TILEDWINDOW,
                       0,                  /*  x - ignored for tiled
                                               windows */
                       0,                  /*  y - ignored for tiled
                                               windows */
                       0,                  /*  cx - ignored for tiled
                                               windows */
                       0,                  /*  cy - ignored for tiled
                                               windows */
                       (HWND) NULL,        /* no parent */
                       (HMENU) NULL,       /* use class menu */
                       (HANDLE) hInstance, /* handle to window
                                               instance */
                       (LPSTR) NULL        /* no parameters to pass
                                               on */
                       );
```

```
ShowWindow(hWnd, cmdShow);                    /* Make window visible */
UpdateWindow(hWnd);

/* Poll messages from the event queue and dispatch them */
    while (GetMessage((LPMSG) &message, NULL, 0, 0)) {
        TranslateMessage((LPMSG) &message);
        DispatchMessage((LPMSG) &message);
        }

    return (int) message.wParam;  /* return control to Windows */
}


long FAR PASCAL MakeFontWndProc(hWnd, message, wParam, lParam)
HWND hWnd;
unsigned message;
WORD wParam;
LONG lParam;
{
  switch (message) {
    case WM_DESTROY:
        PostQuitMessage(0);  /* tell Windows ready to terminate */
        break;

    case WM_PAINT:
        DisplayMessage(hWnd);

    default: /* let Windows process message */
        return DefWindowProc(hWnd, message, wParam, lParam);
        break;
    }

  return (0L);
}
```

The majority of the routines in MAKEFONT are no different
from their counterparts in the first Windows application that was
examined. The MakeFontInit routine defines the window's class and
the desired font. Note the values assigned to the various fields of the
font structure:

```
BOOL MakeFontInit(hInstance)
HANDLE hInstance;
{
    NPWNDCLASS  pClass;

    pClass = (NPWNDCLASS) LocalAlloc(LPTR, sizeof(WNDCLASS));

    pClass->hCursor        = LoadCursor(NULL, IDC_ARROW);
    pClass->hIcon          = LoadIcon(hInstance, (LPSTR) ICON_NAME);
    pClass->lpszClassName  = (LPSTR) APPLICATION_NAME;
    pClass->hbrBackground  = (HBRUSH) GetStockObject(WHITE_BRUSH);
    pClass->hInstance      = hInstance;
    pClass->style          = CS_HREDRAW | CS_VREDRAW;
    pClass->lpfnWndProc    = MakeFontWndProc;

    if (!RegisterClass((LPWNDCLASS)pClass))
        return FALSE;
```

```
    LocalFree((HANDLE) pClass);  /* return space to heap */

    lpFont = (LPLOGFONT) &lFont;

    lFont.lfHeight = 32;
    lFont.lfWidth = 64;
    lFont.lfEscapement = 0;
    lFont.lfOrientation = 0;
    lFont.lfWeight = 400;
    lFont.lfItalic = 16;
    lFont.lfUnderline = 0;
    lFont.lfStrikeOut = 0;
    lFont.lfCharSet = ANSI_CHARSET;
    lFont.lfOutPrecision = OUT_DEFAULT_PRECIS;
    lFont.lfClipPrecision = CLIP_DEFAULT_PRECIS;
    lFont.lfQuality = DRAFT_QUALITY;
    lFont.lfPitchAndFamily = FIXED_PITCH;

    return TRUE;                 /* registration successful */
}
```

The DisplayMessage routine creates and selects the new font in order to display the message FONT TEST. Upon completion, the routine sets the current font to its previous state.

```
DisplayMessage (hWnd)
  HWND hWnd;
  {
    HDC hDC;
    HANDLE hFont, hOldFont;

    char message[255];

    hDC = GetDC (hWnd);

    hFont = CreateFontIndirect (lpFont);
    hOldFont = SelectObject (hDC, hFont);

    TextOut (hDC, 10, 10, message,
             sprintf (message, "FONT TEST"));

    SelectObject (hDC, hOldFont);
    DeleteObject (hFont);

    ReleaseDC (hWnd, hDC);
  }
```

The following is the resource script file for MAKEFONT:

```
NAME    MAKEFONT

DESCRIPTION 'Windows FONT Application'

STUB    'WINSTUB.EXE'
```

```
CODE      MOVEABLE
DATA      MOVEABLE MULTIPLE

HEAPSIZE  512
STACKSIZE 4096

EXPORTS
    MakeFontDlgWndProc a1
```

The module definition file for MAKEFONT is as follows:

```
#include "windows.h"

MAKEFONT ICON   MAKEFONT.ICO
```

TEXTMET

The TEXTMET routine creates a font similar to that used in MAKEFONT but in a much smaller size. Once the font is created, the routine invokes the Windows GetTextMetrics function to obtain specifics about the font. The information returned from the routine is placed into a structure of type TEXTMETRIC that contains the following:

```
short  tmHeight
short  tmAscent
short  tmDescent
short  tmInternalLeading
short  tmExternalLeading
short  tmAveCharWidth
short  tmMaxCharWidth
short  tmWeight
byte   tmItalic
byte   tmUnderlined
byte   tmStruckOut
byte   tmFirstChar
byte   tmLastChar
byte   tmDefaultChar
byte   tmBreakChar
byte   tmPitchAndFamily
byte   tmCharSet
short  tmOverhang
short  tmDigitizedAspectX
short  tmDigitizedAspectY
```

Upon invocation, TEXTMET displays the following:

FONT height: 6	FONT struck out: 0
FONT ascent: 5	FONT first character: 32
FONT descent: 1	FONT last character: 255
FONT internal leading: 0	FONT default character: 128
FONT external leading: 0	FONT break character: 32
FONT average width: 8	FONT pitch and family: 48
FONT max char width: 8	FONT character set: 0
FONT weight: 400	FONT overhang: 2
FONT italic: 1	FONT digitized x aspect: 48
FONT underlined: 0	FONT digitized y aspect: 96

The C program to implement TEXTMET is as follows:

```
#include "windows.h"

#define APPLICATION_NAME "TEXTMET"
#define ICON_NAME "TEXTMET"

long FAR PASCAL TextMetDlgWndProc(HWND, unsigned, WORD, LONG);

LOGFONT lFont;
LPLOGFONT lpFont;

DisplayMetrics (hWnd)
  HWND hWnd;
  {
    HDC hDC;
    HANDLE hFont, hOldFont;
    TEXTMETRIC TextM;
    LPTEXTMETRIC lpTextM;

    char message[255];

    hDC = GetDC (hWnd);
    lpTextM = (LPTEXTMETRIC) &TextM;
```

```
hFont = CreateFontIndirect (lpFont);
hOldFont = SelectObject (hDC, hFont);
GetTextMetrics (hDC, (TEXTMETRIC FAR *) lpTextM);

TextOut (hDC, 0, 10, message,
         sprintf (message, "FONT height: %d", TextM.tmHeight));

TextOut (hDC, 0, 20, message,
         sprintf (message, "FONT ascent: %d", TextM.tmAscent));

TextOut (hDC, 0, 30, message,
         sprintf (message, "FONT descent: %d", TextM.tmDescent));

TextOut (hDC, 0, 40, message,
         sprintf (message, "FONT internal leading: %d",
                 TextM.tmInternalLeading));

TextOut (hDC, 0, 50, message,
         sprintf (message, "FONT external leading: %d",
                 TextM.tmExternalLeading));

TextOut (hDC, 0, 60, message,
         sprintf (message, "FONT average width: %d",
                 TextM.tmAveCharWidth));

TextOut (hDC, 0, 70, message,
         sprintf (message, "FONT max char width: %d",
                 TextM.tmMaxCharWidth));

TextOut (hDC, 0, 80, message,
         sprintf (message, "FONT weight: %d", TextM.tmWeight));

TextOut (hDC, 0, 90, message,
         sprintf (message, "FONT italic: %d",
         LOBYTE(TextM.tmItalic)));

TextOut (hDC, 0, 100, message,
         sprintf (message, "FONT underlined: %d",
         LOBYTE(TextM.tmUnderlined)));

TextOut (hDC, 300, 10, message,
         sprintf (message, "FONT struck out: %d",
         LOBYTE(TextM.tmStruckOut)));

TextOut (hDC, 300, 20, message,
         sprintf (message, "FONT first character: %d",
         LOBYTE(TextM.tmFirstChar)));

TextOut (hDC, 300, 30, message,
         sprintf (message, "FONT last character: %d",
         LOBYTE(TextM.tmLastChar)));

TextOut (hDC, 300, 40, message,
         sprintf (message, "FONT default character: %d",
                 LOBYTE(TextM.tmDefaultChar)));

TextOut (hDC, 300, 50, message,
         sprintf (message, "FONT break character: %d",
         LOBYTE(TextM.tmBreakChar)));

TextOut (hDC, 300, 60, message,
         sprintf (message, "FONT pitch and family: %d",
                 LOBYTE(TextM.tmPitchAndFamily)));

TextOut (hDC, 300, 70, message,
         sprintf (message, "FONT character set: %d",
```

```
                    LOBYTE(TextM.tmCharSet)));

    TextOut (hDC, 300, 80, message,
            sprintf (message, "FONT overhang: %d", TextM.tmOverhang));

    TextOut (hDC, 300, 90, message,
            sprintf (message, "FONT digitized x ascpect: %d",
                    TextM.tmDigitizedAspectX));

    TextOut (hDC, 300, 100, message,
            sprintf (message, "FONT digitized y ascpect: %d",
                    TextM.tmDigitizedAspectY));

    SelectObject (hDC, hOldFont);
    DeleteObject (hFont);

    ReleaseDC (hWnd, hDC);
}


BOOL TextMetDigInit(hInstance)
HANDLE hInstance;
{
    NPWNDCLASS  pClass;

    pClass = (NPWNDCLASS) LocalAlloc(LPTR, sizeof(WNDCLASS));

    pClass->hCursor         = LoadCursor(NULL, IDC_ARROW);
    pClass->hIcon           = LoadIcon(hInstance, (LPSTR) ICON_NAME);
    pClass->lpszClassName   = (LPSTR) APPLICATION_NAME;
    pClass->hbrBackground   = (HBRUSH) GetStockObject(WHITE_BRUSH);
    pClass->hInstance       = hInstance;
    pClass->style           = CS_HREDRAW | CS_VREDRAW;
    pClass->lpfnWndProc     = TextMetDigWndProc;

    if (!RegisterClass((LPWNDCLASS)pClass))
        return FALSE;

    LocalFree((HANDLE) pClass); /* return space to heap */

    lpFont = (LPLOGFONT) &lFont;

    lFont.lfHeight = 4;
    lFont.lfWidth = 8;
    lFont.lfEscapement = 0;
    lFont.lfOrientation = 0;
    lFont.lfWeight = 400;
    lFont.lfItalic = 16;
    lFont.lfUnderline = 0;
    lFont.lfStrikeOut = 0;
    lFont.lfCharSet = ANSI_CHARSET;
    lFont.lfOutPrecision = OUT_DEFAULT_PRECIS;
    lFont.lfClipPrecision = CLIP_DEFAULT_PRECIS;
    lFont.lfQuality = DRAFT_QUALITY;
    lFont.lfPitchAndFamily = FIXED_PITCH;

    return TRUE;                    /* registration successful */
}

int PASCAL WinMain(hInstance, hPrevInstance, lpszCmdLine, cmdShow)
HANDLE hInstance, hPrevInstance;
LPSTR lpszCmdLine;
```

```
int cmdShow;
{
  MSG    message;
  HWND   hWnd;

  if (!hPrevInstance)    /* initialize if this is the first instance */
    if (!TextMetDigInit(hInstance))
      return FALSE;      /* failure to initialize -- return to Windows */

  hWnd = CreateWindow((LPSTR) APPLICATION_NAME,
                      (LPSTR) APPLICATION_NAME,
                      WS_TILEDWINDOW,
                      0,                      /*  x - ignored for tiled
                                                 windows */
                      0,                      /*  y - ignored for tiled
                                                 windows */
                      0,                      /*  cx - ignored for tiled
                                                 windows */
                      0,                      /*  cy - ignored for tiled
                                                 windows */
                      (HWND) NULL,            /* no parent */
                      (HMENU) NULL,           /* use class menu */
                      (HANDLE) hInstance,     /* handle to window
                                                 instance */
                      (LPSTR) NULL            /* no parameters to pass
                                                 on */
                      );

  ShowWindow(hWnd, cmdShow);                  /* Make window visible */
  UpdateWindow(hWnd);

  /* Poll messages from the event queue and dispatch them */
  while (GetMessage((LPMSG) &message, NULL, 0, 0)) {
      TranslateMessage((LPMSG) &message);
      DispatchMessage((LPMSG) &message);
      }

  return (int) message.wParam;  /* return control to Windows */
}


long FAR PASCAL TextMetDigWndProc(hWnd, message, wParam, lParam)
HWND hWnd;
unsigned message;
WORD wParam;
LONG lParam;
{
  switch (message) {
    case WM_DESTROY:
        PostQuitMessage(0);  /* tell Windows ready to terminate */
        break;

    case WM_PAINT:
        DisplayMetrics (hWnd);

    default:  /* let Windows process message */
        return DefWindowProc(hWnd, message, wParam, lParam);
        break;
    }

  return (0L);
}
```

Note that the DisplayMetrics routine is the only difference between this program and MAKEFONT.

The resource script file for TEXTMET contains the following:

```
#include "windows.h"

TEXTMET ICON   TEXTMET.ICO
```

The contents of the module definition file for TEXTMET are as follows:

```
NAME    TEXTMET

DESCRIPTION 'Windows FONT Application'

STUB    'WINSTUB.EXE'

CODE    MOVEABLE
DATA    MOVEABLE MULTIPLE

HEAPSIZE  512
STACKSIZE 4096

EXPORTS
    TextMetWndProc a1
```

FONTDIG

The FONTDIG routine displays a digital clock on the screen, as follows:

It uses the GDI LineTo routine to produce the box around the clock. (The LineTo routine is described in Chapter 16.) In addition, FONT-DIG uses the third Windows input source, the system timer, to update the screen every two seconds. The routine SetTimer associates an alarm with a specific window. When the timer completes, Windows sends a WM—TIMER message to the application. In this case, the application will simply update the screen and set another timer for two seconds later.

The following C program implements FONTDIG:

```
#include "windows.h"
#include <dos.h>          /* needed to interface with DOS */

#define APPLICATION_NAME "FONTDIG"
#define ICON_NAME "FONTDIG"

long FAR PASCAL FontDigWndProc(HWND, unsigned, WORD, LONG);

int hours, minutes;     /* system time */
LOGFONT lFont;
LPLOGFONT lpFont;

void GetSystemTime (hours, minutes)
  int *hours, *minutes;
{
    union REGS inregs, outregs;

    inregs.h.ah = 0x2C;       /* Display system time */
    intdos (&inregs, &outregs);
    *hours = outregs.h.ch;
    *minutes = outregs.h.cl;
}


DisplayTime (hWnd, hours, minutes)
  HWND hWnd;
  int hours, minutes;
  {
    HDC hDC;
    HANDLE hFont, hOldFont;

    char message[255];

    hDC = GetDC (hWnd);

    GetSystemTime (&hours, &minutes);

    DrawRectangle (hDC, 5, 5, 320, 42);

    hFont = CreateFontIndirect (lpFont);
    hOldFont = SelectObject (hDC, hFont);
```

```
    TextOut (hDC, 10, 10, message,
             sprintf (message, "%d:%02d", hours, minutes));

    SelectObject (hDC, hOldFont);
    DeleteObject (hFont);

    ReleaseDC (hWnd, hDC);
}


DrawRectangle (hDC, x, y, xsize, ysize)
  HDC hDC;
  int x, y, xsize, ysize;
{
  MoveTo (hDC, x, y);
  LineTo (hDC, x+xsize, y);
  LineTo (hDC, x+xsize, y+ysize);
  LineTo (hDC, x, y+ysize);
  LineTo (hDC, x, y);
}



BOOL FontDigInit(hInstance)
HANDLE hInstance;
{
    NPWNDCLASS  pClass;

    pClass = (NPWNDCLASS) LocalAlloc(LPTR, sizeof(WNDCLASS));

    pClass->hCursor        = LoadCursor(NULL, IDC_ARROW);
    pClass->hIcon          = LoadIcon(hInstance, (LPSTR) ICON_NAME);
    pClass->lpszClassName  = (LPSTR) APPLICATION_NAME;
    pClass->hbrBackground  = (HBRUSH) GetStockObject(WHITE_BRUSH);
    pClass->hInstance      = hInstance;
    pClass->style          = CS_HREDRAW | CS_VREDRAW;
    pClass->lpfnWndProc    = FontDigWndProc;

    if (!RegisterClass((LPWNDCLASS)pClass))
        return FALSE;

    LocalFree((HANDLE) pClass); /* return space to heap */

    lpFont = (LPLOGFONT) &lFont;

    lFont.lfHeight = 32;
    lFont.lfWidth = 64;
    lFont.lfEscapement = 0;
    lFont.lfOrientation = 0;
    lFont.lfWeight = 400;
    lFont.lfItalic = 0;
    lFont.lfUnderline = 0;
    lFont.lfStrikeOut = 0;
    lFont.lfCharSet = ANSI_CHARSET;
    lFont.lfOutPrecision = OUT_DEFAULT_PRECIS;
    lFont.lfClipPrecision = CLIP_DEFAULT_PRECIS;
    lFont.lfQuality = DRAFT_QUALITY;
    lFont.lfPitchAndFamily = FIXED_PITCH;

    return TRUE;                /* registration successful */
}


int PASCAL WinMain(hInstance, hPrevInstance, lpszCmdLine, cmdShow)
HANDLE hInstance, hPrevInstance;
LPSTR lpszCmdLine;
```

```
int cmdShow;
{
  MSG    message;
  HWND   hWnd;

  if (!hPrevInstance)    /* initialize if this is the first instance */
    if (!FontDigInit(hInstance))
        return FALSE;     /* failure to initialize -- return to Windows */

  hWnd  =   CreateWindow((LPSTR) APPLICATION_NAME,
                         (LPSTR) APPLICATION_NAME,
                         WS_TILEDWINDOW,
                         0,                    /*  x - ignored for tiled
                                                   windows */
                         0,                    /*  y - ignored for tiled
                                                   windows */
                         0,                    /*  cx - ignored for tiled
                                                   windows */
                         0,                    /*  cy - ignored for tiled
                                                   windows */
                         (HWND) NULL,          /* no parent */
                         (HMENU) NULL,         /* use class menu */
                         (HANDLE) hInstance,   /* handle to window
                                                  instance */
                         (LPSTR) NULL          /* no parameters to pass
                                                   on */
                         );


    ShowWindow(hWnd, cmdShow);                 /* Make window visible */
    UpdateWindow(hWnd);

    SetTimer (hWnd, 100, 1, NULL);

    /* Poll messages from the event queue and dispatch them */
    while (GetMessage((LPMSG) &message, NULL, 0, 0)) {
        TranslateMessage((LPMSG) &message);
        DispatchMessage((LPMSG) &message);
        }

    return (int) message.wParam;  /* return control to Windows */
}


long FAR PASCAL FontDigWndProc(hWnd, message, wParam, lParam)
HWND hWnd;
unsigned message;
WORD wParam;
LONG lParam;
{
  switch (message) {
    case WM_DESTROY:
        PostQuitMessage(0);  /* tell Windows ready to terminate */
        break;
    case WM_TIMER:
        GetSystemTime (&hours, &minutes);
        DisplayTime (hWnd, hours, minutes);
        SetTimer (hWnd, 100, 2000, NULL);
        break;

    default:  /* let Windows process message */
        return DefWindowProc(hWnd, message, wParam, lParam);
        break;
    }

  return (0L);
}
```

The first routine, GetSystemTime, uses the DOS services to return the hour and minute of the current system time:

```
void GetSystemTime (hours, minutes)
 int *hours, *minutes;
{
    union REGS inregs, outregs;

    inregs.h.ah = 0x2C;          /* Display system time */
    intdos (&inregs, &outregs);
    *hours = outregs.h.ch;
    *minutes = outregs.h.cl;
}
```

The DisplayTime routine is invoked every two seconds to update the screen with the new system time:

```
DisplayTime (hWnd, hours, minutes)
  HWND hWnd;
  int hours, minutes;
  {
    HDC hDC;
    HANDLE hFont, hOldFont;

    char message[255];

    hDC = GetDC (hWnd);

    GetSystemTime (&hours, &minutes);

    DrawRectangle (hDC, 5, 5, 320, 42);

    hFont = CreateFontIndirect (lpFont);
    hOldFont = SelectObject (hDC, hFont);

    TextOut (hDC, 10, 10, message,
             sprintf (message, "%d:%02d", hours, minutes));

    SelectObject (hDC, hOldFont);
    DeleteObject (hFont);

    ReleaseDC (hWnd, hDC);
  }
```

This routine first selects the larger font and displays the system time. Upon completion, it restores the previous font. Next, the FontDlgInit routine defines both the window class for the application and the large font that will be used to display the system time:

```
BOOL FontDlgInit(hInstance)
HANDLE hInstance;
{
    NPWNDCLASS  pClass;

    pClass = (NPWNDCLASS) LocalAlloc(LPTR, sizeof(WNDCLASS));

    pClass->hCursor           = LoadCursor(NULL, IDC_ARROW);
    pClass->hIcon             = LoadIcon(hInstance, (LPSTR) ICON_NAME);
    pClass->lpszClassName     = (LPSTR) APPLICATION_NAME;
    pClass->hbrBackground     = (HBRUSH) GetStockObject(WHITE_BRUSH);
    pClass->hInstance         = hInstance;
    pClass->style             = CS_HREDRAW | CS_VREDRAW;
    pClass->lpfnWndProc       = FontDlgWndProc;

    if (!RegisterClass((LPWNDCLASS)pClass))
        return FALSE;

    LocalFree((HANDLE) pClass); /* return space to heap */

    lpFont = (LPLOGFONT) &lFont;

    lFont.lfHeight = 32;
    lFont.lfWidth = 64;
    lFont.lfEscapement = 0;
    lFont.lfOrientation = 0;
    lFont.lfWeight = 400;
    lFont.lfItalic = 0;
    lFont.lfUnderline = 0;
    lFont.lfStrikeOut = 0;
    lFont.lfCharSet = ANSI_CHARSET;
    lFont.lfOutPrecision = OUT_DEFAULT_PRECIS;
    lFont.lfClipPrecision = CLIP_DEFAULT_PRECIS;
    lFont.lfQuality = DRAFT_QUALITY;
    lFont.lfPitchAndFamily = FIXED_PITCH;

    return TRUE;                 /* registration successful */
}
```

The WinMain routine is very similar to the WinMain routines in the other applications examined thus far. The only significant difference is the call to SetTimer that defines the first screen update.

Finally, the routine FontDlgWndProc handles the messages received from Windows. Note the processing for WM _TIMER messages:

```
long FAR PASCAL FontDlgWndProc(hWnd, message, wParam, lParam)
HWND hWnd;
unsigned message;
WORD wParam;
LONG lParam;
{
  switch (message) {
    case WM_DESTROY:
        PostQuitMessage(0);  /* tell Windows ready to terminate */
        break;

    case WM_TIMER:
```

```
        GetSystemTime (&hours, &minutes);
        DisplayTime (hWnd, hours, minutes);
        SetTimer (hWnd, 100, 2000, NULL);
        break;

    default:  /* let Windows process message */
        return DefWindowProc(hWnd, message, wParam, lParam);
        break;
    }

  return (OL);
}
```

The resource script file for the application is as follows:

```
#include "windows.h"

FONTDIG ICON    FONTDIG.ICO
```

The contents of the module definition file for the application are as follows:

```
NAME      FONTDIG

DESCRIPTION 'Windows FONT Application'

STUB      'WINSTUB.EXE'

CODE      MOVEABLE
DATA      MOVEABLE MULTIPLE

HEAPSIZE  512
STACKSIZE 4096

EXPORTS
    FontDigWndProc a1
```

Experiment with this application; you will soon find yourself replacing the analog clock program.

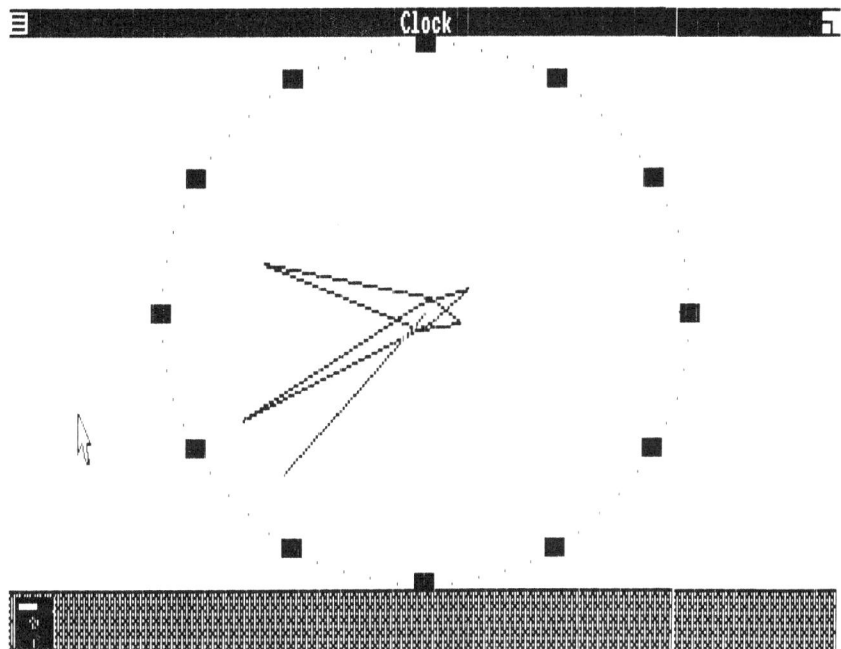

16

USING GDI FUNCTIONS

Windows supports a multitude of graphics capabilities. This chapter examines the GDI (graphic device interface) functions that provide the foundation for these capabilities. Appendix I provides a complete overview of each of the built-in Windows functions. Each of the Windows GDI functions is presented in detail in that appendix. This chapter, therefore, will present only a few of the GDI functions that you can use to create simple graphics programs. Several of the routines called from the applications presented earlier in this text — TextOut, for example — are considered to be GDI routines.

In addition to introducing GDI functions, the C application presented in this chapter illustrates the use of the system timer, the third source for input (in addition to the keyboard and the mouse).

When you examine this program, you should find several routines that you can cut and paste into other Windows applications to increase their capabilities.

Analog Clock

Probably the most familiar Windows application is the analog clock program provided as part of the collection of Windows desktop applications, as shown here:

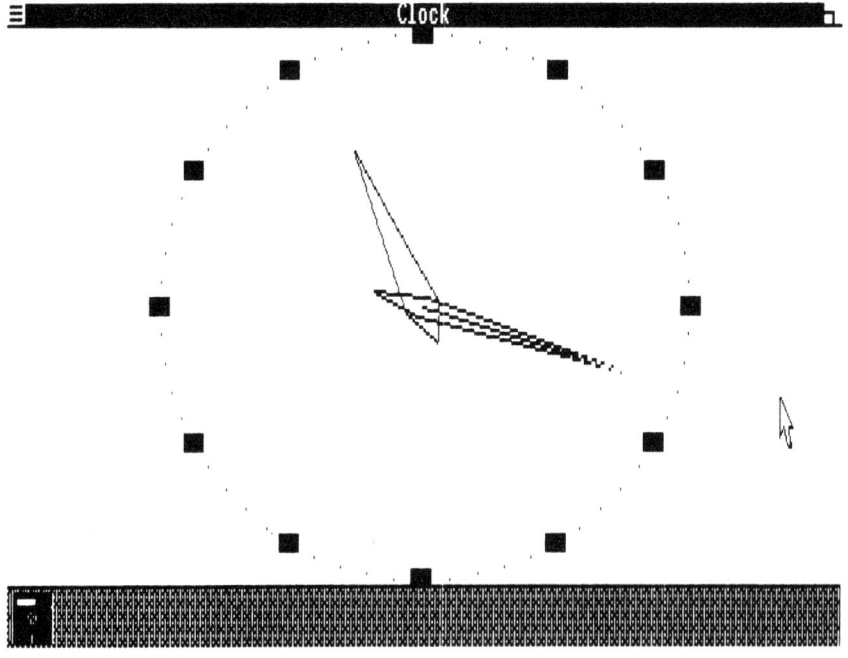

If you load a second copy of the CLOCK.EXE program, you can watch Windows perform multiple applications simultaneously, as follows:

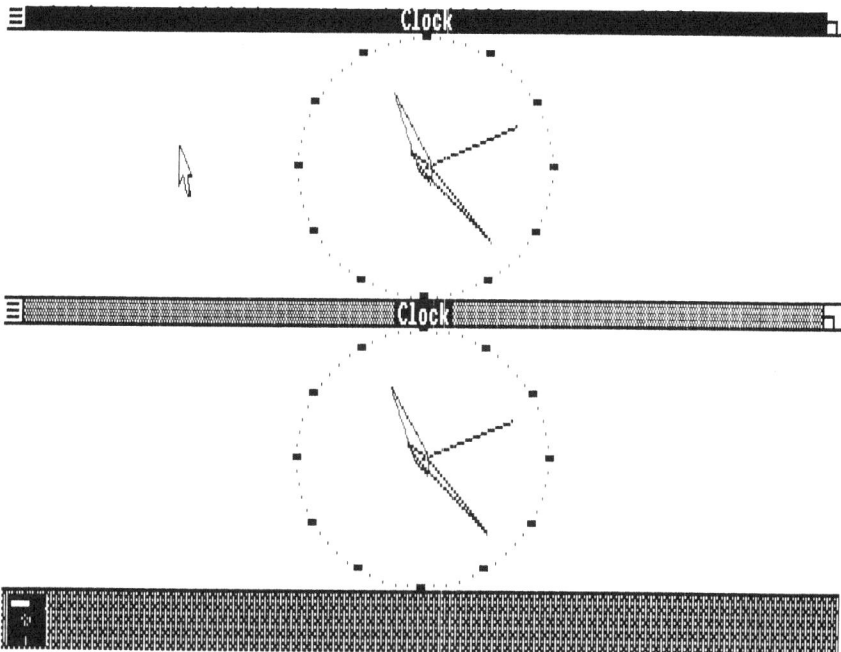

Digital Clock

To keep step with the times, it is important that Windows offer a digital clock in addition to an analog one. The following program, DIGITAL.EXE, displays the digital clock shown here:

Every two seconds the system timer updates the time displayed by the digital clock. If the application is sharing the screen with other Windows applications, the system timer still updates the clock (although the window itself may be inactive), as follows.

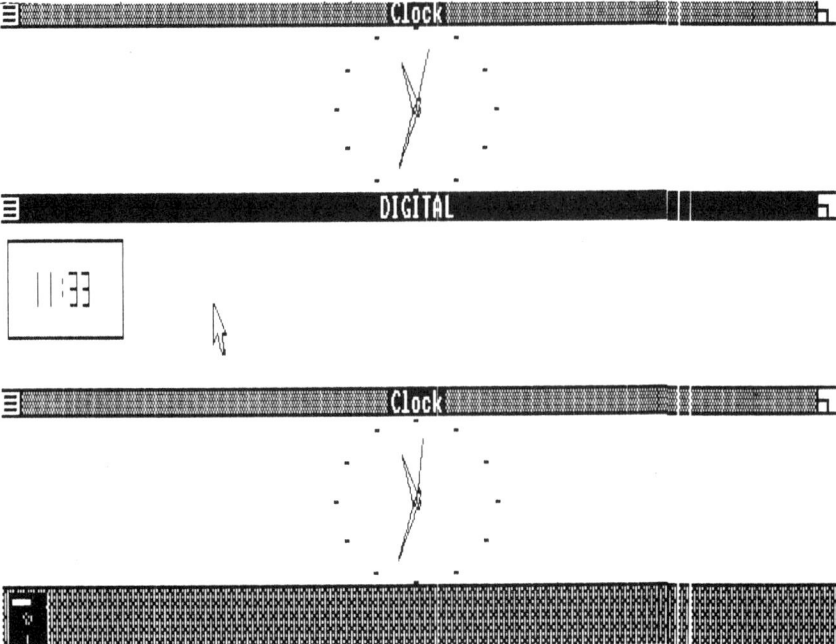

The following C program uses the Windows GDI routines to implement the digital clock:

```
#include "windows.h"
#include <dos.h>          /* needed to interface with DOS */

#define APPLICATION_NAME "DIGITAL"
#define ICON_NAME "DIGITAL"

long FAR PASCAL DigitalWndProc(HWND, unsigned, WORD, LONG);

int hours, minutes;     /* system time */

void GetSystemTime (hours, minutes)
 int *hours, *minutes;
{
    union REGS inregs, outregs;

    inregs.h.ah = 0x2C;       /* Display system time */
    intdos (&inregs, &outregs);
    *hours = outregs.h.ch;
    *minutes = outregs.h.cl;
}
```

```c
void EraseClock (hWnd)
 HWND hWnd;
{
 HBRUSH hBrush, hOldBrush;
 RECT Rect;
 HDC hDC;

 hDC = GetDC (hWnd);

 GetClientRect (hWnd, (LPRECT) &Rect);
 hBrush = CreateSolidBrush(GetSysColor(COLOR_WINDOW));
 hOldBrush = SelectObject(hDC, hBrush);
 FillRect(hDC, (LPRECT) &Rect, hBrush);
 SelectObject (hDC, hOldBrush);
 DeleteObject (hBrush);

 ReleaseDC (hWnd, hDC);
}


DisplayTime (hWnd, hours, minutes)
  HWND hWnd;
  int hours, minutes;
 {
    HDC hDC;
    int tens, ones;

    EraseClock (hWnd);

    hDC = GetDC (hWnd);

GetSystemTime (&hours, &minutes);

DrawRectangle (hDC, 5, 5, 90, 30);

tens = minutes / 10;
ones = minutes % 10;

if ((hours == 1) || (hours == 13))
   DrawOne (hDC, 35, 15, 2, 8, 10);

else if ((hours == 2) || (hours == 14))
   DrawTwo (hDC, 35, 15, 2, 8, 10);

else if ((hours == 3) || (hours == 15))
   DrawThree (hDC, 35, 15, 2, 8, 10);

else if ((hours == 4) || (hours == 16))
   DrawFour (hDC, 35, 15, 2, 8, 10);

else if ((hours == 5) || (hours == 17))
   DrawFive (hDC, 35, 15, 2, 8, 10);

else if ((hours == 6) || (hours == 18))
   DrawSix (hDC, 35, 15, 2, 8, 10);

else if ((hours == 7) || (hours == 19))
   DrawSeven (hDC, 35, 15, 2, 8, 10);

else if ((hours == 8) || (hours == 20))
   DrawEight (hDC, 35, 15, 2, 8, 10);

else if ((hours == 9) || (hours == 21))
   DrawNine (hDC, 35, 15, 2, 8, 10);
```

```
else if ((hours == 10) || (hours == 22))
  {
    DrawOne (hDC, 25, 15, 2, 8, 10);
    DrawZero (hDC, 35, 15, 2, 8, 10);
  }

else if ((hours == 11) || (hours == 23))
  {
    DrawOne (hDC, 25, 15, 2, 8, 10);
    DrawOne (hDC, 35, 15, 2, 8, 10);
  }
else if ((hours == 0) || (hours == 24))
  {
    DrawOne (hDC, 25, 15, 2, 8, 10);
    DrawTwo (hDC, 35, 15, 2, 8, 10);
  }

if (tens == 0)
    DrawZero (hDC, 50, 15, 2, 8, 10);

else if (tens == 1)
    DrawOne (hDC, 50, 15, 2, 8, 10);

else if (tens == 2)
    DrawTwo (hDC, 50, 15, 2, 8, 10);

else if (tens == 3)
    DrawThree (hDC, 50, 15, 2, 8, 10);

else if (tens == 4)
    DrawFour (hDC, 50, 15, 2, 8, 10);

else if (tens == 5)
    DrawFive (hDC, 50, 15, 2, 8, 10);

if (ones == 0)
    DrawZero (hDC, 60, 15, 2, 8, 10);

else if (ones == 1)
    DrawOne (hDC, 60, 15, 2, 8, 10);

else if (ones == 2)
    DrawTwo (hDC, 60, 15, 2, 8, 10);

else if (ones == 3)
    DrawThree (hDC, 60, 15, 2, 8, 10);

else if (ones == 4)
    DrawFour (hDC, 60, 15, 2, 8, 10);

else if (ones == 5)
    DrawFive (hDC, 60, 15, 2, 8, 10);

else if (ones == 6)
    DrawSix (hDC, 60, 15, 2, 8, 10);

else if (ones == 7)
    DrawSeven (hDC, 60, 15, 2, 8, 10);

else if (ones == 8)
    DrawEight (hDC, 60, 15, 2, 8, 10);

else if (ones == 9)
    DrawNine (hDC, 60, 15, 2, 8, 10);
```

```
   MoveTo (hDC, 47, 17);
   LineTo (hDC, 47, 19);

   MoveTo (hDC, 47, 21);
   LineTo (hDC, 47, 23);

   ReleaseDC (hWnd, hDC);
}

DrawRectangle (hDC, x, y, xsize, ysize)
  HDC hDC;
  int x, y, xsize, ysize;
 {
  MoveTo (hDC, x, y);
  LineTo (hDC, x+xsize, y);
  LineTo (hDC, x+xsize, y+ysize);
  LineTo (hDC, x, y+ysize);
  LineTo (hDC, x, y);
 }


BOOL DigitalInit(hInstance)
HANDLE hInstance;
{
    NPWNDCLASS  pClass;

    pClass = (NPWNDCLASS) LocalAlloc(LPTR, sizeof(WNDCLASS));

    pClass->hCursor          = LoadCursor(NULL, IDC_ARROW);
    pClass->hIcon            = LoadIcon(hInstance, (LPSTR) ICON_NAME);
    pClass->lpszClassName    = (LPSTR) APPLICATION_NAME;
    pClass->hbrBackground    = (HBRUSH) GetStockObject(WHITE_BRUSH);
    pClass->hInstance        = hInstance;
    pClass->style            = CS_HREDRAW | CS_VREDRAW;
    pClass->lpfnWndProc      = DigitalWndProc;

    if (!RegisterClass((LPWNDCLASS)pClass))
        return FALSE;

    LocalFree((HANDLE) pClass); /* return space to heap */
    return TRUE;                /* registration successful */
}

DrawOne (hDC, x, y, xstart, xend, yend)
 HDC hDC;
 int x, y, xstart, xend, yend;
{
   MoveTo (hDC, x+(xend-xstart)/2, y);
   LineTo (hDC, x+(xend-xstart)/2, y+yend+1);
}



DrawTwo (hDC, x, y, xstart, xend, yend)
 HDC hDC;
 int x, y, xstart, xend, yend;
{
   MoveTo (hDC, x+xstart, y);
   LineTo (hDC, x+xend, y);
   LineTo (hDC, x+xend, y+yend/2);
   LineTo (hDC, x+xstart, y+yend/2);
   LineTo (hDC, x+xstart, y+yend);
   LineTo (hDC, x+xend, y+yend);
}
```

```
DrawThree (hDC, x, y, xstart, xend, yend)
 HDC hDC;
 int x, y, xstart, xend, yend;
{
   MoveTo (hDC, x+xstart, y);
   LineTo (hDC, x+xend, y);
   LineTo (hDC, x+xend, y+yend/2);
   LineTo (hDC, x+xstart, y+yend/2);
   MoveTo (hDC, x+xend, y+yend/2);
   LineTo (hDC, x+xend, y+yend);
   LineTo (hDC, x+xstart, y+yend);
}


DrawFour (hDC, x, y, xstart, xend, yend)
 HDC hDC;
 int x, y, xstart, xend, yend;
{
   MoveTo (hDC, x+xstart, y);
   LineTo (hDC, x+xstart, y+yend/2);
   LineTo (hDC, x+xend, y+yend/2);
   MoveTo (hDC, x+xend-1, y);
   LineTo (hDC, x+xend-1, y+yend+1);
}


DrawFive (hDC, x, y, xstart, xend, yend)
 HDC hDC;
 int x, y, xstart, xend, yend;
{
   MoveTo (hDC, x+xstart, y);
   LineTo (hDC, x+xend, y);
   MoveTo (hDC, x+xstart, y);
   LineTo (hDC, x+xstart, y+yend/2);
   LineTo (hDC, x+xend, y+yend/2);
   LineTo (hDC, x+xend, y+yend);
   LineTo (hDC, x+xstart, y+yend);
}

DrawSix (hDC, x, y, xstart, xend, yend)
 HDC hDC;
 int x, y, xstart, xend, yend;
{
   MoveTo (hDC, x+xstart, y);
   LineTo (hDC, x+xend, y);
   MoveTo (hDC, x+xstart, y);
   LineTo (hDC, x+xstart, y+yend/2);
   LineTo (hDC, x+xend, y+yend/2);
   LineTo (hDC, x+xend, y+yend);
   LineTo (hDC, x+xstart, y+yend);
   LineTo (hDC, x+xstart, y+yend/2);
}

DrawSeven (hDC, x, y, xstart, xend, yend)
 HDC hDC;
 int x, y, xstart, xend, yend;
{
   MoveTo (hDC, x+xstart, y);
   LineTo (hDC, x+xend, y);
   LineTo (hDC, x+xstart, y+yend+1);
}


DrawEight (hDC, x, y, xstart, xend, yend)
 HDC hDC;
 int x, y, xstart, xend, yend;
{
```

```
   MoveTo (hDC, x+xstart, y);
   LineTo (hDC, x+xend, y);
   MoveTo (hDC, x+xstart, y);
   LineTo (hDC, x+xstart, y+yend/2);
   LineTo (hDC, x+xend, y+yend/2);
   LineTo (hDC, x+xend, y+yend);
   LineTo (hDC, x+xstart, y+yend);
   LineTo (hDC, x+xstart, y+yend/2);
   MoveTo (hDC, x+xend, y);
   LineTo (hDC, x+xend, y+yend/2);
}


DrawNine (hDC, x, y, xstart, xend, yend)
 HDC hDC;
 int x, y, xstart, xend, yend;
{
   MoveTo (hDC, x+xstart, y);
   LineTo (hDC, x+xend, y);
   MoveTo (hDC, x+xstart, y);
   LineTo (hDC, x+xstart, y+yend/2);
   LineTo (hDC, x+xend, y+yend/2);
   LineTo (hDC, x+xend, y+yend+1);
   MoveTo (hDC, x+xend, y);
   LineTo (hDC, x+xend, y+yend/2);
}


DrawZero (hDC, x, y, xstart, xend, yend)
 HDC hDC;
 int x, y, xstart, xend, yend;
{
   MoveTo (hDC, x+xstart, y);
   LineTo (hDC, x+xend, y);
   LineTo (hDC, x+xend, y+yend);
   LineTo (hDC, x+xstart, y+yend);
   LineTo (hDC, x+xstart, y);
}


int PASCAL WinMain(hInstance, hPrevInstance, lpszCmdLine, cmdShow)
HANDLE hInstance, hPrevInstance;
LPSTR lpszCmdLine;
int cmdShow;
{
  MSG    message;
  HWND   hWnd;

  if (!hPrevInstance)    /* initialize if this is the first instance */
    if (!DigitalInit(hInstance))
       return FALSE;      /* failure to initialize -- return to Windows */

  hWnd  = CreateWindow((LPSTR) APPLICATION_NAME,
                       (LPSTR) APPLICATION_NAME,
                       WS_TILEDWINDOW,
                       0,                  /*  x - ignored for tiled
                                               windows */
                       0,                  /*  y - ignored for tiled
                                               windows */
                       0,                  /*  cx - ignored for tiled
                                               windows */
                       0,                  /*  cy - ignored for tiled
                                               windows */
                       (HWND) NULL,        /* no parent */
                       (HMENU) NULL,       /* use class menu */
```

```
                    (HANDLE) hInstance,  /* handle to window
                                               instance */
                    (LPSTR) NULL         /* no parameters to pass
                                               on */
                    );

    ShowWindow(hWnd, cmdShow);                /* Make window visible */
    UpdateWindow(hWnd);

    SetTimer (hWnd, 100, 1, NULL);

    /* Poll messages from the event queue and dispatch them */
    while (GetMessage((LPMSG) &message, NULL, 0, 0)) {
        TranslateMessage((LPMSG) &message);
        DispatchMessage((LPMSG) &message);
        }

    return (int) message.wParam;  /* return control to Windows */
}


long FAR PASCAL DigitalWndProc(hWnd, message, wParam, lParam)
HWND hWnd;
unsigned message;
WORD wParam;
LONG lParam;
{
    PAINTSTRUCT ps;

    switch (message) {
        case WM_DESTROY:
            PostQuitMessage(0);    /* tell Windows ready to terminate */
            break;

        case WM_TIMER:
            GetSystemTime (&hours, &minutes);
            DisplayTime (hWnd, hours, minutes);
            SetTimer (hWnd, 100, 2000, NULL);
            break;

        default:  /* let Windows process message */
            return DefWindowProc(hWnd, message, wParam, lParam);
            break;
    }

    return (0L);
}
```

The first routine, GetSystemTime, simply invokes the DOS system service that returns the current system time. The digital clock is not concerned with seconds, and so only the hours and minutes are returned to the calling routine.

The next routine, EraseClock, is called before each clock update to ensure that the previously displayed time is erased. The routine creates a brush with the same color as the window background, and fills the client region of the window, resulting in a blank window. The code for this routine is as follows:

USING GDI FUNCTIONS

```
void EraseClock (hWnd)
 HWND hWnd;
{
 HBRUSH hBrush, hOldBrush;
 RECT Rect;
 HDC hDC;

 hDC = GetDC (hWnd);

 GetClientRect (hWnd, (LPRECT) &Rect);
 hBrush = CreateSolidBrush(GetSysColor(COLOR_WINDOW));
 hOldBrush = SelectObject(hDC, hBrush);
 FillRect(hDC, (LPRECT) &Rect, hBrush);
 SelectObject (hDC, hOldBrush);
 DeleteObject (hBrush);

 ReleaseDC (hWnd, hDC);
}
```

The DisplayTime routine is called each time the system timer completes. It retrieves the current system time and then invokes the routines DrawZero through DrawNine as required to display the time.

The DrawRectangle routine uses the GDI functions MoveTo and LineTo to draw the rectangle specified by the x and y coordinates received from the calling function.

The next routine, DigitalInit, is similar to the other window utilization routines examined thus far.

```
BOOL DigitalInit(hInstance)
HANDLE hInstance;
{
    NPWNDCLASS  pClass;

    pClass = (NPWNDCLASS) LocalAlloc(LPTR, sizeof(WNDCLASS));

    pClass->hCursor         = LoadCursor(NULL, IDC_ARROW);
    pClass->hIcon           = LoadIcon(hInstance, (LPSTR) ICON_NAME);
    pClass->lpszClassName   = (LPSTR) APPLICATION_NAME;
    pClass->hbrBackground   = (HBRUSH) GetStockObject(WHITE_BRUSH);
    pClass->hInstance       = hInstance;
    pClass->style           = CS_HREDRAW | CS_VREDRAW;
    pClass->lpfnWndProc     = DigitalWndProc;

    if (!RegisterClass((LPWNDCLASS)pClass))
        return FALSE;

    LocalFree((HANDLE) pClass); /* return space to heap */
    return TRUE;                /* registration successful */
}
```

The routines DrawZero through DrawNine use the MoveTo and LineTo routines to draw the numbers 0 through 9 that make up the hours and minutes of the digital display. The code for the DrawZero routine, for example, is as follows:

```
DrawZero (hDC, x, y, xstart, xend, yend)
 HDC hDC;
 int x, y, xstart, xend, yend;
{
    MoveTo (hDC, x+xstart, y);
    LineTo (hDC, x+xend, y);
    LineTo (hDC, x+xend, y+yend);
    LineTo (hDC, x+xstart, y+yend);
    LineTo (hDC, x+xstart, y);
}
```

These routines use a 10×10 grid of pixels.

The WinMain routine is almost identical to the other WinMain routines discussed so far. Note, however, the following statement:

```
SetTimer (hWnd, 100, 1, NULL);
```

It initiates a system timer that, upon completion, will return the value 100. The 1 specifies that the timer should complete in one millisecond, and NULL specifies the time-handling function. System timers, like windows and dialog boxes, provide for a default handling function. In this case, the NULL value directs Windows to place the WM_TIMER message in the message queue. The routine DigitalWndProc processes WM_TIMER messages.

```
Long FAR PASCAL DigitalWndProc(hWnd, message, wParam, lParam)
HWND hWnd;
unsigned message;
WORD wParam;
LONG lParam;
{
   PAINTSTRUCT ps;

   switch (message) {
     case WM_DESTROY:
          PostQuitMessage(0);  /* tell Windows ready to terminate */
          break;

     case WM_TIMER:
          GetSystemTime (&hours, &minutes);
          DisplayTime (hWnd, hours, minutes);
          SetTimer (hWnd, 100, 2000, NULL);
          break;

     default:  /* let Windows process message */
          return DefWindowProc(hWnd, message, wParam, lParam);
          break;
     }

   return (0L);
}
```

Each time the system timer completes, DIGITAL invokes the routine GetSystemTime to obtain the current system time, displays the time via the DisplayTime routine, and sets another system timer to complete in two seconds.

The following DIGITAL.RC file contains the application's resource script definitions:

```
#include "windows.h"

DIGITAL ICON    DIGITAL.ICO
```

The following DIGITAL.DEF file contains the application's module definitions:

```
NAME     DIGITAL

DESCRIPTION 'Windows GDI Application'

STUB     'WINSTUB.EXE'

CODE     MOVEABLE
DATA     MOVEABLE MULTIPLE

HEAPSIZE  512
STACKSIZE 4096

EXPORTS
    DigitalWndProc @1
```

Compile the program in the manner previously shown for all C applications.

The Windows GDI is critical to the success of a Windows application. Admittedly, the program presented in this chapter is a fairly simple one. However, it lays a foundation that you should expand upon by experimenting with each of the GDI functions. Browse through each of the GDI functions presented in Appendix I.

APPENDIXES

A

ASCII CODES

Table A-1 lists the ASCII codes for characters.

DEC	OCTAL	HEX	ASCII	DEC	OCTAL	HEX	ASCII
0	000	00	NUL	6	006	06	ACK
1	001	01	SOH	7	007	07	BEL
2	002	02	STX	8	011	08	BS
3	003	03	ETX	9	011	09	HT
4	004	04	EOT	10	012	0A	LF
5	005	05	ENQ	11	013	0B	VT

Table A-1. ASCII Character Codes

DEC	OCTAL	HEX	ASCII	DEC	OCTAL	HEX	ASCII
12	014	0C	FF	53	065	35	5
13	015	0D	CR	54	066	36	6
14	016	0E	SO	55	067	37	7
15	017	0F	SI	56	070	38	8
16	020	10	DLE	57	071	39	9
17	021	11	DC1	58	072	3A	:
18	022	12	DC2	59	073	3B	;
19	023	13	DC3	60	074	3C	<
20	024	14	DC4	61	075	3D	=
21	025	15	NAK	62	076	3E	>
22	026	16	SYN	63	077	3F	?
23	027	17	ETB	64	100	40	@
24	030	18	CAN	65	101	41	A
25	031	19	EM	66	102	42	B
26	032	1A	SUB	67	103	43	C
27	033	1B	ESC	68	104	44	D
28	034	1C	FS	69	105	45	E
29	035	1D	GS	70	106	46	F
30	036	1E	RS	71	107	47	G
31	037	1F	US	72	110	48	H
32	040	20	SPACE	73	111	49	I
33	041	21	!	74	112	4A	J
34	042	22	"	75	113	4B	K
35	043	23	#	76	114	4C	L
36	044	24	$	77	115	4D	M
37	045	25	%	78	116	4E	N
38	046	26	&	79	117	4F	O
39	047	27	'	80	120	50	P
40	050	28	(	81	121	51	Q
41	051	29	)	82	122	52	R
42	052	2A	*	83	123	53	S
43	053	2B	+	84	124	54	T
44	054	2C	,	85	125	55	U
45	055	2D	—	86	126	56	V
46	056	2E	.	87	127	57	W
47	057	2F	/	88	130	58	X
48	060	30	0	89	131	59	Y
49	061	31	1	90	132	5A	Z
50	062	32	2	91	133	5B	[
51	063	33	3	92	134	5C	\
52	064	34	4	93	135	5D	]

Table A-1. ASCII Character Codes (*continued*)

DEC	OCTAL	HEX	ASCII	DEC	OCTAL	HEX	ASCII
94	136	5E	^	111	157	6F	o
95	137	5F	—	112	160	70	p
96	140	60	'	113	161	71	q
97	141	61	a	114	162	72	r
98	142	62	b	115	163	73	s
99	143	63	c	116	164	74	t
100	144	64	d	117	165	75	u
101	145	65	e	118	166	76	v
102	146	66	f	119	167	77	w
103	147	67	g	120	170	78	x
104	150	68	h	121	171	79	y
105	151	69	i	122	172	7A	z
106	152	6A	j	123	173	7B	{
107	153	6B	k	124	174	7C	|
108	154	6C	l	125	175	7D	}
109	155	6D	m	126	176	7E	~
110	156	6E	n	127	177	7F	DEL

Table A-1. ASCII Character Codes (*continued*)

B

SHAKER

The Windows Software Development Kit provides you with a tool called SHAKER.EXE to aid you in applications testing. Once invoked from the MS-DOS Executive, Shaker randomly allocates sections of global memory, forcing Windows to rearrange the movable code and data segments of other applications. This in turn helps you verify that your application properly locks down code and data segments each time it attempts to access them.

From the MS-DOS Executive, invoke the SHAKER.EXE program. Your screen will contain the following:

Select the Parameters menu, as follows:

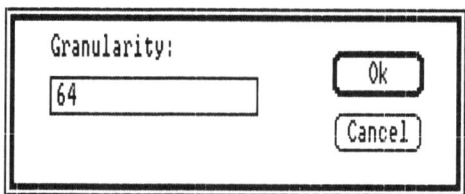

The Allocation Granularity option allows you to specify (in bytes) the size of the objects that Shaker will allocate. Upon selection, the following dialog box appears:

The Time Interval option allows you to specify the number of CPU clock ticks that must occur before Shaker can allocate an object. When you select this option, the following dialog box appears:

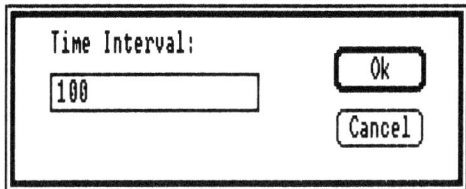

The Max Objects option sets the maximum number of objects that Shaker can allocate. Upon selection this option displays the following dialog box:

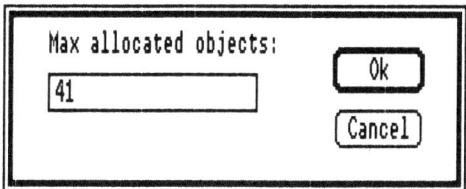

The Show State menu enables or disables the display of object handles as Shaker allocates them. Upon selection, the menu displays the following:

The On option enables the display of handles, whereas Off disables the display.

The Start menu begins the allocation of objects by Shaker. If the handle display state is on, selecting the Start option results in a screen display like the following:

Handle	Size	Handle	Size	Handle	Size	Handle	Size
0	0	23A	80	1DE	7C0	1FA	6C0
1CE	80			21E	6C0	0	0
22E	140	1EA	A00	20E	A00	1DA	14C0
21A	4C0	222	14C0	226	7C0	246	14C0
1C2	140	0	0	1F6	4C0	1D6	6C0
242	6C0	0	0	22A	1BC0		
23E	4C0	232	A00	206	1BC0		
236	FC0	1E6	140	24A	1C0		
1E2	1BC0	1EE	FC0	1C6	A00		
20A	140	1F2	80	202	7C0		
1FE	14C0	212	FC0	0	0		
1D2	4C0	1CA	FC0	216	80		

The Stop menu terminates Shaker.

Finally, the Step menu causes Shaker to allocate one object and then terminate, as opposed to the normal constant rate of object allocation.

Shaker and Heapwalker (see Appendix C) are used hand in hand for testing of your applications memory management. Take a few minutes to understand the functional aspects of Shaker.

APPENDIX

C

HEAPWALKER

The concurrent nature of Windows requires that several programs coexist in memory simultaneously. The Windows Software Development Kit provides you with a utility program called Heapwalker that allows you to examine the *global heap*. Essentially, the global heap consists of all of the available system memory. It may contain blocks that have been allocated to store code or data segments for the currently active programs.

Walk Menu

Invoke the program HEAPWALK.EXE. Select the Walk menu; your screen should contain the following menu options:

```
Walk
Walk
GC(0) and Walk
GC(-1) and Walk
GC(-1) and Hit A:
Allocate all of memory
Free allocated memory
Free 1K of allocated memory
```

The scroll bar at the right of the screen allows you to view the objects that reside in the heap.

All of the options in the Walk menu display the segment address of each object, the size of the object in bytes, the current number of task locks on the object (L3, for example), an optional discardable flag (D), the owner of the object, the object's type (code, data, resource, or shared), and additional information about the object (such as the resource type or the segment number for code segments). The Walk option displays this information as follows:

```
≡                        Luke Heapwalker                              ⌐
 Walk   Sort   Object   File
3E00   480              KERNEL        DATABASE                          ▲
3E1E   26432            KERNEL        CODE      1
4492   4032             MSDOS         TASK                              ▓
458E   512              KERNEL        SHARED
45AE   160          D   DISPLAY       RESOURCE  ICON
45B8   288          D   MSDOS         RESOURCE  STRING
45CA   320              HEAPWALK      DATABASE
45DE   128          D   MSDOS         RESOURCE  DIALOG
45E6   160          D   DISPLAY       RESOURCE  CURSOR
45F0   416              HEAPWALK      TDB
460A   32           D   USER          RESOURCE  MENU
460C   224              USER          SHARED
461A   160          D   MSDOS         RESOURCE  ICON
4624   64               GDI           SHARED
4628   256              GDI           SHARED
4638   192              SYSTEM        DATABASE
4644   1152             SYSTEM        CODE      1
468C   192              KEYBOARD      DATABASE
4698   960              KEYBOARD      DATA
46D4   960              KEYBOARD      CODE      2
                                                                        ▼
```

The GC(0) and Walk option compacts all of the objects in the heap
prior to performing the walk. It does not allocate any memory. The
GC(−1) and Walk option allocates all of the available memory in the
heap (forcing the removal of discardable objects) and then performs
the walk. The GC(−1): and Hit A: option is used for internal testing.
Many programmers use the Allocate all of memory option to test
their out-of-memory condition-handling code. Before displaying the
contents of the global heap, this option forces Heapwalker to first
allocate all of the available free space.

  The Free allocated memory option releases all of the memory
allocated by the Allocate all of memory option. Finally, the Free 1K
of allocated memory option releases allocated memory a 1K block at a
time, displaying the contents of the global heap. Many programmers
use this option to simulate near-out-of-memory conditions.

Sort Menu

The Sort menu allows you to specify how the objects contained in the global heap should be displayed on the screen. By default, Heapwalker displays objects by address, as shown here:

If you select the Module option, Heapwalker will display objects sorted by module name, as follows:

```
≡                          Luke Heapwalker                              ⌐
  Walk   Sort   Object   File
 62AE   480              BURGERMASTER    SHARED                         ▲
 49A0   288              COMM            DATA
 49B2   2688             COMM            CODE        1
 4992   224              COMM            DATABASE
 59C0   224              COURA           DATABASE
 5A1C   224              COURC           DATABASE
 59EE   224              COURD           DATABASE
 479C   7616             DISPLAY         CODE        1
 4772   672              DISPLAY         DATA
 4750   544              DISPLAY         DATABASE
 5AD8   160              DISPLAY         RESOURCE    CURSOR
 5ABA   160              DISPLAY         RESOURCE    ICON
 45E6   160          D   DISPLAY         RESOURCE    CURSOR
 45AE   160          D   DISPLAY         RESOURCE    ICON
 5AC4   160          D   DISPLAY         RESOURCE    CURSOR
 5ACE   160          D   DISPLAY         RESOURCE    CURSOR
 4A66   1888             FONTS           RESOURCE    FONT
 4A5A   192              FONTS           DATABASE
 667C   9504             FREE
 5B96   11040            GDI             DATA
 E4E0   400              GDI             SHARED                         ▼
```

The Size option directs Heapwalker to display the objects in sequence from largest to smallest, as shown here:

```
≡                        Luke Heapwalker                          ⌐
 Walk  Sort   Object  File
 5076  35072          USER           CODE       1                  ▲
 3E1E  26432          KERNEL         CODE       1
 4B84  16512          GDI            CODE       1
 6E1C  15264      D   MSDOS          CODE       4
 62DE  14816   L1     HEAPWALK       DATA
 71D6  14496      D   MSDOS          CODE       3
 5FBA  11680          USER           DATA
 5B96  11040          GDI            DATA
 667C   9504          FREE
 68CE   9152      D   HEAPWALK       CODE       1
 479C   7616          DISPLAY        CODE       1
 7B00   6112      D   USER           CODE       2
 7706   5280      D   USER           CODE       8
 7D98   5248      D   GDI            CODE       5
 7914   4544      D   USER           CODE       4
 4492   4032          MSDOS          TASK
 4F8C   3744          USER           DATABASE
 7A30   3328      D   USER           CODE       3
 6CE8   3296      D   USER           CODE      13
 7642   3136      D   USER           CODE       9      ▼
```

Object Menu

The Object menu allows you to examine specific objects in detail. The
Show option displays the contents of the object in hexadecimal and
ASCII formats, as follows:

```
≡                            62AF
0000 00 00 00 00 73 00 FE 3D FE 7F 00 80 00 00 20 00   ....s.N=N....    ▲
0010 C2 01 20 00 FB 63 00 00 00 00 AE 01 29 00 BA 03   B. .{c.....)..
0020 6B 00 .F 62 00 01 49 5E 20 00 97 5B 04 00 BB 5F   k./b..I^ ..[..._
0030 04 00 .B 5A 04 00 D7 5E 20 00 F9 7F 09 00 BB 7F   ..kZ..W^ .y..
0040 09 00 D9 5A 00 00 CF 5A 01 00 C5 5A 01 00 AD 5F   ..YZ..OZ..EZ..-
0050 20 00 A7 5F 20 00 A1 5F 20 00 9B 5F 20 00 29 46    ._ .._ .._ ..)F
0060 20 00 B3 5F 20 00 89 5F 20 00 DD 4A 20 00 95 5F    .3_ .._ ..jJ
0070 20 00 E7 45 01 00 BB 5A 00 00 8F 5F 20 00 51 47    .gE..Z.._ .QG   ▼
```

You select objects for display by double-clicking the mouse select button once the object name appears in reverse video on the screen. Notice the scroll bar on the right side of the window. This allows you to move easily through the contents of an object.

The Local Walk option examines a data segment and displays the offset (in bytes) of the object into the data segment, the size of the object (in bytes), the object's current allocation status (BUSY or FREE), and the object type (fixed or movable). The object selected must be a data segment. If you select an object that is not a data segment, Heapwalker will display the following dialog box:

The LC (−1) and Local Walk option compacts the local objects before performing the walk.

Write Menu

The Write menu allows you to write the contents of the global heap to the file HEAPWALK.OUT. The file will contain objects from the heap, as shown in Figure C-1.

Heapwalker is very useful for testing and provides useful memory management-information. Traverse each of Heapwalker's options; you will be impressed with its capabilities.

6E7A	49056		HEAPWALK	TASK	
5030	35072		USER	CODE	1
3DD8	26432		KERNEL	CODE	1
4B3E	16512		GDI	CODE	1
6A7E	16320	D	USER	DATA	
5E8A	15936	D	CALENDAR	DATA	
63A6	15936	D	CALENDAR	DATA	
7A74	13536		FREE		
5BD8	11040	D	GDI	DATA	
7DC2	9152	D	HEAPWALK	CODE	1
67B0	8896	L1 D	HEAPWALK	DATA	
4756	7616		DISPLAY	CODE	1
444C	4032		MSDOS	TASK	
4F46	3744		USER	DATABASE	
5B2C	2752	D	MSDOS	DATA	
62FC	2720		KERNEL	SHARED	
496C	2688		COMM	CODE	1
4A9A	2624		GDI	DATABASE	
626E	2272		GDI	SHARED	
69DC	2176		FREE		
4A20	1888		FONTS	RESOURCE	FONT
45FE	1152		SYSTEM	CODE	1
4568	1120		CALENDAR	DATABASE	
58D2	1088		MSDOS	DATABASE	
4652	960		KEYBOARD	DATA	
468E	960		KEYBOARD	CODE	2
593C	704		USER	SHARED	
472C	672		DISPLAY	DATA	
678A	608		BURGERMASTER	SHARED	
470A	544		DISPLAY	DATABASE	
5916	544		MSDOS	CODE	1
46EA	512		MOUSE	CODE	2
4548	512		KERNEL	SHARED	

Figure C-1. Contents of HEAPWALK.OUT file

APPENDIX

D

MANAGING
IMPORT LIBRARIES

Most programmers already have a deep appreciation of the use of library files during program development. The Windows Software Development Kit allows you to create import libraries that can be linked dynamically to an application by using LINK4.

To create an import library, include EXPORTS and LIBRARY statements in the module definition file. The LIBRARY entry specifies the name of the library module resource and has the format shown on the next page.

LIBRARY library __filename

Below the EXPORTS statement, add the name of each callable routine within the library file, as follows:

```
EXPORTS
    ROUTINE1
    ROUTINE2
```

To reference the library routines from within an applications program, you must either specify the routines under the IMPORTS statement in the application's module definition file:

```
IMPORTS
    ROUTINE1.FILENAME
    ROUTINE2.FILENAME
```

or use the LoadLibrary procedure to load the module. The latter method (loading the library via LoadLibrary) is preferred.

The Windows Software Development Kit provides two utility programs, IMPLIB.EXE and EXEHDR.EXE, that are used in manipulating Windows libraries. The first creates the library file, as follows:

```
IMPLIB file.lib file.def
```

The program opens the module definition file specified and examines it for exported routines with which to build the library file named file.lib. The second program, EXEHDR.EXE, examines an EXE file to determine whether it contains a Windows program or library routine. The format of the command is

```
EXEHDR filename.exe
```

The *Programmer's Utility Guide* explains each program in detail. For now, note their existence and functionality.

As you create libraries for Windows applications, keep the following facts in mind:

□ Routines in a library must be compiled such that the data segment differs from the stack segment.

□ Many of the C run-time library routines (ones that perform string manipulation, for example) are incompatible with Windows libraries. You may need to develop your own routines to replace them.

Refer to the documentation provided with the Windows Software Development Kit; you should find that Windows libraries help decrease your application development time.

E

MEMORY MANAGEMENT

The multitasking nature of Windows and its shared memory requirements force the programmer to be more aware of memory management within each Windows application. As you have seen, Windows resources can be assigned attributes that make them

FIXED	Object remains in a fixed location.
MOVABLE	Object can be moved during memory compaction.
DISCARDABLE	Object can be discarded from memory when it is no longer required.

For most applications, you will obtain the greatest degree of system utilization by allowing Windows to move or discard resources when such operations are required.

Windows provides each executing application with an area of memory called the *local heap*. The application can allocate space in this region for strings, arrays, and other data structures. Upon termination of the application, Windows automatically releases local memory back to the system pool.

Likewise, Windows provides a *global heap* that is available to all of the currently executing Windows applications. As with the local heap, applications can allocate, lock, or modify blocks of memory contained within the global heap. Unlike the local heap, however, the application is responsible for releasing all global memory allocated during program application.

Although applications can allocate memory from both the global and local heaps, there are still times when the application requires more dynamic memory than is currently available. During such occurrences, Windows attempts to satisfy the memory allocation request by removing memory marked as discardable until a sufficient number of memory bytes exists. If, upon discarding all of the memory marked as discardable, insufficient memory exists for the memory allocation request, Windows returns an error status value.

Appendix I provides the memory management routines that allow an application to control the local and global heaps. Within that appendix you will find routines that perform data segment binding, and local and global heap allocation and locking, along with routines that discard and compact memory blocks.

Memory management is a complex undertaking. Use the tools provided with the Windows Software Development Kit, Heapwalker, and Shaker to become more conversant with Windows memory utilization.

VIRTUAL KEYS

This appendix lists the values that Windows assigns to each of its virtual keys. Windows defines 256 virtual keys from 0 to 255. It separates these keys into two sets: one, known as Windows-defined virtual keys, ranges from 0 to 127; the other, called OEM-defined keys, consists of the values 128 to 255. Within the set of Windows-defined virtual keys, not all keys are required. The ones that are not required are denoted by an * symbol in Table F-1. Some OEMs sometimes choose to define SHIFT- and CTRL-key combinations in the OEM-definable set of virtual keys.

Numeric Value	Key Pressed
1*	Left mouse select button
2*	Right mouse select button
3	ESC key
4*	Middle mouse select button
5	Not defined
6	Not defined
7	Not defined
8	BACKSPACE key
9	TAB key
10	Not defined
11	Not defined
12*	Clear EOL (not implemented on IBM keyboard)
13	ENTER key
14	Not defined
15	Not defined
16	SHIFT key
17	CTRL key
18	ALT key
19	SCROLL LOCK key
20	CAPS LOCK key
21	Not defined
22	Not defined
23	Not defined
24	Not defined
25	Not defined
26	Not defined
27	ESC key
28	Not defined
29	Not defined
30	Not defined
31	Not defined

Table F-1. Virtual Keys

Numeric Value	Key Pressed
32	SPACEBAR
33	Numeric keypad PGUP key
34	Numeric keypad PGDN key
35	Numeric keypad END key
36	Numeric keypad HOME key
37	Numeric keypad LEFT ARROW key
38	Numeric keypad UP ARROW key
39	Numeric keypad RIGHT ARROW key
40	Numeric keypad DOWN ARROW key
41*	Select key (not implemented on IBM keyboard)
42*	Print key (PRTSC key on IBM keyboard)
43*	Numeric keypad ENTER key
44	Not defined
45	Numeric keypad INS key
46	Numeric keypad DEL key
47*	Help key (not implemented on IBM keyboard)
48-95	Standard ASCII values
96*	Numeric keypad 0 key
97*	Numeric keypad 1 key
98*	Numeric keypad 2 key
99*	Numeric keypad 3 key
100*	Numeric keypad 4 key
101*	Numeric keypad 5 key
102*	Numeric keypad 6 key
103*	Numeric keypad 7 key
104*	Numeric keypad 8 key
105*	Numeric keypad 9 key
106*	Numeric keypad * key
107*	Numeric keypad + key
108*	Numeric keypad , key (not implemented on IBM keyboard)
109*	Numeric keypad − key

Table F-1. Virtual Keys (*continued*)

Numeric Value	Key Pressed
110*	Numeric keypad . key
111*	Numeric keypad / key
112	Function key F1
113	Function key F2
114	Function key F3
115	Function key F4
116	Function key F5
117	Function key F6
118	Function key F7
119	Function key F8
120*	Function key F9
121*	Function key F10
122*	Function key 11
123*	Function key 12
124*	Function key 13
125*	Function key 14
126*	Function key 15
127*	Function key 16

Table F-1. Virtual Keys (*continued*)

G

INSTALLING WINDOWS

The Windows installation will vary, depending on your system configuration, either dual double-density disk drives or a hard disk. This appendix will first examine the dual floppy disk installation.

Floppy Disk Installation

To create a Windows environment for a dual floppy system, perform the following steps:

1. To perform the installation correctly, you must create a backup copy of each Windows disk. Have six blank disks available.

2. The Windows system installation requires a DOS system disk that contains the command DISKCOPY.COM. Have a bootable DOS disk available.

3. Windows will create two disks. The first is the Windows Startup disk that you will use to invoke Windows. The second is the Windows System disk. Have two blank disks available.

4. Boot DOS.

5. At the DOS prompt, place the Windows Setup disk in drive A and issue the command

A> SETUP

6. Perform the installation by following this text.

Windows will respond to the SETUP command with

```
Setup prepares Microsoft Windows to run on your computer.
It also helps you set up your disks in the most efficient way for:

    - starting Microsoft Windows
    - running Windows applications
    - printing from Microsoft Windows
```

```
When you're
ready:
```

TO	PRESS
Continue	C
Quit	Q

If you are not ready to continue the Windows installation, press Q. Windows will return you to the DOS prompt. Otherwise, to continue the installation, press ENTER. Windows will display

```
You can set up Microsoft Windows to run from a floppy disk or
from a hard disk.  Please indicate the type of disk you want.
```

```
When you're
ready:
```

TO	PRESS
Setup on a floppy disk	F
Setup on a hard disk	H
Quit	Q

At this point, Windows has no way of knowing whether you desire a hard disk or floppy disk system installation. In this case, press F. Windows will begin the floppy disk system installation by displaying

```
To setup Microsoft Windows on a floppy disk you need:

     - the Microsoft Windows Setup disk
     - the Microsoft Windows Build disk
     - the Microsoft Windows Utilities disk
     - the Microsoft Windows Font disk

You need to know the following:

     - what kind of pointer device (mouse) you have, if any
     - what kind of graphics adaptor you have
     - what kind of printer(s) you have, if any
     - how each printer is connected to your computer
```

```
When you're
ready:        ┌─────────────────────────────────────────┐
              │ TO                          PRESS        │
              ├─────────────────────────────────────────┤
              │ Continue                      C          │
              │ Quit                          Q          │
              └─────────────────────────────────────────┘
```

If you do not know the information required, press Q and continue the installation at a later time. Otherwise, press ENTER, and Windows will respond with

```
                        Setup Menu
┌─────────────────────────────────────────────────────────────┐
│ TO                                            PRESS           │
├─────────────────────────────────────────────────────────────┤
│ Backup master disks                             B             │
│    Allows you to make copies of your master disks.            │
│                                                               │
│ Set up Windows System                           S             │
│    Allows you to configure Windows to your system.            │
│                                                               │
│ Quit                                            Q             │
└─────────────────────────────────────────────────────────────┘
If this is the first time you have used Setup, do these in order.
```

Since this is the first time that you are performing a Windows system installation, select option B. Windows will prompt you to place your DOS system disk in drive A, as follows:

```
The backup procedure works by running your copy of the DOS utility
DISKCOPY.COM.  Please put your DOS disk in drive A:
```

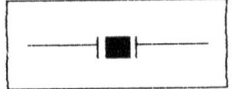

```
                    Put your DOS disk
                      into drive A:
```

```
When you're
ready:
```

TO	PRESS
Continue	C
Return to Setup menu	M

With the DOS system disk in drive A, press ENTER to continue. The
Windows installation is ready to create your backup disk. Place a
blank disk into drive B and press ENTER. The following is displayed:

```
This procedure copies or "backs up" your master disks so that
you may store them away for safekeeping.
```

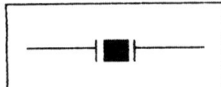   

```
     Put the master disk            Put a blank disk
        into drive A:                 into drive B:
```

```
When you're
ready:
```

TO	PRESS
Continue	C
Return to Setup menu	M

The familiar DISKCOPY prompt now will be displayed on your
screen.

```
          Insert SOURCE Diskette in Drive A :

          Insert TARGET Diskette in Drive B :

          Press any key when ready . . .
```

Place your Windows Setup disk in drive A and a blank disk in drive B. Press ENTER to continue the backup process. When the process is finished, DISKCOPY will display

```
Insert SOURCE Diskette in Drive A :

Insert TARGET Diskette in Drive B :

Press any key when ready . . .

Copying 40 tracks
9 Sectors/Track, 2 Side(s)


Copy another diskette (Y/N)?
```

Press Y at the prompt and repeat this process for each of the Windows disks. When the process is finished, place your original Windows disks in a safe location. You will use the backup disks from now on. The Windows installation will now return to the following menu:

Setup Menu

TO	PRESS
Backup master disks Allows you to make copies of your master disks.	B
Set up Windows System Allows you to configure Windows to your system.	S
Quit	Q

If this is the first time you have used Setup, do these in order.

You are ready to create the Windows System disk. Press S. Windows will now prompt you to enter the type of keyboard your system is using.

```
In order to operate correctly, Microsoft Windows needs to know
what kind of keyboard you have.

Follow these        - Find your keyboard on this list.
steps:              - Type the number for your keyboard.
                      (Or enter M to return to Setup menu)
                    - Press the ─┘ key.

 1: United States   11: France        21: Portugal
 2: Argentina       12: Ireland       22: Spain
 3: Australia       13: Italy         23: Sweden
 4: Austria         14: Japan         24: United Kingdom
 5: Belgium         15: Lebanon       25: Venezuela
 6: Brazil          16: Luxembourg    26: West Germany
 7: Canada          17: Mexico        27: AT&T 6300 or 6300 PLUS
 8: Chile           18: Netherlands
 9: Denmark         19: Norway
10: Finland         20: Peru

        keyboard: 1
```

In this case, Windows is adjusting itself for possible KEYBxx.COM files. Select the appropriate keyboard number and press ENTER.

Next, the Windows installation will prompt you for the type of mouse (pointing device) that you will be using.

```
In order to operate correctly, Microsoft Windows needs to know
what kind of pointing device you have.

Follow these        - Find your pointing device on this list.
steps:              - Type the number for your pointing device.
                      (Or enter M to return to Setup menu)
                    - Press the ─┘ key.

1: No pointing device
2: Microsoft Mouse (Bus/Serial)
3: Mouse Systems or VisiOn Mouse (COM1)
4: Mouse Systems or VisiOn Mouse (COM2)
5: Logitech Serial Mouse
6: Kraft Joystick Mouse
7: the Lite-Pen Company - Lightpen
8: FTG Data Systems Lightpen and Single Pixel Board
9: AT&T Mouse 6300 (plugs into keyboard)

        pointing device: 1
```

If you don't have a mouse, simply press ENTER, thus selecting the default value of 1. Lastly, the installation asks what type of graphics adapter your system is using.

```
In order to operate correctly, Microsoft Windows needs to know
what kind of graphics adapter you have.

Follow these          - Find your graphics adapter on this list.
steps:                 - Type the number for your graphics adapter.
                         (Or enter M to return to Setup menu)
                       - Press the ⏎ key.

1: IBM (or compatible) Color/Graphics Adapter or COMPAQ Personal Computer
2: Hercules Graphics Card (or compatible) with Monochrome Display
3: Enhanced Graphics Adapter (EGA) with Monochrome Personal Computer Display
4: EGA with Enhanced Color Display (Black and White only)
5: EGA with Enhanced Color Display or Personal Computer Color Display
6: EGA (more than 64K) with Enhanced Color Display
7: AT&T PC 6300 or PC 6300 PLUS Display Adapter
8: AT&T Display Enhancement Board
9: Micro Display Systems GENIUS Graphics Adapter

        graphics adapter: 1
```

After you have responded to the three previous prompts, the Windows installation is ready to build the Windows System disk. Place the Windows Setup disk in drive A and a blank disk in drive B.

```
Setup is now ready to create the Windows System disk.
Please insert a blank disk in drive B:
```

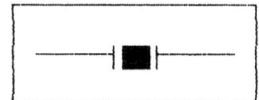

```
            Put a blank disk
            into drive B:
```

```
When you're
ready:
```

TO	PRESS
Continue	C

The Windows installation will copy files from the Setup disk to your Windows System disk, displaying

```
Setup is copying files from the Setup disk to the
Windows System disk.
```

When the process is finished, the procedure will prompt

```
Setup now needs to read the Build disk.
Please insert it in drive A:
```

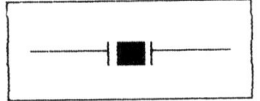

```
              Put the Build disk
                into drive A:
```

When you're
ready:

TO	PRESS
Continue	C

Place the backup copy of your Windows Build disk in drive A. Press ENTER to continue. The Windows installation procedure will begin copying files to your Windows System disk, displaying the following:

```
Setup is copying files from the Build disk to the
Windows System disk.
```

When this process is finished, Windows will display

```
Your new System disk is ready.  Later you will add to it some
information about your hardware.  For now, please remove the
System disk from drive B: and label it "Microsoft Windows System disk"
```

When you're
ready:

TO	PRESS
Continue	C

Figure G-1. New Windows System disk

Remove the disk from drive B and label it as shown in Figure G-1.

The Windows installation procedure is now ready to build your Windows Startup disk. Place a blank disk in drive B and press ENTER to continue.

```
Setup is now ready to create the Windows Startup disk.
Please insert a blank disk in drive B:
```

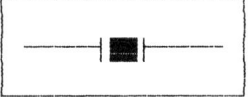

```
                        Put a blank disk
                        into drive B:
```

```
When you're
ready:
```

TO	PRESS
Continue	C

The installation will now prompt you to specify whether or not the Windows installation disk should be a bootable disk. Normally, you will want this disk to be bootable. Press Y and then press ENTER.

The installation will prompt you to place your DOS system disk in drive A, as follows:

```
Setup will now install a copy of DOS on your Windows Startup disk.
Please place your DOS disk into drive A:
```

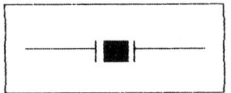

```
                      Put your DOS disk
                        into drive A:
```

When you're
ready:

TO	PRESS
Install DOS	Y
Do not install DOS	N

Windows now will complete the creation of your Startup disk by copying the required files to it.

```
    Setup is writing the Windows startup files to the
    Windows Startup disk.
```

After the files have been copied, the installation procedure will display

```
Your new Startup disk is ready.  Please remove it from drive
B: and label it "Microsoft Windows Startup disk"
```

When you're
ready:

TO	PRESS
Continue	C

Remove the disk from drive B and label it as in Figure G-2.

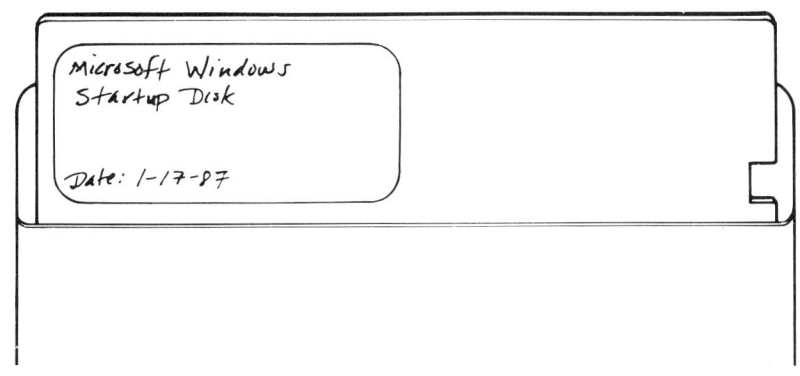

Figure G-2. New Windows Startup disk

Next, the installation will complete the creation of your Windows System disk.

```
In this procedure, Setup goes to the Utilities disk for the
printer drivers and related fonts needed for the hardware you will
specify.  Setup then adds the information to your System disk.
```

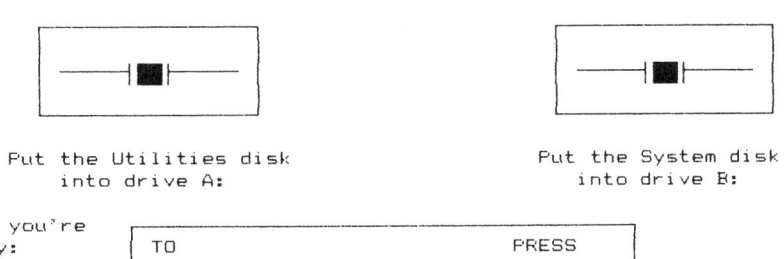

```
     Put the Utilities disk                    Put the System disk
          into drive A:                          into drive B:

When you're
ready:         ┌──────────────────────────────────────────────┐
               │  TO                          PRESS            │
               ├──────────────────────────────────────────────┤
               │  Continue                      C              │
               └──────────────────────────────────────────────┘
```

In drive A, place the backup copy of your Windows Utilities disk and
in drive B, the Windows System disk that you have been creating.
Press ENTER when you have done so. The Windows installation will
prompt you, asking whether or not you want to configure a printer or
plotter to be used with Windows, as follows:

```
Would you like to set up a printer/plotter?
```

```
When you're
ready:        ┌─────────────────────────────────────────────┐
              │  TO                              PRESS       │
              │                                              │
              │  Set up a printer/plotter         Y          │
              │  Continue                         N          │
              └─────────────────────────────────────────────┘
```

If you have a printer, press Y; otherwise, press N. If you select a
printer configuration, the installation will display

```
In order to print correctly, Microsoft Windows needs to know what
kind of printer or plotter you have.

Follow these            - Find your printer in this list.
steps:                  - Type the number for your printer.
                          (Or enter M to return to Setup menu)
                        - Press the ─┘ key.

 1: Epson FX-80         11: NEC P2/P3          21: HP 7550A
 2: Epson MX-80 Graftrax 12: C-Itoh 8510       22: Generic / Text Only
 3: Epson LQ-1500       13: Toshiba P1351      23: PostScript/LaserWriter
 4: IBM Graphics        14: Star SG-10         24: HP ThinkJet (2225 C-D)
 5: IBM Proprinter      15: TI 850             25: Xerox 4020
 6: Okidata 92/93 (IBM) 16: TI 855
 7: Okidata 192/193 (IBM) 17: HP LaserJet
 8: Okidata 92/93 (Std) 18: HP LaserJet+
 9: Okidata 192/193 (Std) 19: HP 7470A
10: NEC 3550            20: HP 7475A

        Printer: 1
```

If your printer appears on the screen, enter its number. If your printer does not appear on the screen, select the printer that most closely
behaves like your printer. Refer to your printer reference manual for
more details.

Next, the procedure will prompt you to enter the port to which
your printer is connected.

```
Now Windows needs to know which port this printer or plotter is
connected to.  (If you're unsure which port you are using,
check the owner's guide for your device.)

Follow these         - Find the output port for this printer/plotter.
steps:                - Type the number for your printer/plotter.
                        (Or enter M to return to Setup menu)
                      - Press the ─┘ key.

1: LPT1:
2: LPT2:
3: LPT3:
4: COM1:
5: COM2:
6: None

          Output port: 1
```

Normally, the printer is connected to LPT1. After you have specified
the port, Windows will copy its utility files to your Windows System
disk.

```
Setup is copying files from the Utilities disk to the
Windows System disk.
```

The installation provides you with the opportunity to configure
multiple printers.

```
Would you like to set up another printer/plotter?
```

When you're
ready:

```
┌─────────────────────────────────────────────┐
│ TO                               PRESS        │
├─────────────────────────────────────────────┤
│ Set up another printer            Y           │
│ Continue                          N           │
└─────────────────────────────────────────────┘
```

If you have additional printers, press Y; otherwise, press N.

The installation procedure will now prompt you for the Font disk.

```
Setup now needs to read the Font disk.
Please insert it in drive A:
```

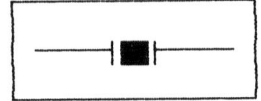

```
                           Put the Font disk
                            into drive A:
```

```
When you're
ready:
```

TO	PRESS
Continue	C

Place the Windows Font disk in drive A and press ENTER to continue the file copy.

```
        Setup is copying files from the Font disk to the
        Windows System disk.
```

Windows will now redisplay the menu, as follows:

```
                        Setup Menu
```

TO	PRESS
Backup master disks Allows you to make copies of your master disks.	B
Set up Windows System Allows you to configure Windows to your system.	S
Quit	Q

```
If this is the first time you have used Setup, do these in order.
```

Press Q. Your Windows installation is complete. The installation will display

```
Microsoft Windows is set up to operate on your computer.

You can now start Windows.

To start Microsoft Windows:

     - Put the Windows Startup disk in drive A:
     - Put the Windows System disk in drive B:
     - Type WIN
     - Press the ⌐ key.

A>
```

Hard Disk Installation

The Windows fixed disk installation is similar to the floppy disk
installation. Because of the significant number of Windows users
using hard disks, however, it is worth examining the complete hard
disk installation here. Using Windows from a hard disk greatly sim-
plifies your efforts, since all of the files reside on the fixed disk. To
install Windows on your fixed disk, perform the following:

1. Boot DOS and be sure that you have adequate disk space on the
   hard disk (approximately 1.5 M).

2. Place the Windows Setup disk in drive A and issue the command

   A> SETUP

3. Perform the installation by following this text.

The Windows installation procedure will respond to the SETUP
command with the following:

```
Setup prepares Microsoft Windows to run on your computer.
It also helps you set up your disks in the most efficient way for:

    - starting Microsoft Windows
    - running Windows applications
    - printing from Microsoft Windows
```

```
When you're
ready:        ┌─────────────────────────────────────────────┐
              │  TO                            PRESS         │
              │                                              │
              │  Continue                       C            │
              │  Quit                           Q            │
              └─────────────────────────────────────────────┘
```

If you are not ready to perform the Windows system installation, press Q, and the installation procedures will return you to the DOS prompt. Otherwise, continue the installation by pressing ENTER. The setup procedure will respond with

```
You can set up Microsoft Windows to run from a floppy disk or
from a hard disk.  Please indicate the type of disk you want.
```

```
When you're
ready:        ┌─────────────────────────────────────────────┐
              │  TO                            PRESS         │
              │                                              │
              │  Setup on a floppy disk         F            │
              │  Setup on a hard disk           H            │
              │  Quit                           Q            │
              └─────────────────────────────────────────────┘
```

In this case, you are performing a hard disk installation, so press H. The Windows installation will display

```
Now Setup will copy the Windows files to your hard disk.

Please type below the full pathname of the directory
where you would like SETUP to put the Windows files.

To accept \WINDOWS as the directory:
    - press the ↵ key.

To specify a different directory:
    - Use the Backspace key to delete characters
    - Type the new directory name (for example: C:\PROGRAMS)
    - press the ↵ key.

[C:\WINDOWS                                              ]
```

By default, the Windows system installation creates a directory called WINDOWS in the root directory of your fixed disk. To specify an alternate directory name, type in the name you desire. If the directory name WINDOWS is acceptable, press ENTER to continue the installation. The installation procedure will continue by displaying

```
To setup Microsoft Windows on a hard disk you need:

    - the Microsoft Windows Setup disk
    - the Microsoft Windows Build disk
    - the Microsoft Windows Utilities disk
    - the Microsoft Windows Font disk
    - the Microsoft Windows Desktop Applications disk
    - the Microsoft Write Program  disk

You need to know the following:

    - what kind of pointer device (mouse) you have, if any
    - what kind of graphics adaptor you have
    - what kind of printer(s) you have, if any
    - how each printer is connected to your computer


When you're
ready:
```

TO	PRESS
Continue	C
Quit	Q

Press ENTER to continue the installation or Q to return to DOS.
Next, the procedure will prompt you for the system keyboard.

```
In order to operate correctly, Microsoft Windows needs to know
what kind of keyboard you have.

Follow these          - Find your keyboard on this list.
steps:                 - Type the number for your keyboard.
                         (Or enter Q to quit Setup)
                       - Press the  ↵  key.

 1: United States    11: France          21: Portugal
 2: Argentina        12: Ireland         22: Spain
 3: Australia        13: Italy           23: Sweden
 4: Austria          14: Japan           24: United Kingdom
 5: Belgium          15: Lebanon         25: Venezuela
 6: Brazil           16: Luxembourg      26: West Germany
 7: Canada           17: Mexico          27: AT&T 6300 or 6300 PLUS
 8: Chile            18: Netherlands
 9: Denmark          19: Norway
10: Finland          20: Peru

     keyboard: 1
```

Enter the number associated with the keyboard format that your system will be using. The procedure now prompts you for the pointing device that you will be using. (If you have not purchased a mouse yet, you should purchase either the Logitech Bus or C7 [Serial] mouse.)

```
In order to operate correctly, Microsoft Windows needs to know
what kind of pointing device you have.

Follow these        - Find your pointing device on this list.
steps:              - Type the number for your pointing device.
                      (Or enter Q to quit Setup)
                    - Press the ⏎ key.

1: No pointing device
2: Microsoft Mouse (Bus/Serial)
3: Mouse Systems or VisiOn Mouse (COM1)
4: Mouse Systems or VisiOn Mouse (COM2)
5: Logitech Serial Mouse
6: Kraft Joystick Mouse
7: the Lite-Pen Company - Lightpen
8: FTG Data Systems Lightpen and Single Pixel Board
9: AT&T Mouse 6300 (plugs into keyboard)

        pointing device: 1
```

Lastly, the Windows installation will prompt you to specify the graphics adapter present on your system.

```
In order to operate correctly, Microsoft Windows needs to know
what kind of graphics adapter you have.

Follow these        - Find your graphics adapter on this list.
steps:              - Type the number for your graphics adapter.
                      (Or enter Q to quit Setup)
                    - Press the ⏎ key.

1: IBM (or compatible) Color/Graphics Adapter or COMPAQ Personal Computer
2: Hercules Graphics Card (or compatible) with Monochrome Display
3: Enhanced Graphics Adapter (EGA) with Monochrome Personal Computer Display
4: EGA with Enhanced Color Display (Black and White only)
5: EGA with Enhanced Color Display or Personal Computer Color Display
6: EGA (more than 64K) with Enhanced Color Display
7: AT&T PC 6300 or PC 6300 PLUS Display Adapter
8: AT&T Display Enhancement Board
9: Micro Display Systems GENIUS Graphics Adapter

        graphics adapter: 1
```

After you have responded to these three prompts, the installation procedure will begin copying files from the Setup disk to the WINDOWS directory on your hard disk.

```
Setup is copying files from the Setup disk to the
C:\WINDOWS\ directory.
```

Next, the procedure will load files from the Windows Build disk.

```
Setup now needs to read the Build disk.
Please insert it in drive A:
```

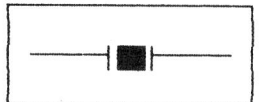

```
'Put the Build disk
    into drive A:
```

When you're
ready:

TO	PRESS
Continue	C

Place the Windows Build disk into drive A and press ENTER. The procedure will copy files from the Build disk, displaying

```
Setup is copying files from the Build disk to the
C:\WINDOWS\ directory.
```

When this process is finished, the installation procedure will copy files from the Windows Utilities disk to your fixed disk.

```
Setup now needs to read the Utilities disk.
Please insert it in drive A:
```

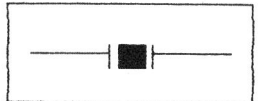

```
Put the Utilities disk
    into drive A:
```

When you're
ready:

TO	PRESS
Continue	C

Place the Utilities disk in drive A and press ENTER.

The installation procedure now allows you to specify the printer that you will be using in conjunction with Windows. Type Y to configure your printer.

```
Would you like to set up a printer/plotter?
```

When you're
ready:

TO	PRESS
Set up a printer/plotter	Y
Continue	N

The procedure will display

```
In order to print correctly, Microsoft Windows needs to know what
kind of printer or plotter you have.

Follow these          - Find your printer in this list.
steps:                 - Type the number for your printer.
                         (Or enter 0 to quit Setup)
                       - Press the ⏎ key.

 1: Epson FX-80        11: NEC P2/P3          21: HP 7550A
 2: Epson MX-80 Graftrax 12: C-Itoh 8510      22: Generic / Text Only
 3: Epson LQ-1500      13: Toshiba P1351      23: PostScript/LaserWriter
 4: IBM Graphics       14: Star SG-10         24: HP ThinkJet (2225 C-D)
 5: IBM Proprinter     15: TI 850             25: Xerox 4020
 6: Okidata 92/93 (IBM) 16: TI 855
 7: Okidata 192/193 (IBM) 17: HP LaserJet
 8: Okidata 92/93 (Std) 18: HP LaserJet+
 9: Okidata 192/193 (Std) 19: HP 7470A
10: NEC 3550           20: HP 7475A

        Printer: 1
```

If your printer is in the list of printers, enter its number and press ENTER. Otherwise, select the printer that behaves most like your printer. Refer to your printer reference manual.

Next, the installation will prompt you to specify the port to which your printer is attached.

```
Now Windows needs to know which port this printer or plotter is
connected to.  (If you're unsure which port you are using,
check the owner's guide for your device.)

Follow these          - Find the output port for this printer/plotter.
steps:                 - Type the number for your printer/plotter.
                         (Or enter 0 to quit Setup)
                       - Press the ⌐⌐ key.

1: LPT1:
2: LPT2:
3: LPT3:
4: COM1:
5: COM2:
6: None

        Output port: 1
```

Normally, the port is LPT1. The procedure continues by copying files
from the disk to your fixed disk, displaying

```
Setup is copying files from the Utilities disk to the
C:\WINDOWS\ directory.
```

Next, the installation procedure allows you to configure multiple
printers. If you have multiple printers, press Y and repeat the previous process. Otherwise, the installation continues by prompting you
to place the Windows Font disk in drive A.

```
Setup now needs to read the Font disk.
Please insert it in drive A:
```

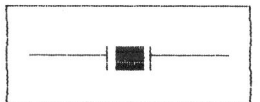

```
Put the Font disk
into drive A:
```

```
When you're
ready:
```

TO	PRESS
Continue	C

Place the disk in drive A and press ENTER to continue.

```
. Setup is copying files from the Font disk to the
  C:\WINDOWS\ directory.
```

After the Font copy is finished, the installation procedure will prompt for the Desktop Applications disk as follows:

```
Setup now needs to read the Desktop Applications disk.
Please insert it in drive A:
```

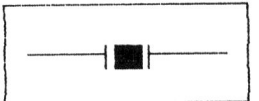

```
Put the Desktop Applications disk
         into drive A:
```

```
When you're
ready:
```

TO	PRESS
Continue	C
Quit	Q

Place the disk in drive A and press ENTER.

```
Setup is copying files from the Desktop Applications disk to the
C:\WINDOWS\ directory.
```

Lastly, the Windows installation will prompt you for the Write Program disk, which contains the Write word processor.

```
Setup now needs to read the Microsoft Write Program  disk.
Please insert it in drive A:
```

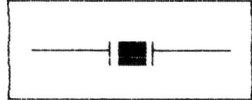

```
          Put the Microsoft Write Program  disk
                   into drive A:
```

```
When you're
ready:
```

TO	PRESS
Continue	C
Quit	Q

Place the disk in drive A and press ENTER.

```
Setup is copying files from the Microsoft Write Program  disk to the
C:\WINDOWS\ directory.
```

The Windows installation is complete, and the procedure will display

```
Microsoft Windows is set up to operate on your computer.
You are now in the Windows directory.

To start Microsoft Windows:

    - Type WIN
    - Press the ⏎ key.

C>
```

H

DESKTOP APPLICATIONS

As you may recall from Chapter 1, Windows provides the following desktop applications:

☐ Clock displays an analog clock with the current system time.

☐ Calculator provides a simple calculator.

☐ Calendar provides an appointment calendar.

☐ Cardfile allows you to organize facts on index cards.

☐ Notepad allows you to create a "To Do" list.

☐ Terminal provides terminal emulation for bulletin-board systems.

☐ Reversi provides a challenging game.

You can load each desktop application as an icon or load the application for immediate execution. In addition, each desktop application has its own System menu that provides the following type of information:

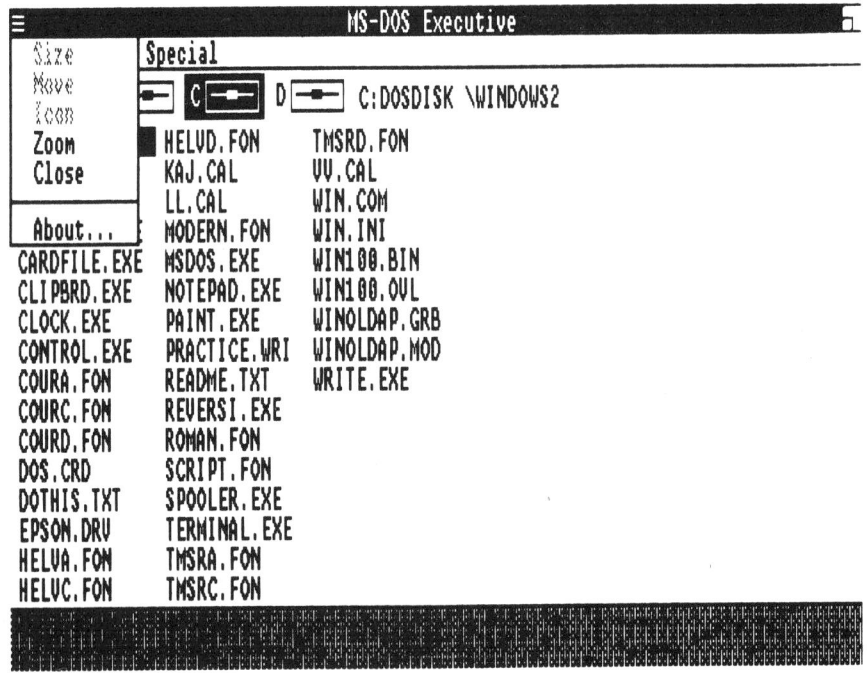

At the end of this appendix you will see each of the options on the System menu and note their effects upon the screen when multiple applications are displayed simultaneously, as shown here:

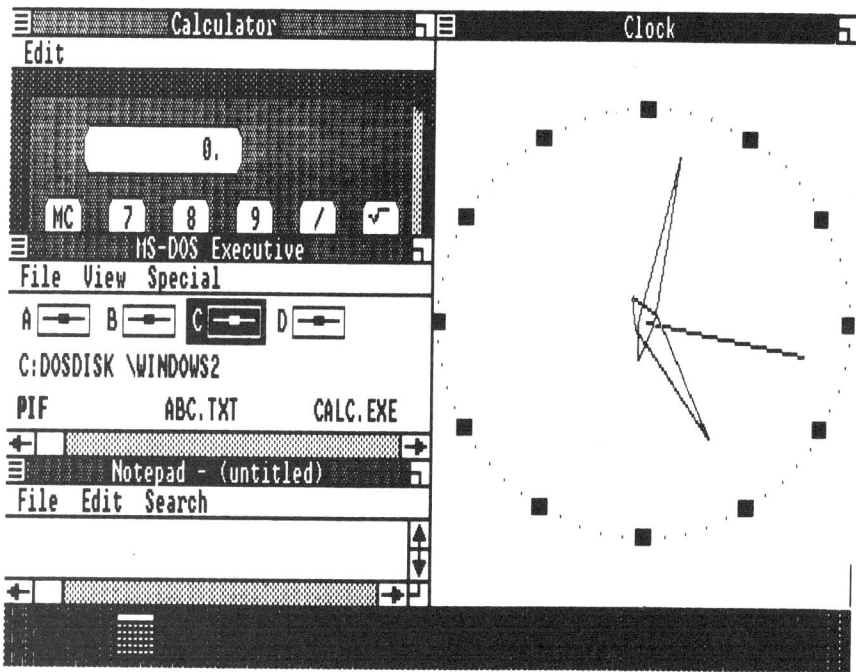

Clock

With Windows, items normally found on a desk are also available on your computer, in the form of programs called desktop applications. The first desktop application to be discussed is the analog clock. Invoke Microsoft Windows by issuing the following command:

A> WIN

Windows will display

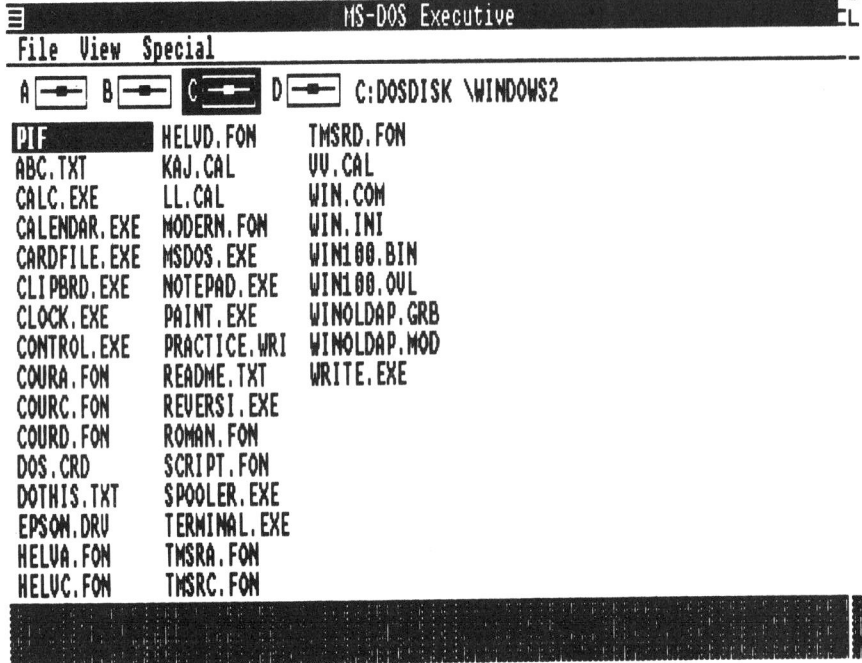

Select CLOCK.EXE as the default Windows file either by using the cursor keys or by pointing at the file with your system mouse and pressing the select button. To invoke the program, simply press the ENTER key on your keyboard, or press the mouse select button twice, as illustrated here:

Keyboard Selection of Executable Program

Select the file desired via the cursor arrow keys. Press the ENTER key to execute the program.

Mouse Selection of Executable Program

Select the file desired via the select button on the mouse. Double-clicking the select button executes the program.

In this case, Windows will respond with

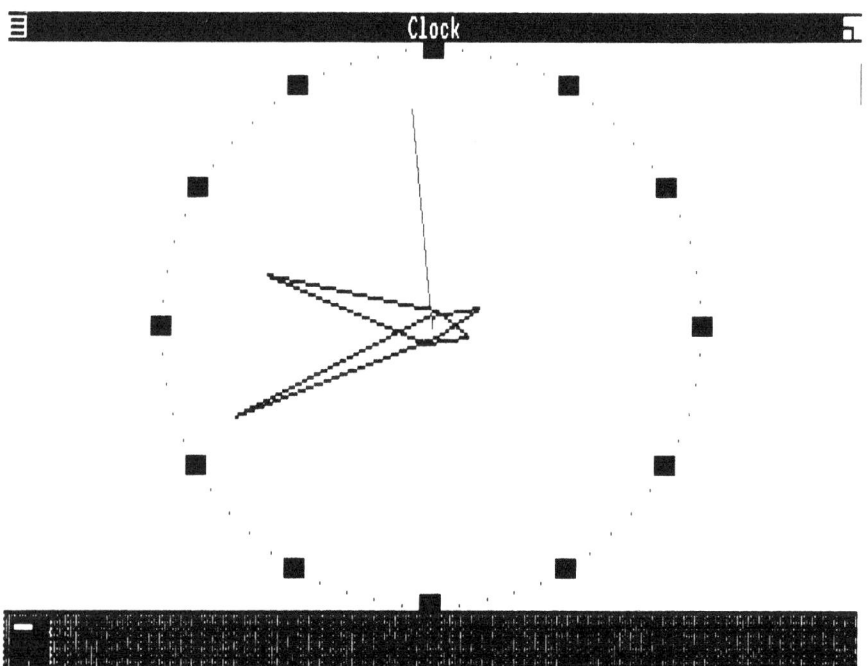

Note the MS-DOS Executive icon in the lower left corner of the screen. It is possible to expand the clock display to the full size of the screen (covering up the icon section) by selecting the Zoom option from the System menu. Remember that the System menu is invoked by pressing ALT-S, or by selecting the menu with your mouse. If you expand the clock, Windows will display

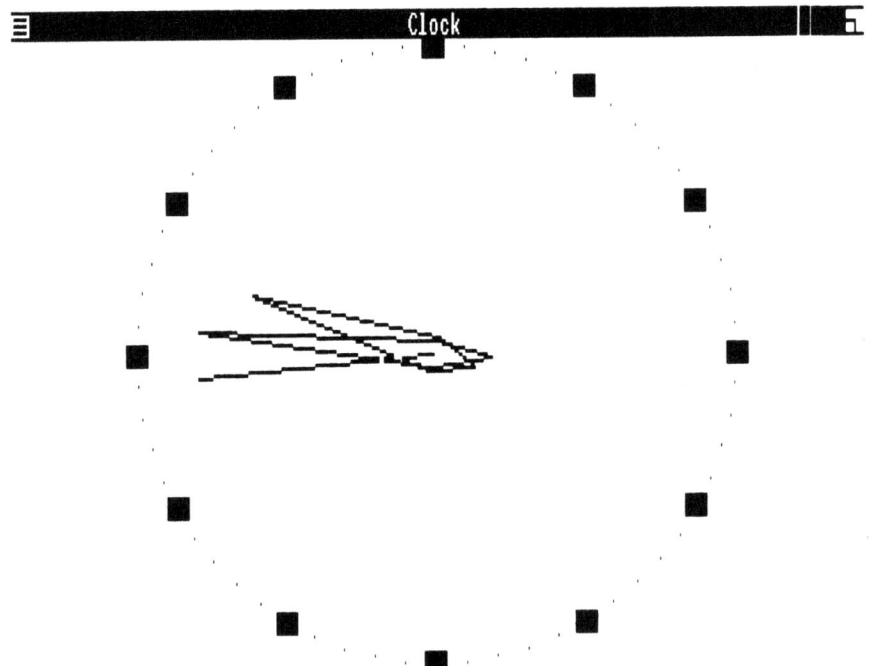

In this case the Zoom option works as a toggle. Pressing it again will redisplay the icon area. Later in this appendix, you will gain greater control over the size of windows when you display several windows simultaneously. Save the Clock program as an icon and return to the MS-DOS Executive.

Calculator

From the MS-DOS Executive, invoke the program CALC.EXE in the same manner as you invoked CLOCK.EXE. Windows will display

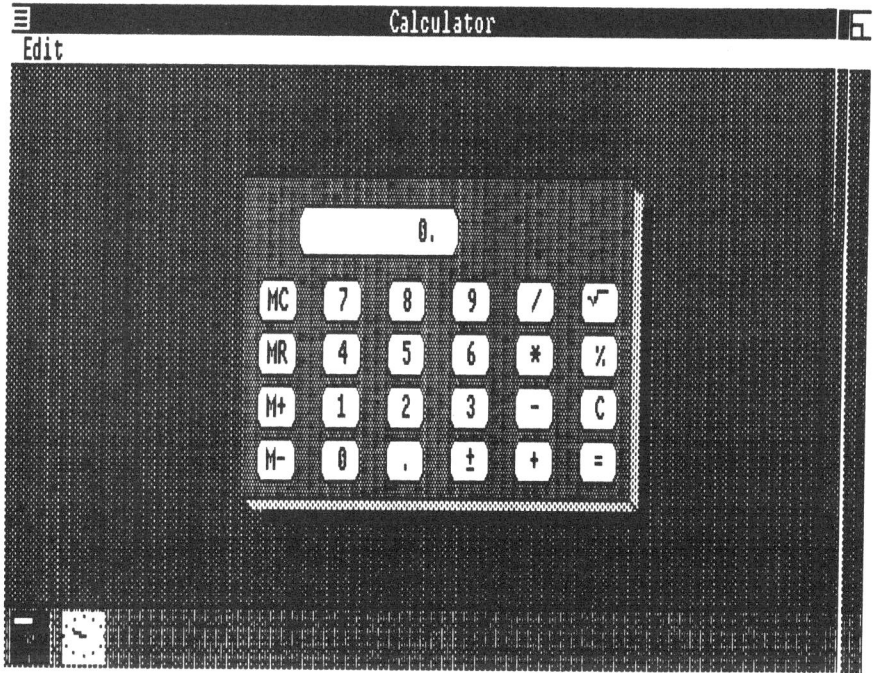

This is your desktop calculator. The Calculator accepts the data entered from either the numbers along the top row of your keyboard or from the numeric keypad. To use the numeric keypad, press the NUMLOCK key on your keyboard (see Figure H-1). To add the numbers 45.66 and 3.77, for example, simply enter the number 45.66 and press the plus (+) key on the numeric keypad (see Figure H-2). Next, enter the number 3.77 and press the equal (=) sign on the top row of your keyboard. The Windows Calculator should now display

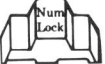

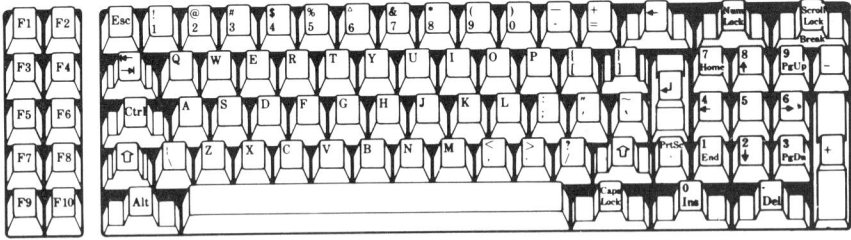

Figure H-1. Location of NUMLOCK key on keyboard

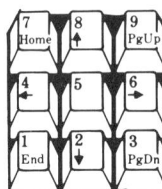

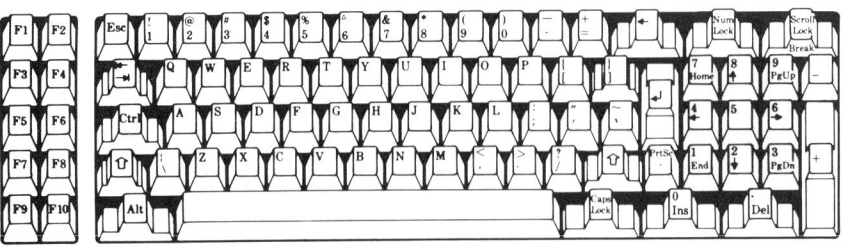

Figure H-2. Location of numeric keypad on keyboard

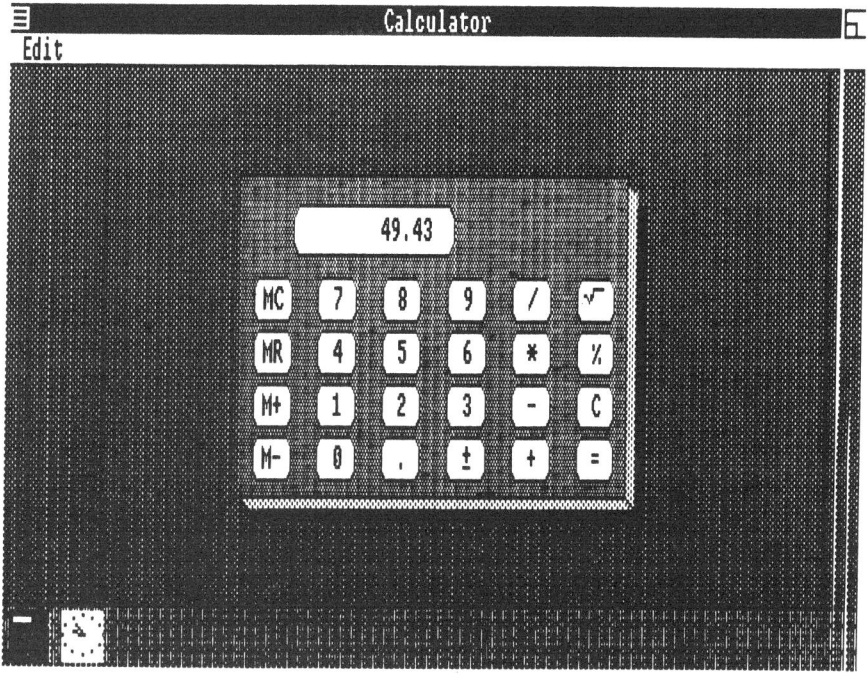

The Calculator works the same way for subtraction, multiplication, and division. The Calculator also provides a square root key. Before you can fully utilize the Windows Calculator, however, you should know that Windows associates the following keyboard entries with the Calculator:

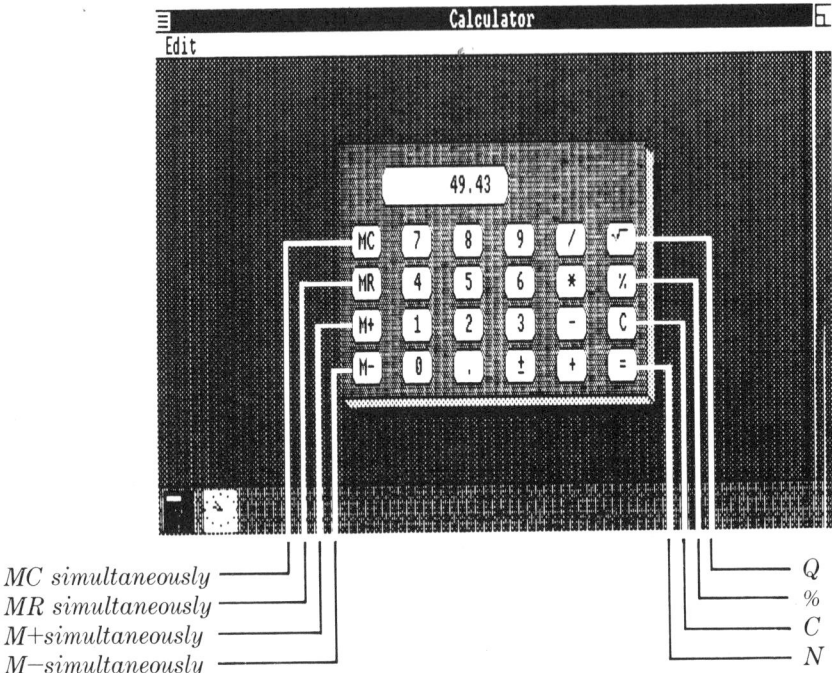

MC *simultaneously*

MR *simultaneously*

M+*simultaneously*

M−*simultaneously*

Q

%

C

N

One of the most useful features of the Calculator is to display the hexadecimal equivalent of a decimal value, as shown here:

Displaying Hexadecimal Equivalents

Enter the decimal value via the numeric keys. Press the H key and CALC will display the hexadecimal equivalent.

For example, enter the value 255 as follows:

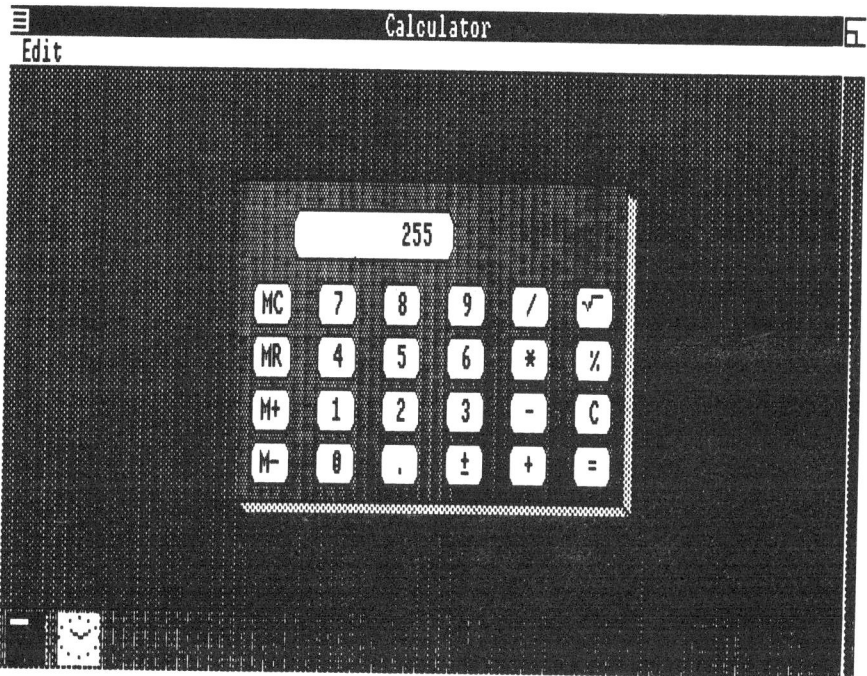

Next, press the H key. The Calculator will display the hexadecimal equivalent of the value 255, as follows:

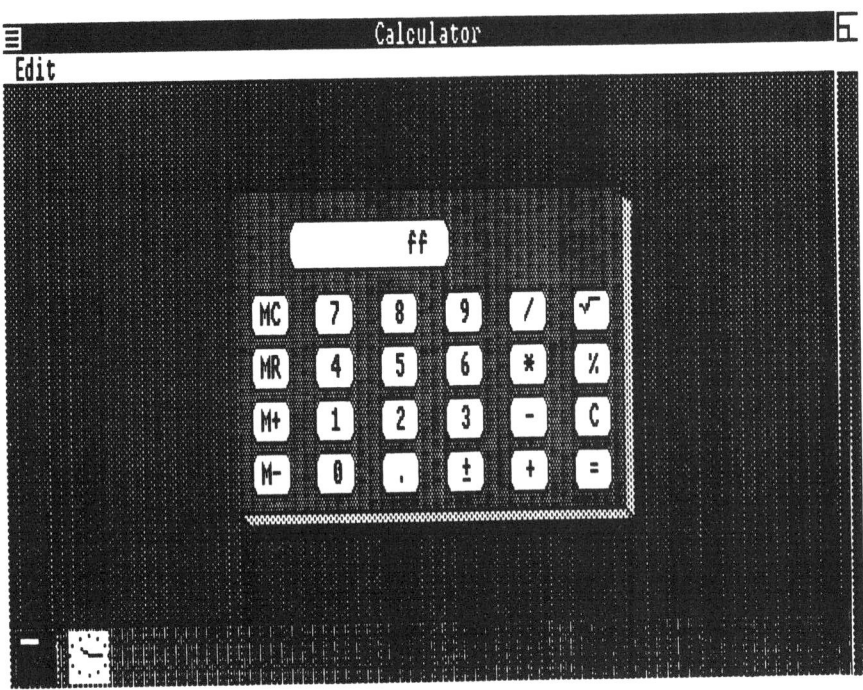

Later in this chapter you will see how to integrate calculations with other Windows applications via the Windows Clipboard. For now, save the Calculator as an icon as shown here:

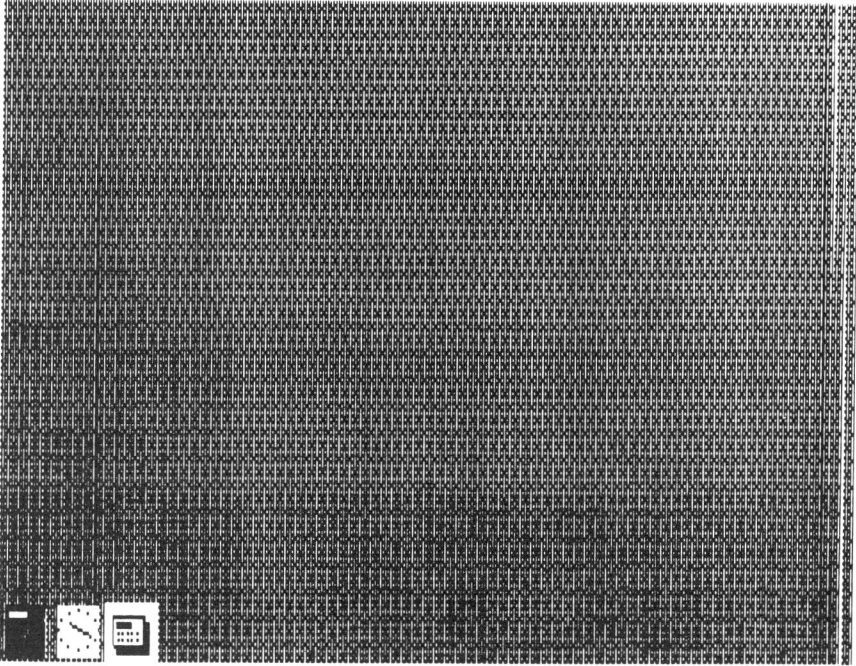

Calendar

The Calendar program provides you with a complete appointment calendar on your computer. With this program you can look up specific dates from January 1980 into the twenty-first century. In addition, Calendar allows you to select appointments or track your daily routine for each of these dates.

From the MS-DOS Executive, invoke CALENDAR.EXE. Windows will display

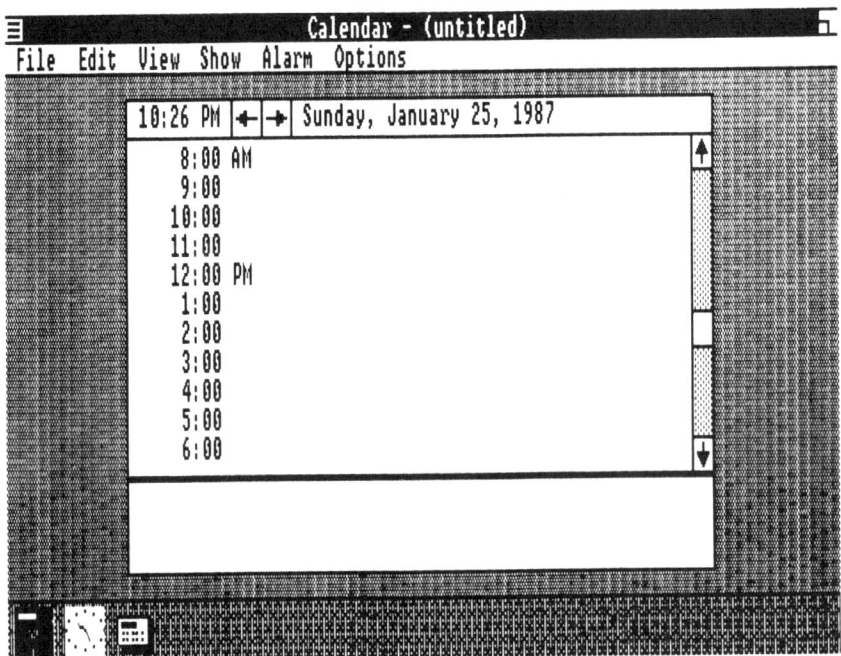

Calendar would list today's appointments here. Examine the menu bar provided with Calendar. The first menu that you will select is File, which provides the following capabilities:

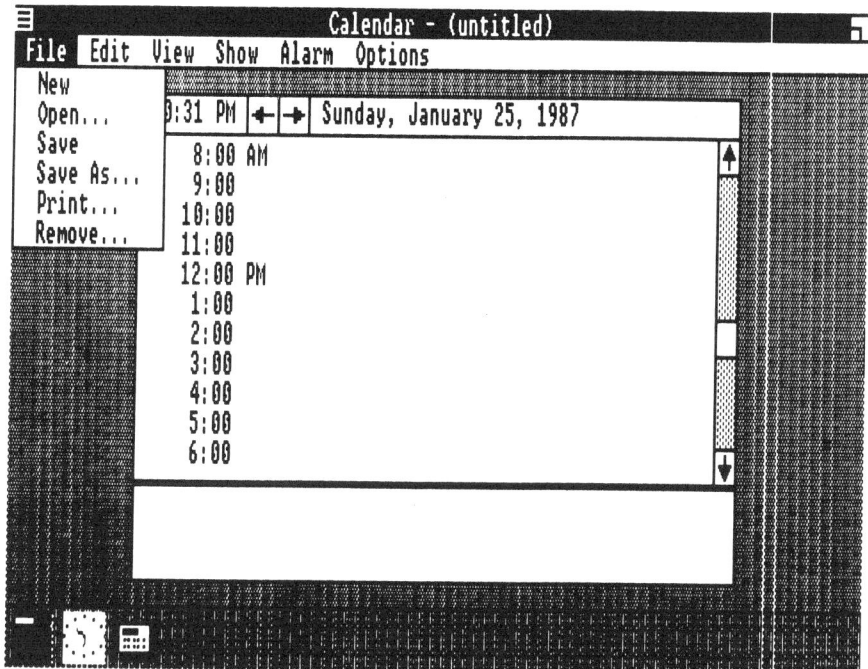

The first File option, New, allows you to create a new calendar file. As you will see, the Calendar allows you to specify several calendar files.

Visualize these files simply as different appointment books (see Figure H-3). For example, if several people were sharing the same computer, each would want individual appointment calendars. Likewise, you might want separate appointment calendars for work and school. In such instances, each time you enter Calendar, you must specify which file to use.

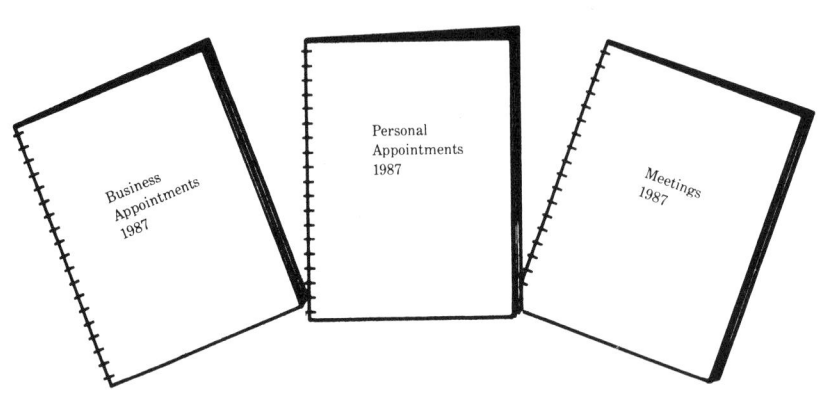

Figure H-3. Sample appointment books

The second File option, Open, allows you to specify which appointment file that Calendar is to use. When you invoke Open, the screen displays the following:

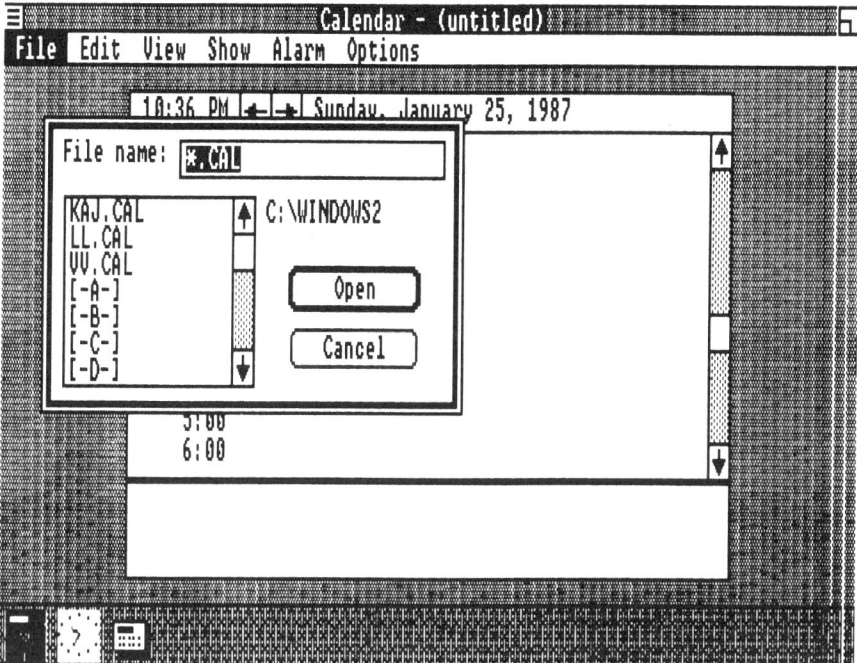

If calendar files exist, Calendar will display their names. To select a file, use your mouse or cursor keys, or simply type the name of the file desired. Each time you modify your appointment calendar, you must save the changes back to disk. You can change appointment calendars by adding, deleting, or modifying appointments.

The Save and Save As options of the File menu save to an appointment file the changes made to a calendar. When you invoke Save or Save As, the screen will display the following dialog box:

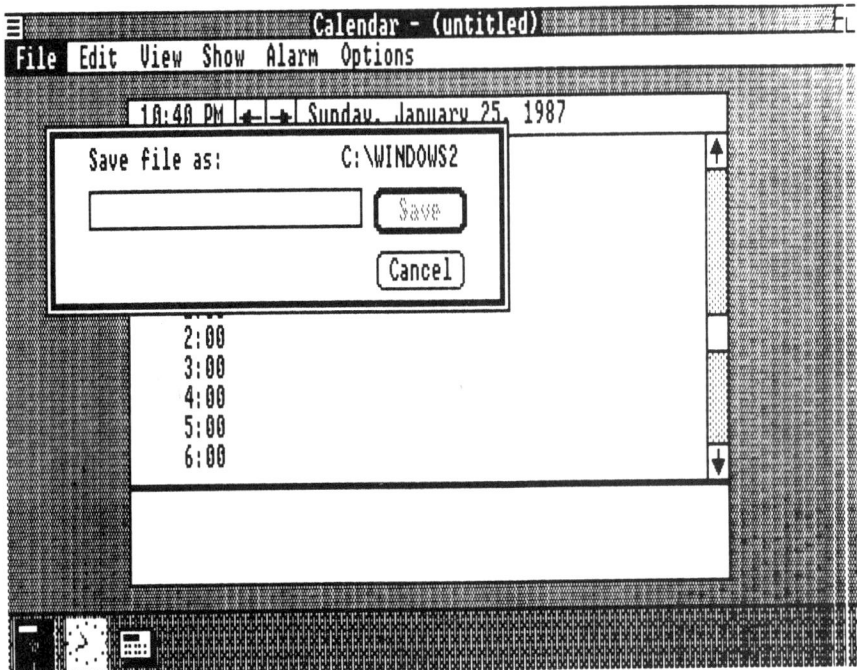

Simply enter the name of the file you want the calendar saved to and press ENTER. Or, you may simply press ENTER to save the file named on the screen.

The Calendar's Print option is a powerful command. When you invoke Print, the following dialog box will be displayed:

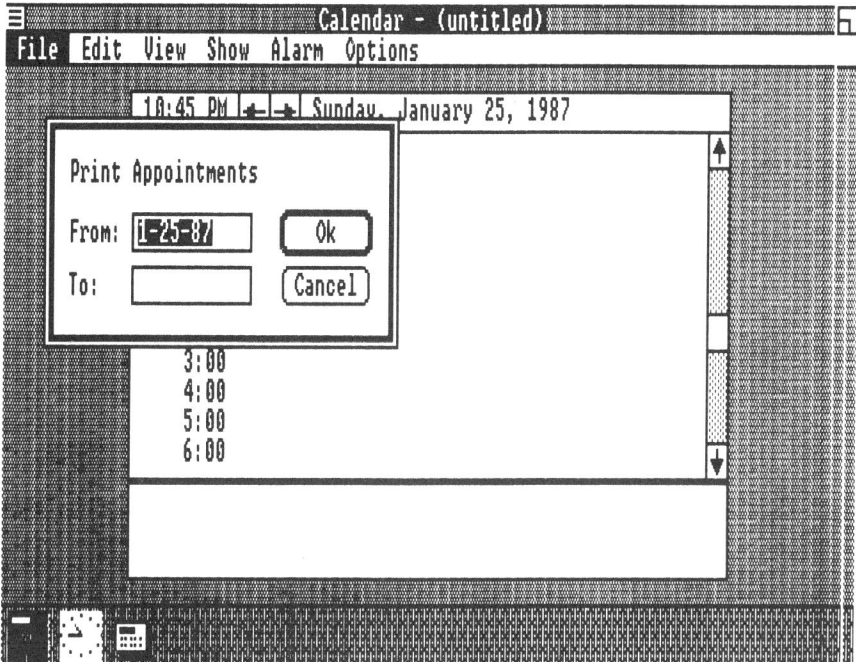

This dialog box allows you to specify the range of dates for which you want to print appointments. The Print option creates a file containing the appointments in the specified range and sends the file to the Windows Spooler. If you do not want to print any files, simply select the Cancel option or press the ESC key.

The Remove option works much like Print. When you invoke Remove, the command displays the following command box:

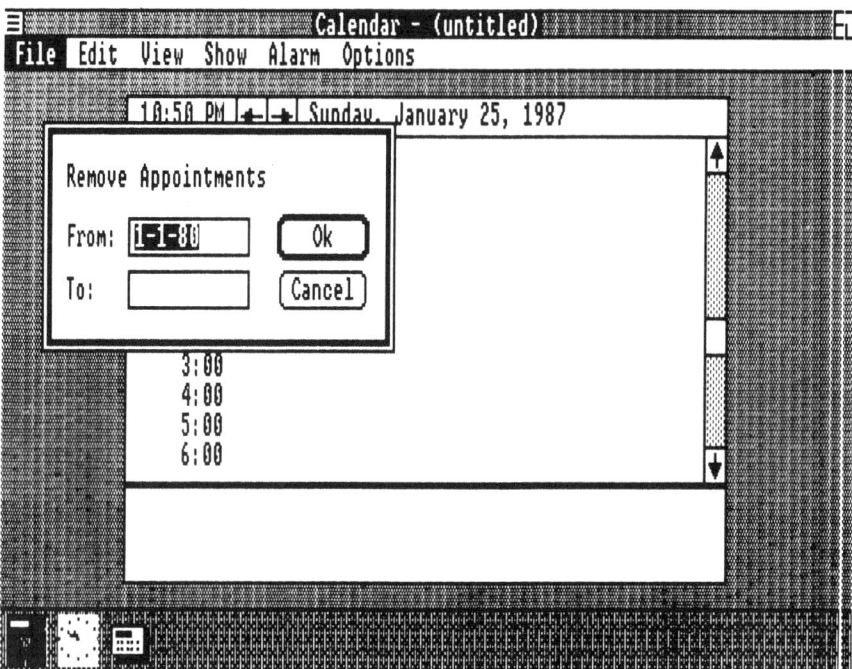

Enter the starting date from which to remove the appointments. Next, press the TAB key or point your mouse to the ending date box. Enter the date at which you want the appointment deletion to end and press ENTER. All of the appointments in the specified range will be deleted. If you don't want to delete any appointments, simply press the ESC key, or point to the Cancel option and press the select button on your mouse.

The second menu option, Edit, allows you to reschedule appointments. When you invoke Edit, it displays the following menu:

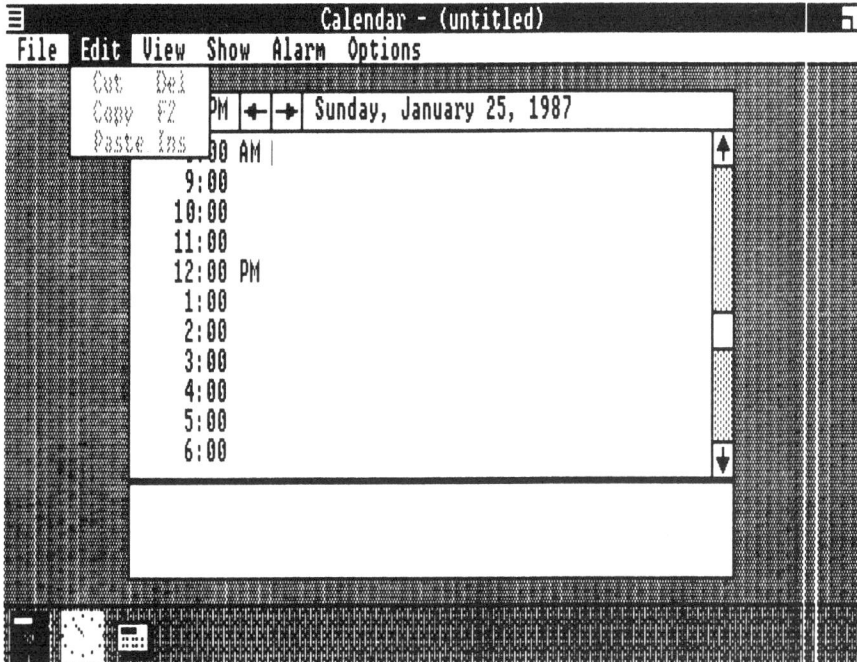

Note that menu options that are not currently available are shown in light characters on the screen.

To demonstrate the use of each Edit option, enter the following appointment at 8:00 A.M.

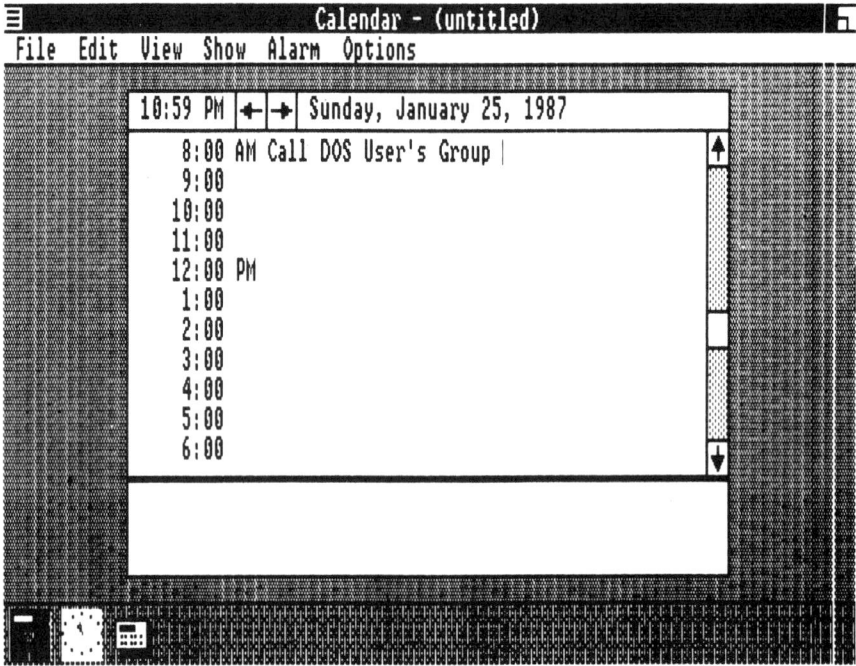

If you must reschedule the appointment for noodisappear from the appointment calendar. Next, move the appointment cursor to noon. Again select the Edit menu and choose the Paste option. The appointment is moved to the desired location, and the screen will contain the following:

Keyboard Selection of Paint Tools

Use the TAB key to move right through the tools or the SHIFT and TAB keys to move left.

Mouse Selection of Paint Tools

Point at the paint tool desired and press the mouse select button.

Next, select the Edit menu. Because you have selected an appointment to be moved, fewer options are shown in light characters. In this case, select the Cut option. The appointment should disappear from the appointment calendar. Next, move the appointment cursor to noon. Again select the Edit menu and choose the Paste option. The appointment is moved to the desired location, and the screen will contain the following:

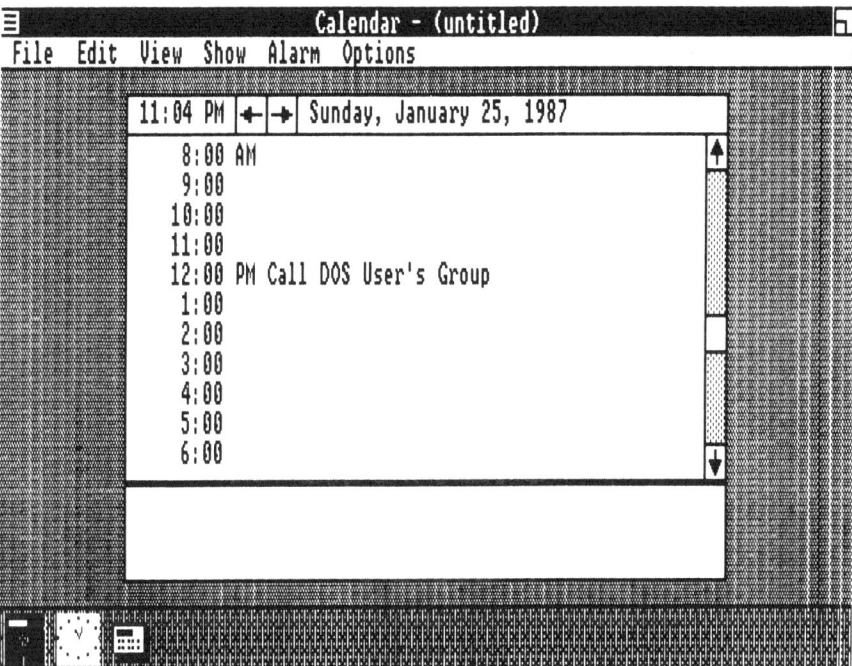

The same procedure can be used to move appointments from one day to the next, to delete appointments, and with the Copy option, to duplicate appointments. This process is called *cutting and pasting*. Windows applications can "cut" out a portion of the text from one location and either omit it or "paste" it in a new location.

The Calendar's View menu allows you to examine either a day or a month calendar. When you invoke View, the screen will display the following:

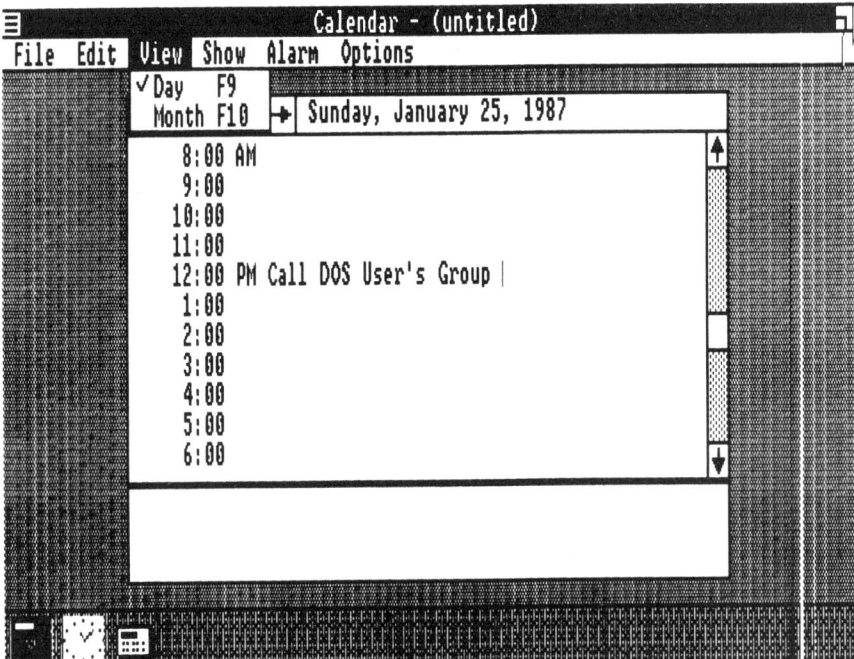

The F9 and F10 included in the menu tell you that Calendar predefines the function keys F9 and F10 to perform the options displayed.
Press the F10 key; Calendar will display the following:

```
┌──────────────────────────────────────────────────────────┐
│≡              Calendar - (untitled)                      ⌐│
│File  Edit  View  Show  Alarm  Options                     │
├──────────────────────────────────────────────────────────┤
│  11:13 PM          Sunday, January 25, 1987               │
│                    January 1987                        ▲  │
│      S      M      T      W      T      F      S          │
│   ┌─────┬─────┬─────┬─────┬─────┬─────┬─────┐             │
│   │     │     │     │     │  1  │  2  │  3  │             │
│   ├─────┼─────┼─────┼─────┼─────┼─────┼─────┤             │
│   │  4  │  5  │  6  │  7  │  8  │  9  │ 10  │             │
│   ├─────┼─────┼─────┼─────┼─────┼─────┼─────┤             │
│   │ 11  │ 12  │ 13  │ 14  │ 15  │ 16  │ 17  │             │
│   ├─────┼─────┼─────┼─────┼─────┼─────┼─────┤             │
│   │ 18  │ 19  │ 20  │ 21  │ 22  │ 23  │ 24  │             │
│   ├─────┼─────┼─────┼─────┼─────┼─────┼─────┤             │
│  〉25 〈│ 26  │ 27  │ 28  │ 29  │ 30  │ 31  │  ▼          │
│   └─────┴─────┴─────┴─────┴─────┴─────┴─────┘             │
│                                                            │
└──────────────────────────────────────────────────────────┘
```

Experiment with the cursor keys (and the PG UP and PG DN keys) along with the mouse to toggle the dates displayed. Select the month to display. Note the box beneath the calendar. Calendar allows you to place a three-line note at the bottom of the calendar, as shown here:

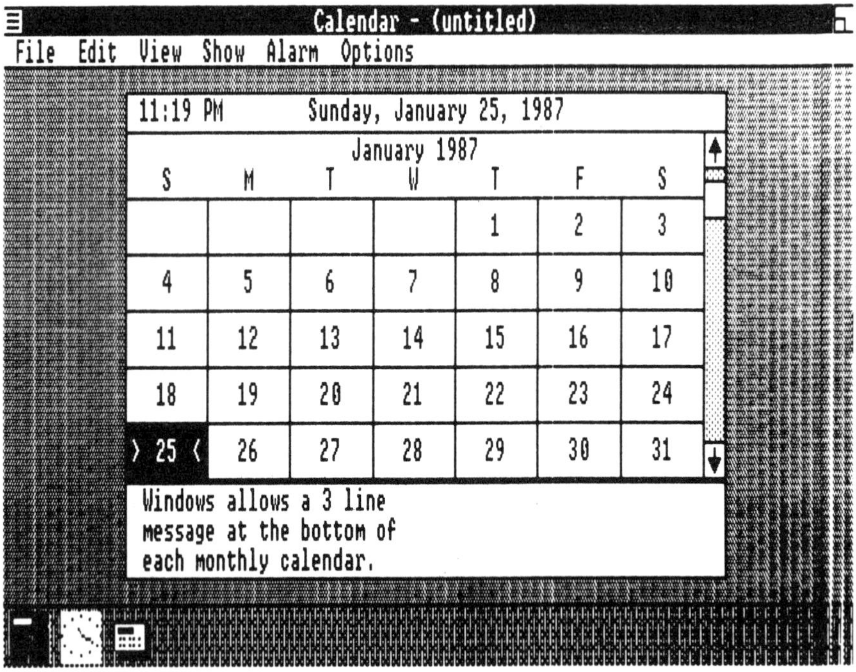

The Calendar's Show menu provides the following capabilities:

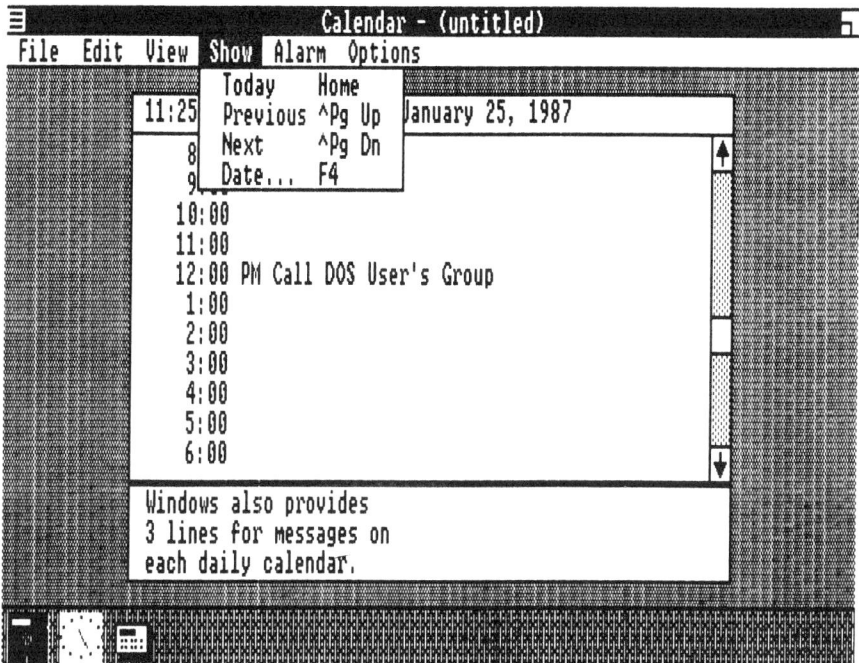

Note the predefined keys for each option. Again, experiment with each of the keys to note their effects on the date displayed. If you select the Date option, Calendar will display the following dialog box:

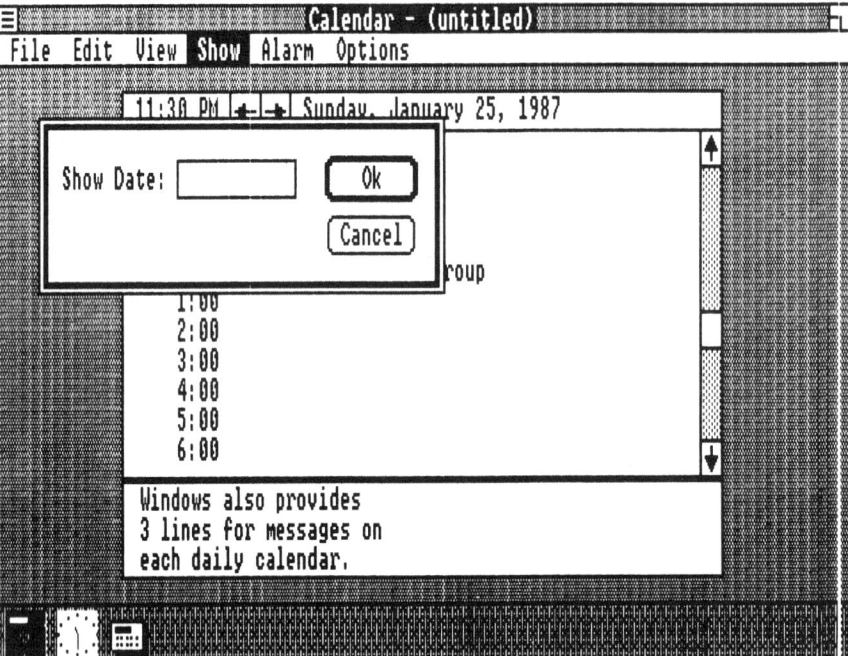

Enter the date for which you want to display appointments and press
ENTER.

One of the best features of the Windows appointment calendar is
that it allows you to set alarms for important appointments. The
Alarm menu provides the following capabilities:

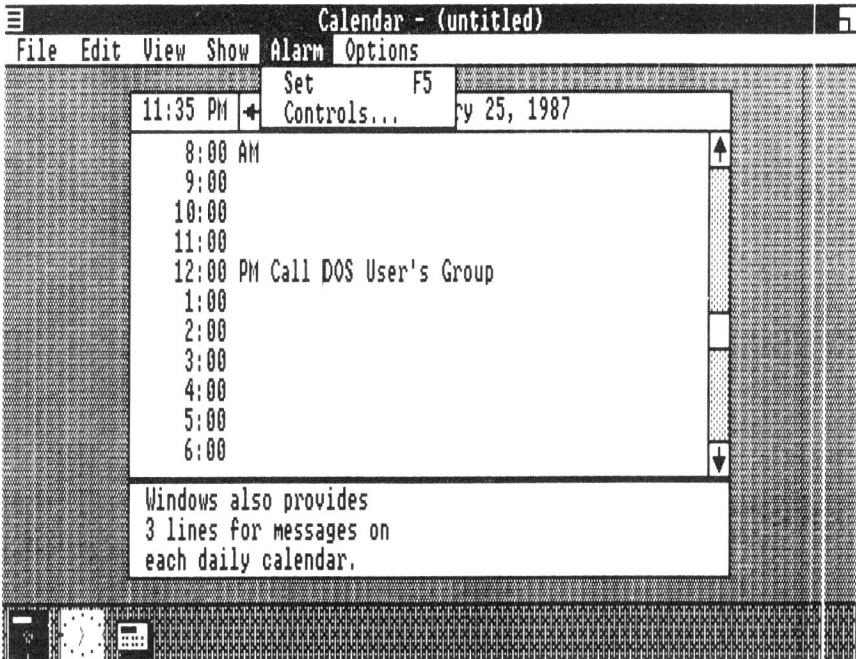

The Set option sets an alarm for the appointment currently referenced by the appointment cursor. For example, place the cursor at the 12:00 P.M. appointment and select the Set option from the Alarm menu. Calendar will display a bell next to the time to notify you that an alarm has been set.

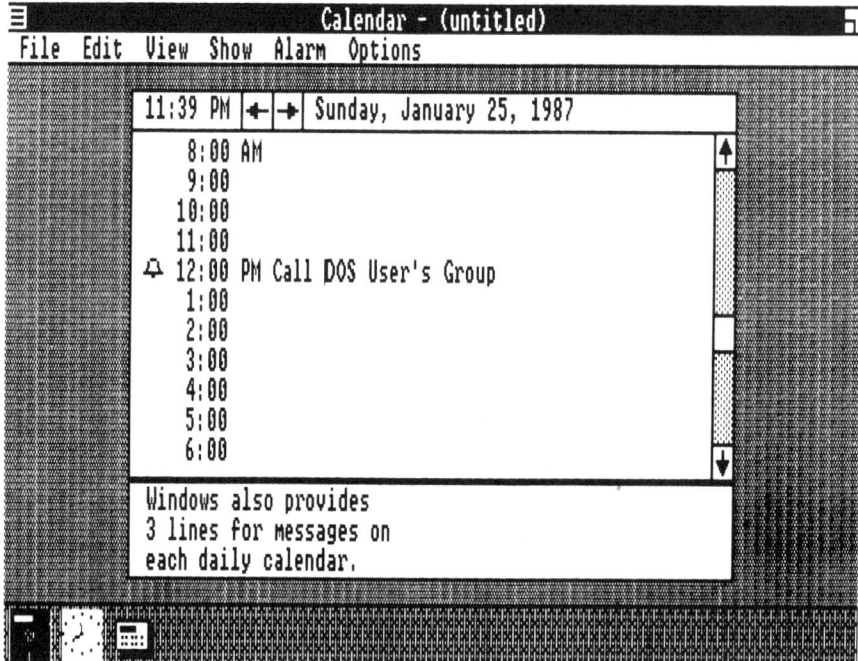

Later, when the time for the appointment arrives, the computer
beeps and displays the following dialog box:

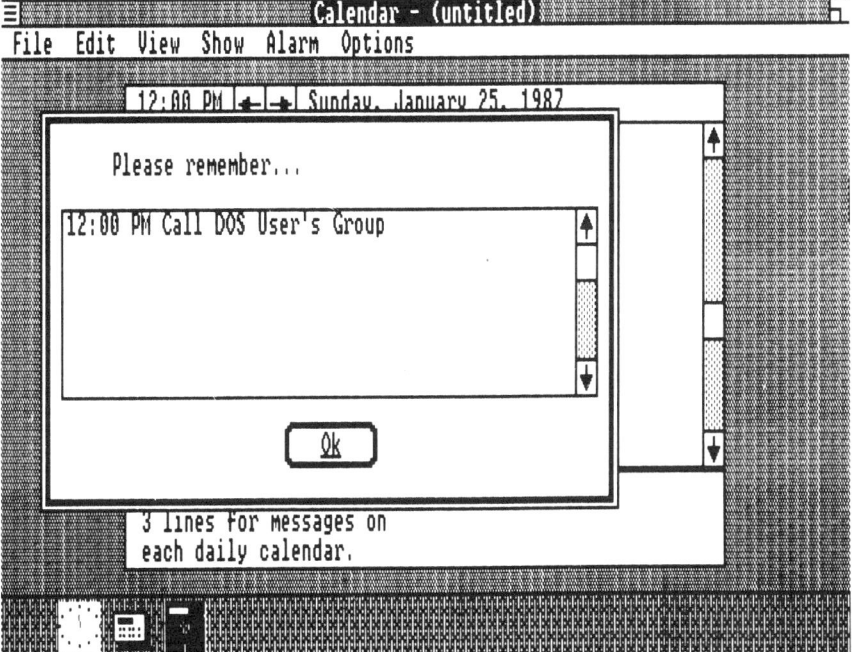

If at the designated time the Calendar package is active only as an icon, the computer will beep and the icon will flash. The Calendar program must, however, reside in memory either as an icon or as an executable image.

The Controls option of the Alarm menu allows you to specify a number of minutes (0-10) before the appointment; the computer will then beep at that time, notifying you of the appointment. In addition, this option allows you to specify whether you want the computer to beep each time an alarm occurs. If you disable beeping, the dialog box is still displayed as long as Calendar is active, or the icon will flash. If you select the Controls option, the following dialog box will appear:

Simply enter the number of minutes before the appointment, or press the TAB key to enable or disable sound. Once the Sound option is selected, pressing the SPACEBAR will toggle sound on and off.

The last option, the Options menu, provides the following:

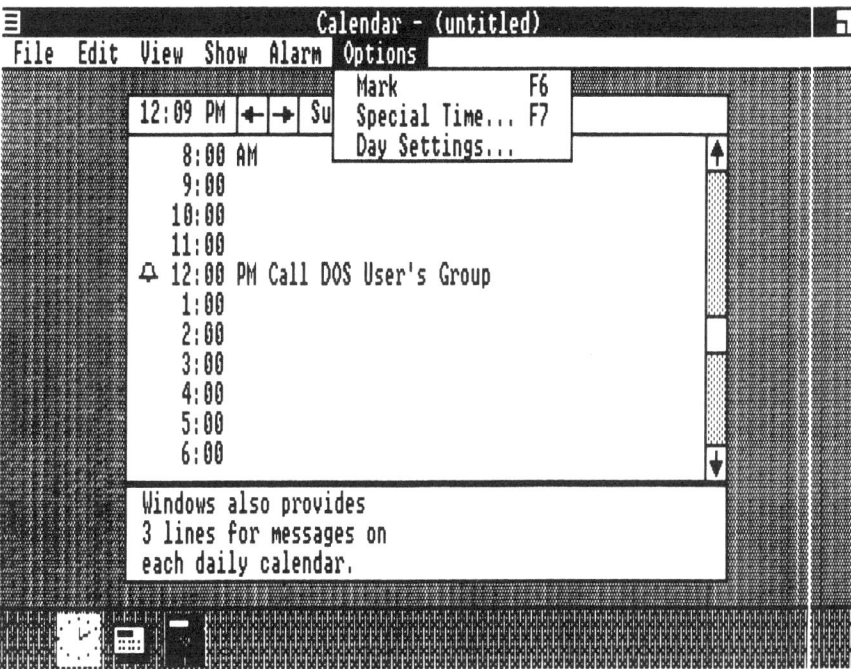

The Mark option places a box around an important date on the monthly appointment calendar. For example, if you select a mark for the current date, Calendar will display the monthly calendar as follows:

```
≡            Calendar - (untitled)              °        ⌐
File  Edit  View  Show  Alarm  Options

  12:14 PM        Sunday, January 25, 1987
                     January 1987                    ▲
     S      M      T      W      T      F      S
                                 1      2      3
     4      5      6      7      8      9     10
    11     12     13     14     15     16     17
    18     19     20     21     22     23     24
  ⟩[25]⟨   26     27     28     29     30     31      ▼
  Windows also provides
  3 lines for messages on
  each daily calendar.
```

The Mark option works as a toggle. The first time that you select the option, the box is displayed. Selecting the option a second time removes the box.

The Special Time option allows you to enter a time that is not included on the daily appointment calendar. For example, if you are to call New York at 7:05, you can select the Special Time option and enter the following:

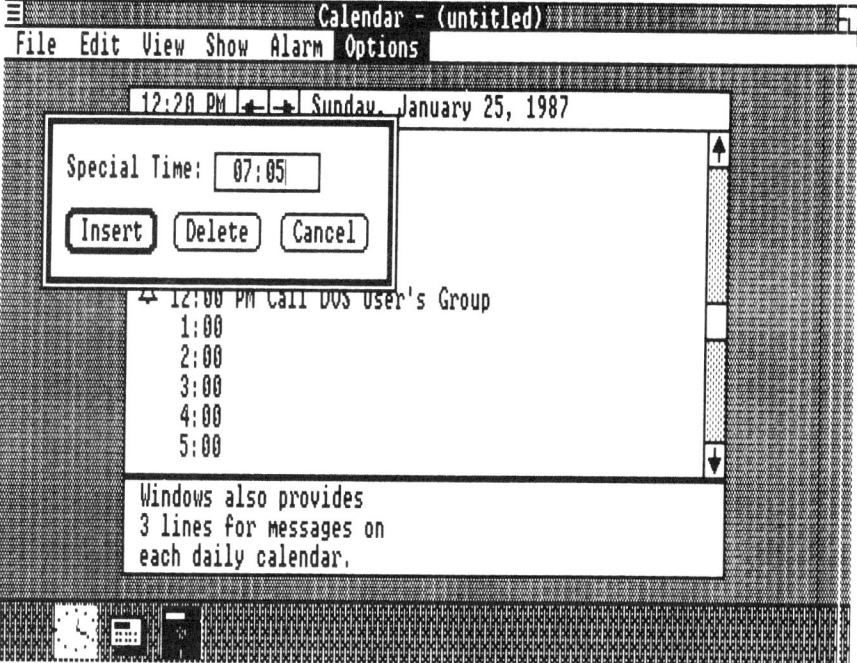

The daily appointment calendar will now display

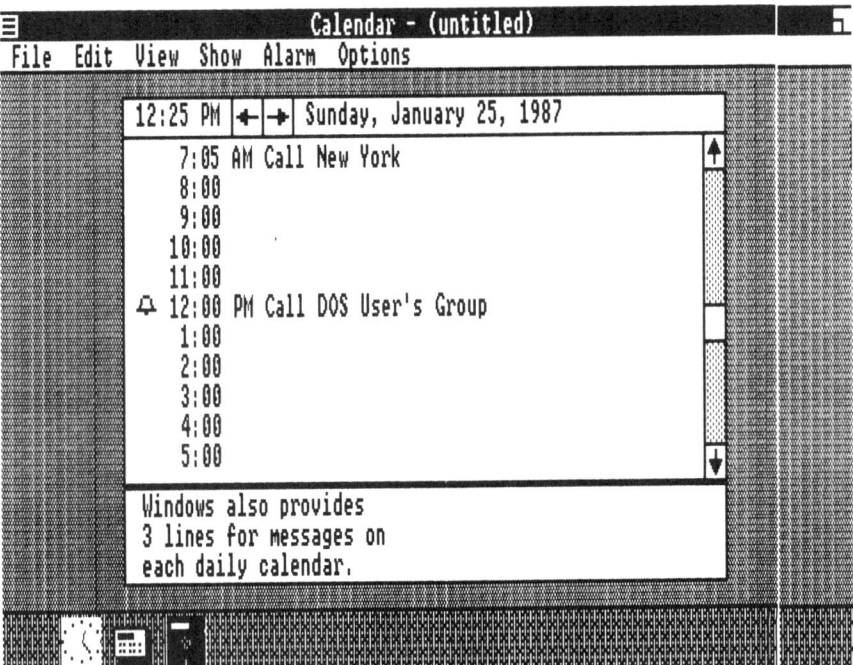

Windows also provides 3 lines for messages on each daily calendar.

The Day Settings option allows you to configure the appointment calendar to meet your specific requirements. When you invoke Day Settings, it will display the following dialog box:

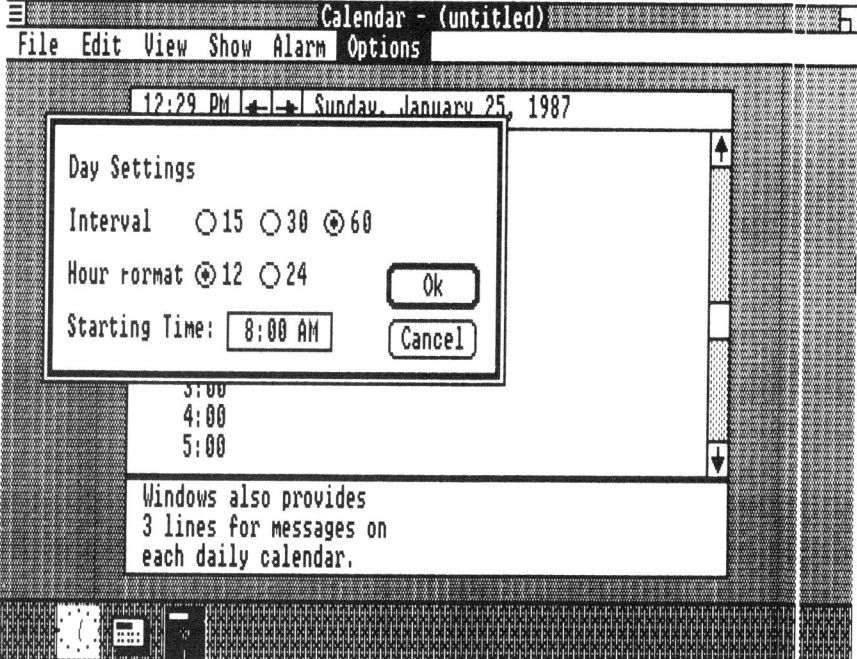

Interval is the number of minutes that you want to appear between appointments on the calendar. By default, Calendar uses 60 minutes. If, however, you require an interval of 15 or 30 minutes, you can do so here. After you select 15-minute intervals, for example, your daily appointment calendar will appear as follows:

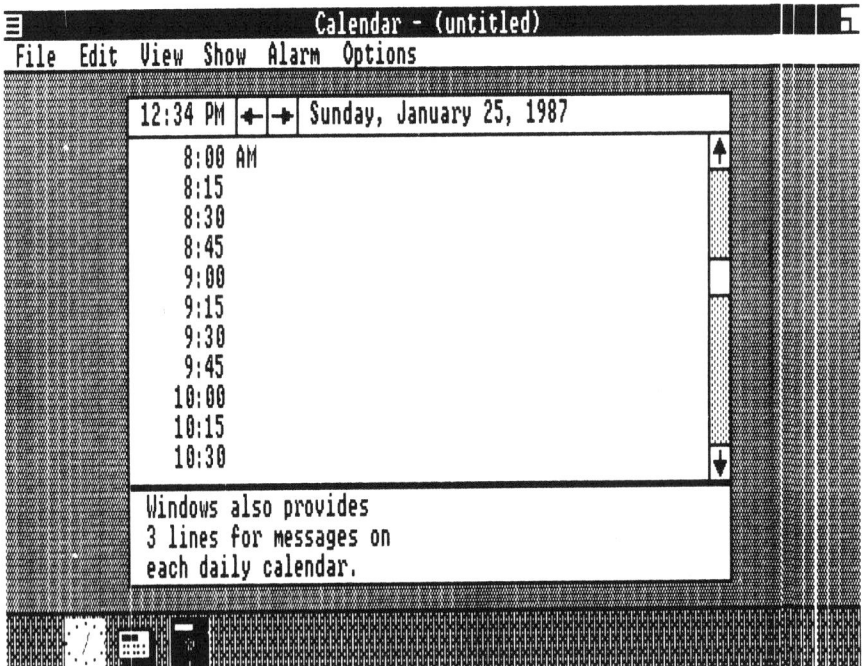

If you select the 24-hour format, the calendar will use International time (0:00-23:00 hours). The Starting Time specifies the first time that you want to appear on your daily calendar. By default, Calendar uses 8:00 A.M.

Cardfile

The Windows Cardfile program allows you to create an on-line tracking system of 3×5 index cards. Simply record your information on the card, and Windows will automatically sort the cards for you.

From the MS-DOS Executive, run CARDFILE.EXE. Windows will display a 3×5 index card as follows:

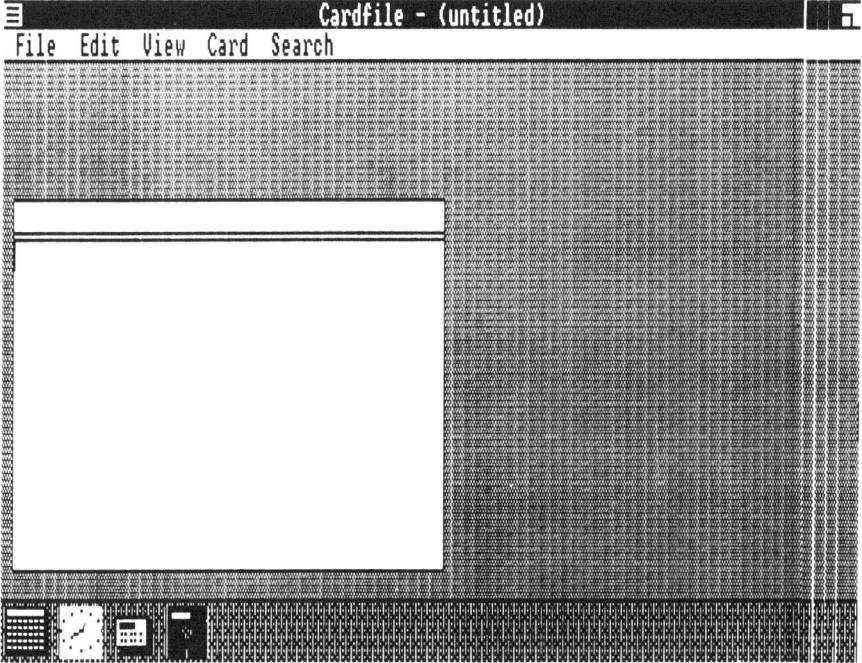

Cardfile works much like the Windows Calendar program. For example, the File menu provides the following options:

Cardfile allows you to track 3×5 index cards for various subjects by means of an index card file. For example, you may have a series of index cards for DOS commands in the file DOS.CRD and a set of cards containing BASIC commands in the file BASIC.CRD.

The New option allows you to create a new deck of cards for recording information. Once a card file exists, you access it with the Open option. Cardfile will display the following dialog box:

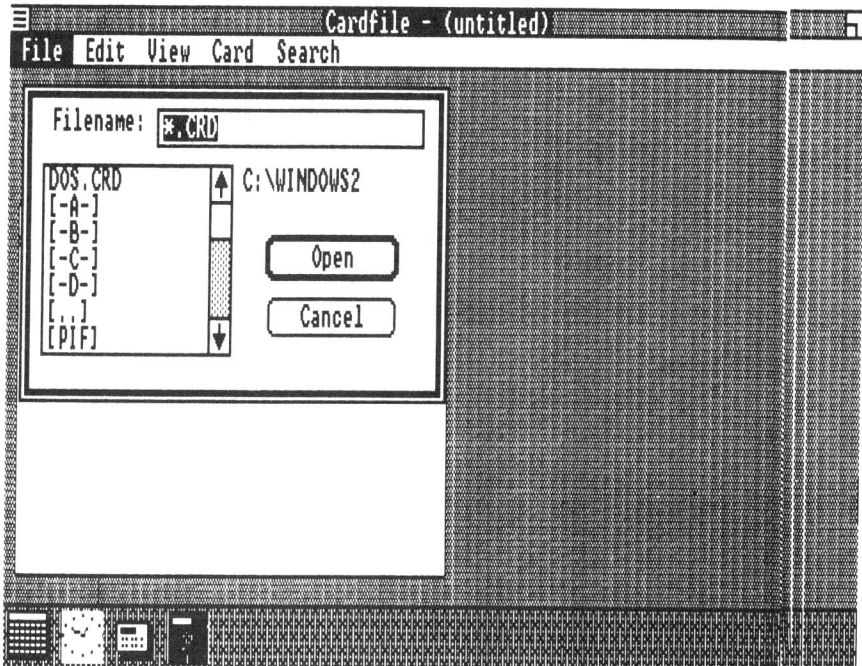

Simply enter the name of the card file you desire and press ENTER. After you modify entries in a card file, you must use the Save and Save As commands to record the updated information in a file. Each displays the following dialog box:

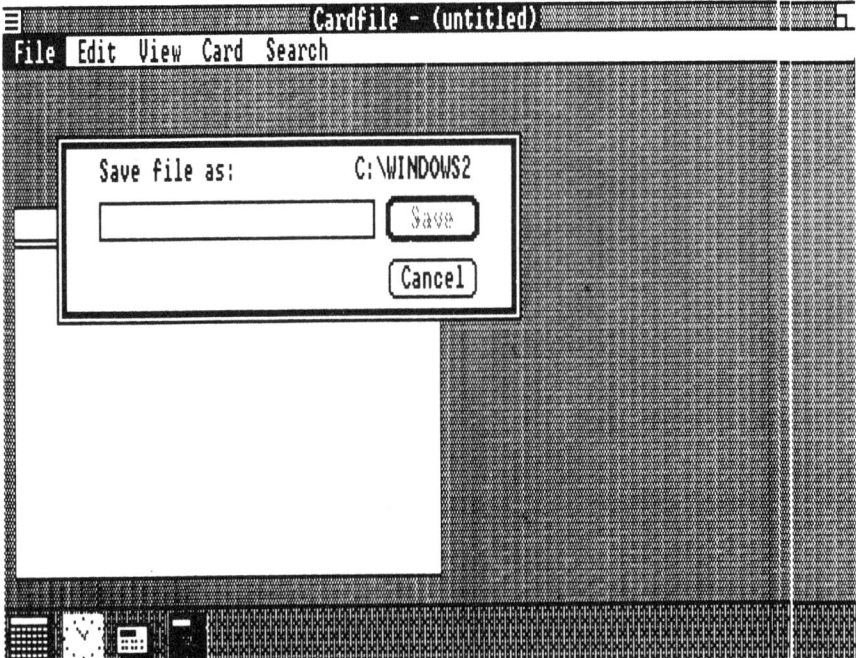

The Print option prints the first card in the deck in the following format:

```
DOS CLS Command
━━━━━━━━━━━━━━━━━━━━━━━━━━━━━━━━━━━━━━━━━━━━

The DOS CLS Command erases the contents
of the screen display and places the
cursor at the home position.

CLS does not affect video attributes.


A> CLS
```

The Print All option prints all of the cards in the deck.

The Merge option of the File menu allows you to include cards from another card file in your current deck. Cardfile will automatically sort the new cards. When you invoke Merge, it will display the following dialog box:

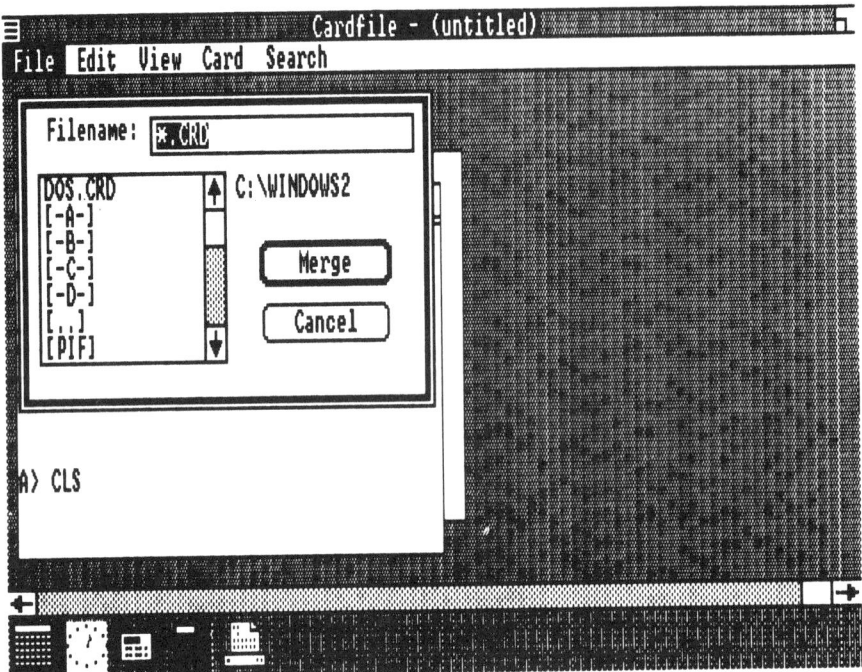

Simply enter the name of the file from which you want to include the cards.

The Edit menu allows you to easily delete, move, copy, or change text within the 3×5 card deck. When you invoke Edit, it will display the following:

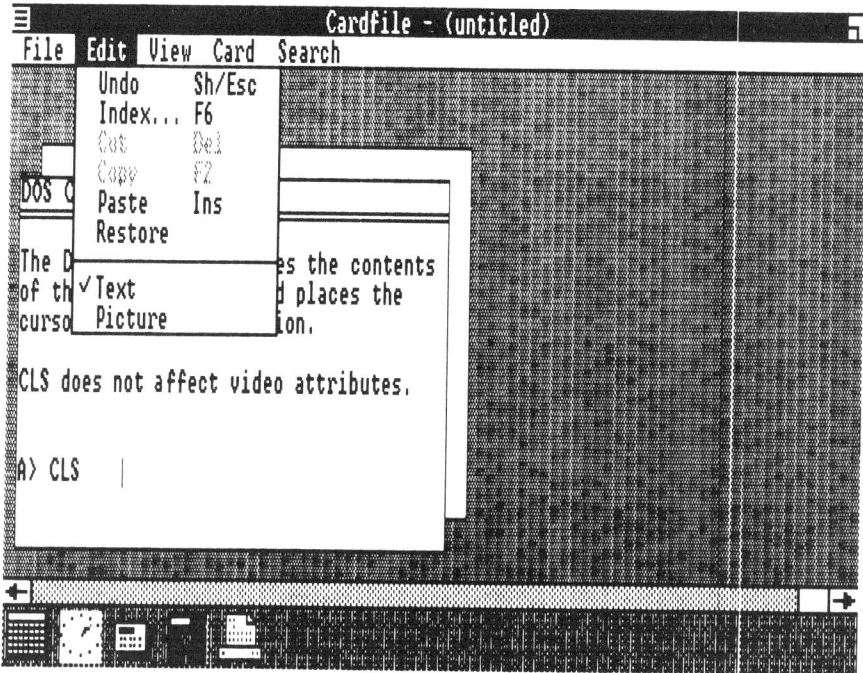

Note the predefined function keys for certain commands.

The first Edit command, Undo, allows you to reverse your latest change to a card. For example, if you use Cut to delete a section of text, Undo allows you to put it back.

The Index option is probably the most-used Edit option. Index allows you to enter the index label in the top line on the current card. Cardfile does not allow you to place the cursor on the index line of a 3 × 5 card; you must select Index to place it there. Once selected, Index will display the following dialog box:

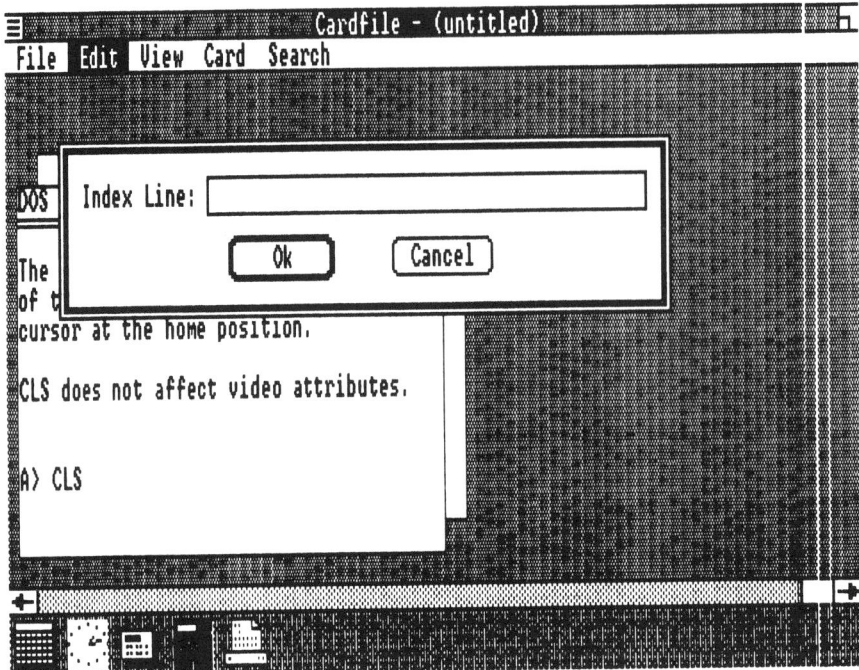

Simply enter the index label you desire and press ENTER.

The Cut option is similar to the Cut option used in Calendar. To move text, simply select the text as follows:

> **Keyboard Selection of Text**
>
> Place the cursor at the first character to select. Use the SHIFT and cursor arrow key to select the characters desired

> **Mouse Selection of Text**
>
> Place the cursor at the first character to select. Use the mouse select button to select the characters desired.

Next, invoke the Edit menu and select the Cut option. The selected text will disappear from the screen.

The Copy command works much like Cut, but rather than moving text, Copy creates a second copy of it. Again, select the text in the same manner as in the previous example. Place the cursor at the desired target location and invoke the Edit menu. Selecting the Copy option results in a duplicate of the text placed at the desired location.

The Paste option works with information contained in the Windows Clipboard, which will be discussed in detail later in this chapter. For now, however, understand that Paste works in conjunction with Cut. After you use Cut to select the text to be moved from one location to another, place the cursor at the desired location. Invoke the Edit menu and select the Paste option; the text will be moved as desired. As you will find, it is possible to use Cut and Paste to move information from one card to another.

The Restore option works with the top card on the deck. If you have modified the top card, Restore allows you to restore its original contents.

The last Edit options, Text and Picture, specify the type of the contents on the Clipboard. As you will see later in this chapter, it is possible to cut pictures from one application and place them in a second. Text specifies that the contents of the clipboard are text characters. If the Clipboard instead contains art, use the Picture option before you issue a Paste command.

The View menu specifies how the cards are to be displayed on the screen. When you invoke View, the screen displays

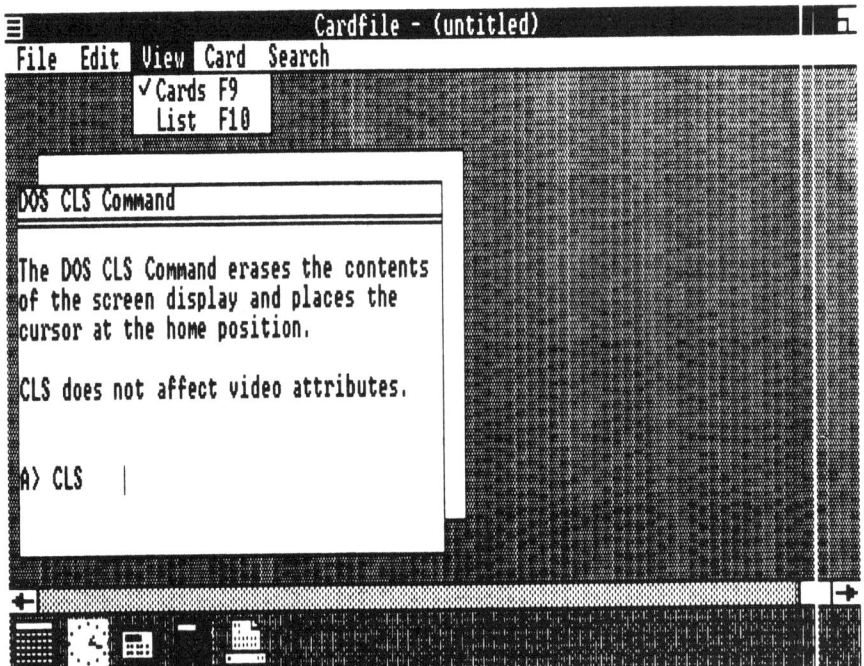

The Cards option will display the index cards in the following manner:

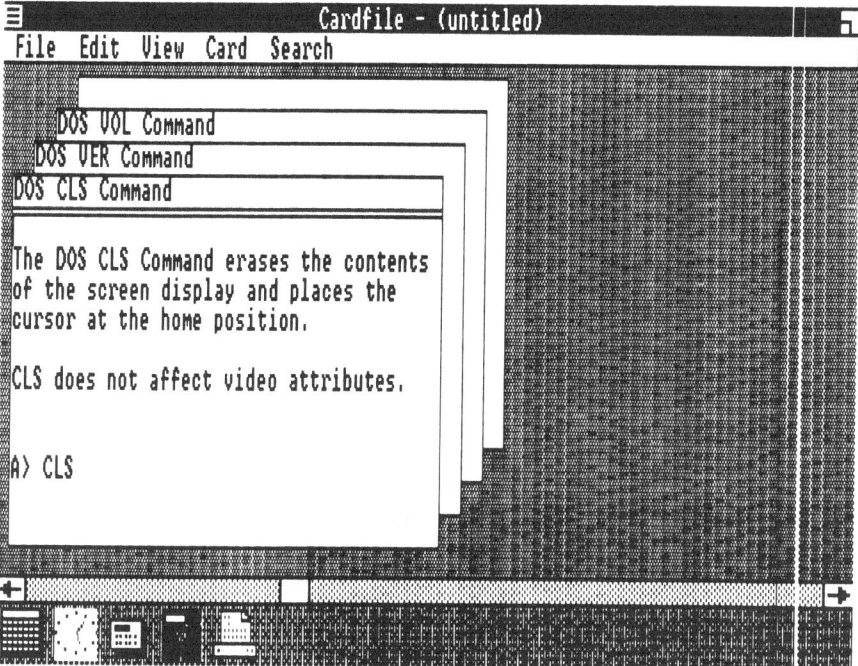

The List option displays the index section of each card as follows:

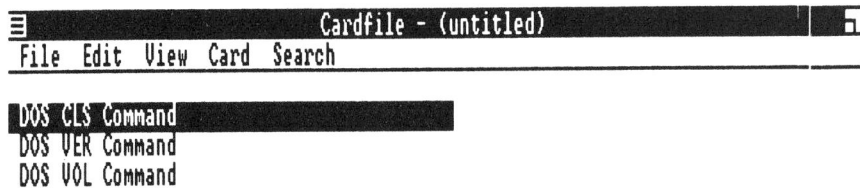

The Cardfile's Card menu allows you to add, delete, or duplicate cards, and it can use the first telephone number found on a card to dial a Hayes or Hayes-compatible modem automatically. When you invoke Card, it displays the following:

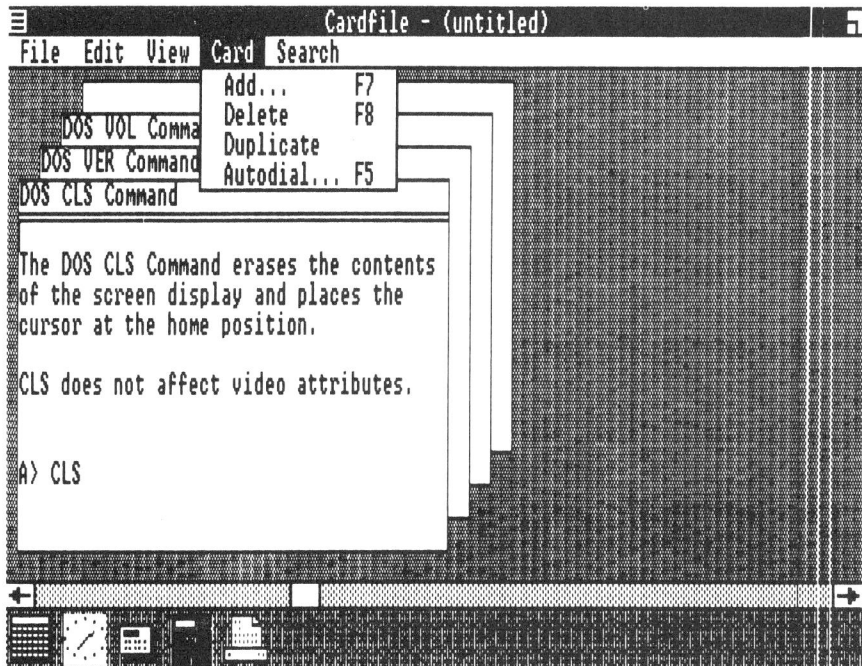

The Add option creates a new card and places it at the front of the deck, as follows:

The Delete option deletes the card on the top of the deck. Duplicate creates an identical copy of the card at the top of the deck. The Autodial option searches the contents of the top card on the deck for a number greater than six characters and automatically dials it. For example, in the case of

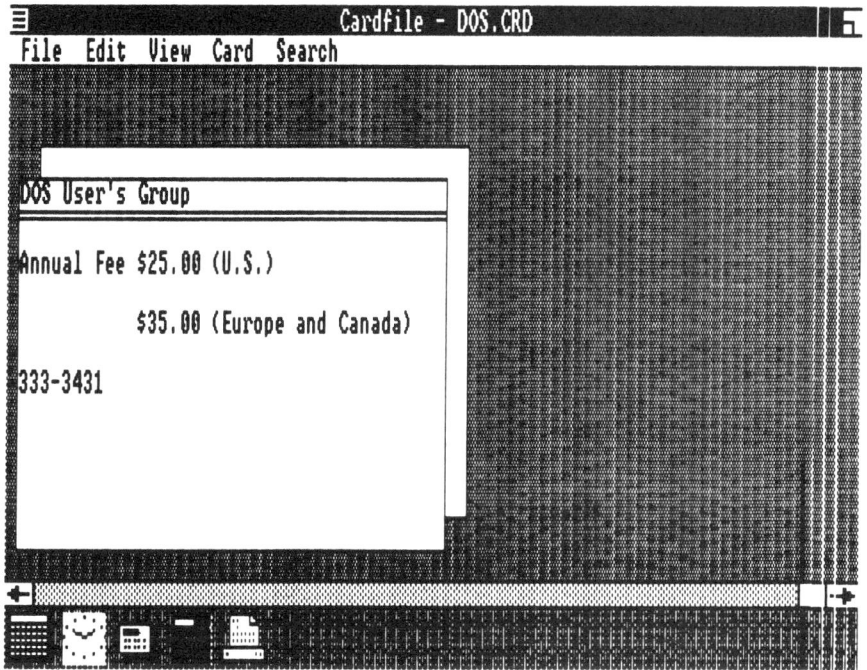

Autodial will dial the number 333-3431.

The last menu, Search, allows you to perform quick lookups of cards in the deck. When you invoke it, the Search menu will display the following:

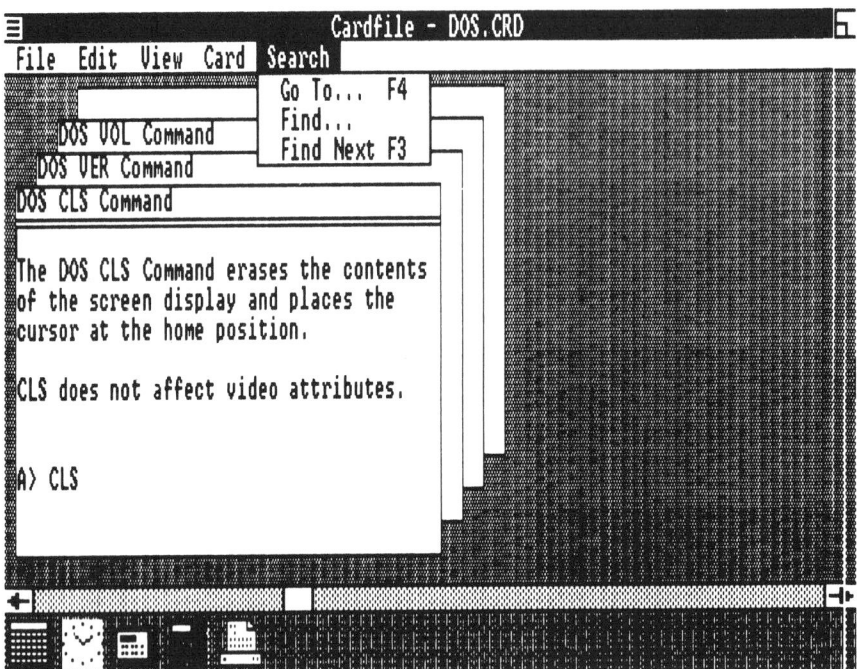

The Go To option will find the card containing the index you enter
in the following dialog box:

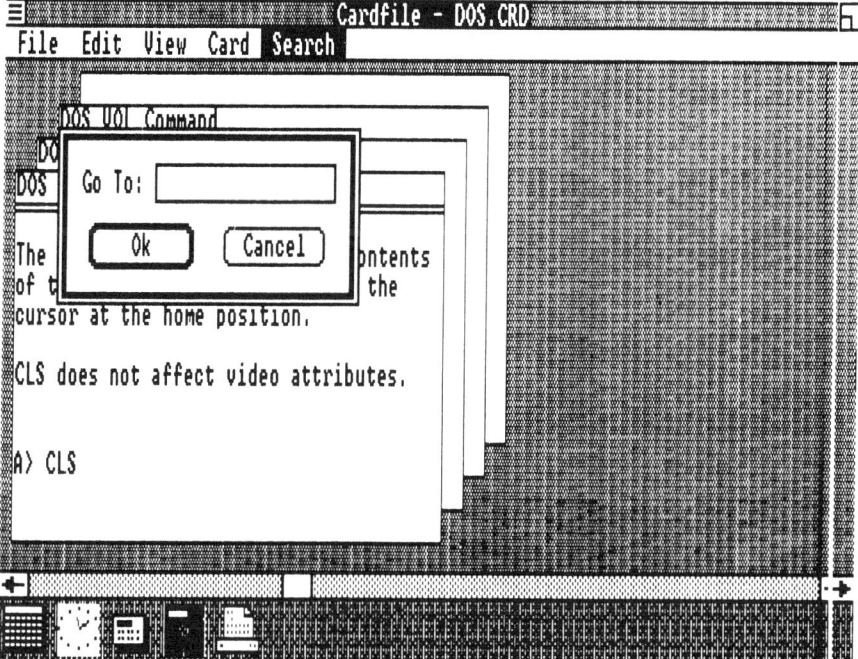

Simply enter as much of the index as you remember and press ENTER. Cardfile will place the card with the index that matches your text on the top of the deck.

The Find option displays the following dialog box:

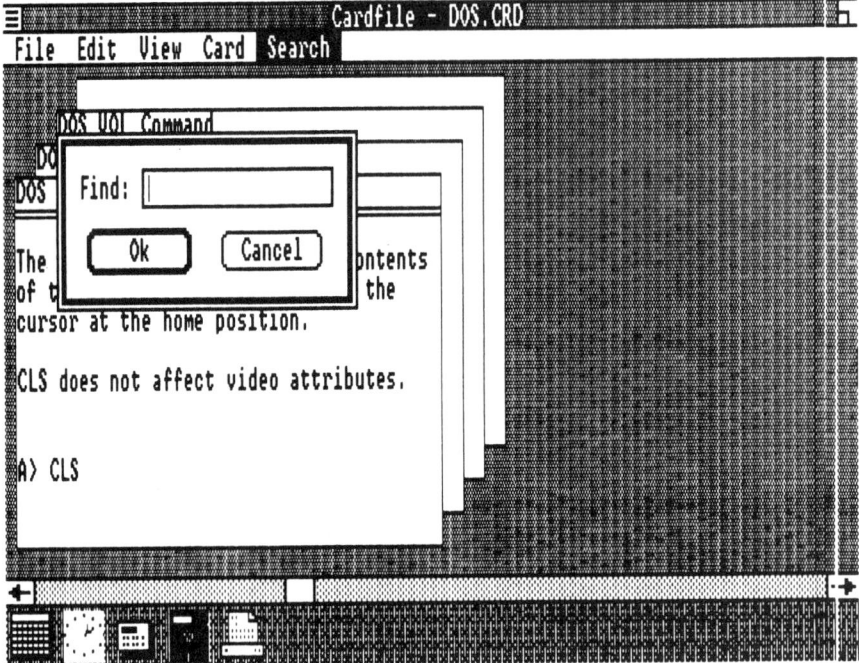

Enter the string for which you want Cardfile to search the deck of cards and press ENTER. When Cardfile encounters the first card having the string, it will place it at the top of the deck. The Find Next command continues the search for the previously defined string.

One of the best uses of Cardfile is to create a list of DOS commands and their specific functions. Then, when you later need to access a command, simply bring up its card file for a quick reference, as shown here:

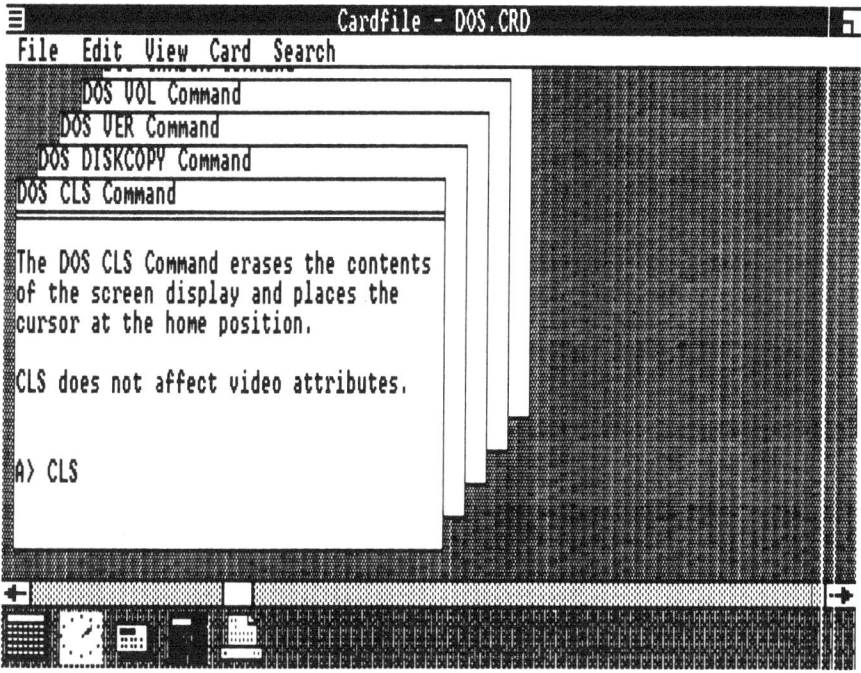

Notepad

Windows allows you to create memos and small documents with
NOTEPAD.EXE. From the MS-DOS Executive, run NOTEPAD
.EXE; Windows will respond with the following:

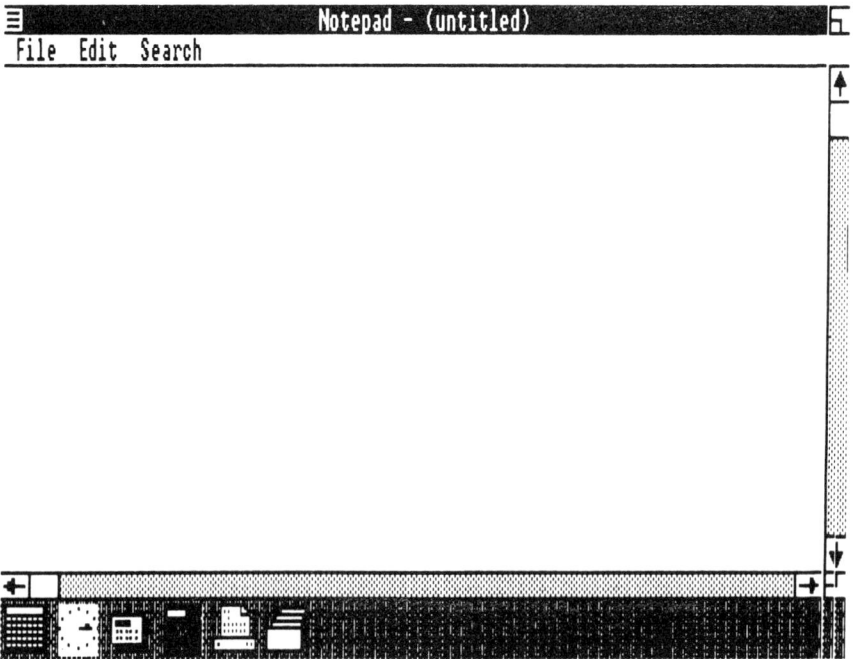

The screen represents a three-page notepad. The menu options provided with Notepad are very similar to the menus examined thus far. Select the File menu, and Notepad will display the following:

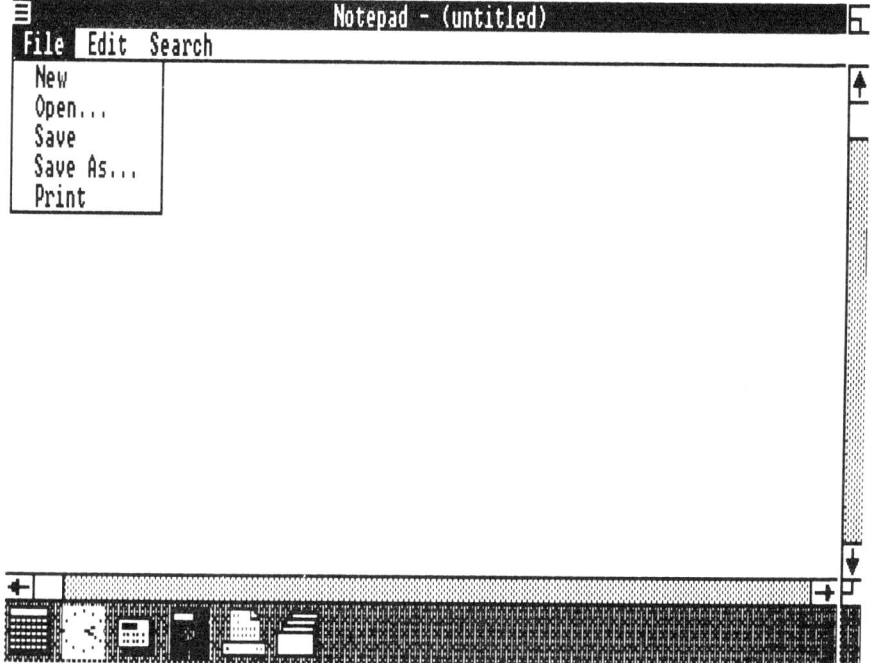

The New option gives you a new pad on which to write notes. Notepad allows you to store all of your memos in separate files.

Once you have created a memo, you can later access it with the Open option. When you invoke Open, it will display the following:

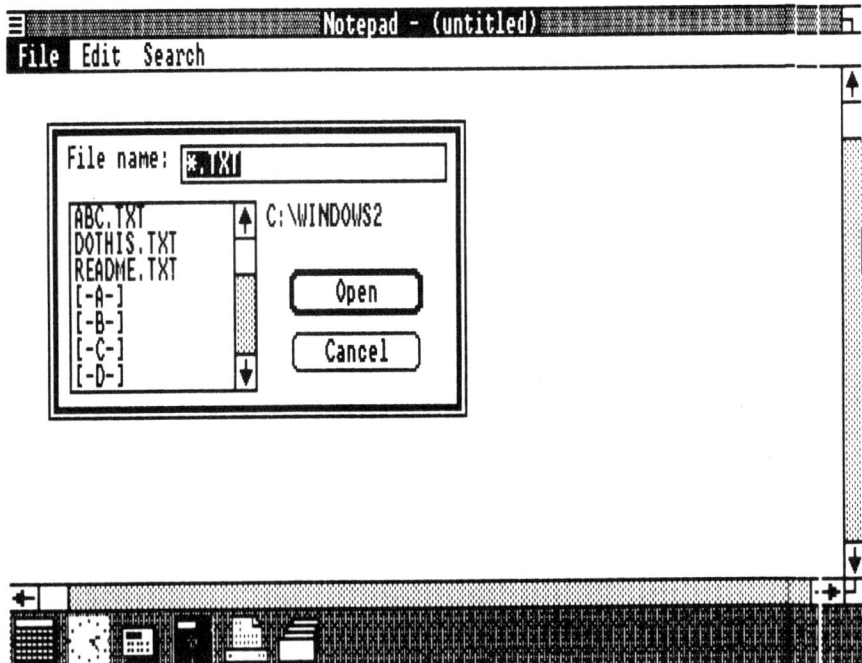

Select the file name that you desire, or simply enter it and then press
ENTER.

The Save and Save As options allow you to save changes that you
have made to memos. Each option displays the following dialog box:

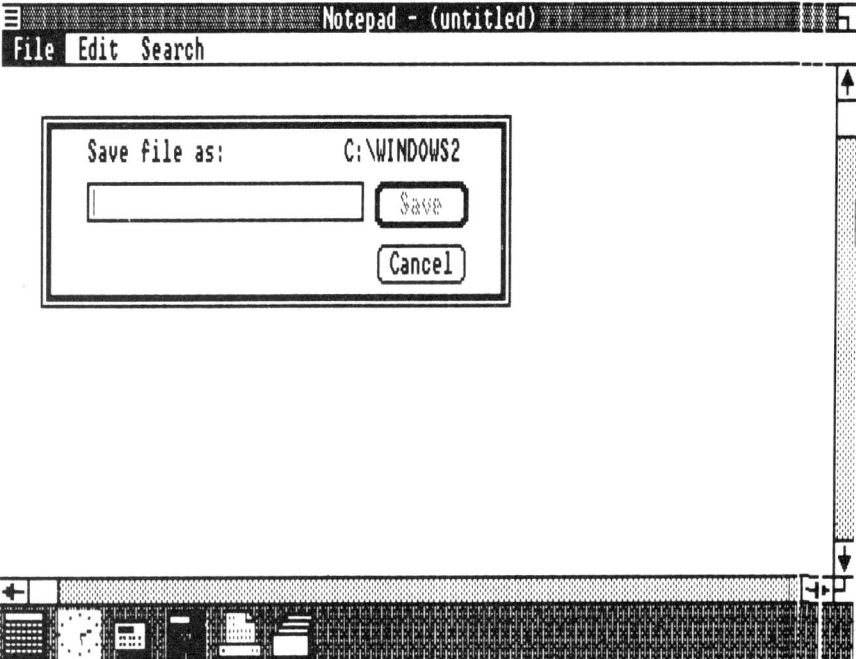

Notepad uses the extension TXT by default. Once you have completed
your memo, the Print option sends it to the Windows Spooler.

Invoking the Edit menu will display the following:

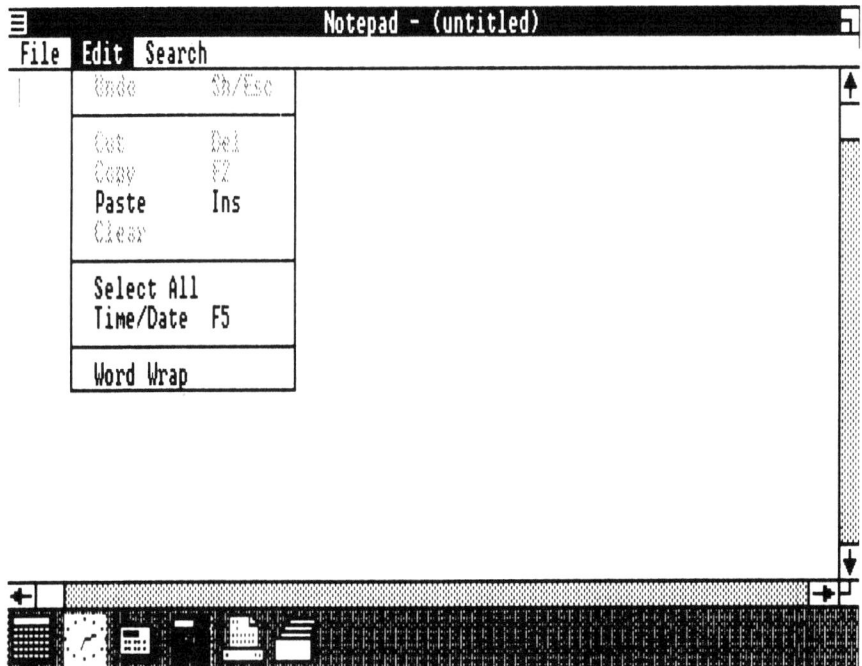

The Undo option is like the Undo option in the Windows Cardfile program: it reverses the previous option. For example, if you enter a line of text while editing a memo, Undo will allow you to delete the line in one simple step.

The Cut, Copy, and Paste options all work as in the Windows Cardfile program. Cut selects a section of text to be moved or deleted, erasing it from the screen. Copy selects a section of text for duplication. Paste restores a section of text that has been cut or copied to a new location.

The Clear option simply deletes a section of text. The Select All option is used when you want to copy the entire memo to the Clipboard (discussed in detail later in this appendix).

The Time/Date option inserts the current system date and time at the current cursor position. It is good practice to time- and date-stamp all of your memos.

Last, the Word Wrap option directs Notepad to automatically wrap text at the right column so that you do not need to press ENTER at the end of each line. Word Wrap works as a toggle. The first time that you select it, Notepad will begin wrapping sentences; selecting the option a second time turns off Word Wrap.

Select the Notepad Search menu. Notepad will display the following:

Selecting the first option, Find, results in the following dialog box, which prompts you for a text string to search for within the memo.

Simply enter the words that you are looking for and press ENTER.
The Find Next option continues the search for keywords.

Here are two example memos entered on the Notepad. The first is a "To Do" list:

```
┌─────────────────────────────────────────────────────────────────┐
│≡              Notepad - (untitled)                           [L]│
├─────────────────────────────────────────────────────────────────┤
│ File  Edit  Search                                            [▲]│
├─────────────────────────────────────────────────────────────────┤
│ Task                          Priority                        [▲]│
│                                                               [ ]│
│ Recompile Windows Program        1                            [ ]│
│ Create New Object Libraries      1                            [ ]│
│                                                               [ ]│
│ Complete Documentation           2                            [ ]│
│ Order New Binders                2                            [ ]│
│ Check Previous Orders            2                            [ ]│
│                                                               [ ]│
│ Process Accounts Receivable      3                            [ ]│
│                                                               [ ]│
│ Process Accounts Payable         4                            [ ]│
│ Send Out Fliers                  4                            [ ]│
│                                                               [ ]│
│ Print Source Files               5                            [ ]│
│                            I                                  [▼]│
├─────────────────────────────────────────────────────────────────┤
│[←][ ]                                                      [→][ ]│
└─────────────────────────────────────────────────────────────────┘
```

The second is an interoffice memo:

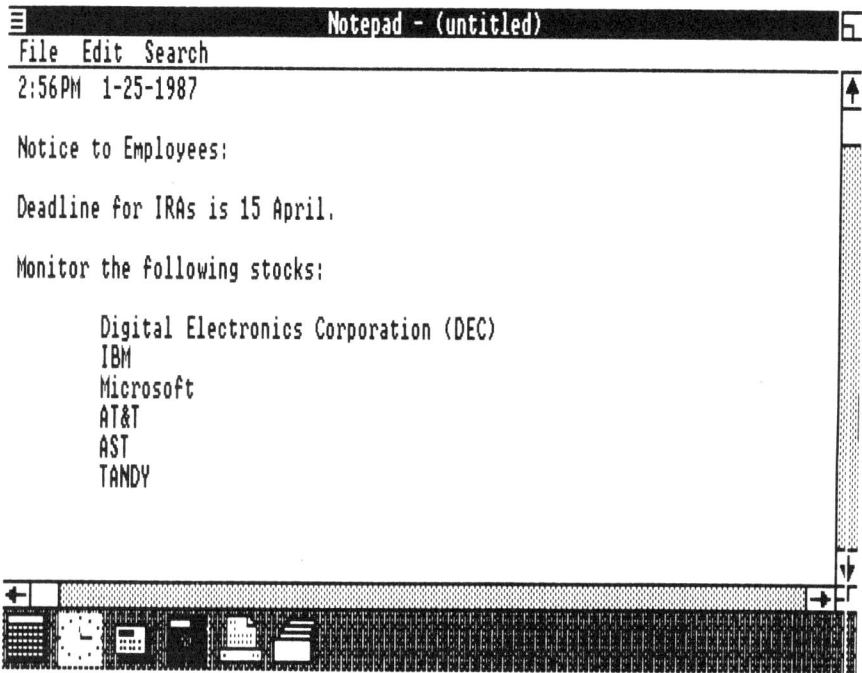

Terminal

Windows offers more than its desktop features; its terminal-emulation program allows you to connect and share information with remote computers over telephone lines. If you don't have a modem connected to your system, you may want to skip this section. If you do have a modem, you should find the Windows communication package very

simple to use. From the MS-DOS Executive invoke the program
TERMINAL.EXE. Windows will display the following:

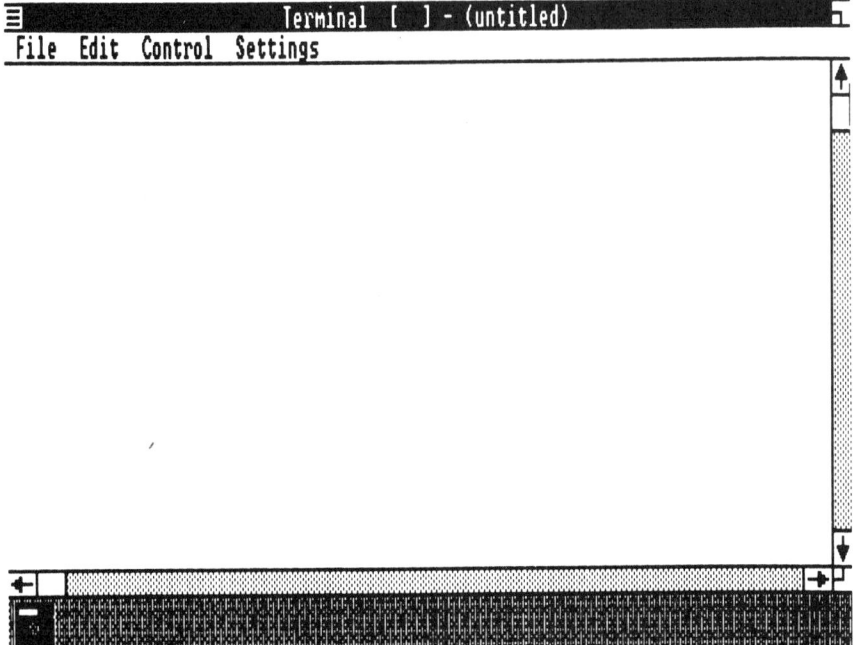

The screen format should look familiar by now. First select the File menu. Terminal will display the following:

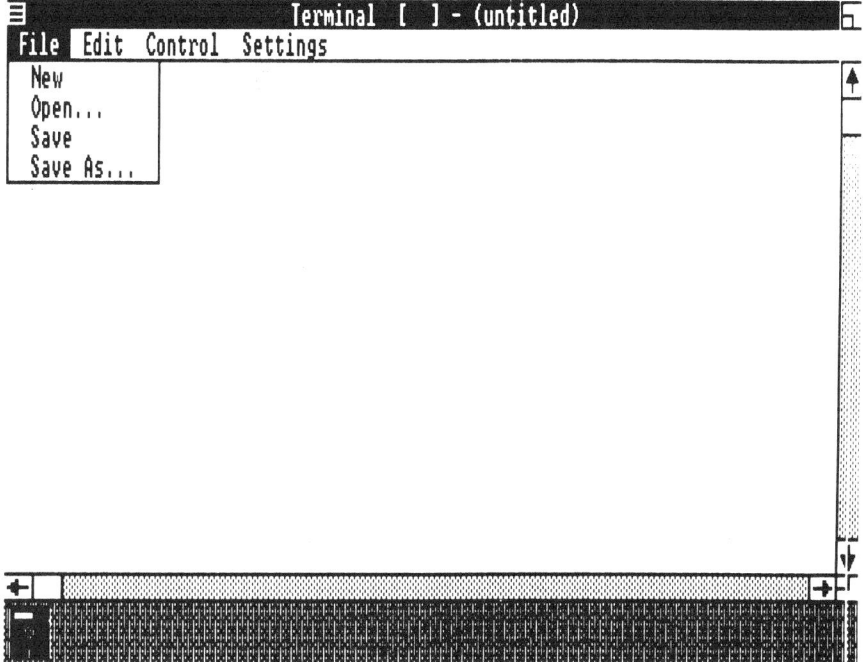

One of the most useful features of the Windows communication package is that once you configure your system for a particular bulletin board or on-line service, you can save the configuration in a file. The New option allows you to create a new configuration file. The

Open option opens an existing configuration file and loads its communications options. When you invoke Terminal, it will display the following:

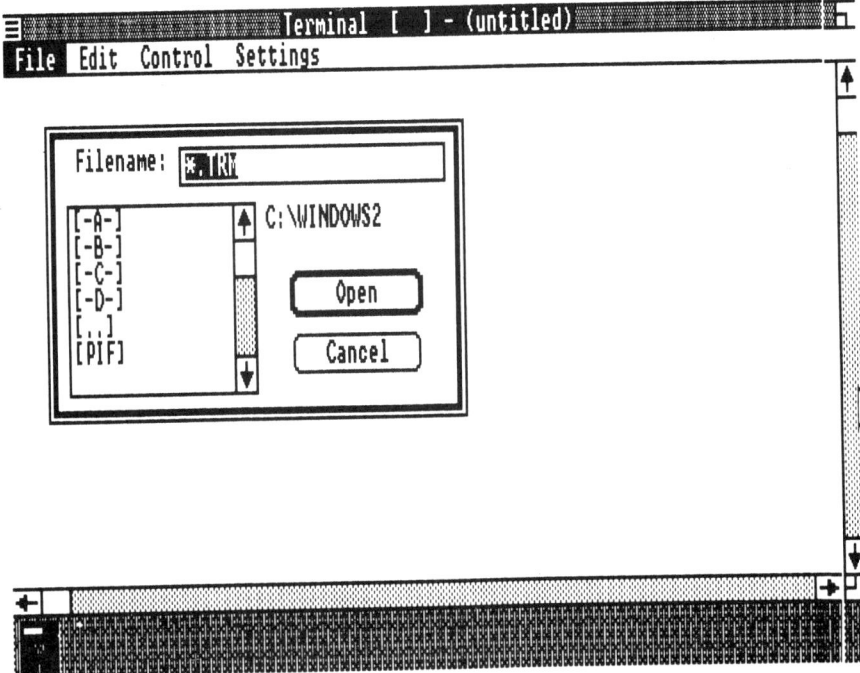

Select the file that you desire, or simply enter it and press ENTER. Once you have created or modified a configuration file, the Terminal

Save and Save As options allow you to save the changes to a file. Both options will display the following dialog box:

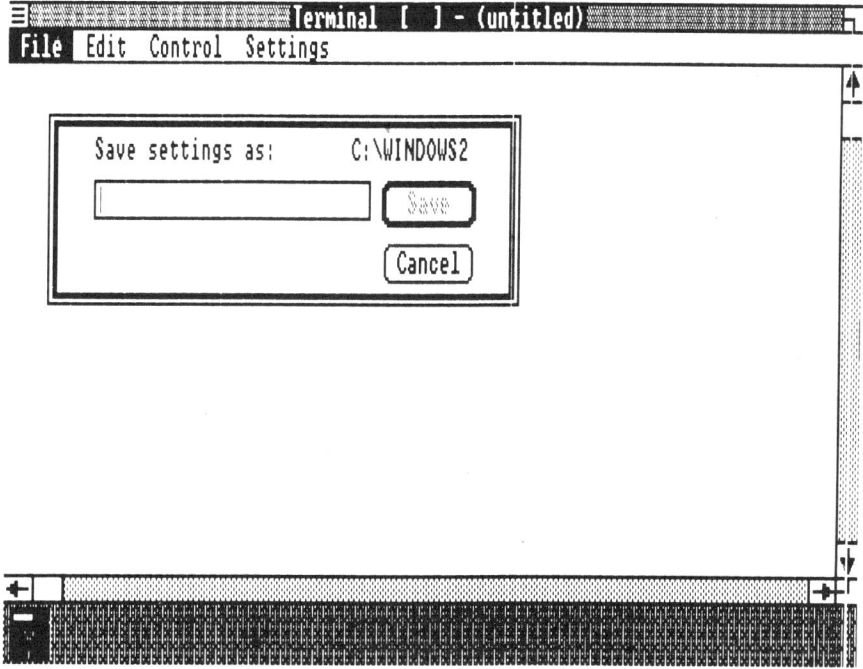

Simply type in the name of the file to which you want the configuration saved.

Select the Terminal Edit menu. Terminal will display the following:

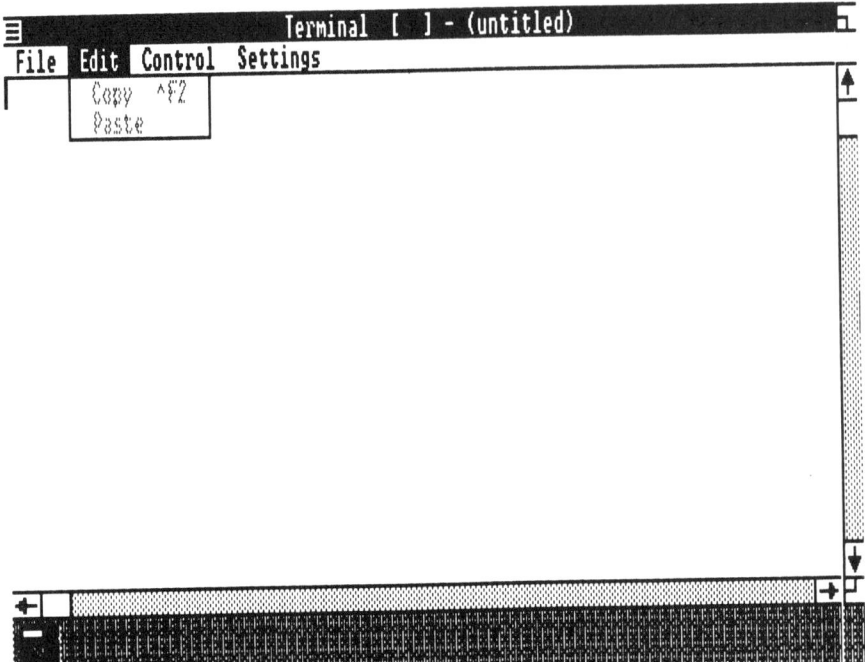

These options allow you to exchange information between Windows applications via the Clipboard. The Terminal Control menu provides the following capabilities:

```
 ≣          Terminal [ ] - (untitled)                    🔒
 File  Edit  Control  Settings
 ┌──────────┬─────────────────┐                          ▲
 │          │ Connect    ^F3  │                          │
 │          │ Print      ^F4  │                          │
 │          │ Capture    ^F5  │                          │
 │          │ Pause      ^F6  │                          │
 │          ├─────────────────┤                          │
 │          │ Break      ^F7  │                          │
 │          └─────────────────┘                          │
 │                                                        │
 │                                                        │
 │                                                        │
 │                                                        ▼
 ←  □                                                  → 
 ─
```

The Connect option uses all of the configuration options specified in the file and dials the number that you have specified for the desired service. To terminate the session at a later time, simply select Connect again. Connect works as a toggle. The first time you select Connect it establishes a connection; the second time it terminates the connection.

The Print option causes all the information received (and displayed on the screen) to be echoed to the printer. The option uses the Windows Spooler, so you are not constrained by a slow printer. This option also works as a toggle.

The Terminal Capture option allows you to capture into a file you can later edit all of the information received. When you invoke Capture, it displays the following dialog box:

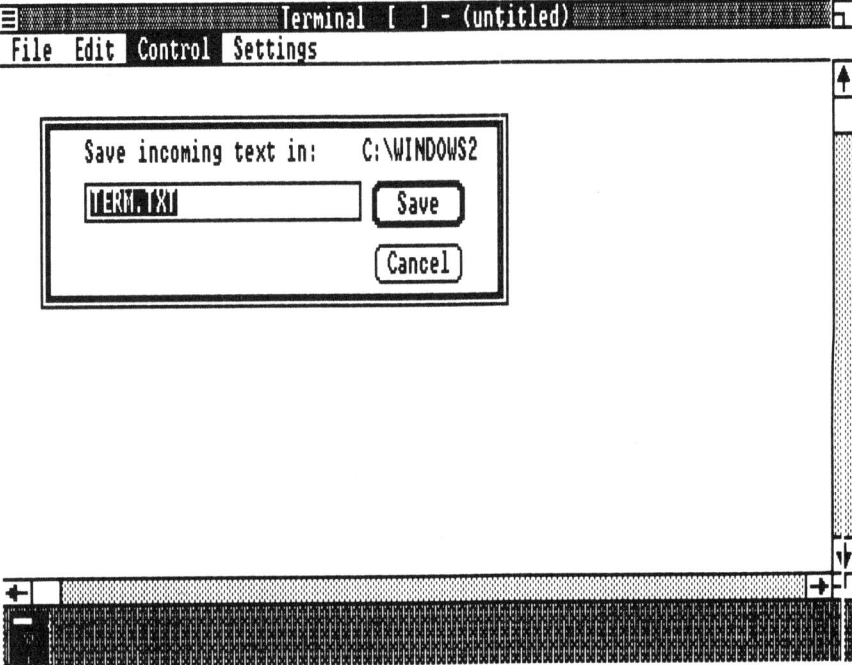

Enter the name of the file in which you want to record the data, or press ENTER to use the default name.

The first time you select the Pause option, the screen stops scrolling; the second time, scrolling resumes.

The last option, Break, sends a break signal to the host computer, requesting that it terminate the current application. Again, note the predefined keys for each option.

Select the Terminal Settings menu. Terminal will display the following:

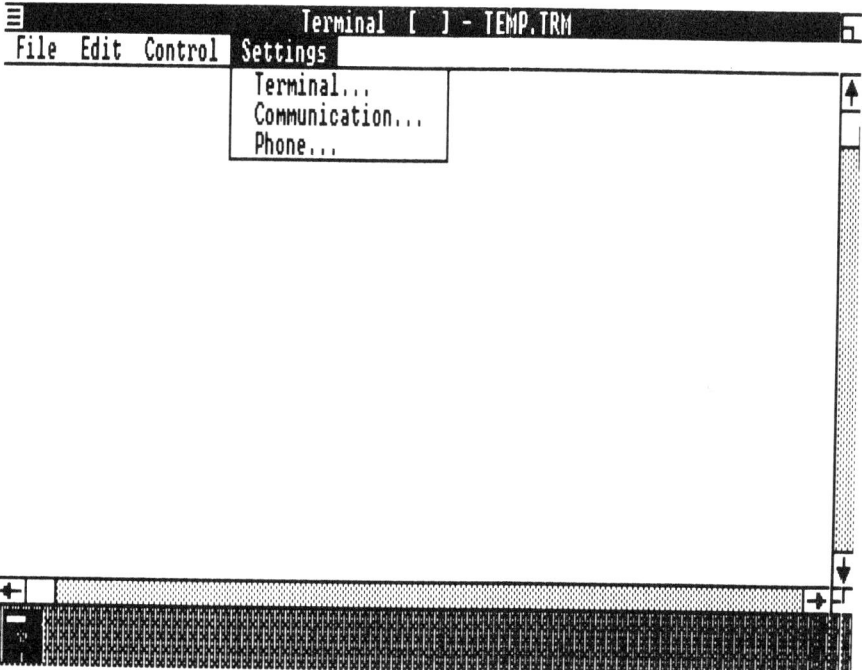

These options allow you to configure your system to meet the tele-communications requirements of the service to which you are connected. Select the Terminal option, and the Terminal program will display the following:

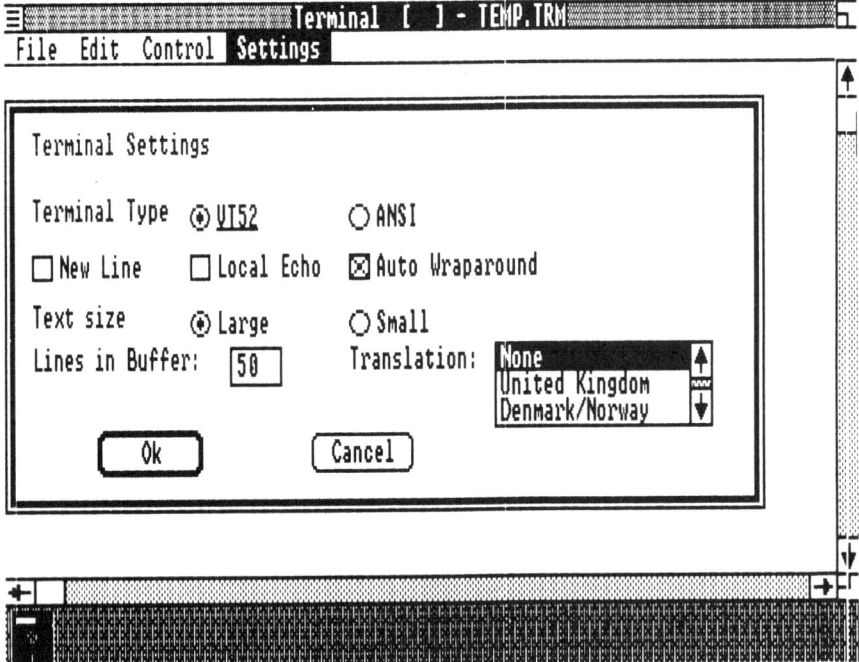

Most services will specify the terminal types that they support. VT52 and ANSI have been the standards for several years. Refer to the service documentation for more details.

The New Line option causes your computer to replace each line feed sequence with a carriage return-line feed. Some computers do not return the cursor to the beginning of the line when a new line begins, so select this option to compensate for this.

The Local Echo option is used when the service with which you are communicating does not echo the keys that you type as you type them. In this case, your terminal must do the echoing for you.

The Auto Wraparound option directs Terminal to automatically wrap each line at column 80.

Many advanced users will buffer in memory the information received and later scroll through it.

The Text size option allows you to reduce the size of the text on the screen to allow more information to be displayed.

The Lines in Buffer option allows you to specify the size of the buffer. Simply type in a value of up to 999 lines and press ENTER.

The Communication option displays the following:

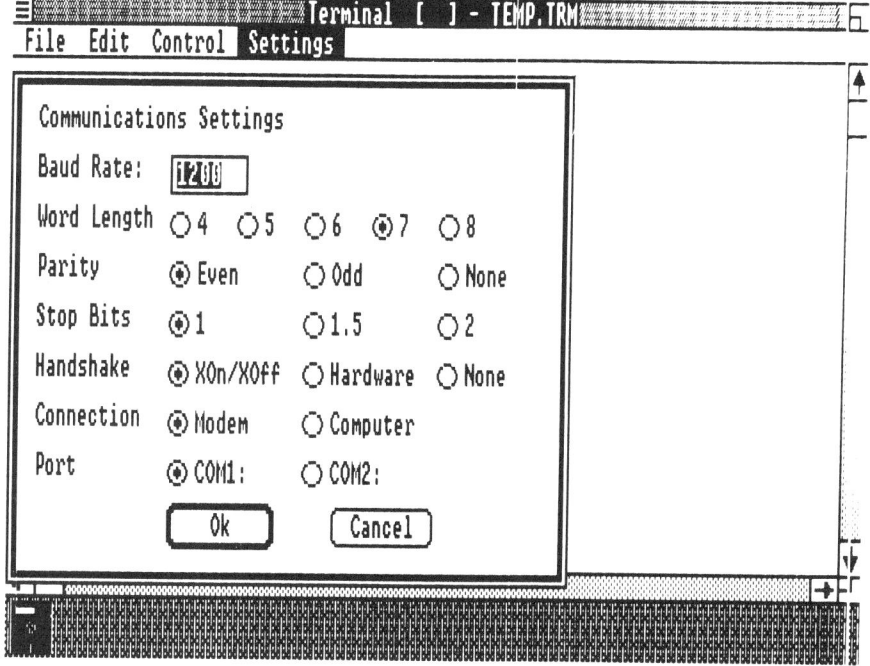

Refer to the documentation of your specific service for this section. The only parameter that is independent of the service is Port, which specifies to what communications port your modem is attached, either COM1 or COM2.

The last option, Phone, displays the following:

```
≡▓▓▓▓▓▓▓▓▓▓▓▓▓▓▓▓▓Terminal [ ] - TEMP.TRM▓▓▓▓▓▓▓▓▓▓▓▓▓▓▓5
 File  Edit  Control  Settings                              ▲
┌──────────────────────────────────┐                       ▓
│                                  │                       ▓
│  Phone Settings                  │                       ▓
│                                  │                       ▓
│  Connect to: ┌─────────────────┐ │                       ▓
│              └─────────────────┘ │                       ▓
│  Dial Type   ⊙Tone  ○Pulse       │                       ▓
│                                  │                       ▓
│  Speed       ○Slow  ⊙Fast        │                       ▓
│  Wait for Tone (2-15):  ┌─┐      │                       ▓
│                         │2│      │                       ▓
│                         └─┘      │                       ▓
│  Wait for Answer (1-256): ┌──┐   │                       ▓
│                           │60│   │                       ▓
│                           └──┘   │                       ▓
│    ┌──────────┐   ┌──────────┐   │                       ▓
│    │    Ok    │   │  Cancel  │   │                       ▼
└──────────────────────────────────┘
```

Enter the telephone number of the service in the Connect to box. Dial Type refers to your phone type. A push-button phone is a tone phone, and a rotary phone is a pulse phone. Speed refers to how fast the number should be dialed. Wait for Tone specifies the number of seconds that Terminal will wait for a dial tone. Likewise, Wait for Answer specifies the number of seconds that Terminal will let the phone ring.

If you have a modem connected to your system, you should find that the Windows Terminal program provides all of the functions you will need.

Reversi

Windows also provides a board game called Reversi. From the MS-DOS Executive, run the program REVERSI.EXE. Windows will display the following:

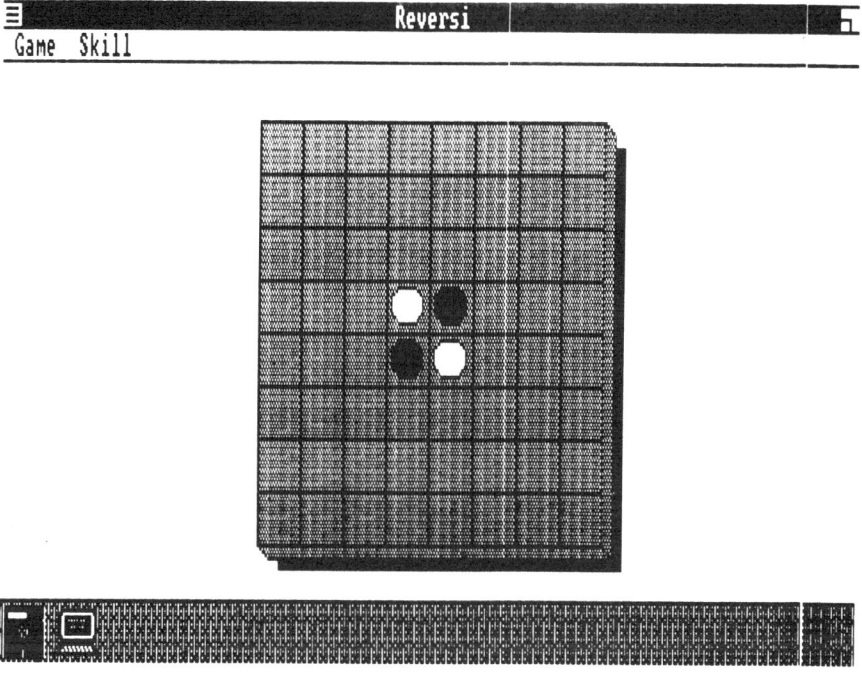

If you have played Othello, you should find Reversi to be quite challenging.

I

CALLING SEQUENCES AND ARGUMENTS

The following appendix provides the calling sequences and arguments for each of the Windows functions.

Window Manipulation Routines

The following are window manipulation routines.

Main Routine

The following is the main manipulation routine.

WinMain (hInstance, hPrevInstance, lpCmdLine, nCmdShow);

Function Entry point for all Windows applications. Normally, WinMain defines, creates, and displays the window for an application, and then begins a message-processing loop.

Value Returned Integer value containing wParam for the last message processed.

Parameters

hInstance: Handle to the new instance of the window.

hPrevInstance: Handle to a previous instance of this window class.

lpCmdLine: Long pointer to NULL-terminated command line.

nCmdShow: Integer value that specifies whether the window should be displayed, left iconic, or hidden.

Notes WinMain does not have to be exported in the module definition file.

Message Routines

The following are message routines in Windows.

PostQuitMessage (nExitCodeValue);

Function Inform Windows that the application wishes to terminate execution, assigning the value of nExitCodeValue to wParam of the WM_QUIT nmessage.

Value Returned   None.

Parameter

nExitCodeValue: Integer value specifying the exit status code.

GetMessage (lpMessage, hWnd, wMsgFilterMin, wMsgFilterMax);

Function   Retrieve a message from the applications message queue. If no messages are present, the routine yields control to another application.

Value Returned   Boolean value of FALSE when the message WM—QUIT is received; otherwise, the value TRUE is returned.

Parameters

lpMessage: Long pointer to data structure of type MSG.

hWnd: Handle to the window whose messages are being processed.

wMsgFilterMin: Integer value specifying the lowest message to be examined.

wMsgFilterMax: Integer value specifying the highest message to be examined.

PeekMessage (lpMessage, hWnd, wMsgFilterMin, wMsgFilterMax, bRemoveMsg);

Function   Check the application queue for a message and if a message is present, place the message into the MSG structure referenced by lpMessage.

Value   Returned   Boolean value of TRUE if a message is present; otherwise, FALSE.

Parameters

lpMessage: Long pointer to data structure of type MSG.

hWnd: Handle to the window whose messages are being processed.

wMsgFilterMin: Integer value specifying the lowest message to be examined.

wMsgFilterMax: Integer value specifying the highest message to be examined.

bRemoveMsg: Boolean value of TRUE if a found message should be removed from the application queue.

Notes   PeekMessage cannot process WM_PAINT messages.

WaitMessage ( );

Function   Suspend application execution and release control to other applications until a new message is in the applications message queue.

Value Returned   None.

Parameters   None.

GetMessagePos ( );

Function   Return the mouse coordinates of the last message retrieved by GetMessage.

Value Returned   Long integer specifying the coordinates of the mouse at the time of the last message retrieval by GetMessage. The high-order word contains the y coordinate and the low-order word contains the x coordinate.

Parameters   None.

GetMessageTime ( );

Function   Return the time of the last message retrieved by Get-Message.

Value Returned   Long integer specifying the system time of the last message obtained by GetMessage.

Parameters   None.

GetCurrentTime ( );

Function   Return the number of milliseconds since the system boot.

Value Returned   Long integer containing the number of milliseconds since the system was booted.

Parameters   None.

TranslateMessage (lpMessage);

Function   Translate a virtual keystroke into character messages.

Value Returned   Boolean value of TRUE if the message was translated; otherwise, FALSE.

Parameter
lpMessage: Long pointer to a data structure of type MSG that contains the message to translate.

Notes   Character messages translated are placed in the application message queue.

TranslateAccelerator (hWnd, hAccTable, lpMessage);

Function   Process keyboard accelerators for menu commands.

Value Returned   Boolean value TRUE if the message is translated as an accelerator.

Parameters

hWnd: Handle to the window to which the message was sent.

hAccTable: Handle to the table defining the accelerators for the current application.

lpMessage: Long pointer to the message to translate.

Notes   Do not translate a translated accelerator with Translate-Message.

DispatchMessage (lpMessage);

Function   Send the message specified to the window's message-processing procedure.

Value Returned   Long-integer value specifying the result of the message-processing function.

Parameter

lpMessage: Long pointer to a data structure of type MSG that contains the message to dispatch.

SendMessage (hWnd, wMessage, wParam, lParam);

Function   Send a message to one or more windows and wait until processed.

Value Returned Long-integer value from the window message-processing routine that received the message.

Parameters

hWnd: Handle to the window to receive the message. If the value is 0xFFFF, the message is sent to every window.

wMessage: Integer value specifying the message to be sent.

wParam: Integer value for the wParam field of the message.

lParam: Long-integer value specifying the lParam field of the message.

PostMessage (hWnd, wMessage, wParam, lParam);

Function Place a message in one or more window's message queues.

Value Returned Long-integer value from the window message-processing routine that received the message.

Parameters

hWnd: Handle to the window to receive the message. If the value is 0xFFFF, the message is sent to every top level window.

wMessage: Integer value specifying the message to be sent.

wParam: Integer value for the wParam field of the message.

lParam: Long-integer value specifying the lParam field of the message.

ReplyMessage (lReply);

Function Reply to message sent by SendMessage without returning control to the routine SendMessage.

Value Returned None.

Parameter

lReply: Long integer specifying the result of the message processing.

PostAppMessage (hTask, wMessage, wParam, lParam);

Function   Post a message to the task referenced by the handle hTask without waiting for the receiving task to process the message.

Value Returned   Boolean value of TRUE if the message is posted; otherwise, FALSE.

Parameters

hTask: Handle to the task to receive the message.

wMessage: Integer value specifying the message to be sent.

wParam: Integer value for the wParam field of the message.

lParam: Long-integer value specifying the lParam field of the message.

RegisterWindowMessage (lpStr);

Function   Define a new systemwide message.

Value Returned   Integer value representing the message registered, or the value 0 if an error occurs.

Parameter

lpStr: Long pointer to an ASCIIZ string defining the new message.

Window Routine

The following is a window routine.

WndProc (hWnd, wMessage, wParam, lParam);

Function   Process messages received from Windows or the main function via Dispatch Message.

Value Returned   Long integer specifying the result of the message processing.

Parameters

hWnd: Handle to the window receiving the message.

wMessage: Integer value specifying the message received.

wParam: Integer value for the wParam field of the message.

lParam: Long-integer value specifying the lParam field of the message.

Default Window Routine

The following is the default window routine.

DefWindowProc (hWnd, wMessage, wParam, lParam);

Function   Process all messages not explicitly processed by the application.

Value Returned   Integer value specifying the result of the message processing.

Parameters

hWnd: Handle to the window receiving the message.

wMessage: Integer value specifying the message received.

wParam: Integer value for the wParam field of the message.

lParam: Long-integer value specifying the lParam field of the message.

Windows Class Routines

The following are Windows class routines.

RegisterClass (lpWinClass);

Function Register a window class for later use. A *window class* defines the attributes of a window.

Value Returned Boolean value of TRUE if the window is registered; otherwise, FALSE.

Parameter
lpWndClass: Long pointer to a data structure of type WNDCLASS that defines the attributes of the window to register.

GetClassName (hWnd, lpClassName, nMaxCount);

Function Return the class name of the window specified by hWnd.

Value Returned Integer value specifying the number of characters actually copied into the buffer referenced by lpClassName.

Parameters
hWnd: Handle to the window of which to return the class name.

lpClassName: Long pointer to the buffer into which the window class name is copied.

nMaxCount: Integer value specifying the maximum number of bytes that lpClassName can store.

GetClassWord (hWnd, nIndex);

Function Return the word at the location in the WNDCLASS structure indexed by nIndex.

Value Returned Integer value retrieved from the WNDCLASS structure.

Parameters

hWnd: Handle to the window for which to return the item.

nIndex: Integer value specifying an index into the WNDCLASS structure, as follows:

GCW_CBCLSEXTRA
GCW_CBWNDEXTRA
CGW_HBRBACKGROUND
CGW_HCURSOR
CGW_HICON
CGW_HINSTANCE
CGW_STYLE

GetClassLong (hWnd, nIndex);

Function Return the long integer at the location in the WNDCLASS structure indexed by nIndex.

Value Returned Long-integer value retrieved from the WNDCLASS structure.

Parameters

hWnd: Handle to the window for which to return the item.

nIndex: Integer value specifying an index into the WNDCLASS structure, as follows:

GCL_MENUNAME
GCL_WNDPROC

SetClassWord (hWnd, nIndex, wNewWord);

Function   Replace the word at the location in the WNDCLASS data structure indexed by nIndex with the value contained in wNewWord.

Value Returned   Integer value that specifies the previous value of the word indexed.

Parameters

hWnd: Handle to the window for which to update the word.

nIndex: Integer index into the WNDCLASS data structure, as follows:
GCW_CBCLSEXTRA
GCW_CBWNDEXTRA
CGW_HBRBACKGROUND
CGW_HCURSOR
CGW_HICON
CGW_HINSTANCE
CGW_STYLE

nNewWord: Integer value specifying the replacement value.

SetClassLong (hWnd, nIndex, wNewLong);

Function   Replace the long-integer value at the location in the WNDCLASS data structure indexed by nIndex with the value contained in wNewWord.

Value Returned   Long-integer value that specifies the previous value of the long integer indexed.

Parameters

hWnd: Handle to the window for which to update the word.

nIndex: Integer index into the WNDCLASS data structure, as follows:

GCL—MENUNAME
GCL—WNDPROC

nNewLong: Long-integer value specifying the replacement value.

CallWindowProc (lpPrevWndfunct, hWnd, wMessage, wParam, lParam);

Function Pass a message to the function specified by lpPrevWnd-funct to support window subclassing.

Value Returned Long integer specifying the result of the message processing.

Parameters

lpPrevWndfunct: Long pointer to the previous window routine.

hWnd: Handle to the window passing the message.

wMessage: Integer value identifying the message.

wParam: Integer value containing the wParam field for the message.

lParam: Long-integer value containing the lParam field for the message.

Window Creation Routines

The following are Windows creation routines.

CreateWindow (lpClassName, lpWindowName, dwStyle, nX, nY, nWidth, nHeight, hWndParent, hMenu, hInstance, lpParam);

Function Create a tiled, child, or pop-up window.

Value Returned Handle to the window created, or the value NULL if an error occurred.

Parameters

lpClassName: Long pointer to an ASCIIZ string specifying the window class name.

lpWindowName: Long pointer to an ASCIIZ string specifying the window name.

dwStyle: Integer value specifying the style of the window.

nX: Integer value specifying the x coordinate of the window, if applicable.

nY: Integer value specifying the y coordinate of the window, if applicable.

nWidth: Integer value specifying the width of the window in logical units.

nHeight: Integer value specifying the height of the window in logical units.

hWndParent: Handle to a parent window.

hMenu: Handle to a window's menu.

hInstance: Handle to instance associated with the window.

lpParam: Long pointer to a long value that is passed to the application via the WM—CREATE message.

IsWindow (hWnd);

Function Return TRUE if the window associated with the handle hWnd is a valid existing window.

Value Returned Boolean value TRUE if the window is a valid existing window; otherwise, FALSE.

Parameter

hWnd: Handle to the window in question.

DestroyWindow (hWnd);

Function Send a WM—DESTROY message to the window associated with the handle hWnd.

Value Returned Boolean value of TRUE if the window is destroyed; otherwise, the value is FALSE.

Parameter
hWnd: Handle to the window to delete.

GetWindowWord (hWnd, nIndex);

Function Return information about the window associated with the handle hWnd.

Value Returned Integer value specifying the information requested about the window.

Parameters
hWnd: Handle to the desired window.

nIndex: Integer index to the desired value, as follows:
GWW—HINSTANCE   Handle to the instance owning the window
GWW—HWNDPARENT Handle to the parent window
GWW—HWNDPARENT Handle to the parent window
GWW—HWNDTEXT   Handle to the window's caption
GWW—ID   Window control identification

GetWindowLong (hWnd, nIndex);

Function Return information about the window associated with the handle hWnd.

Value Returned Long-integer value specifying the information requested about the window.

Parameters

hWnd: Handle to the desired window.

nIndex: Integer index to the desired value, as follows:

GWL—STYLE	Window style
GWL—WNDPROC	Long pointer to the window function

SetWindowWord (hWnd, nIndex, wNewWord);

Function   Replace information about the window associated with the handle hWnd.

Value Returned   Integer value of the previous window value.

Parameters

hWnd: Handle to the desired window.

nIndex: Integer index to the desired value:

GWW—HINSTANCE	Handle to the instance owning the window
GWW—HWNDPARENT	Handle to the parent window
GWW—HWNDTEXT	Handle to the window's caption
GWW—ID	Window control identification

wNewWord: Integer value specifying the replacement value.

SetWindowLong (hWnd, nIndex, wNewWord);

Function   Replace information about the window associated with the handle hWnd.

Value Returned   Long-integer value of the previous window value.

Parameters

hWnd: Handle to the desired window.

nIndex: Integer index to the desired value, as follows:

GWL_STYLE   Window style

GWL_WNDPROC   Long pointer to the window function

wNewLong: Long-integer value specifying the replacement value.

Window Display and Movement Routines

The following are routines for window display and movement.

ShowWindow (hWnd, nCmdShow);

Function   Display or hide the window associated with the window handle hWnd.

Value Returned   Boolean value of TRUE if the window was previously visible; otherwise, FALSE.

Parameters

hWnd: Handle to the desired window.

nCmdShow: Integer value specifying the desired operation, as follows:

HIDE_WINDOW   Do not display window

SHOW_FULLSCREEN   Use entire screen for window display

SHOW_ICONWINDOW   Display a previously iconic window

SHOW_OPENWINDOW   Display a window for the first time

SHOW_OPENNOACTIVE   Display the window but do not activate it

OpenIcon (hWnd);

Function   Open and display an iconic window removing its icon from the icon area.

Value Returned Boolean value of TRUE if the window is opened; otherwise, FALSE.

Parameter
hWnd: Handle to the desired window.

Notes This function cannot open child and pop-up windows.

CloseWindow (hWnd);

Function Close the window associated with the window handle hWnd.

Value Returned Boolean value TRUE if the window is closed; otherwise, FALSE.

Parameter
hWnd: Handle to the desired window.

Notes Closing a tiled window results in the window being removed from the screen and the icon being placed in the icon area.

MoveWindow (hWnd, nX, nY, nWidth, nHeight, nRepaint);

Function Send a WM—SIZE message to the window associated with the window handle hWnd. The location and size of the window are specified by the parameters passed to MoveWindow.

Value Returned None.

Parameters
hWnd: Handle to the desired window.

nX, nY: Integer values specifying the desired x and y coordinate of the upper-left corner of the window.

nWidth: Integer value specifying the width of the window.

nHeight: Integer value specifying the height of the window.

nRepaint: Boolean value that, when TRUE, requests the window be repainted.

BringWindowToTop (hWnd);

Function Bring a pop-up or child window to the top of the stack of overlapping windows.

Value Returned None.

Parameter
hWnd: Handle to the desired window.

SetActiveWindow (hWnd);

Function Select a tiled or pop-up window as the active window.

Value Returned Handle to the previously active window.

Parameter
hWnd: Handle to the desired window.

IsWindowVisible (hWnd);

Function Return TRUE if the window specified is visible; otherwise, FALSE.

Value Returned Boolean value TRUE if the window associated with the window handle hWnd is currently visible; otherwise, FALSE.

Parameter
hWnd: Handle to the desired window.

AnyPopup ( );

Function   Return TRUE if a pop-up window is currently visible on the screen.

Value Returned   Boolean value TRUE if a pop-up window is currently visible on the screen.

Parameters   None.

IsIconic (hWnd);

Function   Return whether the window associated with the window handle hWnd is currently iconic.

Value Returned   Boolean value TRUE if the desired window is currently iconic; otherwise, FALSE.

Parameter
hWnd: Handle to the desired window.

EnumWindows (lpEnumfunct, lParam);

Function   Enumerate the windows on the screen by passing handles for each window to an application-defined callback function.

Value Returned   Boolean value of TRUE if all of the windows have been enumerated.

Parameters
lpEnumfunct: Long pointer to application-defined callback function.

lParam: Long integer passed to the callback routine for enumeration.

Notes Windows are enumerated in the following order:

Tiled windows
Iconic windows
Pop-up windows
Hidden pop-up windows

The format for the application-defined callback function is

callback (hWnd, lParam);

EnumChildWindows (hWndParent, lpEnumfunct, lParam);

Function Enumerate the child windows of a parent in a manner similar to the routine EnumWindows.

Value Returned Boolean value TRUE if all of the child windows have been enumerated; otherwise, FALSE.

Parameters

hWndParent: Handle to the parent window.

lpEnumfunct: Long pointer to application-defined callback function.

lParam: Long integer passed to the callback routine for enumeration.

Notes See EnumWindows.

Dialog Box Routines

The following routines allow applications to create, delete, and manipulate dialog boxes and the controls they contain.

CreateDialog (hInstance, lpTemplateName, hWndParent, lpDialogfunct);

Function   Create a modeless dialog box.

Value Returned   Handle to the newly created dialog box, or NULL if an error occurred.

Parameters

hInstance: Handle to the module instance containing the dialog box.

lpTemplateName: Long pointer to an ASCIIZ string naming the dialog template.

hWndParent: Handle to the window owning the dialog box.

lpDialogfunct: Long pointer to the dialog box processing function.

Notes   The dialog box processing function must be of the form

funct (hWnd, wMessage, wParam, lParam);

IsDialogMessage (hDlg, lpMessage);

Function   Return TRUE if the message is intended for the modeless dialog box associated with the dialog handle hDlg; otherwise, FALSE.

Value Returned   Boolean value TRUE if the message is meant for the specified dialog box.

Parameters

hDlg: Handle to the desired dialog box.

lpMessage: Long pointer to a data structure of type MSG that contains the message to be processed.

DialogBox (hInstance, lpTemplateName, hWndParent, lpDialogfunct);

Function   Create a modal dialog box.

Value Returned   Integer value of -1 if insufficient memory existed to create the dialog box; otherwise, the value returned by the applications dialog box function.

Parameters

hInstance: Handle to the module instance containing the dialog box.

lpTemplateName: Long pointer to an ASCIIZ string naming the dialog template.

hWndParent: Handle to the window owning the dialog box.

lpDialogfunct: Long pointer to the dialog box processing function.

Notes   The dialog box processing function must be of the form

funct (hWnd, wMessage, wParam, lParam);

EndDialog (hDlg, nResult);

Function   Destroy the window associated with a modal dialog box and free the resources that it had allocated.

Value Returned   None.

Parameters

hDlg: Handle to the desired dialog box.

nResult: Integer value returned by the routine initiating the call.

DlgDirList (hDlg, lpPath, nIDListBox, nIDStatic, wFiletype);

Function   Create a list of files and directories.

Value Returned   Boolean value TRUE if the listing was made; otherwise, FALSE.

Parameters

hDlg: Handle to the dialog box window.

lpPath: Long pointer to an ASCIIZ string containing the drive and path to use for the directory listing.

nIDListBox: Integer value specifying the list box control.

nIDStatic: Integer value specifying the identification of a static text displayed for drive and directory.

wFiletype: DOS file attributes of the desired file type.

DlgDirSelect (hDlg, lpStr, nIDListBox);

Function   Copy the selection from a list box built by DlgDirSelect into the buffer referenced by lpStr.

Value Returned   Boolean value TRUE if the current selection is a DOS directory; otherwise, FALSE.

Parameters

hDlg: Handle to the dialog box window.

lpStr: Long pointer to a buffer to contain the selected file name.

nIDListBox: Integer value specifying the list control box.

GetDlgItem (hDlg, nIDDlgItem);

Function   Return a handle to the specified dialog box control.

Value Returned Handle to the specified control, or NULL if an error occurred.

Parameters

hDlg: Handle to the dialog box window.

nIDDlgItem: Integer value specifying the desired control.

SetDlgItemInt (hDlg, nIDDlgItem, wValue, bSigned);

Function Set the value of the selected dialog box control to the value contained in wValue.

Value Returned None.

Parameters

hDlg: Handle to the dialog box window.

nIDDlgItem: Integer value specifying the control to modify.

wValue: Integer value to assign to the control.

bSigned: Boolean value that, when TRUE, states that the value in wValue is a signed integer; otherwise, unsigned.

GetDlgItemInt (hDlg, nIDDlgItem, lpTranslated, bSigned);

Function Translate a dialog text into an integer value.

Value Returned Integer value containing the translated value.

Parameters

hDlg: Handle to the dialog box window.

nIDDlgItem: Integer value specifying the desired control.

lpTranslated: Long pointer to a Boolean value that, when TRUE, states no errors occurred; otherwise, the text contained noninteger characters.

bSigned: Boolean value that, when TRUE, states that the value to be retrieved is a signed value.

SetDlgItemText (hDlg, nIDDlgItem, lpStr);

Function   Set a dialog text to the contents of the string referenced by lpStr.

Value Returned   None.

Parameters

hDlg: Handle to the dialog box window.

nIDDlgItem: Integer value specifying the desired control.

lpStr: Long pointer to an ASCIIZ string containing the text to assign to the control.

GetDlgItemText (hDlg, nIDDlgItem, lpStr, nMaxBytes);

Function   Copy the contents of a dialog text to the buffer referenced by lpStr.

Value Returned   Integer value specifying the actual number of bytes copied into the buffer.

Parameters

hDlg: Handle to the dialog box window.

nIDDlgItem: Integer value specifying the desired control.

lpStr: Long pointer to the buffer receiving the copy.

nMaxBytes: Integer value specifying the size of the buffer.

CheckDlgButton (hDlg, nIDButton, wCheck)

Function   Place or remove a check mark from a control button.

Value Returned   None.

Parameters

hDlg: Handle to the dialog control window.

nIDButton: Integer value specifying the desired control.

wCheck: Integer value specifying the desired action.

Notes   If wCheck is 0, the check mark is removed; otherwise, a check mark is placed on the button. For three-state buttons, the following applies:

0   Remove the check mark
1   Place a check mark
2   Gray the button

IsDlgButtonChecked (hDlg, nIDButton);

Function   Determine if a control button has a check mark next to it.

Value Returned   Integer value defining the state of the button.

Parameters

hDlg: Handle to the dialog box window.

nIDButton: Integer value specifying the desired control button.

Notes   If the value returned is 1, a check mark exists next to the button. For three-state buttons, the following return value applies:

0 Check mark not set

1 Check mark set

2 Check mark disabled

CheckRadioButton (hDlg, nIDFirstButton, nIDLastButton, nIDCheckButton);

Function Place a check mark next to the button referenced by nIDCheckButton, and remove check marks from all of the other buttons in the functions nIDFirstButton to nIDLastButton.

Value Returned None.

Parameters

hDlg: Handle to the dialog box window.

nIDFirstButton: Integer value specifying the first button in the range of buttons from which to remove check marks.

nIDLastButton: Integer value specifying the last button in the range of buttons from which to remove check marks.

nIDCheckButton: Integer value specifying the button by which to place a check mark.

SenDDlgItemMessage (hDlg, nIDDlgItem, wMessage, wParam, lParam);

Function Send the specified message to the control in the dialog box associated with the handle hDlg.

Value Returned Integer value returned by the dialog box function.

Parameters

hDlg: Handle to the dialog box window.

nIDDlgItem: Integer value specifying the desired control.

wMessage: Integer value specifying the message to be sent.

wParam: Integer value specifying the value of the wParam field of the message.

lParam: Long-integer value specifying the value of the lParam field of the message.

MapDialogRect (hDlg, lpRect);

Function Convert the dialog box coordinates specified in the data structure of type RECT referenced by lpRECT to client coordinates.

Value Returned None.

Parameters

hDlg: Handle to the dialog box window.

lpRECT: Long pointer to a data structure of type RECT that contains the dialog box coordinates.

Clipboard Routines

The following are the Clipboard routines in Windows.

OpenClipboard (hWnd);

Function Open the Windows Clipboard for examination by the application, restricting Clipboard access by other applications.

Value Returned Boolean value of TRUE if the Clipboard is successfully opened; otherwise, FALSE.

Parameter

hWnd: Handle to the window opening the Clipboard.

CloseClipboard ( );

Function   Close the Clipboard, allowing other applications to access it.

Value Returned   Boolean value of TRUE if the Clipboard is successfully closed; otherwise, FALSE.

Parameters   None.

EmptyClipboard ( );

Function   Empty the contents of the Clipboard, freeing a handle to the data that it contained.

Value Returned   Boolean value of TRUE if the Clipboard is successfully emptied; otherwise, FALSE.

Parameters   None.

GetClipboardOwner ( );

Function   Return a handle to the window currently owning the Clipboard.

Value Returned   Handle to the window owning the Clipboard, or the value NULL if an error occurred.

Parameters   None.

SetClipboardData (wFormat, hMem);

Function Define the data to be displayed in the Clipboard.

Value Returned Handle to the data returned by the Clipboard, or the NULL value if an error occurred.

Parameters

wFormat: Integer value specifying the format of the data (see Chapter 14).

hMem: Handle to the memory block containing the data to be placed into the Clipboard.

Notes Once the handle hMem is passed to the Clipboard, the memory block becomes property of the Clipboard and should not be manipulated by the application.

GetClipboardData (wFormat);

Function Return a handle to the data contained in the Clipboard.

Value Returned Handle to the data contained in the Clipboard in the format specified by wFormat.

Parameters

wFormat: Integer value specifying the desired data format.

RegisterClipboardFormat (lpFormatName);

Function Register the Clipboard data format name contained in the string referenced by lpFormatName in the list of Clipboard data formats.

Value Returned Integer value referencing the new data format, or the value 0 if an error occurred.

Parameter

lpFormatName: Long pointer to the ASCIIZ string containing the name of the new Clipboard data format.

CountClipboardFormats ( );

Function Return a count of the number of available Clipboard data formats.

Value Returned Integer value specifying the number of Clipboard data formats supported by the Clipboard.

Parameters None.

GetClipboardFormatName (wFormat, lpFormatName, nMaxBytes);

Function Return the ASCIIZ name of the Clipboard data format specified by the value in wFormat.

Value Returned Integer value specifying the actual number of bytes copied into the buffer.

Parameters

wFormat: Integer value specifying the Clipboard data format of which to return the name.

lpFormatName: Long pointer to the buffer to store the format name.

nMaxBytes: Integer value specifying the maximum size of the buffer.

EnumClipboardFormats ( );

Function   Enumerate the Clipboard data formats currently available.

Value Returned   Integer value specifying the Clipboard data format, or the value 0 if the last format has been enumerated.

Parameter

wFormat: Integer value specifying a known format. When set to 0, the first format is returned.

SetClipboardViewer (hWnd);

Function   Place the window handle contained in hWnd into the chain of Clipboard viewers that are notified when changes to the Clipboard occur.

Value Returned   Handle to the next window in the Clipboard viewer chain.

Parameter

hWnd: Handle to the desired window.

GetClipboardViewer ( );

Function   Return the handle of the first window in the Clipboard viewer chain.

Value Returned   Handle to the first window in the Clipboard viewer chain.

Parameters   None.

ChangeClipboardChain (hWnd, hWndNext);

Function Remove the window associated with the handle hWnd from the Clipboard viewer chain.

Value Returned Boolean value of TRUE if the window is removed, or FALSE if an error occurred.

Input Routines

The following are input routines for Windows.

SetFocus (hWnd);

Function Assign the Windows input focus to the window specified by the window handle hWnd.

Value Returned Handle to the window previously controlling the input focus, or NULL if no previous control exists.

Parameter
hWnd: Handle to the window receiving the input focus.

GetFocus ( );

Function Return the handle to window currently owning the input focus.

Value Returned Handle to window owning the input focus.

Parameters None.

GetKeyState (nVirtualKey);

Function   Specify the state of the virtual key specified — up, down, or toggled.

Value Returned   Integer value specifying the state of the virtual key.

Parameter
nVirtualKey: Integer value specifying the virtual key of interest.

Notes   The following are the key states:

High-order bit set	Key is depressed
Low-order bit set	Key is toggled
Otherwise	Key is up

SetCapture (hWnd);

Function   Direct Windows to send all future mouse inputs to the window associated with hWnd.

Value Returned   Handle to the window previously capturing all mouse inputs, or the value 0 if no window previously existed.

Parameter
hWnd: Handle to the window to capture mouse inputs.

ReleaseCapture ( );

Function   Terminate the capturing of mouse inputs by the window previously assigned by the routine SetCapture and resume standard input processing.

Value Returned   None.

Parameters   None.

SetTimer (hWnd, nIDEvent, wElapse, lpTimerfunct);

Function   Set a system timer.

Value Returned   Integer value specifying the new timer event, or the value 0 if an event has not been set.

Parameters

hWnd: Handle to the desired window.

nIDEvent: Integer value identifying the timer event.

wElapse: Integer value specifying the time in milliseconds until the timer event.

lpTimerfunct: Long pointer to the application-defined timer function.

Notes   The timer function should be of the following form:

timerfunct (hWnd, wMessage, nIDEvent, dwTime);

If the timer function is NULL, the window associated with the timer receives a WM—TIMER message each time the event occurs.

KillTimer (hWnd, nIDEvent);

Function   Kill the timer event referenced by nIDEvent.

Value Returned   Boolean value of TRUE if the event has been successfully killed; otherwise, FALSE.

Parameters

hWnd: Handle to the window associated with the timer event.

nIDEvent: Integer value specifying the timer event to kill.

EnableWindow (hWnd, bEnableFlag);

Function   Enable or disable the window associated with hWnd from receiving keyboard and mouse input.

Value Returned   Boolean value of TRUE if the window has been enabled or disabled as specified.

Parameters

hWnd: Handle to the window desired.

bEnableFlag: Boolean value that, when TRUE, enables input.

IsWindowEnabled (hWnd);

Function   Determine whether the specified window can receive keyboard and mouse input.

Value Returned   Boolean value of TRUE when the specified window is enabled for mouse and keyboard input; otherwise, the value is FALSE.

Parameter

hWnd: Handle to the desired window.

Menu Manipulation Routines

The following are menu manipulation routines.

SetMenu (hWnd, hMenu);

Function   Sets the window menu for the window associated with hWnd to the menu referenced by the handle hMenu.

Value Returned Boolean value of TRUE if the menu is set successfully; otherwise, FALSE.

Parameters

hWnd: Handle to the desired window.

hMenu: Handle to the new desired menu.

GetMenu (hWnd);

Function Returns a handle to the menu associated with hWnd.

Value Returned Handle to the window menu, or the value NULL if no menu exists.

Parameter

hWnd: Handle to the desired window.

DestroyMenu (hMenu);

Function Destroy the menu associated with the handle hMenu.

Value Returned Boolean value of TRUE if the menu is destroyed; otherwise, FALSE.

Parameter

hMenu: Handle to the menu to destroy.

ChangeMenu (hMenu, wIDItem, lpNewItem, wIDNewItem, wChange);

Function Append, insert, delete, or modify a menu item in the menu associated with hMenu.

Value Returned   Boolean value of TRUE if the menu is successfully changed; otherwise, FALSE.

Parameters

hMenu: Handle to the menu to modify.

wIDItem: Integer value identifying the menu item to modify.

lpNewItem: Long pointer to either a bitmap, handle to a menu, or string depending upon the value of wChange. The default is a long pointer to a string.

wIDNewItem: Integer value identifying the new menu item.

wChange: Integer value specifying how to change the menu, as follows:

MF_APPEND	Append the item
MF_BITMAP	Use a bitmap as the item
MY_BYPOSITION	WIDItem specifies the position number of the item, not its identification value
MF_BYCOMMAND	WIDItem specifies the item identification value
MF_CHANGE	Replace the item
MF_CHECKED	Place a check mark next to the item
MF_DELETE	Remove the item
MF_DISABLED	Disable the menu item
MF_ENABLED	Enable the menu item
MF_GRAYED	Display item in gray
MF_INSERT	Insert the item below the specified line
MF_MENUBARBREAK	Place divider before the menu item
MF_MENUBREAK	Place the item on a new line
MF_POPUP	Associate a pop-up menu with the menu item
MF_SEPARATOR	Draw a horizontal dividing line
MF_STRING	lpNewItem points to a string
MF_UNCHECKED	Remove a check mark from the menu item

DrawMenuBar (hWnd);

Function Redraw the menu bar associated with the window referenced by hWnd.

Value Returned None.

Parameter
hWnd: Handle to the desired window.

CheckMenuItem (hMenu, wIDItem, wCheck);

Function Place a check mark next to the specified menu item.

Value Returned Boolean value of TRUE if the item was previously checked.

Parameters
hMenu: Handle to desired menu.

wIDItem: Integer value identifying the item to check.

wCheck: Integer value specifying how the item is checked, as follows:

MF—BYCOMMAND	wIDItem specifies an identification value
MF—BYPOSITION	wIDItem specifies a position number
MF—CHECKED	Add a check mark
MF—UNCHECKED	Remove a check mark

Notes Top-level menu items cannot be checked.

EnableMenuItem (hMenu, wIDEnableItem, wEnable);

Function Enable, disable, or gray a menu item.

Value Returned   Boolean value containing the previous state of the menu item.

Parameters

hMenu: Handle to the desired menu.

wIDEnableItem: Integer value specifying the desired menu item.

wEnable: Integer value specifying how the item is modified, as follows:

MF—BYCOMMAND	wIDEnableItem specifies an identification value
MF—BYPOSITION	wIDEnableItem specifies a position number
MF—DISABLED	Menu item is disabled
MF—ENABLED	Menu item is enabled
MF—GRAYED	Menu item is grayed

HiliteMenuItem (hWnd, hMenu, wIDItem, wHilite);

Function   Highlight or remove highlight for the specified window item.

Value Returned   Boolean value of TRUE if the item is highlighted; otherwise, FALSE.

Parameters

hWnd: Handle to the desired window.

hMenu: Handle to the desired message.

wIDItem: Integer value specifying the menu item to highlight.

wHilite: Integer value specifying how the menu item is highlighted, as follows:

MF—BYCOMMAND	wIDEnableItem specifies an identification value

MF_BYPOSITION	wIDEnableItem specifies a position number
MF_HILITE	Highlight the menu item
MF_UNHILITE	Highlight is removed for the menu item

GetSubMenu (hMenu, nPosition);

Function Retrieve a handle to a pop-up menu.

Value Returned Handle to a pop-up menu, or NULL if no such menu exists.

Parameters

hMenu: Handle to the desired menu.

nPosition: Integer value specifying the index to the pop-up menu.

GetSystemMenu (hWnd, bAction);

Function Allow access to the system menu for modification.

Value Returned Handle to the system menu if the value of bAction is TRUE; otherwise, a handle to a copy of the system menu is returned.

Parameters

hWnd: Handle to the desired window.

bAction: Boolean value that, when TRUE, modifies the system menu; otherwise, modifies a copy of the system menu.

GetMenuString (hMenu, wIDItem, lpStr, nMaxBytes, wFlag);

Function Return the character string associated with the specified menu item.

Value Returned   Copy the character string prompt associated with the specified menu item into the buffer referenced by lpStr.

Parameters

hMenu: Handle to the desired menu.

wIDItem: Integer value specifying the desired menu item.

lpStr: Long pointer to a buffer receiving the character string copy.

nMaxBytes: Integer value specifying the maximum size of the buffer.

wFlag: Integer value specifying how wIDItem is interpreted, as follows:

MF—BYCOMMAND   wIDEnableItem specifies an identification value

MF—BYPOSITION   wIDEnableItem specifies a position number

Window Painting Routines

The following routines prepare the client area of a window for GDI (Graphics Device Interface) functions.

GetDC (hWnd);

Function   Return the display context for the client area of the window referenced by hWnd.

Value Returned   Handle to the client area if the function is successful; otherwise, the NULL value.

Parameter

hWnd: Handle to the desired window.

Notes   Only five display contexts are available in Windows at a given time.

GetWindowDC (hWnd);

Function   Return the display context for the entire window.

Value Returned   Handle to the display context for the specified window, or a NULL value if an error occurred.

Parameter
hWnd: Handle for the desired window.

ReleaseDC (hWnd, hDC);

Function   Release the specified display context.

Value Returned   Integer value of 1 if the display context is released; otherwise, the value is 0.

Parameters
hWnd: Handle to the desired window.

hDC: Handle to the display context to release.

BeginPaint (hWnd, lpPaint);

Function   Prepare specified window for painting and fill the data structure pointed to by lpPaint with information about the area to paint.

Value Returned   Handle to the display context for specified window.

Parameters
hWnd: Handle to the desired window.

lpPaint: Long pointer to a data structure of the type PAINTSTRUCT that contains information about the region to paint.

EndPaint (hWnd, lpPaint);

Function Mark the end of the repainting for the specified window.

Value Returned None.

Parameters

hWnd: Handle to the desired window.

lpPaint: Long pointer to a data structure of the type PAINT-STRUCT that contains information about the region to paint.

UpdateWindow (hWnd);

Function Ensure that the appearance of the specified window is up-to-date.

Value Returned None.

Parameter

hWnd: Handle to the window to be updated.

Notes UpdateWindow sends a WM—PAINT message to the window message-processing procedure.

GetUpdateRect (hWnd, lpRect, bEraseFlag);

Function Return the rectangle bounding the region of the window that needs updating.

Parameters

hWnd: Handle to the desired window.

lpRect: Long pointer to a data structure of type RECT that contains the rectangle bounding the area of the screen to be updated.

bEraseFlag: Boolean value that, when TRUE, directs Windows to erase the background of the update area prior to the update.

InvalidateRect (hWnd, lpRect, bEraseFlag);

Function   Mark for repainting the rectangle bounding the region of the window that needs updating.

Parameters

hWnd: Handle to the desired window.

lpRect: Long pointer to a data structure of type RECT that contains the rectangle bounding the area of the screen to be updated.

bEraseFlag: Boolean value of TRUE when the rectangle should be erased; otherwise, FALSE.

InvalidateRgn (hWnd, hRgn, bEraseFlag);

Function   Marks a region of the window for repainting.

Value Returned   None.

Parameters

hWnd: Handle to the desired window.

hRgn: Handle to the region to be repainted.

bEraseFlag: Boolean value that, when TRUE, directs Windows to erase the screen.

ValidateRect (hWnd, lpRect);

Function   Release an area previously marked for painting.

Value Returned   None.

Parameters

hWnd: Handle to the desired window.

lpRect: Long pointer to a data structure of type RECT that defines the area to be released.

ValidateRgn (hWnd, hRgn);

Function   Release a region previously marked for painting.

Value Returned   None.

Parameters

hWnd: Handle to the desired window.

hRgn: Handle to a region to be released.

Module Management Routines

The following routines provide the Windows interface for module management.

GetModuleHandle (lpModuleName);

Function   Returns a handle to the module name specified by lpModuleName.

Value Returned   Handle to the module specified by lpModuleName.

Parameter

lpModuleName: Long pointer to an ASCIIZ string that contains the name of the desired module.

Notes   If the module specified is not found, NULL is returned.

GetModuleUsage (hModule);

Function   Returns a count of the number of references to a module.

Value Returned   Integer value containing the number of references to a module.

Parameter
hModule: Handle to the desired module.

Notes   hModule is obtained via GetModuleHandle.

GetModuleFileName (hModule, lpFilename, nSize);

Function   Return the file name from which the module specified was loaded.

Value Returned   Integer value containing the number of characters in the file name.

Parameters
hModule: Handle to the desired module.

lpFilename: Long pointer to the buffer in which the file name is stored.

nSize: Integer value specifying the length of the buffer pointed to by lpFilename.

Notes   hModule is obtained via GetModuleHandle.

GetInstanceData (hInstance, pData, nCount);

Function   Copy data from a previous instance of the application.

Value Returned   Integer value specifying the number of bytes of data actually copied.

Parameters

hInstance: Handle to the instance from which the data is copied.

pData: Pointer to the receiving buffer.

nCount: Integer value specifying the number of bytes to copy.

GetProcAddress (hModule, lpProcName);

Function   Return the memory address of the function pointed to by lpProcName.

Value Returned   Long pointer to function's entry point.

Parameters

hModule: Handle to the module containing the function.

pProcName: Long pointer to an ASCIIZ string that contains the file name desired.

Notes   If the function name is invalid, or not found, the NULL is returned.

GetCodeHandle (lpProc);

Function   Return a handle to the code segment containing the function referenced by lpProc.

Value Returned   hCode: Handle to a code segment.

Parameter

lpProc: Long pointer to a function.

Notes   If the code segment is not loaded, GetCodeHandle will attempt to load it.

MakeProcInstance (lpProc, hInstance);

Function   Bind the data segment used by the module referenced by hInstance to the function referenced by lpProc.

Value Returned   Long pointer to the function if the bind is successful.

Parameters
lpProc: Long pointer to the function.

hInstance: Handle to the module containing the data segment to bind to the function.

Notes   If the bind is not successful, the NULL value is returned. If the function is exported from another module, use the routine GetProcAddress instead.

FreeProcInstance (lpProc);

Function   Free (unbind) a function from a specific data segment that it was bound to via the routine MakeProcInstance.

Value Returned   None.

Parameter
lpProc: Long pointer to the function to be freed.

LoadLibrary (lpLibFileName);

Function   Load the library module contained in the file specified.

Value Returned   Handle to the loaded module in memory.

Parameter
lpLibFileName: Long pointer to an ASCIIZ string containing the library module to load.

Notes If the file specified is invalid, NULL is returned. A return value of less than 32 is a DOS error code.

FreeLibrary (hLibModule);

Function Decrease the reference count of the library module specified by one.

Value Returned None.

Parameter
hLibModule: Handle to the desired library module.

GetVersion ( );

Function Returns the Windows major and minor version numbers.

Value Returned Integer value where the high byte contains the minor version number and the low byte contains the major version number.

Parameters None.

Notes For Windows 1.03, 1 is the major number while 03 is the minor number.

Catch (lpCatchBuf);

Function Copies the current execution environment to the buffer referenced by lpCatchBuf.

Value Returned Integer value (if 0, the environment was copied).

Parameter
lpCatchBuf: Long pointer to the buffer to store the environment.

Notes The environment contains the state of all system registers and the instruction counter.

Throw (lpCatchBuf, nThrowBack);

Function Restore the execution environment to the values contained in the buffer lpCatchBuf.

Value Returned None.

Parameters

lpCatchBuf: Long pointer to the system environment to be restored. The environment was obtained via the routine Catch.

nThrowBack: Integer value to be returned to the routine Catch.

Memory Management Functions

These routines provide control over the global and local heaps (see Appendix E on Windows memory management).

GlobalAlloc (wFlags, dwBytes);

Function Allocate the number of bytes specified from general system memory.

Value Returned Handle to the memory allocated.

Parameters

wFlags: Integer value specifying how the memory should be allocated, as follows:

GMEM—FIXED	Memory is fixed
GMEM—MOVABLE	Memory can be moved

GMEM—ZEROINIT	Initialize to 0
GMEM—DISCARDABLE	Memory is discardable
GMEM—NODISCARD	Cannot discard objects
GMEM—NOCOMPACT	No memory compaction

dwBytes: Long integer specifying the number of bytes of memory to allocate.

Notes If the function cannot allocate the memory as specified, the NULL value is returned.

GlobalCompact (dwMinFree);

Function Compact memory until dwMinFree bytes of free memory are available.

Value Returned Long integer specifying the number of bytes in the largest free block of memory.

Parameter

dwMinFree: Long integer specifying the number of free bytes desired.

Notes If dwMinFree is 0, the size of the largest block is returned, but memory compaction does not occur.

GlobalDiscard (hMem);

Function Discard the global memory block referenced by hMem.

Value Returned Handle that is 0 if successful discard; otherwise, equal to hMem.

Parameter

hMem: Handle to the block of global memory to discard.

Notes   GlobalDiscard cannot unlock locked memory.

GlobalLock (hMem);

Function   Lock and return the absolute memory address of the block referenced by hMem.

Value Returned   Long pointer to the first byte of the memory block.

Parameter
hMem: Handle to the memory block desired in global memory.

Notes   If the lock is not successful, the NULL value is returned. Locked memory cannot be moved or discarded.

GlobalReAlloc (hMem, dwBytes, wFlags);

Function   Reallocate the memory block referenced by hMem either by increasing or decreasing its size or flags.

Value Returned   Handle to the newly reallocated memory.

Parameters
hMem: Handle to the current block of memory.

dwBytes: Number of bytes of memory to allocate.

wFlags: Flags specifying how the memory is to be allocated. (See the routine GlobalAlloc.)

Notes   If the block cannot be reallocated, the NULL value is returned.

GlobalSize (hMem);

Function Return the size (in bytes) of the global memory block referenced by hMem.

Value Returned Long integer that contains the number of bytes in the block.

Parameter
hMem: Handle to the block of global memory.

Notes A 0 is returned if the handle specified is invalid.

GlobalUnlock (hMem);

Function Unlock the block of global memory referenced by hMem.

Value Returned Boolean value that is TRUE if the block is still locked, or 0 if the unlock was successful.

Parameter
hMem: Handle to the block of memory to unlock.

Notes Once unlocked, the block can again be moved or discarded.

GlobalFlags (hMem);

Function Return the system flags for the block of memory referenced by hMem.

Value Returned Integer value specifying the memory allocation flags for the specific block of memory. The high-order byte contains

GMEM_SWAPPED	Block swapped to disk
GMEM_DISCARDED	Block has been discarded
GMEM_DISCARDABLE	Block can be discarded

Likewise, the low-order byte contains the reference count for the block.

Parameter

hMem: Handle to the block of memory of interest.

LocalAlloc (wFlags, wBytes);

Function   Allocate the number of bytes specified from the local heap.

Value Returned   Handle to the memory allocated.

Parameters

wFlags: Integer value specifying how the memory should be allocated, as follows:

LMEM_FIXED	Memory is fixed
LMEM_MOVABLE	Memory can be moved
LMEM_ZEROINIT	Initialize to 0
LMEM_DISCARDABLE	Memory is discardable
LMEM_NODISCARD	Cannot discard objects
LMEM_NOCOMPACT	No memory compaction

wBytes: Integer specifying the number of bytes of memory to allocate.

Notes   If the function cannot allocate the memory as specified, NULL is returned.

LocalCompact (wMinFree);

Function   Compact local memory until wMinFree bytes of free memory are available.

Value Returned Integer specifying the number of bytes in the largest free block of local memory.

Parameter
wMinFree: Integer specifying the number of free bytes desired.

Notes If wMinFree is 0, the size of the largest block is returned, but memory compaction does not occur.

LocalDiscard (hMem);

Function Discard the local memory block referenced by hMem.

Value Returned Handle that is 0 if successful discard; otherwise, equal to hMem.

Parameter
hMem: Handle to the block of local memory to discard.

Notes LocalDiscard cannot unlock locked memory.

LocalLock (hMem);

Function Lock and return the absolute memory address of the block referenced by hMem.

Value Returned Pointer to the first byte of the memory block.

Parameter
hMem: Handle to the memory block desired in local memory.

Notes If the lock is not successful, the NULL value is returned. Locked memory cannot be moved or discarded.

LocalFreeze (dummy__variable);

Function   Prevent the local heap from being compacted.

Value Returned   None.

Parameter
dummy__variable: Not used.

Notes   This routine is used in conjunction with LocalMelt.

LocalMelt (dummy__variable);

Function   Allow local heap compaction.

Value Returned   None.

Parameter
dummy__variable: Not used.

Notes   This routine is used in conjunction with LocalFreeze.

LocalReAlloc (hMem, wBytes, wFlags);

Function   Reallocate the memory block referenced by hMem either by increasing or decreasing its size or flags.

Value Returned   Handle to the newly reallocated memory.

Parameters
hMem: Handle to the current block of memory.

wBytes: Number of bytes of memory to allocate.

wFlags: Flags specifying how the memory is to be allocated. (See the routine LocalAlloc.)

Notes If the block cannot be reallocated, the NULL value is returned.

LocalSize (hMem);

Function Return the size (in bytes) of the local memory block referenced by hMem.

Value Returned Integer that contains the number of bytes in the block.

Parameter
hMem: Handle to the block of local memory.

Notes A 0 is returned if the handle specified is invalid.

LocalUnlock (hMem);

Function Unlocks the block of local memory referenced by hMem.

Value Returned Boolean value that is TRUE if the block is still locked, or 0 if the unlock was successful.

Parameter
hMem: Handle to the block of memory to unlock.

Notes Once unlocked, the block can again be moved or discarded.

LocalHandleDelta (nNewDelta);

Function Define the number of table entries dynamically allocated when the local heap manager runs out of handle table entries.

Value Returned Integer value specifying the current handle delta.

Parameter
nNewDelta: Integer value specifying the desired handle delta.

LockData (dummy—variable);

Function   Lock the current data segment in memory.

Value Returned   Handle to the locked data segment.

Parameter
dummy—variable: Not used.

Notes   Once the data segment is locked, it cannot be moved in memory.

UnlockData (dummy—variable);

Function   Unlock the current data segment in memory.

Value Returned   None.

Parameter
dummy—variable: Not used.

Notes   This routine is the counterpart to LockData.

LocalFlags (hMem);

Function   Return the system flags for the block of memory referenced by hMem.

Value Returned   Integer value specifying the memory allocation flags for the specific block of memory. The high-order byte contains

LMEM—DISCARDED   Block has been discarded
LMEM—DISCARDABLE Block can be discarded

Likewise, the low-order byte contains the reference count for the block.

Parameter

hMem: Handle to the block of memory of interest.

Task Management Routines

The following functions allow Windows applications to control tasks and task attributes.

GetCurrentTask ();

Function   Return a handle to the current task.

Value Returned   Handle to the current task.

Parameters   None.

Notes   If the function is not successful, the NULL value is returned.

Yield ();

Function   Halts the current task and passes control to the first waiting task found.

Value Returned   Boolean value of TRUE if a waiting task is started; otherwise, the value is FALSE.

Parameters   None.

Notes   Yield should not be used in conjunction with message processing. Use Get/Peek/Wait Message instead.

SetPriority (hTask, nChangeAmount);

Function   Increment or decrement the execution priority of the task referenced by hTask.

Value Returned   Integer value specifying the new task priority.

Parameters
hTask: Handle to the desired task.

nChangeAmount: Integer value specifying the amount to increment or decrement the task's priority.

Notes   Initial priority is 0. The highest task priority is -15 and the lowest is 15.

Resource Manager Functions

This series of routines allows Windows applications to manage Windows resources (icons, cursors, fonts, menus, and bitmaps).

AddFontResource (lpFilename);

Function   Add the font contained in the file name specified to the Windows font table.

Value Returned   Integer value specifying the number of fonts added.

Parameter
lpFilename: Long pointer to the file name containing the fonts.

Notes   Use the routine RemoveFontResource to remove the font from the Windows font resource table.

RemoveFontResource (lpFilename);

Function Remove an added font from the Windows font resource table.

Value Returned Boolean value of TRUE if the function is successful; otherwise, FALSE.

Parameter

lpFilename: Long pointer to the file name of the font resource to remove.

LoadBitmap (hInstance, lpBitmapName);

Function Load the bitmap resource specified from the executable file referenced by hInstance.

Value Returned Handle to the new bitmap.

Parameters

hInstance: Handle to the instance of the executable module that contains the bitmap.

lpBitmapName: Long pointer to the name of the bitmap resource.

Notes The bitmap is stretched or compressed to match the system's aspect ratio and resolution. The bitmap is automatically removed when the application terminates.

LoadCursor (hInstance, lpCursorName);

Function Load the cursor resource from the executable module referenced by hInstance into the Windows resource table.

Value Returned Handle to the new cursor.

Parameters

hInstance: Handle to the instance of the module containing the desired cursor.

lpCursorName: Long pointer to the ASCIIZ name of the desired cursor resource.

Notes To access a predefined Windows cursor, set hInstance to NULL and assign lpCursor Name to one of the following:

IDC_ARROW	Standard Windows cursor
IDC_BEAM	I-beam cursor
IDC_CROSS	Crosshair cursor
IDC_ICON	Icon cursor
IDC_UPARROW	Vertical arrow cursor
IDC_WAIT	Hourglass cursor

LoadIcon (hInstance, lpIconName);

Function Load the specified icon resource from the module referenced by hInstance.

Value Returned Handle to the newly loaded icon.

Parameters

hInstance: Handle to the instance of the module containing the icon resource.

lpIconName: Long pointer to the ASCIIZ icon resource name.

Notes To access the Windows predefined icons, set hInstance to NULL and assign lpIconName one of the following values:

IDI_APPLICATION	Default application icon
IDI_ASTERISK	Asterisk
IDI_EXCLAMATION	Exclamation mark
IDI_HAND	Hand icon
IDI_QUESTION	Question mark

LoadMenu (hInstance, lpMenuName);

Function   Load the specified menu from the executable module referenced by hInstance.

Value Returned   Handle to the newly loaded menu.

Parameters

hInstance: Handle to the instance of the module containing the menu resource desired.

lpMenuName: Long pointer to the ASCIIZ menu name resource.

Notes   If the function is not successful, the NULL value is returned.

LoadString (hInstance, wId, lpBuffer, nBufferSize);

Function   Load the string specified from the string table defined in the resource file.

Value Returned   Integer value specifying the number of bytes copied into the string buffer.

Parameters

hInstance: Handle to the instance of the module containing the string definitions.

wId: Integer value specifying the string to load.

lpBuffer: Long pointer to the buffer to contain the string.

nBufferSize: Integer value specifying the number of bytes that the buffer can store.

Notes   If the function returns 0, the string specified did not exist.

LoadAccelerators (hInstance, lpTableName);

Function   Load the accelerators associated with an application menu.

Value Returned   Handle to the accelerator table loaded.

Parameters

hInstance: Handle to the module instance containing the accelerator table.

lpTableName: Long pointer to the accelerator table name.

Notes   If the table has been previously loaded, the function returns a handle to the previous table.

FindResource (hInstance, lpName, lpType);

Function   Determine the location of the resource specified in the resource file.

Value Returned   Handle to the resource specified.

Parameters

hInstance: Handle to the module containing the resource.

lpName: Long pointer to the ASCIIZ name of the resource desired.

lpType: Long pointer to an ASCIIZ string specifying the resource type. For predefined resources use the following:

RT_ACCELERATOR	Accelerator resource
RT_BITMAP	Bitmap resource
RT_CURSOR	Cursor resource
RT_DIALOG	Dialog box resource
RT_FONT	Font resource
RT_ICON	Icon resource
RT_MENU	Menu resource
RT_STRING	String resource

Notes If the resource is not found, the NULL value is returned. If the high-order word of lpType is 0, the low-order word specifies the integer identification of the resource desired. Likewise, if the first character is a "#" sign, the remaining characters must signify a decimal value that represents the resource.

LoadResource (hInstance, hResource);

Function Load the resource specified by hResource from the file associated with hInstance.

Value Returned Handle to the resource specified.

Parameters

hInstance: Handle to the instance of the module containing the desired resource.

hResource: Handle to the resource to be loaded.

Notes If the function cannot load the resource, NULL is returned. If the resource has already been loaded, a handle to the previous resource is returned.

AllocResource (hInstance, hResource, nSize);

Function Allocate UNINITIALIZED memory for the specified resource.

Value Returned Handle to the memory location allocated.

Parameters

hInstance: Handle to the instance of the module containing the desired resource.

hResource: Handle to the desired resource.

nSize: Number of bytes required for override size.

Notes If the function cannot allocate memory for the resource, the NULL value is returned. If it is 0, nSize is ignored.

LockResource (hResource);

Function Lock the resource specified in memory. A locked resource cannot be moved or discarded.

Value Returned Long pointer to first byte of the locked resource.

Parameter
hResource: Handle to the resource to lock.

Notes Locking a resource increments its reference count. The resource remains locked until its reference count is 0.

FreeResource (hRes);

Function Remove a locked resource from memory making available to Windows the memory it had allocated.

Value Returned Boolean value that is TRUE if the resource has not been freed; otherwise, FALSE.

Parameter
hRes: Handle to the resource data to be removed.

Notes FreeResource actually only decrements a resource's reference count. Once the count is 0, the resource can be removed from memory.

AccessResource (hInstance, hResource);

Function Open the resource file associated with hResource and move the file pointer to the beginning of the file that allows the application to read the file.

Value Returned Handle to the file containing the resource desired.

Parameters

hInstance: Handle to the instance of the module containing the desired resource.

hResource: Handle to the resource desired.

Notes The file is opened for read access only. If the file cannot be opened, -1 is returned.

SizeofResource (hInstance, hResource);

Function Return the number of bytes required for the specified resource.

Value Returned Integer value containing the size of the resource in bytes.

Parameters

hInstance: Handle to the instance of the module containing the resource desired.

hResource: Handle to the resource of which to return the size.

Notes If the resource is not found, the NULL value is returned.

SetResourceHandler (hInstance, lpType, lpLoadFunc);

Function   Define the function to load resources.

Value Returned   Long pointer to the user-defined function.

Parameters
hInstance: Handle to the instance of module containing the desired resource.

lpType: Long pointer to an integer value that specifies the resource type.

lpLoadFunc: Long pointer to the user-defined load function.

Notes   If the function is not successful, the NULL value is returned.

String Translation Functions

The following routines aid Windows programs in string manipulation.

AnsiToOem (lpANSIStr, lpOEMStr);

Function   Translate a string in the ANSI character set to a string in the OEM character set.

Value Returned   Boolean value that is TRUE if the translation was successful; otherwise, FALSE.

Parameters
lpANSIStr: Long pointer to the ASCIIZ ANSI string.

lpOEMStr: Long pointer to the ASCIIZ OEM string.

OemToAnsi (lpOEMStr, lpANSIStr);

Function   Translate a string in the OEM character set to a string in the ANSI character set.

Value Returned   Boolean value that is TRUE if the translation was successful; otherwise, FALSE.

Parameters

lpOEMStr: Long pointer to the ASCIIZ OEM string.

lpANSIStr: Long pointer to the ASCIIZ ANSI string.

AnsiUpper (lpStr);

Function   Convert an ANSI string to uppercase characters.

Value Returned   cChar: If the parameter is a single character, the return value is the uppercase character. If the parameter is a string, the return value is a long pointer to the string.

Parameter

lpStr: Long pointer to an ASCIIZ string to convert to uppercase, or a long integer whose low-order word contains a character to be converted.

AnsiLower (lpStr);

Function   Convert an ANSI string to lowercase characters.

Value Returned   cChar: If the parameter is a single character, the return value is the lowercase character. If the parameter is a string, the return value is a long pointer to the string.

Parameter

lpStr: Long pointer to an ASCIIZ string to convert to lowercase, or a long integer whose low-order word contains a character to be converted.

AnsiNext (lpCurrentChar);

Function   Return the next character in the string.

Value Returned   Long pointer to the next character in a string.

Parameter

lpCurrentChar: Long pointer to the current character in an ASCIIZ string.

Notes   If no characters remain in the string, the long pointer will point to NULL.

AnsiPrev (lpStart, lpCurrentChar);

Function   Return the previous character in the string.

Value Returned   Long pointer to the previous character in a string.

Parameters

lpStart: Long pointer to the first character in an ASCIIZ string.

lpCurrentChar: Long pointer to the current character in an ASCIIZ string.

Notes   If the character is at the beginning of the string, the value returned will equal lpStart.

Atom Manager Functions

This series of routines manipulates atoms. An *atom* is an integer value that represents a string. Windows applications that perform a large amount of string manipulation often utilize atoms.

InitAtomTable (nSize);

Function   Initialize the atom hash table with the initial size specified by nSize.

Value Returned   Boolean value of TRUE if the function is successful; otherwise, the value is FALSE.

Parameter
nSize: Integer value specifying the size of the atom hash table.

Notes   The default table size is 37.

AddAtom (lpStr);

Function   Add the character string referenced by lpStr to the atom hash table and return an integer value that uniquely identifies the string.

Value Returned   Integer value identifying the string added to the atom hash table.

Parameter
lpStr: Long pointer to the ASCIIZ string to be placed in the atom hash table.

Notes If the function is not successful, the NULL value is returned.

DeleteAtom (nAtom);

Function Remove the atom specified from the atom hash table.

Value Returned If the function is successful, NULL is returned. Otherwise, the value nAtom is returned.

Parameter
nAtom: Integer value used to uniquely reference an atom.

Notes This routine actually decrements the atom reference count. Once the count is 0, the atom is removed.

FindAtom (lpStr);

Function Return the index of the string referenced by lpStr within the atom table.

Value Returned If the string is not found, the value NULL is returned. Otherwise, the integer value that uniquely references the string is returned.

Parameter
lpStr: Long pointer to the ASCIIZ string desired.

GetAtom (nAtom, lpBuffer, nSize);

Function Return the character string associated with the atom, nAtom.

Value Returned Number of bytes copied into the buffer referenced by lpBuffer. If the atom does not exist, the value 0 is returned.

Parameters

nAtom: Integer value that uniquely references the atom desired.

lpBuffer: Long pointer to the buffer to store the atom's name.

nSize: Size of the storage buffer.

MAKEINTATOM (wInteger);

Function Create an integer atom to represent a numeric string in the form #digits.

Value Returned Integer value that uniquely represents the atom.

Parameter

wInteger: Integer value that specifies the value of the atom's character string.

Notes MAKEINTATOM is a macro and hence all uppercase.

Windows Initialization File (WIN.INI) Routines

The following routines provide an interface from Windows applications to WIN.INI, the Windows initialization file.

GetProfileInt (lpApplicationName, lpKeyName, nDefault);

Function Return an integer key associated with an application from the file WIN.INI. The routine searches WIN.INI for a string matching the ASCIIZ string referenced by lpApplication Name and if the application is found, continues searching for the key name and a value.

Value Returned Integer value of the key value if it was found; otherwise, the value of nDefault.

Parameters

lpApplicationName: Long pointer to an ASCIIZ string containing the application name for which to search WIN.INI.

lpKeyName: Long pointer to an ASCIIZ string containing the name of a key value.

nDefault: Integer value for the default key value if one is not found in WIN.INI.

Notes WIN.INI must contain entries in the following form:

[Application—name]
        key—name=integer—value

GetProfileString (lpApplicationName, lpKeyName, lpDefault, lpReturnedStr, nSize);

Function Return a character string from the applications profile in WIN.INI.

Value Returned Number of characters copied into the buffer referenced by lpReturnedStr.

Parameters

lpApplicationName: Long pointer to an ASCIIZ string containing the application name for which to search WIN.INI.

lpKeyName: Long pointer to an ASCIIZ string containing the name of a key value.

lpDefault: Long pointer to an ASCIIZ string containing the default character string to use if an entry is not found in WIN.INI.

lpReturnedStr: Long pointer to an ASCIIZ string that contains either the character string associated with the key name from WIN.INI, or the contents of the string referenced by lpDefault.

nSize: Integer value specifying the size of the buffer.

Notes WIN.INI must have entries in the following form:

[Application—name]
      key—name=string

WriteProfileString (lpApplication, lpKeyName, lpStr);

Function Place an entry for the profile string referenced by lpString into the Windows initialization file WIN.INI.

Value Returned Boolean value TRUE if the routine is successful; otherwise, FALSE.

Parameters

lpApplication: Long pointer to an ASCIIZ string containing the name of the application.

lpKeyName: Long pointer to an ASCIIZ string containing the name of a key value.

lpStr: Long pointer to an ASCIIZ string containing the desired profile string.

Notes The string entry will be of the following form:

[Application—name]
      key—name=string

Debugging Function

The following routine is a useful debugging tool.

FatalExit (error__code);

Function   Display an error code and the symbolic stack, and prompt the programmer how to proceed.

Value Returned   Integer value returned only when the user chooses to ignore the error message.

Parameter
error__code: Integer value containing the error code to display.

Notes   Programmer options to the error are the following:

a   Terminate Windows
b   Simulate an NMI interrupt entering the debugger
i   Ignore the error

Communication Routines

This series of routines provides data communication support for Windows applications. With these routines, most of the data communication complexities become transparent to the programmer.

OpenComm (lpCommName, nInQueue, nOutQueue);

Function   Open the communications device referenced by lpComm-Name and return a communications identification to the device.

Value Returned Integer value to be associated with the device.

Parameters

lpCommName: Long pointer to an ASCIIZ string containing the name of the communications device.

nInQueue: Integer value defining the size of the input queue.

nOutQueue: Integer value defining the size of the output queue.

Notes nCid can contain the following error codes:

IE—BADID	Unsupported identification
IE—BAUDRATE	Unsupported baud rate
IE—BYTESIZE	Invalid byte size
IE—DEFAULT	Invalid default parameters
IE—HARDWARE	Hardware not present
IE—MEMORY	Cannot allocate queues
IE—NOPEN	Device not open

CloseComm (nCid);

Function Close the communication device associated with nCid and release any memory allocated for queues.

Value Returned Integer value containing the result of the close. The value is 0 if the device closed successfully, or −1 if an error occurred.

Parameter

nCid: Integer value associated with the device to be closed.

ReadComm (nCid, lpBuffer, nSize);

Function Read nSize characters from the device associated with nCid into the buffer referenced by lpBuffer.

Value Returned Byte value specifying the actual number of bytes read.

Parameters

nCid: Integer value associated with the device from which to read.

lpBuffer: Long pointer to the input buffer.

nSize: Integer value specifying the number of bytes to read.

Notes If an error occurs, a negative value is returned. Use the routine GetCommError for more specifics.

WriteComm (nCid, lpBuffer, nSize);

Function Write nSize characters to the device associated with nCid from the buffer referenced by lpBuffer.

Value Returned Byte value specifying the actual number of bytes written.

Parameters

nCid: Integer value associated with the device to which to write.

lpBuffer: Long pointer to the output buffer.

nSize: Integer value specifying the number of bytes to write.

Notes If an error occurs, a negative value is returned. Use the routine GetCommError for more specifics.

UngetCommChar (nCid, cChar);

Function Place the character contained in cChar back into the input queue.

Value Returned Integer value of 0 if the routine was successful. Otherwise, a negative value is returned.

Parameters

nCid: Integer value associated with the device for which to place the character back into the input buffer.

cChar: Byte value to be placed back into the input buffer.

Notes Consecutive calls to UngetCommChar without an intermediate read are not

TransmitCommChar (nCid, cChar);

Function Mark the character contained in cChar for immediate transmission by placing it at the front of the output queue.

Value Returned Integer value of 0 if the function was successful. Otherwise, a negative value is returned.

Parameters

nCid: Integer value associated with the device to which to transmit.

cChar: Byte value of the character to be transmitted.

Notes A character typically cannot be transmitted until the previous character placed in the output queue by TransmitCommChar has completed transmission.

BuildCommDCB (lpDefinition, lpDCB);

Function Build a device control block based upon the definition string contained in lpDefinition.

Value Returned Integer value of 0 if the DCB is built. Otherwise, a negative value is returned.

Parameters

lpDefinition: Long pointer to the definition string.

lpDCB: Long pointer to the device control block to be created.

Notes   See the DCB structure in Chapter 7. The string referenced by lpDefinition must have the same format as the DOS MODE command.

GetCommState (nCid, lpDCB);

Function   Store the values associated with the device referenced by nCid into the fields of the DCB record referenced by lpDCB.

Value Returned   Integer value of 0 if the function was successful; otherwise, a negative value.

Parameters
nCid: Integer value associated with the device.

lpDCB: Long pointer to the DCB to fill with the current device values.

SetCommState (lpDCB);

Function   Set the values associated with the device referenced by the identification field of the DCB record associated with lpDCB to the values contained in the fields of the DCB record.

Value Returned   Integer value of 0 if the function was successful; otherwise, a negative value.

Parameter
lpDCB: Long pointer to the DCB to which to set the current device values.

GetCommError (nCid, lpStatus);

Function Get the device status and error codes associated with the device reference by nCid and place them into a record of type COMSTAT referenced by lpStatus.

Value Returned Integer value containing the error codes that have occurred since the last GetCommError.

Parameters

nCid: Integer value associated with the device.

lpStatus: Long pointer to a record of type COMSTAT.

Notes Error codes include the following:

CE_BREAK	Hardware break condition detected
CE_CTSTO	Clear-to-send timeout
CE_DNS	Parallel device not selected
CE_DSRTO	Data-set-ready timeout
CE_FRAME	Hardware framing error
CD_IOE	Parallel device I/O error
CE_MODE	Requested mode is not supported
CE_OOP	Parallel device out of paper
CE_OVERRUN	Character not read before next character arrived
CE_PTO	Parallel device timeout
CE_RLSDTO	Receive-line signal detect timeout
CE_RXOVERRUN	Receive queue overflow
CE_RXPARITY	Hardware parity error
CE_TXFULL	Transmit queue full

SetCommEventMask (nCid, nEventMask);

Function Retrieve or enable the event mask for the device associated with nCid.

Value Returned   Long pointer to the current state of the event mask.

Parameters

nCid: Integer value associated with the device.

nEventMask: Integer value that specifies the events to be enabled, as follows:

EV_BREAK	Set when break is detected on input
EV_CTS	Set when clear-to-send signal changes states
EV_DSR	Set when data-set-ready signal changes states
EV_PERR	Set when printer error occurs
EV_ERR	Set when line-status error occurs
EV_RING	Set when ring indicator is detected
EV_RLSD	Set when receive-line signal detect signal changes states
EV_RXCHAR	Set when character received
EV_RXFLAG	Set when received character is specified in the device control block
EV_TXEMPTY	Set when output queue is empty

GetCommEventMask (nCid, nEventMask);

Function Retrieve the event mask for the device associated with nCid.

Value Returned Integer value containing the current state of the event mask.

Parameters

nCid: Integer value associated with the device.

nEventMask: Integer value that specifies the events set, as follows:

EV_BREAK	Set when break is detected on input
EV_CTS	Set when clear-to-send signal changes states
EVDSR	Set when data-set-ready signal changes states
EV_ERR	Set when line-status error occurs
EV_RLSD	Set when receive-line signal detect signal changes states
EV_RXCHAR	Set when character received
EV_RXFLAG	Set when received character is specified in the device control block
EV_TXEMPTY	Set when output queue is empty

FlushComm (nCid, nQueue);

Function Flush all characters from the transmit or receive queue.

Value Returned Integer value of 0 if the function was successful. Otherwise, a negative value is returned.

Parameters

nCid: Integer value associated with the device.

nQueue: Integer value specifying the input or output queue, as follows:

| 0 | Output queue |
| 1 | Input queue |

ClearCommBreak (nCid);

Function Place transmission line in nonbreak state to restore transmission.

Value Returned Integer value of 0 if the routine was successful. Otherwise, a negative value is returned.

Parameter

nCid: Integer value associated with the device.

EscapeCommFunction (nCid, nFunction);

Function Direct the device associated with nCid to carry out the function specified by nFunction.

Value Returned Integer value of 0 if the function was successful. Otherwise, a negative value is returned.

Parameters

nCid: Integer value associated with the device.

nFunction: Integer value specifying the function to be performed, as follows:

CLRDTR	Clear data-terminal-ready signal
CLRRTS	Clear request-to-send signal
RESETDEV	If possible, reset the device
SETDTR	Assert data-terminal-ready signal
SETRTS	Assert request-to-send signal
SETXOFF	Behave as if XOFF were received
SETXON	Behave as if XON were received

Sound Functions

The following routines provide the sound interface from Windows applications.

OpenSound ( );

Function Opens access to the play device, restricting other applications from opening the device.

Value Returned Integer value specifying the number of voices available.

Parameters None.

CloseSound ( );

Function Closes access to the play device, flushing all queues and freeing memory allocated to contain the queues. The play device is then available to other applications.

Value Returned None.

Parameters None.

SetVoiceQueueSize (nVoice, nBytes);

Function Allocate a queue of nBytes for the voice queue referenced by nVoice. The default size is 192 bytes (approximately 32 notes).

Value Returned Integer value specifying the result of the routine, as follows:

S—ERRMACT   Music currently playing
S—SEROFM   Insufficient memory

Parameters

nVoice: Integer value that specifies the desired voice queue.

nBytes: Number of bytes to allocate for the voice queue.

Notes Windows locks voice queues in memory. Queue size cannot be set while music is playing.

SetVoiceAccent (nVoice, nTempo, nVolume, nMode, nPitch);

Function   Specify the attributes of the voice queue referenced by nVoice.

Value Returned   Integer value specifying the result of the routine, as follows:

S_SERDMD	Invalid mode
S_SERDTP	Invalid tempo
S_SERDVL	Invalid volume
S_SERQFUL	Voice queue full

Parameters

nVoice: Integer value specifying the voice queue desired.

nTempo: Integer value specifying the number of quarter notes played per minute (default is 120).

nVolume: Integer value (0-255) specifying voice volume.

nMode: Integer value specifying how notes are played, as follows:

S_LEGATO
S_NORMAL
S_STACCATO

nPitch: Integer value (0-83) specifying each note's pitch.

SetVoiceEnvelope (nVoice, nShape, nRepeat);

Function   Queue an envelope (wave shape and repeat count) in the voice queue associated with nVoice.

Value Returned   Integer value specifying the result of the routine, as follows:

S_SERDRC   Invalid repeat count
S_SERDSH   Invalid shape
S_SERQFUL   Voice queue full

Parameters

nVoice: Integer value specifying the desired voice queue.

nShape: Integer index to an OEM wave-shape table.

nRepeat: Integer value specifying the number of repetitions.

SetSoundNoise (nSource, nDuration);

Function   Define the source and noise duration for the play device.

Value Returned   Integer value of 0 if the routine is successful, or the value S_SERDSR if the source is invalid.

Parameters

nSource: Integer value specifying the noise source, as follows:

S_PERIOD512	Frequency is N/512 less coarse hiss
S_PERIOD1024	Frequency is N/1024
S_PERIOD2048	Frequency is N/2048 coarse hiss
S_PERIODVOICE	Frequency is from channel 3
S_WHITE512	Frequency is N/512 less coarse hiss
S_WHITE1024	Frequency is N/1024
S_WHITE2048	Frequency is N/2048 coarse hiss
S_WHITEVOICE	Frequency is from channel 3

nDuration: Integer value specifying in clock ticks the duration of the noise.

SetVoiceNote (nVoice, nValue, nLength, nDotCount);

Function   Queue a note with the attributes specified in the queue associated with nVoice.

Value Returned   Integer value specifying the result of the routine, as follows:

S_SERDCC	Invalid dot count
S_SERDLN	Invalid note
S_SERDNT	Invalid note length
S_SERQFUL	Voice queue full

Parameters

nVoice: Integer value associated with the desired voice queue.

nValue: Integer value (0-83) specifying the note.

nLength: Integer value specifying the reciprocal of the note.

nDotCount: Integer value specifying in counts the duration of the note.

Notes   If nValue is 0, a rest occurs.

SetVoiceSound (nVoice, lFrequency, nDuration);

Function   Queue the sound frequency and duration in the voice queue associated with nVoice.

Value Returned   Integer value specifying the result of the routine, as follows:

S_SERDDR	Invalid duration
S_SERDFQ	Invalid frequency
S_SERDVL	Invalid volume
S_SERQFUL	Voice queue full

Parameters

nVoice: Integer value associated with the desired voice queue.

lFrequency: Long integer specifying the desired frequency in KHz.

nDuration: Integer value specifying the duration in clock ticks.

StartSound ( );

Function Start play of each voice queue.

Value Returned Integer value specifying the result of the function.

Parameters None.

StopSound ( );

Function Stop play of each voice queue.

Value Returned Integer value specifying the result of the function.

Parameters None.

WaitSoundState (nState);

Function Pause until the play driver enters the state specified by nState.

Value Returned Integer value of 0 if the function is successful, or the value S—SERDST if the device is invalid.

Parameter

nState: Integer value specifying the desired state, as follows:

S—ALLTHRESHOLD	All queues have reached threshold
S—QUEUEEMPTY	All queues empty
S—THRESHOLD	A voice queue has reached threshold

SyncAllVoices ( );

Function Queue a sync mark in each queue.

Value Returned Integer value specifying the result of the routine (0 if successful or S—SERQFUL if a voice queue is full).

Parameters None.

Notes Play is turned off until each voice queue finds a sync mark.

CountVoiceNotes (nVoice);

Function Return the number of notes in the voice queue associated with nVoice.

Value Returned Integer value specifying the number of notes in the queue.

Parameter
nVoice: Integer value associated with the desired voice queue.

GetThresholdEvent ( );

Function Return a flag that specifies the most recent threshold event.

Value Returned Long pointer to an integer value that specifies a threshold event.

Parameters None.

GetThresholdStatus ( );

Function Return the threshold event status for each voice.

Value Returned Integer value specifying the status flags of the current threshold event.

Parameters None.

Notes   Each bit in the returned integer value represents the status for a specific voice queue. If clear, the associated voice queue has reached the threshold event. Otherwise, the bit is set.

SetVoiceThreshold (nVoice, nNotes);

Function   Set the threshold value for a given voice queue.

Value Returned   Integer value of 0 if the function is successful, or 1 if the specified notes are out of range.

Parameters

nVoice: Integer value associated with the desired voice queue.

nNotes: Integer value specifying the number of notes in the threshold level.

Utility Functions

This series of routines is a miscellaneous collection of programming utilities. Note the functional aspects of each routine. You should be able to reduce your development time by using them.

HIBYTE (nInt);

Function   Return the high-order byte of the integer value specified by nInt.

Value Returned   A byte value containing the high-order byte of nInt.

Parameter

nInt: Integer value of which to return the high byte.

LOBYTE (nInt);

Function Return the low-order byte of the integer value specified by nInt.

Value Returned A byte value containing the low-order byte of nInt.

Parameter
nInt: Integer value of which to return the low-order byte.

HIWORD (lInt);

Function Return the high-order word of the long-integer value specified by lInt.

Value Returned Integer value containing the high-order word of lInt.

Parameter
lInt: Long-integer value of which to return the high-order word.

LOWORD (lInt);

Function Return the low-order word of the long-integer value specified by lInt.

Value Returned Integer value containing the low-order word of lInt.

Parameter
lInt: Long-integer value of which to return the low-order word.

MAKELONG (nLow, nHigh);

Function Return a long integer that contains nLow as its low-order word and nHigh as its high-order word.

Value Returned Long word containing the concatenated integer values in the specified order.

Parameters

nLow: Integer value containing the desired low-order word.

nHigh: Integer value containing the desired high-order word.

MAKEINTRESOURCE (nInt);

Function Convert the integer value contained in nInt from a long pointer to a string type.

Value Returned Long pointer to an ASCIIZ string.

Parameter

nInt: Integer value to convert into a long pointer to an ASCII string.

MAKEPOINT (lInt);

Function Convert the long-integer value contained in lInt into the x and y coordinates of a point structure.

Value Returned Point structure containing x and y coordinates.

Parameter

lInt: Long integer value whose high-order word contains a y coordinate and whose low-order word is an x coordinate.

GetRValue (rgbColor);

Function Return a byte that contains the red value from an RGB value.

Value Returned Byte containing the red value from an RGB value.

Parameter

rgbColor: Long-integer value containing an RGB value.

GetBValue (rgbColor);

Function   Return a byte that contains the blue value from an RGB value.

Value Returned   Byte containing the blue value from an RGB value.

Parameter

rgbColor: Long-integer value containing an RGB value.

GetGValue (rgbColor);

Function   Return a byte that contains the green value from an RGB value.

Value Returned   Byte containing the green value from an RGB value.

Parameter

rgbColor: Long-integer value containing an RGB value.

min (Val1, Val2);

Function   Return the minimum of the values Val1 and Val2.

Value Returned   Minimum value of Val1 and Val2.

Parameters

Val1, Val2: Arbitrary values of which to return the minimum.

max (Val1, Val2);

Function Return the maximum of the values Val1 and Val2.

Value Returned Maximum value of Val1 and Val2.

Parameters
Val1, Val2: Arbitrary values of which to return the maximum.

File Manipulation Routines

The following routines provide access to DOS files from within Windows applications. The routines provide a great deal more functional flexibility than is normally available from standard high-level programming languages.

OpenFile (lpFileName, lpOFSTRUCT, wStyle);

Function Create, open, reopen, or delete the specified file based upon the value of wStyle.

Value Returned File handle if successful, or the value −1 if an error occurred.

Parameters
lpFileName: Long pointer to an ASCIIZ string that contains the name of the desired file.

lpOFSTRUCT: Long pointer to a data structure of type OFSTRUCT.

wStyle: Integer value specifying the desired action, as follows:

OF__CANCEL   Add a cancel prompt to the file dialog box

OF_CREATE	Create the specified file
OF_DELETE	Delete the specified file
OF_EXIST	Tests file existence
OF_PARSE	Fill the OFSTRUCT structure only
OF_PROMPT	Prompt the user whether to create the file if the file does not exist
OF_READ	Open for read access only
OF_READWRITE	Open for the file for read/write access
OF_REOPEN	Use the reopen buffer to open the file
OF_VERIFY	Verify date-and-time stamp has not changed
OF_WRITE	Open for write access only

GetTempFile (cDrive, lpPrefixStr, wUnique, lpTempName);

Function   Create a temporary file.

Value Returned   Integer value that contains the unique numeric value used in the temporary file name.

Parameters

cDrive: Byte value specifying the desired drive for the file.

lpPrefixStr: Long pointer to an ASCIIZ string that contains the three-letter prefix of the file name.

wUnique: Integer value that specifies how to create the file name.

lpTempName: Long pointer to the temporary file name.

Notes   The file name created will be of the form

drive: \path \~pppxxxx.TMP

where *ppp* is the prefix, and *xxxx* is the unique number assigned to the file.

GetTempDrive (cDrive);

Function   Return the optimal drive on which to create a temporary file.

Value Returned   Byte value that specifies the optimal drive.

Parameter
cDrive: Byte value that when 0, directs GetTempDrive to return the current drive; otherwise, the optimal drive is returned.

Notes   Windows defines the optimal drive as the disk drive with the best access time.

Graphics Device Interface (GDI) Routines

The following routines provide the complete calling sequences and parameters used in the GDI routines.

Display Context Routines

The following routines are used for display context.

CreateDC (lpDriver, lpDevice, lpOutput, lpInitData);

Function   Create a display context for the device specified.

Value Returned   Handle to a display context.

Parameters

lpDriver: Long pointer to an ASCIIZ string that contains the name of the file containing the required device driver.

lpDevice: Long pointer to an ASCIIZ string that contains the name of the desired device.

lpOutput: Long pointer to an ASCIIZ that specifies the device or file for the physical output medium.

lpInitData: Long pointer to device-specific initialization data for the device. The pointer is NULL if the device requires no initialization.

Notes Device names follow standard DOS conventions with the terminating colon being optional.

CreateCompatibleCD (hDC);

Function Return a memory device context that is compatible with the device context associated with hDC.

Value Returned Handle to the memory device context. If the context is compatible with the display screen, NULL is returned.

Parameter

hDC: Handle to the device context for which to create the compatible memory device context.

CreateIC (lpDriver, lpDevice, lpOutput, lpInitData);

Function Create an information context for the device specified. Information context provides quick access to information normally only available through device contexts.

Value Returned Handle to the information context.

Parameters

lpDriver: Long pointer to an ASCIIZ string that contains the name of the file containing the required device driver.

lpDevice: Long pointer to an ASCIIZ string that contains the name of the desired device.

lpOutput: Long pointer to an ASCIIZ that specifies the device or file for the physical output medium.

lpInitData: Long pointer to device-specific initialization data for the device. The pointer is NULL if the device requires no initialization.

Notes Device names follow standard DOS conventions with the terminating colon being optional.

DeleteDC (hDC);

Function Delete the device context associated with hDC.

Value Returned Boolean value of TRUE if the routine is successful; otherwise, FALSE.

Parameter

hDC: Handle to the device context to delete.

SaveDC (hDC);

Function Save current state of a device context to a context stack.

Value Returned Integer value that uniquely identifies the saved display context, or 0 if the function was unsuccessful.

Parameter

hDC: Handle to the device context to save.

Notes Context display state includes fields (such as clipping region) and mapping mode.

RestoreDC (hDC, nSaveDC);

Function Restore the device context associated with hDC to the previous context stored on the device context stack via SaveDC.

Value Returned Boolean value of TRUE if the function is successful; otherwise, FALSE.

Parameters

hDC: Handle to the desired device context.

nSaveDC: Integer value that specifies the device context to be restored.

Output Routines

The following are output routines.

MoveTo (hDC, nX, nY);

Function Move the current position to the specified x and y coordinates.

Value Returned Long-integer value specifying the previous x and y coordinates. The high-order word contains the y coordinate and the low-order word contains the x coordinate.

Parameters

nX: Integer value specifying the desired x coordinate.

nY: Integer value specifying the desired y coordinate.

GetCurrentPosition (hDC);

Function   Return the current x and y coordinates.

Value Returned   Long-integer value specifying the previous x and y coordinates. The high-order word contains the y coordinate and the low-order word contains the x coordinate.

Parameter

hDC: Handle to the device context of which to return the current coordinates.

LineTo (hDC, nX, nY);

Function   Draw a line from the current position to the x and y coordinates specified by nX and nY.

Value Returned   Boolean value of TRUE if the line is drawn; otherwise, FALSE.

Parameters

hDC: Handle to the device context.

nX: Integer value specifying the x coordinate to which to draw a line.

nY: Integer value specifying the y coordinate to which to draw a line.

PolyLine (hDC, lpPoints, nCount);

Function   Draw the set of line segments connecting the points contained in the array referenced by lpPoints.

Value Returned   Boolean value of TRUE if the line segments are drawn; otherwise, FALSE.

Parameters

hDC: Handle to the desired device context.

lpPoints: Long pointer to the array of points to be connected.

nCount: Integer value specifying the number of points in the array.

Notes nCount must be at least 2. Each element of the array referenced by lpPoints must be of the type POINT.

Rectangle (hDC, nX1, nY1, nX2, nY2);

Function Draw the rectangle specified by the points nX1, nY1, nX2, and nY2.

Value Returned Boolean value of TRUE if the rectangle is drawn; otherwise, FALSE.

Parameters

hDC: Handle to the desired device context.

nX1, nY1, nX2, nY2: Integer value specifying the coordinates of the rectangle to display.

Notes The width of the rectangle cannot exceed 32,767 logical units.

RoundRect (hDC, nX1, nY1, nX2, nY2, nX3, nY3);

Function Display a rectangle with rounded corners.

Value Returned Boolean value of TRUE if the rectangle is drawn; otherwise, FALSE.

Parameters

hDC: Handle to the desired device context.

nX1, nY1: Integer values specifying the upper-left corner of the rectangle.

nX2, nY2: Integer values specifying the lower-right corner of the rectangle.

nX3, nY3: Integer values specifying the width and height of the ellipse used to draw the rounded corners.

Notes The width of the rectangle cannot exceed 32,767 logical units.

Polygon (hDC, lpPoints, nCount);

Function Display a polygon consisting of two or more points connected by lines.

Value Returned Boolean value of TRUE if the polygon is drawn; otherwise, FALSE.

Parameters

hDC: Handle to the desired device context.

lpPoints: Long pointer to an array of points specifying the coordinates of the polygon.

nCount: Integer value specifying the number of points in the array.

Notes Each element of the array referenced by lpPoints must be the type POINT.

Ellipse (hDC, nX1, nY1, nX2, nY2);

Function Display an ellipse that bounds the rectangle specified by the points nX1, nY1, nX2, and nY2.

Value Returned Boolean value of TRUE if the ellipse is drawn; otherwise, FALSE.

Parameters

hDC: Handle to the desired device context.

nX1, nY1, nX2, nY2: Integer values specifying the coordinates of a rectangle the ellipse is to bound.

Notes The width of the rectangle specified cannot exceed 32,767 units.

Arc (hDC, nX1, nY1, nX2, nY2, nX3, nY3, nX4, nY4);

Function Display an elliptical arc. The arc bounds the rectangle specified by nX1, nY1, nX2, and nY2. The arc begins at the point nX3, nY3 and terminates at the point nX4, nY4.

Value Returned Boolean value of TRUE if the arc is drawn; otherwise, FALSE.

Parameters

hDC: Handle to the desired device context.

nX1, nY1, nX2, nY2: Integer value specifying the rectangle the arc is to bound.

nX3, nY3: Integer value specifying the starting point of the arc.

nX4, nY4: Integer value specifying the ending point of the arc.

Notes The width of the rectangle specified by nX1, nY1, nX2, and nY2 cannot exceed 32,767 units.

Pie (hDC, nX1, nY1, nX2, nY2, nX3, nY3, nX4, nY4);

Function Display a pie-shaped wedge.

Value Returned Boolean value of TRUE if the wedge is displayed; otherwise, FALSE.

Parameters

hDC: Handle to the desired device context.

nX1, nY1, nX2, nY2: Integer value specifying the rectangle that the wedge is to bound.

nX3, nY3: Integer value specifying the starting point of the arc.

nX4, nY4: Integer value specifying the ending point of the arc.

Notes The width of the rectangle specified cannot exceed 32,767 units.

PatBlt (hDC, nX, nY, nWidth, nHeight, dwRaster);

Function Create a bit pattern on the device referenced by hDC.

Value Returned Boolean value of TRUE if the pattern is drawn; otherwise, FALSE.

Parameters

hDC: Handle to the desired device context.

nX, nY: Integer value specifying the upper left-hand coordinate of the pattern.

nHeight: Integer value specifying the height of the pattern in logical units.

dwRaster: Long integer specifying the raster operation code.

Notes Raster operations range from 0-255.

BitBlt (hDestDC, nX, nY, nWidth, nHeight, hSrcDC, nSrcX, nSrcY, dwRaster);

Function Move a bitmap from the source specified by hSrcDC to the destination specified by hDestDC.

Value Returned Boolean value if the bitmap is drawn; otherwise 0.

Parameters

hDestDC: Handle to the destination device context.

nX, nY: Integer value specifying the upper left-hand corner of the destination bitmap.

nWidth: Integer value specifying the width of the destination bitmap.

nHeight: Integer value specifying the height of the destination bitmap.

hSrcDC: Handle to the source device context.

nSrcX, nSrcY: Integer value specifying the upper left-hand corner of the source bitmap.

dwRaster: Long integer specifying the raster operation.

Notes   Raster operations range from 0-255.

StretchBlt (hDestDC, nX, nY, nWidth, nHeight, hSrcDC, nSrcX, nSrcY, nSrcWidth, nSrcHeight, dwRaster);

Function   Move a bitmap to the source device context associated with hDestDC from the device context associated with hSrcDC, compressing or stretching the bitmap as required to fit into the destination rectangle.

Value Returned   Boolean value of TRUE if the bitmap is displayed; otherwise, FALSE.

Parameters

hDestDC: Handle to the destination device context.

nX, nY: Integer value specifying the upper left-hand corner of the bitmap on the destination device.

nWidth: Integer value specifying the width of the bitmap on the destination device.

nHeight: Integer value specifying the height of the bitmap on the destination display.

hSrcDC: Handle to the source device context.

nSrcX, nSrcY: Integer value specifying the upper left-hand corner of the bitmap on the source device context.

nSrcWidth: Integer value specifying the width of the bitmap on the source device.

nSrcHeight: Integer value specifying the height of the bitmap on the source device.

dwRaster: Long-integer value specifying the raster operation.

Notes Raster operations range from $0-255$.

TextOut (hDC, nX, nY, lpStr, nCount);

Function Write the string referenced by the string lpStr with the current font starting at the location specified by nX, and nY.

Value Returned Boolean value of TRUE if the string is written; otherwise, FALSE.

Parameters

hDC: Handle to the desired device context.

nX: Integer value specifying the x coordinate of the starting location at which to display the string.

nY: Integer value specifying the y coordinate of the starting location at which to display the string.

lpStr: Long pointer to an ASCIIZ string to display.

nCount: Integer value specifying the number of characters to display.

DrawText (hDC, lpStr, nCount, lpRect, wFormat);

Function Display formatted text within the rectangle specified by the Rect data structure referenced by lpRect.

Value Returned   Boolean value of TRUE if the string is displayed; otherwise, FALSE.

Parameters

hDC: Handle to the desired device context.

lpStr: Long pointer to the ASCIIZ string to display.

nCount: Integer value containing the number of characters to display.

lpRect: Long pointer to a RECT data structure that surrounds the displayed text.

wFormat: Integer value specifying the method of text formatting, as follows:

DT_BOTTOM	Bottom justify
DT_CENTER	Center text
DT_EXPANDTABS	Expand tabs
DT_EXTERNALLEADING	External leading in line height
DT_LEFT	Left-justify text
DT_NOCLIP	Draw without clipping
DT_RIGHT	Right-justify text
DT_SINGLELINE	Single line only
DT_TABSTOP	Set tab stops
DT_TOP	Top justify
DT_VCENTER	Vertically center
DT_WORDBREAK	Lines are broken between word breaks

Notes   Format values can be combined with a bitwise OR.

GrayString (hDC, hBrush, lpOutputFunct, lpData, nCount, nX, nY, nWidth, nHeight);

Function   Display a gray character string.

Value Returned Boolean value of TRUE if the string is displayed; otherwise, FALSE.

Parameters

hDC: Handle to the desired device context.

hBrush: Handle to the brush to be used for graying.

lpOutputFunct: Long pointer to the function to be used to draw the string.

lpData: Long pointer to the string to be displayed.

nCount: Integer value containing the number of characters to display.

nX, nY: Integer value specifying the x and y coordinates at which to display the string.

nWidth: Integer value specifying the width of the rectangle enclosing the string.

nHeight: Integer value specifying the height of the rectangle enclosing the string.

Notes The address of the function assigned to lpOutputFunct must be created using MakeProcInstance.

DrawIcon (hDC, nX, nY, hIcon);

Function Display the icon associated with the handle hIcon on the display context referenced by hDC.

Value Returned Boolean value of TRUE if the icon is displayed; otherwise, FALSE.

Parameters

hDC: Handle to the desired device context.

nX, nY: Integer value specifying the x and y coordinates at which to place the icon.

hIcon: Handle to the icon to display.

SetPixel (hDC, nX, nY, rgbColor);

Function   Place in a pixel at the point specified by nX, nY with the color attributes specified in rgbColor.

Value Returned   The RGB value of the pixel displayed if the function is successful. Otherwise, the value -1 if the pixel is clipped.

Parameters

hDC: Handle to the desired device context.

nX, nY: Integer value specifying the x and y coordinates at which to place the pixel.

rgbColor: RGB color value of the desired pixel color.

GetPixel (hDC, nX, nY);

Function   Return the RGB color of the pixel at the x and y location specified.

Value Returned   The RGB color of the specified pixel if the function is successful; otherwise, the value -1.

Parameters

hDC: Handle to the desired device context.

nX, nY: Integer value specifying the x and y location of the desired pixel.

FloodFill (hDC, nX, nY, rgbColor);

Function   Fill the region bounded by rgbColor with the current brush.

Value Returned   Boolean value of TRUE if the function is successful; otherwise, FALSE.

Parameters

hDC: Handle to the desired device context.

nX, nY: Integer value specifying a pixel within the region to fill.

rgbColor: RGB color of the region boundary.

LoadDDA (nX1, nY1, nX2, nY2, lpLineFunct, lpData);

Function   Compute successive points in the line starting at nX1, nY1 and ending at location nX2, nY2 based upon the function referenced by lpLineFunct and the user-supplied data associated with lpData.

Value Returned   None.

Parameters

nX1, nY1: Integer value specifying the starting location of the line.

nX2, nY2: Integer value specifying the ending location of the line.

lpLineFunct: Long pointer to the function that produces the points in the line.

lpData: Long pointer to the application-defined data.

Notes   The line function must be in the form

LineFunct (x, y, lpData);

FillRgn (hDC, hRgn, hBrush);

Function   Fill the region specified by hRgn with the brush specified by hBrush.

Value Returned   Boolean value of TRUE if the region is filled; otherwise, FALSE.

Parameters

hDC: Handle to the desired device context.

hRgn: Handle to the region to fill.

hBrush: Handle to the brush with which to fill the region.

FrameRegion (hDC, hRgn, hBrush, nWidth, nHeight);

Function   Draw a border around the region specified by hRgn with the brush associated with hBrush.

Value Returned   Boolean value of TRUE if the region is framed; otherwise, FALSE.

Parameters

hDC: Handle to the desired device context.

hRgn: Handle to the region to frame.

hBrush: Handle to the brush used to draw the border.

nWidth: Integer value specifying the width of vertical brush strokes.

nHeight: Integer value specifying the height of horizontal brush strokes.

InvertRgn (hDC, hRgn);

Function   Invert the colors in the region specified by hRgn.

Value Returned   Boolean value of TRUE if the colors are inverted; otherwise, FALSE.

Parameters

hDC: Handle to the desired device context.

hRgn: Handle to the region within which to invert the color.

PaintRgn (hDC, hRgn);

Function   Fill the region specified by hRgn with the current brush.

Value Returned   Boolean value of TRUE if the function is successful; otherwise, FALSE.

Parameters

hDC: Handle to the desired device context.

hRgn: Handle to the region to fill.

FillRect (hDC, lpRect, hBrush);

Function   Fill the contents of the rectangle associated with hRect with the specified brush.

Value Returned   None.

Parameters

hDC: Handle to the desired device context.

lpRect: Long pointer to the rectangle to fill.

hBrush: Handle to the brush used for filling.

FrameRect (hDC, lpRect, hBrush);

Function   Frame the rectangle specified by lpRect with the brush provided.

Value Returned   None.

Parameters

hDC: Handle to the desired device context.

lpRect: Long pointer to the rectangle to frame.

hBrush: Handle to the brush used during framing.

InvertRect (hDC, lpRect);

Function   Invert the display bits in the rectangle referenced by lpRECT.

Value Returned   None.

Parameters

hDC: Handle to the desired device context.

lpRect: Long pointer to the rectangle to invert.

Drawing Object Routines

The following are routines for drawing objects.

GetStockObject (nIndex);

Function Retrieve a handle to predefined pens, brushes, or fonts.

Value Returned Handle to the desired object.

Parameter

nIndex: Integer value that specifies the type of desired object, as follows:

BLACK_BRUSH	Black brush
DKGRAY_BRUSH	Dark gray brush
GRAY_BRUSH	Gray brush
HOLLOW_BRUSH	Hollow brush
LTGRAY_BRUSH	Light gray brush
NULL_BRUSH	Null brush
WHITE_BRUSH	White brush
BLACK_PEN	Black pen
NULL_PEN	Null pen
WHITE_PEN	White pen
ANSI_FIXED_FONT	ANSI fixed font
ANSI_VAR_FONT	ANSI variable font
DEVICE_DEFAULT_FONT	Dependent device font
OEM_FIXED_FONT	Dependent OEM font
SYSTEM_FONT	Dependent system font

Notes If the function is not successful, NULL is returned.

CreatePen (nPenStyle, nWidth, rgbColor);

Function Define a logical pen with the specified attributes.

Value Returned Handle to a logical pen if the function is successful; otherwise, NULL is returned.

Parameter

nPenStyle: Integer value specifying the style of the pen, as follows:

0	Solid pen
1	Dashed pen
2	Dotted pen
3	Dashed-and-dotted pen
4	Dashed-and-two-dots pen
5	NULL pen

Notes   Pens with a physical width greater than 1 have either NULL or solid style.

CreatePenIndirect (lpLogPen);

Function   Create a logical pen with the attributes specified in the data structure of type LOGPEN.

Value Returned   Handle to a logical pen if the function is successful; otherwise, the NULL value is returned.

Parameter

lpLogPen: Long pointer to a data structure of type LOGPEN.

Notes   Pens with a physical width greater than 1 have either NULL or solid style.

CreateSolidBrush (rgbColor);

Function   Create a logical brush with the color attributes specified by rgbColor.

Value Returned   Handle to the logical brush created if the function is successful; otherwise, the value NULL is returned.

Parameter

rgbColor: Long integer specifying rgbColor for the logical brush.

CreateHatchBrush (nIndex, rgbColor);

Function Create a logical brush with the hatched pattern and specified color.

Value Returned Handle to the logical brush created if the function is successful; otherwise, the value NULL.

Parameters

nIndex: Integer value specifying the hatch style of the brush, as follows:

HS_BDIAGONAL	45-degree downward hatch
HS_CROSS	Horizontal and vertical hatch
HS_DIAGCROSS	45-degree cross-hatch
HS_FDIAGONAL	45-degree upward hatch
HS_HORIZONTAL	Horizontal hatch
HS_VERTICAL	Vertical hatch

rgbColor: Long integer containing the RGB color of the brush.

CreatePatternBrush (hBitmap);

Function Create a logical brush with the pattern contained in the bitmap referenced by the handle hBitmap.

Value Returned Handle to the logical brush created if the function is successful; otherwise, the value NULL is returned.

Parameter

hBitmap: Handle to the bitmap to be used to create the brush pattern.

Notes   The size for the fill pattern bitmap is 8×8.

CreateBrushIndirect (lpLogBrush);

Function   Create a logical brush based upon the attributes specified in the LOGBRUSH data type referenced by lpLogBrush.

Value Returned   Handle to the logical brush created if the function was successful; otherwise, the NULL value is returned.

Parameter

lpLogBrush: Long pointer to a LOGBRUSH data structure that defines the attributes of the desired logical brush.

CreateBitmap (nWidth, nHeight, nPlanes, nBitCount, lpBits);

Function   Create a bitmap with the specified attributes. The bitmap is later available for selection via SelectObject.

Value Returned   Handle to the bitmap created if the function was successful; otherwise, the NULL value is returned.

Parameters

nWidth: Integer value specifying the width of the bitmap.

nHeight: Integer value specifying the height of the bitmap.

nPlanes: Integer value specifying the number of color planes in the bitmap.

nBitCount: Integer value specifying the number of color bits per pixel.

lpBits: Long pointer to the array containing the initial bitmap values or 0 if the array is an uninitialized bitmap.

CreateBitmapIndirect (lpBitmap);

Function Create a bitmap based upon the attributes specified in the data structure of type BITMAP referenced by lpBitmap.

Value Returned Handle to the bitmap created if the function is successful; otherwise, the NULL value is returned.

Parameter

lpBitmap: Long pointer to a data structure of type BITMAP that contains the bitmap attributes.

CreateCompatibleBitmap (hDC, nWidth, nHeight);

Function Create a bitmap compatible with the device specified by hDC.

Value Returned Handle to the bitmap created if the function is successful; otherwise, the NULL value is returned.

Parameters

hDC: Handle to the desired device context.

nWidth: Integer value specifying the width of the bitmap in pixels.

nHeight: Integer value specifying the height of the bitmap in pixels.

Notes The bitmap has the same number of color planes as the device for which it is created.

SetBitmapBits (hBitmap, dwCount, lpBits);

Function Set the bits of a bitmap to the bits referenced by lpBits.

Value Returned Long integer specifying the actual number of bits copied.

Parameters

hBitmap: Handle to the bitmap to set.

dwCount: Long-integer value specifying the number of bits to copy.

lpBits: Long pointer to an integer array containing the desired bits.

GetBitmapBits (hBitmap, dwCount, lpBits);

Function   Copy the number of bits specified from the bitmap referenced by hBitmap into the array referenced by lpBits.

Value Returned   Long-integer value specifying the actual number of
bits copied.

Parameters

hBitmap: Handle to the bitmap to copy.

dwCount: Long integer specifying the number of bits to copy.

lpBits: Long pointer to an integer array to receive the bits.

SetBitmapDimension (hBitmap, nWidth, nHeight);

Function   Map the width and height of a bitmap to 0.1-mm units.

Value Returned   Long integer value specifying the old dimensions of
the bitmap. The high-order word contains the height and the low-
order word contains the width.

Parameters

hBitmap: Handle to the bitmap to dimension.

nWidth: Integer value specifying the width of the bitmap in 0.1-mm
units.

nHeight: Integer value specifying the height of the bitmap in 0.1-mm
units.

GetBitmapDimension (hBitmap);

Function   Return the width and height of the bitmap associated with hBitmap in 0.1-mm units.

Value Returned   Long integer containing the bitmap dimensions. The high-order word contains the width of the bitmap and the low-order word contains the height.

Parameter

hBitmap: Handle to the bitmap of which to return the dimension.

CreateFont (nHeight, nWidth, nEscapement, nOrientation, nWeight, cItalic, cUnderline, cStrikeOut, nCharSet, nOutputPrecision, nClipPrecision, cQuality, cPitchAndFamily, lpFacename);

Value Returned   Handle to the font created if the function was successful; otherwise, the NULL value is returned.

Parameters

nHeight: Integer value specifying the height of the font in logical units.

nWidth: Integer value specifying the width of the font in logical units.

nEscapement: Integer value specifying the angle of each line in tenths of degrees of each line written.

nOrientation: Integer value of the angle of each character's baseline in tenths of degrees.

nWeight: Integer value specifying the desired weight of the font from 0-1000 (400 is normal, 700 is bold).

cItalic: Byte flag specifying whether the font is italic.

cUnderline: Byte flag specifying whether the font is underlined.

cStrikeOut: Byte flag specifying whether the font is struck through.

nCharSet: Integer value specifying the desired character set, as follows:

ANSI—CHARSET   Standard ANSI character set
OEM—CHARSET   OEM-provided character set

nOutputPrecision: Integer value specifying the desired output precision, as follows:

OUT—CHARACTER—PRECIS
OUT—DEFAULT—PRECIS
OUT—STRING—PRECIS
OUT—STROKE—PRECIS

nClipPrecision: Integer value specifying the clipping precision, as follows:

CLIP—CHARACTER—PRECIS
CLIP—DEFAULT—PRECIS
CLIP—STROKE—PRECIS

cQuality: Byte flag specifying the output quality, as follows:

DEFAULT—QUALITY
DRAFT—QUALITY
PROOF—QUALITY

cPitchAndFamily: Byte flag specifying the font and pitch family. The two low-order bits can be

DEFAULT—PITCH
FIXED—PITCH
VARIABLE—PITCH

The four high-order bits can be

FF—DECORATIVE
FF—DONTCARE
FF—MODERN
FF—ROMAN
FF—SCRIPT
FF—SWISS

lpFacename: Long pointer to an ASCIIZ string containing the font's facename.

CreateFontIndirect (lpLogFont);

Function   Create a font based upon the attributes specified in the data structure LOGFONT referenced by lpLogFont.

Value Returned   Handle to the font created if the routine is successful; otherwise, the NULL value is returned.

Parameter

lpLogFont: Long pointer to a data structure of type LOGFONT that contains the attributes of the desired font.

DeleteObject (hObject);

Function   Delete the object (pen, font, brush, bitmap, or memory region) referenced by hObject.

Value Returned   Boolean value of TRUE if the object is deleted; otherwise, FALSE.

Parameter

hObject: Handle to the object to delete.

Notes   The object must not be selected into a device context when deleted.

Selection Routines

The following are GDI selection routines.

SelectObject (hDC, hObject);

Function   Select the logical object specified as the current object for the specified device context.

Value Returned Handle to object being replaced if the function is successful; otherwise, the NULL value is returned.

Parameters

hDC: Handle to the desired device context.

hObject: Handle to the object to select.

Notes Selected objects are the GDI default objects. Therefore, no more than one object of each type can be selected at one time.

SelectClipRgn (hDC, hRgn);

Function Select the region specified as the current clipping region for clipping operations.

Value Returned Integer value specifying the region type, as follows:

COMPLEXREGION
ERROR
NULLREGION
SIMPLEREGION

Parameters

hDC: Handle to the desired device context.

hRgn: Handle to the region to be used as the current clipping

GetObject (hObject, nCount, lpObject);

Function Fill the buffer referenced by lpObject with the data that defines the attributes of the object referenced by the handle hObject.

Value Returned Integer value specifying the actual number of bytes copied.

Parameters

hObject: Handle to the object of which to copy the attributes.

nCount: Integer value specifying the number of bytes of data to copy.

lpObject: Long pointer to the buffer receiving the contents of the copy.

Notes If hObject refers to a bitmap, only the width, height, and color are returned.

Display Context Attribute Routines

The following routines allow applications to modify the attributes of the display context.

SetRelAbs (hDC, nRelAbsMode);

Function Specify whether GDI coordinates are relative or absolute.

Value Returned Integer value specifying the previous coordinate mode.

Parameters

hDC: Handle to the desired device context.

nRelAbsMode: Integer value specifying the desired mode, as follows:

ABSOLUTE   Absolute coordinate addressing
RELATIVE   Relative coordinate addressing

Notes If the return value is NULL, an error occurred.

GetRelAbs (hDC);

Function Return the current coordinate mode, relative or absolute.

Value Returned Integer value specifying the current coordinate mode, ABSOLUTE or RELATIVE.

Parameter

hDC: Handle to the desired device context.

Notes If the return value is NULL, hDC is not a valid device context.

SetBkColor (hDC, rgbColor);

Function Sets the current background color as specified by rgbColor.

Value Returned Long integer value specifying the previous background color.

Parameters

hDC: Handle to desired device context.

rgbColor: Long integer value specifying the desired background color.

GetBkColor (hDC);

Function Return the current background color.

Value Returned Long integer value specifying the current background color.

Parameter

hDC: Handle to the desired device context.

SetBkMode (hDC, nBackMode);

Function Define background mode for text, hatched brush, or line-style operations. The background mode specifies whether GDI functions overwrite the background before performing the operations specified previously.

Value Returned Integer value specifying the previous background mode.

Parameters

hDC: Handle to the desired device context.

nBackMode: Integer value specifying the desired background mode, as follows:

OPAQUE	Background filled with background color before GDI functions
TRANSPARENT	Background is unaffected

GetBkMode (hDC);

Function Return the current background mode (OPAQUE, TRANSPARENT) for the display context specified by hDC.

Value Returned Integer value specifying the current background mode.

Parameter

hDC: Handle to the desired device context.

SetTextColor (hDC, rgbColor);

Function Define the color to be used for character display.

Value Returned Long integer value containing the previous text color.

Parameters

hDC: Handle to the desired device context.

rgbColor: Long integer to the desired text color.

GetTextColor (hDC);

Function Return the current RGB color used for text display.

Value Returned Long integer containing the RGB color used for text display.

Parameter

hDC: Handle to the desired device context.

SetROP2 (hDC, nDrawMode);

Function Define the current drawing mode.

Value Returned Integer value containing the previous drawing mode.

Parameters

hDC: Handle to the desired device context.

nDrawMode: Integer value specifying the drawing mode. (See the constants R2_* in windows.h.)

Notes Drawing mode is used for raster devices only.

GetROP2 (hDC);

Function   Return the current drawing mode.

Value Returned   Integer value specifying the current drawing mode.

Parameter
hDC: Handle to the desired device context.

SetStretchBltMode (hDC, nStretchMode);

Function   Define the stretch mode for the StretchBlt function.

Value Returned   Integer value containing the previous stretch mode.

Parameters
hDC: Handle to the desired device context.

nStretchMode: Integer value specifying the desired stretch mode, as follows:

BLACKONWHITE	Preserve black pixels at the expense of white pixels
COLORONCOLOR	Throw out eliminated lines
WHITEONBLACK	Preserve white pixels at the expense of black pixels

Notes   COLORONCOLOR is normally used to preserve color bitmaps.

GetStretchBlkMode (hDC);

Function   Return the stretch mode for the device context associated with hDC.

Value Returned   Integer value specifying the current stretching mode.

Parameter
hDC: Handle to the desired device context.

SetPolyFillMode (hDC, nPolyFillMode);

Function   Define the polygon fill mode for the display context associated with hDC.

Value Returned   Integer value specifying the previous polygon fill mode.

Parameters
hDC: Handle to the desired device context.

nPolyFillMode: Integer value specifying the polygon fill mode, as follows:

ALTERNATE   Select alternate mode
WINDING   Select winding mode

Notes   ALTERNATE mode fills every other region in the polygon. WINDING mode fills all regions.

GetPolyFillMode (hDC);

Function   Return the polygon fill mode for the device context associated with hDC.

Value Returned   Integer value specifying the polygon fill mode (ALTERNATE, WINDING).

Parameter
hDC: Handle to the desired device context.

SetMapMode (hDC, nMappingMode);

Function Define the mapping mode for the device context associated with hDC.

Value Returned Integer value specifying the previous mapping mode.

Parameters

hDC: Handle to the desired device context.

nMappingMode: Integer value specifying the desired mapping mode, as follows:

MM_ANSIOTROPIC	Logical unit is mapped to arbitrary units. Viewport specifies plus x and y.
MM_HIENGLISH	Logical unit is 0.001 in. Plus x is right; plus y is up.
MM_HIMETRIC	Logical unit is mapped to 0.01 mm. Plus x is right; plus y is up.
MM_ISOTROPIC	Logical unit is mapped to arbitrary units. Viewport specifies plus x and y.
MM_LOENGLISH	Logical unit is mapped to 0.01 in. Plus x is right; plus y is up.
MM_LOMETRIC	Logical unit is mapped to 0.1 mm. Plus x is right; plus y is up.
MM_TEXT	Logical unit is mapped to a pixel. Plus x is right; plus y is down.
MM_TWIPS	Logical unit is mapped to 1/1440 in. Plus x is right; plus y is up.

GetMapMode (hDC);

Function Return the current mapping mode for the device context associated with hDC.

Value Returned Integer value specifying the current mapping mode.

Parameter

hDC: Handle to the desired device context.

SetWindowOrg (hDC, nX, nY);

Function Define the window origin for the device context associated with hDC.

Value Returned Long integer that specifies the previous x and y coordinates of the window origin. The high-order word contains the y coordinate and the low-order word contains the x coordinate.

Parameters

hDC: Handle to the desired device context.

nX: Integer value specifying the x coordinate of the window origin.

nY: Integer value specifying the y coordinate of the window origin.

Notes GDI will map all points relative to the window origin.

GetWindowOrg (hDC);

Function Return the x and y coordinates of the window origin for the device context associated with hDC.

Value Returned Long integer specifying the coordinates of the window origin. The high-order word contains the y coordinate of the origin and the low-order word contains the x coordinate of the origin.

Parameter

hDC: Handle to the desired device context.

SetWindowExt (hDC, nX, nY);

Function   Set the x and y extents of the window associated with the device context referenced by hDC. *Extents* define how much GDI functions can stretch or compress a logical coordinate system of a window.

Value Returned   Long integer containing the previous x and y extents. The high-order word contains the y extent and the low-order word contains the x extent.

Parameters

hDC: Handle to the desired device context.

nX: Integer value specifying the x extent.

nY: Integer value specifying the y extent.

Notes   The x and y extents also define the window orientation relative to the viewport. If the signs for the window's extents match the signs of the viewport extents, the axes have the same orientation.

Windows ignores calls to SetWindowExt and SetViewportExt when the following mapping modes are set:

MM—HIENGLISH
MM—HIMETRIC
MM—LOENGLISH
MM—LOMETRIC
MM—TEXT
MM—TWIPS

GetWindowExt (hDC);

Function   Return the x and y extents for the window associated with the device context hDC.

Value Returned Long-integer value specifying the current x and y window extents. The high-order word contains the y extent and the low-order word contains the x extent.

Parameter

hDC: Handle to the desired device context.

SetViewportOrg (hDC, nX, nY);

Function Define the viewport origin for the device context associated with hDC.

Value Returned Long integer that specifies the previous x and y coordinates of the viewport origin. The high-order word contains the y coordinate and the low-order word contains the x coordinate.

Parameters

hDC: Handle to the desired device context.

nX: Integer value specifying the x coordinate of the viewport origin.

nY: Integer value specifying the y coordinate of the viewport origin.

Notes GDI will map all points relative to the viewport origin.

GetViewportOrg (hDC);

Function Return the x and y coordinates of the viewport origin for the device context associated with hDC.

Value Returned Long integer specifying the coordinates of the viewport origin. The high-order word contains the y coordinate of the origin and the low-order word contains the x coordinate of the origin.

Parameter

hDC: Handle to the desired device context.

SetViewportExt (hDC, nX, nY);

Function   Set the x and y extents of the viewport associated with the device context referenced by hDC. (Extents define how much GDI functions can stretch or compress a logical coordinate system of a viewport.)

Value Returned   Long integer containing the previous x and y extents. The high-order word contains the y extent and the low-order word contains the x extent.

Parameters

hDC: Handle to the desired device context.

nX: Integer value specifying the x extent.

nY: Integer value specifying the y extent.

Notes   The x and y extents also define the viewport's orientation relative to the window. If the signs for the window's extents match the signs of the viewport extents, the axes have the same orientation.

   Windows ignores calls to SetWindowExt and SetViewportExt when the following mapping modes are set:

MM—HIENGLISH
MM—HIMETRIC
MM—LOENGLISH
MM—LOMETRIC
MM—TEXT
MM—TWIPS

GetViewportExt (hDC);

Function   Return the x and y extents for the viewport associated with the device context hDC.

Value Returned   Long-integer value specifying the current x and y viewport extents. The high-order word contains the y extent and the low-order word contains the x extent.

Parameter

hDC: Handle to the desired device context.

ScaleWindowExt (hDC, nXnum, nXdiv, nYnum, nYdiv);

Function   Modify the current window extents relative to the current extents, as follows:

NewX = (OldX * nXnum) / nXdiv
NewY = (OldY * nYnum) / nYdiv

Value Returned   Long integer value containing the x and y extents for the desired window.

Parameters

hDC: Handle to the desired device context.

nXnum: Integer value specifying the amount by which to multiply the current x extent.

nXdiv: Integer value specifying the amount by which to divide the x extent.

nYnum: Integer value specifying the amount by which to multiply the current y extent.

nYdiv: Integer value specifying the amount by which to divide the y extent.

ScaleViewportExt (hDC, nXnum, nXdiv, nYnum, nYdiv);

Function   Modify the current viewport extents relative to the current extents, as follows:

NewX = (OldX * nXnum) / nXdiv
NewY = (OldY * nYnum) / nYdiv

Value Returned Long-integer value containing the x and y extents for the desired viewport.

Parameters

hDC: Handle to the desired device context.

nXnum: Integer value specifying the amount by which to multiply the current x extent.

nXdiv: Integer value specifying the amount by which to divide the x extent.

nYnum: Integer value specifying the amount by which to multiply the current y extent.

nYdiv: Integer value specifying the amount by which to divide the y extent.

OffsetWindowOrg (hDC, nX, nY);

Function Modify the window origin relative to the current origin values.

Value Returned Long-integer value specifying the previous window origin. The high-order word contains the y coordinate and the low-order word contains the x coordinate.

Parameters

hDC: Handle to the desired device context.

nX: Integer value to add to the current x origin.

nY: Integer value to add to the current y origin.

OffsetViewportOrg (hDC, nX, nY);

Function Modify the viewport origin relative to the current origin values.

Value Returned Long-integer value specifying the previous viewport origin. The high-order word contains the y coordinate and the low-order word contains the x coordinate.

Parameters

hDC: Handle to the desired device context.

nX: Integer value to add to the current x origin.

nY: Integer value to add to the current y origin.

GetBrushOrg (hDC);

Function Return the brush origin for the device context associated with hDC.

Value Returned Long integer that specifies the origin for the brush associated with the display context. The high-order word contains the y coordinate and the low-order word contains the x coordinate.

Parameter

hDC: Handle to the desired device context.

Notes Default brush origin is 0,0.

SetBrushOrg (hDC, nX, nY);

Function Set the origin for brushes selected in the display context associated with hDC.

Value Returned Long-integer value containing the previous brush origin for the device context. The high-order word contains the y coordinate and the low-order word contains the x coordinate.

Parameters

hDC: Handle to the desired display context.

nX: Integer value specifying the desired x coordinate.

nY: Integer value specifying the desired y coordinate.

Notes Do not use SetBrushOrg with stock objects.

UnrealizeObject (hBrush);

Function Reset the origin of the given brush next time it is used.

Value Returned Boolean value of TRUE if the function was successful; otherwise, FALSE.

Parameter
hBrush: Handle to the brush of which to reset the origin.

Notes Do not use UnrealizeObject with stock objects.

Clipping Region Routines

The following are GDI clipping region routines.

GetClipBox (hDC, lpRECT);

Function Return the dimensions of a rectangle that bounds the current clipping region.

Value Returned Integer value specifying the clipping region type, as follows:

COMPLEXREGION
ERROR
NULLREGION
SIMPLEREGION

Parameters

hDC: Handle to the desired device context.

lpRECT: Long pointer to a data structure of type RECT that receives the rectangle specifying the clipping region.

IntersectClipRect (hDC, nX1, nY1, nX2, nY2);

Function Define a new clipping region by intersecting the current clipping region with the rectangle specified by the points nX1, nY1 and nX2, nY2.

Value Returned Integer value specifying the type of clipping region.

Parameters

hDC: Handle to the desired device context.

nX1, nY1: Integer value specifying the upper left-hand corner of the rectangle to intersect with the current clipping region.

nX2, nY2: Integer value specifying the lower right-hand corner of the rectangle to intersect with the current clipping region.

Notes The width of the rectangle to be intersected with the current clipping region cannot exceed 32,767 units.

OffsetClipRgn (hDC, nX, nY);

Function Move the clipping region in the x and y direction as specified.

Value Returned Integer value specifying the type of the new clipping region.

Parameters

hDC: Handle to the desired device context.

nX: Integer value specifying the number of units and direction to move the clipping region.

nY: Integer value specifying the number of units and direction to move the clipping region.

ExcludeClipRegion (hDC, nX1, nY1, nX2, nY2);

Function Define a new clipping region that contains the current clipping region minus the region specified by desired rectangular coordinates.

Value Returned Integer value specifying the type of the new clipping region.

Parameters

hDC: Handle to the desired device context.

nX1, nY1: Integer value specifying the upper left-hand corner of the rectangular region to exclude.

nX2, nY2: Integer value specifying the lower right-hand corner of the rectangular region to exclude.

PtVisible (hDC, nX, nY);

Function Return TRUE if the point specified is within the current clipping region; otherwise, FALSE.

Value Returned Boolean value TRUE if the point specified is contained in the current clipping region; otherwise, FALSE.

Parameters

hDC: Handle to the desired device context.

nX, nY: Integer value specifying a coordinate of a pixel.

RectVisible (hDC, lpRECT);

Function   Return TRUE if the rectangle specified is within the current clipping region; otherwise, FALSE.

Value Returned   Boolean value TRUE if the rectangle specified is contained in the current clipping region; otherwise, FALSE.

Parameters

hDC: Handle to the desired device context.

lpRECT: Long pointer to a data structure of type RECT that defines the rectangle to examine.

Region Routines

The following are the GDI region routines.

CombineRgn (hDestRgn, hSrcRgn1, hSrcRgn2, nCombineMode);

Function   Create a new region by combining two existing regions.

Value Returned   Integer value specifying the type of the newly created region.

Parameters

hDestRgn: Handle to the new region.

hSrcRgn1: Handle to the first region to combine.

hSrcRgn2: Handle to the second region to combine.

nCombineMode: Integer value specifying how regions are combined, as follows:

RGN_AND	Intersection
RGN_COPY	Copy region 1

RGN__DIFF   Difference
RGN__OR   Union
RGN__XOR   Exclusive OR

EqualRgn (hSrcRgn1, hSrcRgn2);

Function Return TRUE if the two regions specified are identical.

Value Returned Boolean value TRUE if both of the regions specified are identical; otherwise, FALSE.

Parameters

hSrcRgn1, hSrcRgn2: Handles to the regions to compare.

OffsetRgn (hRgn, nX, nY);

Function Move the region associated with the region handle hRgn as specified by nX and nY.

Value Returned Integer value specifying the type of the new region.

Parameters

hRgn: Handle to the region to move.

nX: Integer value specifying the number of units and direction to move the region in the x direction.

nY: Integer value specifying the number of units and direction to move the region in the y direction.

CreateRectRgn (nX1, nY1, nX2, nY2);

Function Create the region specified by the rectangular coordinates.

Value Returned   Handle to the new region if the function is successful; otherwise, the value NULL.

Parameters

nX1, *nY1:* Integer values specifying the upper left-hand coordinate of the rectangle defining the region.

nX2, *nY2:* Integer values specifying the lower right-hand coordinate of the rectangle defining the region.

CreateRectRgnIndirect (lpRECT);

Function   Create a region based upon the coordinates in the RECT data structure referenced by lpRECT.

Value Returned   Handle to the newly created region if the function is successful; otherwise, the value NULL.

Parameter

lpRECT: Long pointer to a data structure of type RECT that defines the region to be created.

CreateEllipticRgn (nX1, nY1, nX2, nY2);

Function   Create the region specified by the elliptical coordinates.

Value Returned   Handle to the new region if the function is successful; otherwise, the value NULL.

Parameters

nX1, *nY1:* Integer values specifying the upper left-hand coordinate of the rectangle defining the region.

nX2, *nY2:* Integer values specifying the lower right-hand coordinate of the rectangle defining the region.

CreateEllipticRgnIndirect (lpRECT);

Function Create a region based upon the coordinates in the RECT data structure referenced by lpRECT.

Value Returned Handle to the newly created region if the function is successful; otherwise, the value NULL.

Parameter

lpRECT: Long pointer to a data structure of type RECT that defines the region to be bounded by the ellipse.

CreatePolygonRgn (lpPoints, nCount, nPolyFillMode);

Function Create a polygon region.

Value Returned Handle to the newly created region if the function is successful; otherwise, the value NULL.

Parameters

lpPoints: Long pointer to an integer array of points that specify the polygon coordinates.

nCount: Integer value specifying the number of points in the array referenced by lpPoints.

nPolyFillMode: Integer value specifying the polygon filling mode.

PtInRegion (hRegion, nX, nY);

Function Return TRUE if the pixel specified falls within the provided region.

Value Returned Boolean value TRUE if the pixel specified by nX, nY falls within the region specified by hRegion; otherwise, FALSE.

Parameters

hRegion: Handle to the region to examine.

nX, nY: Integer value specifying the coordinates of the pixel for which to test.

Scrolling Routines

The following are the Windows routines used for scrolling.

ScrollWindow (hWnd, nX, nY, lpRect, lpClipRect);

Function   Scroll the contents of the client area of the specified window the number of units in the x and y direction.

Value Returned   None.

Parameters

hWnd: Handle to the desired window.

nX: Integer value containing the number of units to scroll the window in the x direction.

nY: Integer value containing the number of units to scroll the window in the y direction.

lpRect: Long pointer to a data structure of type RECT that specifies the region of the window to scroll. If NULL, the entire window is scrolled.

lpClipRect: Long pointer to a data structure of type RECT that specifies the clipping region for the scroll.

SetScrollPos (hWnd, nScrollBar, nPosition, bRedrawFlag);

Function   Set the position of the scroll bar elevator.

Value Returned Integer value specifying the previous location of the scroll bar elevator.

Parameters

hWnd: Handle to the window desired.

nScrollBar: Integer value specifying the scroll bar to set, as follows:

SB__CTL	Scroll bar control
SB__HORZ	Horizontal scroll bar
SB__VERT	Vertical scroll bar

nPosition: Integer value specifying the new position of the scroll bar elevator.

bRedrawFlag: Boolean value that, when TRUE, directs Windows to redraw the scroll bar to show the change.

GetScrollPos (hWnd, nScrollBar);

Function Return the current position of the scroll bar elevator for the specified scroll bar.

Value Returned Integer value containing the current scroll bar elevator position.

Parameters

hWnd: Handle to the desired window.

nScrollBar: Integer value specifying the desired scroll bar, as follows:

SB__CTL	Scroll bar control
SB__HORZ	Horizontal scroll bar
SB__VERT	Vertical scroll bar

SetScrollRange (hWnd, nScrollBar, nMinPosition, nMax-Position, bRedrawFlag);

Function Define the scroll bar elevator range for the specified scroll bar.

Value Returned None.

Parameters

hWnd: Handle to the desired window.

nScrollBar: Integer value specifying the desired scroll bar.

nMinPosition: Integer value specifying the minimum value in the scroll range.

nMaxPosition: Integer value specifying the maximum value in the scroll range.

bRedrawFlag: Boolean value that, when TRUE, directs Windows to redraw the scroll bar to show the change.

GetScrollRange (hWnd, nScrollBar, lpMinimumPosition, lpMaximumPosition);

Function Return the scrolling region for the specified scroll bar.

Value Returned None.

Parameters

hWnd: Handle to the desired window.

nScrollBar: Integer value specifying the desired scroll bar, as follows:

SB—CTL   Scroll bar control
SB—HORZ   Horizontal scroll bar
SB—VERT   Vertical scroll bar

lpMinimumPosition: Long pointer to an integer value containing the minimum scroll bar position.

lpMaximumPosition: Long pointer to an integer value containing the maximum scroll bar position.

Property List Routines

The following are the Windows property list routines.

SetProp (hWnd, lpStr, hData);

Function Copy the character string and data containing property list to the window specified by hWnd.

Value Returned Boolean value of TRUE if the function is successful; otherwise, the value is FALSE.

Parameters

hWnd: Handle to the desired window.

lpStr: Long pointer to a character string or atom specifying a character string.

hData: Handle to a data structure used to contain the property list.

GetProp (hWnd, lpStr);

Function Get the character string containing the property list associated with the window specified by hWnd.

Value Returned Boolean value of TRUE if the function is successful; otherwise, the value is FALSE.

Parameters

hWnd: Handle to the desired window.

lpStr: Long pointer to a character string or atom specifying a character string.

Notes If the high-order word of lpStr is 0, the value is treated as an atom.

RemoveProp (hWnd, lpStr);

Function Remove the data associated with specified string from the window property list for the window referenced by hWnd.

Value Returned Handle to a data structure named by the string in lpStr.

Parameters
hWnd: Handle to the desired window.

lpStr: Long pointer to an ASCIIZ string or atom defining the data to remove from the property list.

Notes If the high-order word of lpStr is 0, the value is treated as an atom.

EnumProps (hWnd, lpEnumfunct);

Function Enumerate all of the properties for the specified window.

Value Returned Integer value containing the last value returned by the application-defined callback function.

Parameters
hWnd: Handle to the desired window.

lpEnumfunct: Long pointer to the application-defined callback function.

Notes   The callback function should have the following format:

callback (hWnd, nDummy, pStr, hData);

Window Attribute Functions

The following routines access and modify window attributes.

SetWindowText (hWnd, lpStr);

Function   Set the window caption bar to the string specified by lpStr.

Value Returned   None.

Parameters
hWnd: Handle to the desired window.

lpStr: Long pointer to the string containing the new caption.

GetWindowText (hWnd, lpStr, nMaxBytes);

Function   Copy the window caption into the string referenced by lpStr.

Value Returned   Integer value specifying the actual number of bytes copied into the character string.

Parameters
hWnd: Handle to the desired window.

lpStr: Long pointer to character string to store the caption bar.

nMaxBytes: Integer value specifying the size of character string buffer.

GetWindowTextLength (hWnd);

Function   Return the number of characters in the window caption bar.

Value Returned   Integer value specifying the number of characters in the window caption bar.

Parameter
hWnd: Handle to the desired window.

FindWindow (lpClassName, lpWindowName);

Function   Return a handle to the window whose class is defined by lpClassName and whose name is defined by lpWindowName.

Value Returned   Handle to the desired window, or the value NULL if no such window exists.

Parameters
lpClassName: Long pointer to an ASCIIZ string containing the class name of the desired window.

lpWindowName: Long pointer to an ASCIIZ string containing the window name of the desired window.

GetParent (hWnd);

Function   Retrieve a handle to the parent of the specified window.

Value Returned   Handle to the parent of the specified window, or NULL if no parent exists.

Parameter

hWnd: Handle to the desired window.

GetClientRect (hWnd, lpRect);

Function Copy the coordinates of the client window into the data structure of type RECT referenced by lpRECT.

Value Returned None.

Parameters

hWnd: Handle to the desired window.

lpRect: Long pointer to a data structure of type RECT that contains the coordinates of the client window.

GetWindowRect (hWnd, lpRect);

Function Return the dimensions of the bounding rectangle specified window.

Value Returned None.

Parameters

hWnd: Handle to the desired window.

lpRect: Long pointer to a data structure of type RECT that contains the dimensions of the specified window.

GetSysModalWindow ( );

Function Return the handle of the system modal window if one is present.

Value Returned   Handle to the system modal window, or the NULL value if no such window is present.

Parameters   None.

SetSysModalWindow (hWnd);

Function   Define the system modal window.

Value Returned   Handle to the previous system modal window, or NULL if no such window exists.

Parameter

hWnd: Handle to the desired window.

Error Routines

The following routines simplify error processing within Windows applications.

MessageBox (hWndParent, lpText, lpCaption, wType);

Function   Create and display a message box.

Value Returned   Integer value specifying one of the following constants:

IDABORT
IDCANCEL
IDIGNORE
IDOK
IDNO
IDRETRY
IDYES

Parameters

hWndParent: Handle to the window owning the message box.

lpText: Long pointer to an ASCIIZ string containing the message to be displayed.

lpCaption: Long pointer to an ASCIIZ string containing the message box caption.

wType: Integer value specifying the type of message box (see Chapter 13).

MessageBeep (wType);

Function   Generate a beep via the system bell when a message box of the specified type is displayed.

Value Returned   Boolean value of TRUE if the function is successful; otherwise, FALSE.

Parameter

wType: Integer value specifying the message box type for which to beep the system bell. See Chapter 13 for message box types.

FlashWindow (hWnd, bInvertFlag);

Function   The window border and caption will flash one time.

Value Returned   Boolean value of TRUE if the window was inverted; otherwise, FALSE.

Parameters

hWnd: Handle to the desired window.

bInvertFlag: Boolean value that, when TRUE, directs Windows to invert the window when it is flashed.

Cursor Manipulation Routines

The following routines enhance cursor manipulation in Windows.

SetCursor (hCursor);

Function   Set the cursor shape as specified by hCursor.

Value Returned   Handle to the cursor previously defining the cursor.

Parameter
hCursor: Handle to the new desired cursor.

SetCursorPos (nX, nY);

Function   Set the position of the mouse cursor to the screen coordinates specified by nX and nY.

Value Returned   None.

Parameters
nX, nY: Integer value specifying the x and y coordinates for the desired mouse position.

ClipCursor (lpRect);

Function   Restrict the mouse cursor to a given rectangle on the screen.

Value Returned None.

Parameter

lpRect: Long pointer to a data structure of type RECT that defines the screen region to which the mouse cursor is restricted.

GetCursorPos (lpPoint);

Function Return the current position of the mouse cursor.

Value Returned None.

Parameter

lpPoint: Long pointer to a data structure of type POINT which contains the x and y coordinates of the mouse cursor.

ShowCursor (bShowFlag);

Function Display or hide the system color.

Value Returned Integer value specifying the current cursor display count.

Parameter

bShowFlag: Boolean value that, when TRUE, increases the display count; otherwise, decrements the display count.

Notes When the display count is 0, the cursor is hidden.

Caret Manipulation Routines

The following routines create, delete, display, and modify the system caret.

CreateCaret (hWnd, hBitmap, nWidth, nHeight);

Function   Create a new caret for the specified window. The routine ShowCaret displays the caret.

Value Returned   None.

Parameters

hWnd: Handle to the desired window.

hBitmap: Handle to the bitmap containing the desired caret.

nWidth: Integer value specifying the width of the caret in logical units.

nHeight: Integer value specifying the height of the caret in logical units.

DestroyCaret ( );

Function   Destroy the current caret, releasing any memory that it allocated.

Value Returned   None.

Parameters   None.

HideCaret (hWnd);

Function   Hide the caret associated with the specified window.

Value Returned   None.

Parameter

hWnd: Handle to the desired window.

ShowCaret (hWnd);

Function   Display the caret associated with the specified window.

Value Returned   None.

Parameter
hWnd: Handle to the desired window.

SetCaretPos (nX, nY);

Function   Set the caret to the coordinates specified by nX and nY.

Value Returned   None.

Parameters
nX, nY: Integer value specifying the x and y coordinates of the caret.

SetCaretBlinkTime (nMilliSeconds);

Function   Define the caret blink rate.

Value Returned   None.

Parameter
nMilliSeconds: Integer value specifying the caret blink rate.

GetCaretBlinkRate ( );

Function   Return the current caret blink rate.

Value Returned Integer value specifying the current caret blink rate in milliseconds.

Parameters None.

Coordinate Routines

The following routines convert window and client coordinates.

ClientToScreen (hWnd, lpPoint);

Function Convert the client coordinate contained in the data structure referenced by lpPoint to screen coordinates.

Value Returned None.

Parameters
hWnd: Handle to the desired window.

lpPoint: Long pointer to a data structure of type POINT that contains the point in client coordinates.

ScreenToClient (hWnd, lpPoint);

Function Convert the screen coordinate contained in the data structure referenced by lpPoint to client coordinates.

Value Returned None.

Parameters
hWnd: Handle to the desired window.

lpPoint: Long pointer to a data structure of type POINT that contains the point in screen coordinates.

WindowFromPoint (Point);

Function   Return a handle to the window that contains the specified point.

Value Returned   Handle to the window containing the point, or the NULL value if no such window exists.

Parameter

Point: Point data structure containing desired point.

ChildWindowFrom (hWndParent, Point);

Function   Return a handle to a child window containing the specified point.

Value Returned   Handle to the child window containing the specified point or the NULL value if no such child window exists.

Parameters

hWndParent: Handle to the parent window.

Point: Point data structure containing the desired point.

Rectangle Functions

The following routines support rectangle manipulation from within Windows applications.

SetRect (lpRECT, nX1, nY1, nX2, nY2);

Function   Assign the rectangle specified structure pointed to by lpRECT with the specified coordinates.

Value Returned   None.

Parameters

lpRECT: Long pointer to a data structure of type RECT that is assigned the specified values.

nX1, nY1: Integer value specifying the upper-left rectangle corner.

nX2, nY2: Integer value specifying the lower-right rectangle corner.

SetRectEmpty (lpRECT);

Function   Define the rectangle referenced by lpRECT to empty.

Value Returned   None.

Parameter

lpRECT: Long pointer to a data structure of type RECT.

CopyRect (lpDestinationRect, lpSourceRect);

Function   Copy the contents of the source rectangle to the destination rectangle.

Value Returned   None.

Parameters

lpDestinationRect: Long pointer to a data structure of type RECT receiving the contents of the source rectangle.

lpSourceRect: Long pointer to a data structure of type RECT to be copied.

InflateRect (lpRect, nX, nY);

Function   Expand the rectangle referenced by lpRect by the number of units contained in nX and nY.

Value Returned   None.

Parameters

lpRect: Long pointer to a data structure of type RECT that contains the rectangle to be expanded.

nX, nY: Integer value specifying the number of units to modify the rectangle in the x and y directions.

Notes   The rectangle width must be less than 32,767 units.

IntersectRect (lpDestinationRect, lpSourceRect1, lpSourceRect2);

Function   Create a third rectangle from the intersection of the two rectangles defined by lpSourceRect1 and lpSourceRect2.

Value Returned   Integer value of 0 if the intersection of two rectangles results in an empty rectangle; otherwise, the value is 1.

Parameters

lpDestinationRect: Long pointer to a data structure of type RECT that receives the rectangle defined by the intersection of the two rectangles.

lpSourceRect1, lpSourceRect2: Long pointer to data structures of type RECT to be intersected.

UnionRect (lpDestinationRect, lpSourceRect1, lpSourceRect2);

Function Create a third rectangle from the union of th

e two rectangles defined by lpSourceRect1 and lpSourceRect2.

Value Returned Integer value of 0 if the intersection of two rectangles results in an empty rectangle; otherwise, the value is 1.

Parameters
lpDestinationRect: Long pointer to a data structure of type RECT that receives the rectangle defined by the union of the two rectangles.

lpSourceRect1, lpSourceRect2: Long pointer to data structures of type RECT to be unioned.

OffsetRect (lpRect, nX, nY);

Function Move the rectangle as specified by the x and y offsets.

Value Returned None.

Parameters
lpRect: Long pointer to a data structure of type RECT that defines the rectangle to move.

nX, nY: Integer values specifying the number of units to move the rectangle in the x and y directions.

IsRectEmpty (lpRect);

Function Determine if a rectangle is empty.

Value Returned Boolean value of TRUE if the specified rectangle is empty; otherwise, FALSE.

Parameter

lpRect: Long pointer to a data structure of type RECT that is examined to see if it is empty.

PtInRect (lpRect, Point);

Function Determine if the specified point is contained in the rectangle provided.

Value Returned Boolean value of TRUE if the point is contained in the rectangle; otherwise, FALSE.

Parameters

lpRect: Long pointer to a data structure of type RECT that defines the rectangle to examine for the point.

Point: Point data structure defining the desired point.

System Information Routines

The following are the system information routines for Windows.

GetSystemMetrics (nIndex);

Function Return the value of the system metric indexed by nIndex.

Value Returned Integer value specifying the desired metric.

Parameter

nIndex: Integer value specifying the desired system metric (see SM __* in windows.h).

GetSysColor (nIndex);

Function   Return information about the colors of the selected item.

Value Returned   Long-integer value containing the RGB color of the selected item.

Parameter

nIndex: Integer value containing the index to the desired item, as follows:

COLOR_ACTIVECAPTION
COLOR_BACKGROUND
COLOR_CAPTIONTEXT
COLOR_INACTIVECAPTION
COLOR_MENU
COLOR_MENUTEXT
COLOR_SCROLLBAR
COLOR_WINDOW
COLOR_WINDOWFRAME
COLOR_WINDOWTEXT

SetSysColors (nChanges, lpSysColor, lpColorValues);

Function   Change one or more system colors.

Value Returned   None.

Parameters

nChanges: Integer value specifying the number of changes.

lpSysColor: Long pointer to the integer array of items whose colors are to be changed.

lpColorValues: Long pointer to an integer array of colors desired for each system item.

Window Hook Routine

The following is a Windows hook routine.

SetWindowHook (nFilterType, lpFilterfunct);

Function Install system or application hook functions.

Value Returned Address of the previously defined filter, or NULL if no such filter exists.

Parameters

nFilterType: Integer value specifying the type of hook to be installed, as follows:

WH_MSGFILTER   Invoke the function specified each time a message is received.

WH_KEYBOARD   Invoke the function specified each time keyboard input occurs.

lpFilterfunct: Long pointer to the application-defined function that filters the hooks specified.

Notes Most applications maintain readability and maintainability by eliminating the use of hook functions.

TRADEMARKS

INDEX

The manuscript for this book was prepared and submitted to Osborne **McGraw-Hill** in electronic form. The acquisitions editor for this project was Nancy Carlston, the technical reviewer was Richard Dill, and the project editor was Fran Haselsteiner.

Text design by Pamela Webster, using Century Expanded and Univers.

Cover art by Bay Graphics Design Associates. Color separation by colour image. Cover supplier, Phoenix Color Corp. Book printed and bound by R.R. Donnelley & Sons Company, Crawfordsville, Indiana.

Advanced Turbo C®

by Herbert Schildt

Ready for power programming with Turbo C®? You'll find the expertise you need in *Advanced Turbo C®*, the Borland/Osborne book with the inside edge. In this instruction guide and lasting reference, Herb Schildt, the author of five acclaimed books on C, takes you the final step on the way to Turbo C mastery. Each stand-alone chapter presents a complete discussion of a Turbo C programming topic so you can pinpoint the information you need immediately. *Advanced Turbo C®* thoroughly covers sorting and searching; stacks, queues, linked lists, and binary trees; operating system interfacing; statistics; encryption and compressed data formats; random numbers and simulations; and expression parsers. In addition, you'll learn about converting Turbo Pascal® to Turbo C and using Turbo C graphics. *Advanced Turbo C®* shows you how to put the amazing compilation speed of Turbo C into action on your programs.

$22.95 p
0-07-881280-1, 325 pp., 7³/₈ x 9¹/₄

The Borland-Osborne/McGraw-Hill Programming Series

Advanced Turbo Prolog™ Version 1.1

by Herbert Schildt

Herb Schildt now applies his expertise to Borland's remarkable Turbo Prolog™ language development system, specifically designed for fifth-generation language programming and the creation of artificial intelligence on your IBM® PC. *Advanced Turbo Prolog™* has been extensively revised to include Turbo Prolog version 1.1. The new Turbo Prolog Toolbox™, which offers more than 80 tools and 8,000 lines of source code, is also described in detail. Schildt focuses on helping you progress from intermediate to advanced techniques by considering typical AI problems and their solutions. Numerous sample programs and graphics are used throughout the text to sharpen your skills and enhance your understanding of the central issues involved in AI. Expert systems, problem solving, natural language processing, vision and pattern recognition, robotics, and logic are some of the applications that Schildt explains as he leads you to Turbo Prolog mastery.

$21.95 p
0-07-881285-2, 350 pp., 7³/₈ x 9¹/₄

The Borland-Osborne/McGraw-Hill Programming Series

Turbo Pascal® Programmer's Library

by Kris Jamsa and Steven Nameroff

You can take full advantage of Borland's famous Turbo Pascal® with this outstanding collection of programming routines. Now revised to cover Borland's new Turbo Pascal Numerical Methods Toolbox™, the *Turbo Pascal® Programmer's Library* includes a whole new collection of routines for mathematical calculations. You'll also find new date and time routines. Kris Jamsa, author of *DOS: The Complete Reference* and *The C Library*, and Steven Nameroff give experienced Turbo Pascal users a varied library that includes utility routines for Pascal macros as well as routines for string and array manipulation, records, pointers, and pipes. You'll find I/O routines and a discussion of sorting that covers bubble, shell, and quick-sort algorithms. And there's even more ... routines for the Turbo Toolbox® and the Turbo Graphix Toolbox® packages. It's all here to help you become the most effective Turbo Pascal programmer you can be.

$21.95 p
0-07-881286-0, 625 pp., 7³/₈ x 9¹/₄

The Borland-Osborne/McGraw-Hill Programming Series

Using Turbo C®

by Herbert Schildt

Here's the official book on Borland's tremendous new C compiler. *Using Turbo C®* is for all C programmers, from beginners to seasoned pros. Master programmer Herb Schildt devotes the first part of the book to helping you get started in Turbo C. If you've been programming in Turbo Pascal® or another language, this orientation will lead you right into Turbo C fundamentals. Schildt's emphasis on good programming structure will start you out designing programs for greater efficiency. With these basics, you'll move on to more advanced concepts such as pointers and dynamic allocation, compiler directives, unions, bitfields, and enumerations, and you'll learn about Turbo C graphics. When you've finished *Using Turbo C®*, you'll be writing full-fledged programs that get professional results.

$19.95 p
0-07-881279-8, 350 pp., 7³/₈ x 9¹/₄

The Borland-Osborne/McGraw-Hill Programming Series

Advanced Turbo Pascal®
by Herbert Schildt

Advanced Turbo Pascal® is the book you need to learn superior programming skills for the leading Pascal language development system. Revised and expanded, *Advanced Turbo Pascal®* now covers Borland's newly released Turbo Database Toolbox®, which speeds up database searching and sorting, and the Turbo Graphix Toolbox®, which lets you easily create high-resolution graphics. And, *Advanced Turbo Pascal®* includes techniques for converting Turbo Pascal for use with Borland's hot new compiler, Turbo C®. Schildt provides many programming tips to take you on your way to high performance with Turbo Pascal. You'll refine your skills with techniques for sorting and searching; stacks, queues, linked lists and binary trees; dynamic allocations; expression parsing; simulation; interfacing to assembly language routines; and efficiency, porting, and debugging. For instruction and reference, *Advanced Turbo Pascal®* is the best single resource for serious programmers.

$21.95 p
0-07-881283-6, 350 pp., 7³/₈ x 9¹/₄

The Borland-Osborne/McGraw-Hill Programming Series

Using Turbo Pascal®
by Steve Wood

Using Turbo Pascal® gives you a head start with Borland's acclaimed compiler, which has become a worldwide standard. Programmer Steve Wood has completely rewritten the text and now provides programming examples that run under MS-DOS®, as well as new information on memory resident applications, in-line code, interrupts, and DOS functions. If you're already programming in Pascal or any other high-level language, you'll be able to write programs that are more efficient than ever. *Using Turbo Pascal®* discusses program design and Pascal's syntax requirements, and thoroughly explores Turbo Pascal's features. Then Wood develops useful applications and gives you an overview of some of the advanced utilities and features available with Turbo Pascal. *Using Turbo Pascal®* gives you the skills to become a productive programmer — and when you're ready for more, you're ready for *Advanced Turbo Pascal®*.

$19.95 p
0-07-881284-4, 350 pp., 7³/₈ x 9¹/₄

The Borland-Osborne/McGraw-Hill Programming Series

Using Turbo BASIC®
by Frederick E. Mosher and David I. Schneider

Using Turbo BASIC® is your authoritative guide to Borland's incredible new compiler that offers faster compilation speeds than any other product on the market. *Using Turbo BASIC®* is packed with information for everyone from novices to seasoned programmers. Authors Mosher and Schneider, two accomplished programmers, introduce you to the Turbo BASIC operating environment on the IBM™ PC and PC-compatibles, and discuss the interactive editor and the BASIC language itself. You'll learn about recursion, math functions, graphics and sound functions, and conversions from IBM BASICA to Turbo BASIC. With this excellent step-by-step guide to Borland's new compiler, you'll have the extraordinary power of Turbo BASIC at your fingertips.

$19.95 p
0-07-881282-8, 350 pp., 7³/₈ x 9¹/₄
The Borland-Osborne/McGraw-Hill Programming Series

DOS: The Complete Reference
by Kris Jamsa

Why waste computing time over a baffling PC-DOS™ command or an elusive MS-DOS® function? *DOS: The Complete Reference* has the answers to all of your questions on DOS through version 3.X. This essential resource is for every PC- and MS-DOS user, whether you need an overview of the disk operating system or a reference for advanced programming and disk management techniques. Each chapter begins with a discussion of specific applications followed by a list of commands used in each. All commands are presented in the same clear, concise format: description, syntax, discussion of arguments or options, and examples. For comprehensive coverage, *DOS: The Complete Reference* discusses Microsoft® Windows and EDLIN, and provides two special appendixes covering the ASCII chart and DOS error messages. A ready resource, *DOS: The Complete Reference* is the only DOS consultant you'll need.

$24.95 p
0-07-881259-3, 840 pp., 7³/₈ x 9¹/₄

PC-DOS Tips & Traps
by Dick Andersen, Janice M. Gessin, Fred Warren, and Jack Rodgers

Solve immediate problems and quickly perform specific business tasks on your IBM® PC or PC-compatible with *PC-DOS Tips & Traps*. Written for everyone using PC-DOS 2.1 or MS-DOS 2.11, Andersen provides an array of tips and discusses frequently encountered traps with their solutions. You'll find a broad range of helpful information from initializing your system and formatting disks, to controlling peripherals, and managing the DOS environment. Throughout the book Andersen shows you how to use the DOS Batch files to design your own commands and automate certain tasks. Tips for using DOS utilities including EDLIN for text editing and DEBUG for programming are also discussed. You'll save time and minimize the chance for error with Andersen's insights on the PC- and MS-DOS® operating systems.

$16.95 p
0-07-881194-5, 250 pp., 7³/₈ x 9¹/₄

Your IBM® PC: A Guide to the IBM PC (DOS 2.0) and XT
by Lyle Graham and Tim Field

"Excellent reference for the IBM PC with PC-DOS version 1.0, 1.05 and 1.1. Provides a clear overview of IBM PC hardware and software, step-by-step operating instructions, and an introduction to BASIC programming, color graphics, and sound. Also includes a chapter on trouble-shooting and IBM's PDP (Problem Definition Procedure). Rating: A"
(Computer Book Review)

$18.95 p
0-07-881120-1, 592 pp., 6⅞ x 9¼

PC Secrets: Tips for Power Performance
by James E. Kelley

Power performance is at your command with these secrets for mastering the PC. This collection of shortcuts and solutions to frustrating and frequently encountered problems gives users of the IBM® PC and PC compatibles the inside edge. James Kelley, author of numerous books on the IBM PC, discloses his secrets for controlling hardware, peripherals, DOS, and applications software. You'll learn tips for keyboard harmonics, display enhancements, controlling fixed disks, managing the printer, and manipulating DOS routines that include batch files, directories and subdirectories, as well as system menus. You'll also find programs that help you use WordStar® and Lotus™ 1-2-3™ to greater advantage. With *PC Secrets*, you don't need to be a technical expert to become a PC power user.

$16.95 p
0-07-881210-0, 224 pp., 7⅜ x 9¼

Supercharging Your PC
by Lewis Perdue

Supercharging Your PC is easy with Perdue's expansion guide. Add memory expansion boards, hard disk storage, graphics boards ......Perdue covers all the tricks you can use to get your PC performing at top speed. Every chapter presents a hardware or software solution to an expansion problem. You'll learn how to select and use utility software and hardware enhancements and implement other techniques to gain greater RAM, more disk storage, and better graphics. You'll also find out how to choose a PC clone for maximum reliability and compatibility. Take powerful applications programs such as Lotus® 1-2-3®, dBASE®, and popular graphics software, and make them run faster and more effectively, Perdue shows you how. Best of all, *Supercharging Your PC* has a "do-it-yourself" format—you'll save money while you become a PC expert.

$19.95 p
0-07-881000-0, 320 pp., 6⅜ x 9¼

1-2-3®: The Complete Reference
by Mary Campbell

1-2-3®: The Complete Reference is the authoritative desktop companion for every Lotus® 1-2-3® user. All commands, functions, and procedures are explained in detail and are demonstrated in practical "real-world" business applications. Conventionally organized according to task, this essential reference makes it easy to locate information on topics such as printing, macros, graphics production, and data management. Each chapter thoroughly describes a 1-2-3 task and all the procedures it requires, followed by an alphabetical listing of every command or function applied. Special emphasis is placed on compatible software packages, including Report Writer™, Reflex™ and others, that you can use to extend 1-2-3's capabilities. Campbell, a consultant and writer whose magazine columns appear monthly in *IBM PC UPDATE*, *Absolute Reference*, and *CPA Journal*, draws on her years of 1-2-3 expertise to provide you with this outstanding, comprehensive resource.

$22.95 p
0-07-881005-1, 928 pp., 7⅜ x 9¼

dBASE III PLUS™: The Complete Reference
by Joseph-David Carrabis

This indispensable dBASE III PLUS™ reference will undoubtedly be the most frequently used book in your dBASE III® library. *dBASE III PLUS™: The Complete Reference* is a comprehensive resource to every dBASE III and dBASE III PLUS command, function, and feature. Each chapter covers a specific task so you can quickly pinpoint information on installing the program, designing databases, creating files, manipulating data, and many other subjects. Chapters also contain an alphabetical reference section that describes all the commands and functions you need to know and provides clear examples of each. Carrabis, author of several acclaimed dBASE books, discusses the lastest features of dBASE III PLUS, including networking capabilities; the Assistant, a menu-driven interface; and the Applications Generator, a short-cut feature for creating database files and applications without programming. *dBASE III PLUS™: The Complete Reference* also includes a glossary and handy appendixes that cover error messages, converting from dBASE II to dBASE III PLUS, and add-on utilities.

$22.95 p
0-07-881012-4, 600 pp., 7⅜ x 9¼

**The Osborne/McGraw-Hill Guide to
Using Lotus™ 1-2-3™ Second Edition,
Covers Release 2**
by Edward M. Baras

Your investment in Lotus™ 1-2-3™ can yield the most
productive returns possible with the tips and practical
information in *The Osborne/McGraw-Hill
Guide to Using Lotus™ 1-2-3™.* Now the second
edition of this acclaimed bestseller helps you take full
advantage of Lotus' new 1-2-3 upgrade, Release 2. This
comprehensive guide offers a thorough presentation
of the worksheet, database, and graphics functions. In
addition, the revised text shows you how to create
and use macros, string functions, and many other
sophisticated 1-2-3 features. Step by step, you'll learn
to implement 1-2-3 techniques as you follow application models for financial forecasting, stock portfolio
tracking, and forms-oriented database management.
For both beginners and experienced users, this tutorial
quickly progresses from fundamental procedures to
advanced applications.

$18.95 p
0-07-881230-5, 432 pp., 7³⁄₈ x 9¹⁄₄

Available at fine bookstores and computer stores everywhere.

For a complimentary catalog of all our current publications contact:
Osborne **McGraw-Hill**, 2600 Tenth Street, Berkeley, CA 94710.

Phone inquiries may be made using our toll-free number.
Call 800-227-0900 or 800-772-2531 (in California).
TWX 910-366-7277.

Prices subject to change without notice.

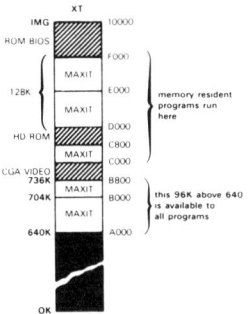
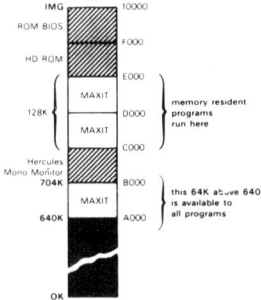